Basic
Bible
Doctrine

Basic Bible Doctrine

Donald S. Fortner

Go *publications*

Go Publications
The Cairn, Hill Top, Eggleston, Co. Durham, DL12 0AU, ENGLAND

© Go Publications 2004
First Published 2004

British Library Cataloguing in Publication Data available

ISBN 0 9527 074 9 7

Printed and bound in Great Britain
by Lightning Source UK Ltd

This book is dedicated to:

Grace Baptist Church *of* Danville
Danville, Kentucky

"Beloved ... My Joy and Crown"

Contents

Foreword

Despite never having met Pastor Don Fortner I have enjoyed his ministry for many years. His preaching is bold, forthright, and challenging. He preaches with conviction such that any who hear him cannot help but be impressed by his passion and his dedication to the gospel of the Lord Jesus Christ.

Pastor Fortner's weekly sermons are recorded, collected and reproduced on video and DVD for friends around the world who gratefully receive his teaching. The recordings contains six or seven sermons on a four hour tape and circulate widely amongst those who appreciate the value of free and sovereign grace.

On one occasion a lady received a video tape of these sermons. She watched the tape from start to finish in a single sitting of almost four hours before returning it to the lender. Anxious to know how the ministry had been received by the new listener her friend asked what she thought of the tape. "Oh," she replied, "the tape was great, I just could not understand why the preacher changed his jacket five times during the sermon."

This story, while amusing, is indicative of the appeal Pastor Fortner's preaching has for many of us. We respond to his engaging and persuasive manner. We appreciate his clear and direct approach. We enjoy the simple presentation of profound truth in each sermon.

Yet, what draws this positive reaction from people all over the world to Don Fortner's preaching is not primarily the man, but the message. It is not the preacher so much as the One preached. Listeners know that each one of these sermons will honour their precious Saviour and lift up the name of the Lord Jesus Christ.

Pastor Fortner's approach to preaching is to emphasise the Lord's glory with clear Biblical teaching. Don believes in free grace. He sees all of God's plan and purpose directed toward one end of glorifying the Lord Jesus in the salvation of sinners. His sermons resonate with God honouring, Christ exalting, Spirit filled doctrine. His is preaching of the highest order for he places the Saviour at the forefront of our attention, the worth of Christ's blood and righteousness on the lips of every saved sinner.

Now, I am delighted to discover the substance of this excellent ministry gathered together in book form. *Basic Bible Doctrine* is a topical presentation of Bible truth concerning Jesus Christ. In it we see His glory, His purpose and His work of salvation. The book deals with all the major doctrinal subjects contained in scripture describing them clearly and comprehensively.

I know of no other book on doctrine that so simply presents and explains what the Bible teaches. This is the book I would recommend to be read alongside holy scripture for any believer seeking to obtain an understanding of Christian doctrine. It is written with the urgency of a preacher, the plainness of a pastor and the passion of a saved sinner wholly immersed in Christ's love and mercy for His people. If you would like a clear, easy to read presentation of basic Bible doctrine, the volume now in your hand will supply your need.

Peter L. Meney
July 2004

'If the foundations be destroyed, what can the righteous do?'
(Psalm 11:3)

Chapter 1

Why Study Doctrine ?

Why should we study doctrine?

People often object to any talk about doctrine and the study of doctrine, because they wrongly imagine that it is an unnecessary cause of strife and division. The fact is, we cannot have any unity at all if we do not have doctrinal unity. Doctrine is not everything in Christianity; but nothing is more important than doctrine. Gospel doctrine is the foundation of all true faith, the basis of all real comfort, and the inspiration for all worship, obedience, and devotion.

I often hear people say, 'Let's not discuss doctrine. Let's just get on with evangelism'. 'Let's not talk about doctrine. Let's just worship the Lord'. 'Don't preach doctrine. Just preach Christ'. That makes about as much sense as a basketball coach saying to his team, 'Boys, don't worry about the baskets, or the ball, or those lines out there on the court. Let's just play basketball'. You cannot have basketball without the baskets, the ball, and the lines; and you cannot have evangelism, worship, and Christianity without doctrine.

The study of doctrine is important, because it is foundational. In Psalm 11:3, David asked, 'If the foundations be destroyed, what can the righteous do?' Obviously, we recognize that 'the foundation of God standeth sure' (2 Timothy 2:19). Yet, we also know that in this dark, apostate age in which wicked religious men and women walk in darkness, without knowledge and without understanding, 'all the foundations of the earth are out of course' (Psalm 82:5). The religion of the world constantly attacks, assaults, and seeks to destroy the foundation of doctrinal truth. When men seek to destroy the very foundations of our faith, what can the righteous do? Here are three things we can and must do ...

1. We must recognize and assert the importance of doctrine in the Word of God. 'Doctrine' is not a dirty word. When we talk about the doctrine of the Bible, we are simply talking about the 'teaching' of the Bible. To say, 'Doctrine is insignificant', is to say that the teachings of the Bible are insignificant. Doctrine is not insignificant. It is vital.

Gospel doctrine is absolutely necessary to saving faith. Faith in Christ is not a leap in the dark. It is walking in the light. That person who is not taught the doctrine of Christ or believes that which is contrary to the doctrine of Christ does not know Christ. This is not a matter of speculation, but of revelation (Romans 16:17-18; 1 Timothy 4:16; 2 John 1:9).

Sound doctrine is necessary for godly behaviour, too. I do not doubt that people may live in an outwardly moral, religious manner without doctrine; but you cannot live for Christ, to the glory of Christ, and after the example of Christ, without the doctrine of Christ. Paul tells us that the doctrine of Christ is that doctrine which is according to godliness (1 Timothy 6:3).

Our comfort as believers living in this world of woe greatly depends upon our grasp of the doctrine of holy scripture (Romans 15:4). Were it not for the teachings of scripture regarding God's sovereignty and grace in predestination and providence, Christ's substitutionary atonement, and the Spirit's efficacious grace, where would we find the strength and comfort we need to face and deal with life in this world?

2. We must recognize the importance of doctrine; and when men would destroy the foundations upon which our souls are built, we must cling to the Word of God.

In this world of chaos, the one thing that stands unchanged, unchanging, and unchangeable is the Word of God. Here is a foundation that cannot be destroyed. 'The foundation of God standeth sure' (Psalm 119:89; Isaiah 40:8). Our house of faith is built not upon the shifting sand of human philosophy, but upon the solid rock of God's own Word.

3. When the foundations are being assaulted from every quarter, we must earnestly contend for the faith once delivered to the saints (Jude 3-4).

If, in these dark days, we would contend for the integrity of the scriptures and the faith of the saints, we must prayerfully study and seek, by the grace of God, to comprehend the teaching (the doctrine) of the Word of God.

The study of doctrine is important, because it is foundational and because the doctrine we are studying is of God. The doctrines we believe, those doctrines taught in holy scripture and believed by all true Christians, are not of men, but of God. These are not mere denominational dogmas, church confessions, doctrinal debates, and theological theses, but the teachings of God himself. Those things which are vital to our souls, vital to the knowledge of God, and vital to salvation are things which could not be known except by divine revelation (1 Peter 1:21)

They can be understood only by divine illumination (1 Corinthians 2:13-14). Both the man who attempts to teach and those who seek to learn the doctrine of holy scripture are totally dependent upon the grace, wisdom, and power of God the Holy Spirit. If he is our Teacher, we shall be taught well; for we are taught of God.

What is the source of true doctrine?

To those who read these pages that question may, at first, appear to be redundant, perhaps even silly; it is not. The fact is, in the minds of most men there are many sources for true doctrine. None, other than the most outlandishly ignorant would suggest that the Bible is not a source of doctrine. Most would assert that it is the primary source. However, very few look upon the Word of God as the only source of doctrine. Even among those who say they do, very few truly look upon the scriptures alone as our only source for true doctrine.

Many, like the Pharisees, build their doctrine upon the Bible and tradition. Those who do so, by their tradition, make void the Word of God. Whenever people attempt to build their doctrine on both the Word of God and tradition, they soon prefer tradition to the Word and make the Word of God to be of none effect (Matthew 15:6-9; 16:12; Mark 7:7, 13).

Others build their doctrine on the Word of God and the creeds of the church. While there may be a proper place and use for creeds and confessions of faith, our faith must not be determined by the creeds of even the best of men. Our faith must stand in the Word of God alone. Bible doctrine is the teaching of holy scripture. Dogma is teaching that is laid down by and imposed upon men by churches. Whenever a church's dogma contradicts the Bible's doctrine, or adds anything to it, it must be rejected as false.

Many build their doctrine upon the plain statements of holy scripture and those things which may be reasonably inferred from the scriptures. There is among Protestants a commonly accepted doctrine called 'the doctrine of necessary consequence', which is largely responsible for much of the heresy we have to deal with today. When men attempt to build doctrine upon both the plain statements of scripture and what they think must be necessarily deduced from scripture, they try to build upon two foundations, one of sand and the other of rock. The result is destruction. When sinful men make their reason the basis of believing something, there is no limit to the nonsense that will be passed off as Bible doctrine.

In this day of charismatic nonsense, multitudes build their doctrine upon the Word of God and experience. Experience is no basis for faith. Saul had a real experience in the house of a witch in Endor; but that experience is not a basis for our doctrine. Neither are our own experiences, good or bad. Martin Luther was exactly right when he said, 'any teaching which does not square with the scriptures is to be rejected even if it snows miracles every day'.

The only basis for doctrine, the only source of divine truth is the Word of God. When we talk about doctrine, the teaching of holy scripture, we have no right to even entertain our own thoughts and opinions, much less express them. In these matters, we dare not speak either more or less than that which is expressly written in the Word of God (Isaiah 8:20; 2 Timothy 3:16-17).

All true doctrine is the doctrine of the Apostles and Prophets. Faithful men teach exactly what they taught. Ours is the doctrine of the Bible, the Old and the New Testaments. We do not simply hold to the doctrine of the New Testament. Our doctrine is the doctrine of the Bible. We recognize that the Bible is one book, with one message, and total uniformity of doctrine. The Old Testament teaches exactly the same thing as the New Testament, only with less clarity and fulness. The Old Testament is the shadow. The New Testament is the substance. The Old Testament is the type. The New Testament is the anti-type. The Old Testament is the promise and prophecy. The New Testament is the fulfilment. Someone once said, 'The Old Testament is the New Testament concealed. The New Testament is the Old Testament revealed'.

The book of Acts is an inspired history of the ministry of the New Testament church for the first thirty years after our Lord's ascension and exaltation. In that inspired history we are given a running narrative of apostolic doctrine and preaching. Every time we read about the preaching of the Apostles in the book of Acts (in all 37 references), the subject preached was Jesus Christ and the resurrection. Every summary of gospel doctrine given in the book of Acts, indeed, in the entire New Testament, reveals an inspired system of doctrine centring around the accomplishment of redemption by the death of Christ and the verification of its accomplishment by his resurrection from the dead. 'The apostles' doctrine', that which they preached everywhere, had five basic, essential points.

1. The total sovereignty of God over all things (Acts 2:23; 4:26-28; 13:26-30).
2. The fact that Jesus of Nazareth is the Christ (Acts 3:13-18).
3. The accomplishment of redemption for God's elect by the death of Christ, verified by his resurrection from the dead (Acts 1:22; 2:24, 32).
4. Salvation by grace alone, through faith alone, without works (Acts 2:38; 3:16; 4:12; 15:11; 16:31).
5. The believer's freedom from the law in Christ (Acts 15:10-11). See Hebrews 8:1-2 and Romans 10:4.

How should we study Bible doctrine?

I will not attempt to lay down any absolute rules as to the best method of Bible study. Many do things in different ways and seem to get along just fine. So I will not suggest that they should change their method of study. However, no matter what method of study we use, there are some rules or guidelines that ought to be followed in the study of doctrine.

1. Study all doctrines contextually. This cannot be over emphasized. Nothing is more dishonest than to study the Word of God by looking for proof texts. We dare not go to the Word of God to prove our doctrine. We go to the Bible to get our doctrine. If you want to know what the Bible teaches about a given subject, go to the place in the Bible where that subject is explained, interpreting all relevant texts in the light of those passages. Honesty compels us to interpret obscure passages by the obvious, not the obvious by the obscure. For example: – If you want to study believer's baptism, you go to Romans 6, not Genesis 17. – If you wish to understand the ordinance of the Lord's Supper, you must go to 1 Corinthians 11, not John 13. – If you desire to know what the Bible teaches about divorce, you must go to 1 Corinthians 7, not Romans 7. – If you want to know what the scriptures teach about redemption, you go to Romans 5, not John 3. If you are interested in predestination, you go to Romans 8 and 9, and Ephesians 1, not Ezekiel 33.

2. Study the Word of God submissively. May God give us grace to bring all things to the touchstone of holy scripture. Let us bow to the Word of God. Always be prepared to give up any doctrine or practice that is not found in holy scripture and to embrace anything revealed in the Book of God, no matter what the sacrifice, no matter what the consequence.

3. To the degree that it is possible, we ought to state our doctrine in the very language of the Bible. I realize that for the sake of clarification and faithful exposition, we sometimes use terms that are not specifically used in the Bible (sovereignty, satisfaction, trinity, substitution, etc.); but we must not allow ourselves to get caught in the trap of either requiring others or being required by others to say things in a specific way. Bible doctrine is both simple and clearly revealed. It is not given in 'code'. The Word of God is not the secrecy of God, but the revelation of God. If a man has to take you around the world to get you around the corner, trying to prove his doctrine, his doctrine is probably wrong.

4. Give no doctrine greater or less prominence and importance than it is given in the scriptures. The dominant theme of holy scripture is the gospel of the grace of God, the message of salvation by grace alone, through faith alone, in Christ alone. The message of the Bible is Jesus Christ and him crucified (Luke 24:27, 44-47; John 1:45; Acts 10:43). If Satan gets our focus off Christ and on to something else, he has won the day.

5. 'Adorn the doctrine of God our Saviour in all things' (Titus 2:10). Let us take great care to conform our lives to our doctrine. Doctrine and duty cannot be separated. Every truth discovered in the Word of God ought to be applied to our lives. If our character and conduct does not reflect the grace and glory of God revealed in the gospel, our doctrine is utterly meaningless.

Test all doctrine by two things, two simple questions. First, who gets the glory – God or man? Second, does the doctrine lead you to, and cause you to, rest in Christ? All true doctrine gives glory to God and abases man. True doctrine directs sinners to Christ to find rest for their souls in him (Jeremiah 6:16).

'I will worship toward thy holy temple, and praise thy name for thy loving kindness and for thy truth: for thou hast magnified thy word above all thy name'.
(Psalm 138:2)

Chapter 2

The Word of God

I do not pretend to know all that is implied by the statement in the verse above; but I am sure of this – God almighty intends for us to understand that he has a very high opinion of his Word. It is something of indescribable value, a Book to be revered, honoured, read, believed, and obeyed. It has not been given to us to be a decoration to adorn your coffee table at home or the communion table at church. The volume of holy scripture came from God and shows us the way back to God. Read it. Study it. Believe it. Obey it. Know it in your head. Store it in your heart. Show it in your life. Sow it in the world. This blessed Book, the Bible, is and must be the Word of God.

Before studying the glorious truths of holy scripture, we must have a firm grasp of the fact that the Bible is indeed of divine origin, inspired, infallible, and authoritative. Unless we recognize that fact we have no authoritative basis for believing anything taught in the Bible. In fact, I am certain that the reason for all the fuzziness, instability, and confusion among religious people in our day is that they fail to recognize the absolute authority of the Word of God in all matters of faith and practice, in all matters of doctrine and conduct.

As we face the heresies, speculations, scepticism, and ignorance of the religious world around us, as well as that of the secular world, we need to be sure of our ground. Doctrinal, spiritual ignorance always leads to spiritual bondage (Isaiah 5:13).

Numerous books have been written demonstrating the fact that the Bible's claim of divine origin, inspiration, and infallibility cannot be denied. Assuming that you recognize this fact, I will show you four things about the Bible which I trust will be blessed of God to your soul and make the Book of God even more precious to you than it is already.

1. The Bible is the inspired, infallible, inerrant Word of God

This is the claim the Bible makes of itself. We must either accept the claim in its entirety or reject it altogether. Either the Bible is the Word of God, or it is a horribly evil hoax by which the souls of men are deceived and ruined. The same must be said concerning all other religious books that claim divine origin. If the Bible is the Word of God, then the Koran, the Book of Mormon, and the claims of modern self-proclaimed prophets must all be rejected as evil deceptions by which the souls of men are destroyed. The Bible claims to be the inspired, infallible, inerrant, complete, sufficient, and final Word of God. It takes but a casual glance at the scriptures to see that this is the claim of the Bible.

– The Bible claims divine origin. It claims to be infallibly inspired, though written by men who were both fallible and sinful (2 Timothy 3:16-17; Hebrews 1:1; 2 Peter 1:21).
– The Bible claims to be a necessary revelation, without which God cannot be known (Romans 10:13-17; 1 Peter 1:23-25). God is Spirit, the eternal, self-existent, incomprehensible Spirit. Though his eternal power and godhead is evident from the things he has made, so that

all are without excuse, he cannot be known unless he makes himself known by special revelation through the Word.

– The Bible claims to be the sufficient, effectual means by which chosen, redeemed sinners are called to life, faith, and everlasting salvation in Christ (Isaiah 55:11; 2 Timothy 3:15; Hebrews 4:12; James 1:18).

– The Bible claims both authority and finality as the Word of God (Isaiah 8:20; Revelation 22:18-19).

When we talk about inspiration, be sure you understand what the scriptures teach about it. We sometimes speak of the men who wrote the scriptures as being inspired. That is not really accurate. Those men were moved and carried along by the Holy Spirit as they wrote; but they were not inspired. It is the Word of God itself, that which those faithful men were employed to write, which is inspired.

We recognize, and the Bible carefully shows us, the flaws of those men. The Book was given through weak, sinful human beings; but their weaknesses, sins, and humanity do not affect the Bible's infallibility. We see the personalities of the writers in their writings; but their personalities do not corrupt the Bible's perfection. The Bible claims to be and is the inspired, infallible, inerrant Word of God.[1]

Few believers have not been asked, 'What about all the places where the statements of the Bible contradict the proven discoveries of science?' Usually, I respond by asking, 'Would you show me which statements you mean?' That usually ends the discussion. I do not claim to be a scientist. I am not even a student of science. Yet, I do make this assertion without the slightest fear of contradiction – There is not a single point of contradiction between the statements of holy scripture and the established facts of science. There is great conflict between the scriptures and scientific theories, but none

---

[1] 'It is utterly inconsistent to extol the Bible as a good book, and at the same time deny its infallibility'. C. D. Cole

between scripture and fact. The theories of science change constantly and constantly contradict one another; but the facts of science and the facts of the Bible are in perfect harmony.

2. The evidences and arguments for the divine origin and inspiration are as comforting as they are irrefutable

Let me give you just a few of the many internal evidences of inspiration. We will not even look at the external evidences, though they are numerous. The internal evidences are sufficient, both to refute the gainsayers and to comfort our souls, as we live by faith in this world of trouble and woe, leaning upon the promises and teachings of our God in holy scripture.

First, the Lord Jesus Christ accepted the Old Testament scriptures as the Word of God. When he dwelt upon the earth, he never made any attempt to prove the validity of the Old Testament, but simply referred to it, quoted it, expounded it, and lived upon it as the Word of God. In fact, he very deliberately quoted from the two books of the Old Testament which are most frequently attacked by infidels: Deuteronomy and Isaiah. Deuteronomy was the book from which he made every quotation when Satan tempted him in the wilderness (Deuteronomy 8:3; 6:16; 6:13; Luke 4:4-12). Isaiah was the book he referred to when he began his public ministry and first announced himself as the Messiah (Isaiah 61:1; Luke 4:16-21).

Second, the uniqueness of the Bible, that is to say the singularity of its teachings, attests to its divine origin. The Book of God is totally different from all other books in the things it reveals and teaches. All who ever drank from this Fountain of Truth have tasted the distinct difference. The Bible tells us what no other book could tell us and what no other book would tell us if it could about certain things.

– The Bible alone gives us an account and revelation of God's character that agrees with and satisfies that which is revealed in creation and stamped upon the consciences of all human beings. Holy scripture tells us that the Lord our God is omnipotent, holy, wise, just, and good.

– The Bible alone gives us an account of man's origin, his sinful nature, his God consciousness, and his sense of immortality. No other attempt to account for these things gives any satisfaction. No book of mere human composition would give such a brutally honest portrayal of human depravity.

– The Bible alone reveals and explains the necessity of Christ's incarnation, obedience, death, and resurrection.

– The Bible alone reveals a plan and scheme of salvation for fallen men that is both honouring to God and satisfactory to the conscience of men. God's plan of salvation (Romans 3:24-26) is the satisfaction of justice by substitutionary redemption and imputed righteousness by his free grace toward sinners in Christ his Son.

Any honest person who reads the Bible with any measure of carefulness and thoroughness will readily acknowledge that it could not possibly be a book of mere human origin. The Bible has the stamp of God upon it.

Third, the frankness and candour with which the Bible deals with its most prominent characters is evidence of its divine origin. All human biographies, if they expose any weaknesses and faults in their subjects, either excuse them or find a way to make them appear insignificant. The Word of God paints a different kind of picture when it describes the lives of its greatest, most eminent characters. It paints their very darkest sides. The Bible makes no attempt to whitewash Noah's drunkenness, Abraham's fear of Abimelech, Lot's incest, Moses' anger, Aaron's idolatry, David's murder and adultery, the disciples' unbelief, Peter's fall, or the strife which divided Paul and Barnabas.

Fourth, the perfect harmony and unity of the Bible is simply an unanswerable argument for its divine origin and a great source of comfort and assurance for our faith. If I should see my great-grandfather, who has been dead since I was a boy, rise up out of the earth that fact would be less miraculous than the existence of God's Word. Listen to this carefully ...

The Bible was written in three languages (Hebrew, Aramaic, and Greek), by some forty different authors, who lived on two separate continents, over a period of more than sixteen hundred years. Parts of it were written in palaces, parts in prisons. Some of it was written by well educated men in great cities, other parts were written by shepherds and fishermen. Parts of it were written during times of war, pestilence, and danger; other parts during times of ecstatic joy. Those who wrote the words of holy scripture were from virtually every walk of life: judges, priests, kings, prophets, prime-ministers, herdsmen, scribes, fishermen, and soldiers. Yet, in spite of all these varying circumstances, conditions, workmen, and ages of time employed in the production of the Book, it stands as one Book. It is perfectly one in all its parts, free from error, and free of contradiction.

Imagine forty persons of different nationalities, possessing various degrees of musical culture, visiting the organ of some great cathedral and at long intervals of time, and without any collusion whatever, striking sixty-six different notes, which when combined yielded the theme of the grandest oratorio ever heard; would it not show that behind these forty different men there was one presiding mind, one great Tone-Master? As we listen to some great orchestra, with its immense variety of instruments playing their different parts, but producing melody and harmony, we realize that at the back of these many musicians there is the personality and genius of the composer. And when we enter the halls of the Divine Academy and listen to the heavenly choirs singing the Song of Redemption, all in perfect accord and unison, we know that it is God himself who has written the music and put this song into their mouths. (A. W. Pink)

There is only one sane explanation for the existence of the Bible:

> For the prophecy came not in old time by the will of man: but holy men of God spake as they were moved by the Holy Ghost.
> (2 Peter 1:21)

Fifth, the multitude of prophecies given in the Bible that have been exactly fulfilled, to the very letter, demand that honest people acknowledge the divine origin of the Bible. Prophecy is the foretelling of future events before they come to pass. This is the acid test of divine revelation. The Lord God himself appeals to fulfilled prophecy throughout the Bible (Deuteronomy 18:22; Isaiah 41:21-23; 2 Peter 1:19-21). Fortune tellers, palm readers, and other practitioners of witchcraft frequently make general predictions that astound men. The Word of God does not make vague, general predictions, but specific, precise predictions, and stakes its veracity upon their fulfilment.

The Lord Jesus Christ was, of course, the central theme of Old Testament prophecy (Psalm 22; Isaiah 53); but there were a multitude of specific prophetic statements made about him in the Old Testament that were exactly fulfilled (Isaiah 7:14; Micah 5:2; Acts 13:29). The prophecy concerning Josiah, the boy king of Judah, was made during the days of Jeroboam and fulfilled three hundred and fifty years later (1 Kings 13:2; 2 Kings 23:15-16). Numerous other fulfilled prophecies could be cited by anyone even casually familiar with holy scripture. These are facts which no one can refute.

Let men cavil as they will, the Bible is the very Word of God. It simply cannot be explained in any other way. It is an open Book. Its truths are not written in the language of scholars, but in the common language of common men. The Bible is the Book for the people. It was delivered by God to his saints, not to the pope, not to priests, not to academics, not to the clergy, but to the saints of God. There is nothing hidden, nothing written in secret codes. Everything is open. If the gospel is veiled, it is not because there is a veil upon the Book of God, but because there is a veil upon the hearts of men (2 Corinthians 4:4).

3. The doctrine of the Bible's inspiration and infallibility has very serious consequences.

If the Bible is indeed the Word of God, its authority cannot be questioned. Its teachings cannot be disputed. All that it says must be received as true, submitted to, and obeyed. Its words must be candidly, honestly, and faithfully interpreted. There must be, on our part, a docility of spirit before God's holy Word. We must bow before God, as he speaks in his Word, with hearts willing to be taught of God, saying with Samuel, 'Speak, Lord, for thy servant heareth' (1 Samuel 3:9).

As this holy Book is of divine origin, so too our understanding of it is the gift of God. Every time we open it, let us pray for grace from God the Holy Spirit to enlighten and illuminate our hearts, that he might open our understanding and cause us to understand the scriptures (Psalm 119:18; John 16:13-16; 1 Corinthians 2:11, 14).

4. The metaphors used to describe the scriptures give us a hint of their great value, usefulness, and profitability.

It is both interesting and profitable to carefully study the various metaphors given in scripture for the Word of God. The Bible is compared to a lamp, or a light (Psalm 119:105, 130; Proverbs 6:23). It is called a mirror (2 Corinthians 3:18; James 1:23). We look into the Bible and see ourselves, not what we think we are, but what we really are: sinful, corrupt, depraved, lost, ruined, and utterly helpless. Holy scripture is compared to a laver, or wash bowl (Ephesians 5:26; Psalm 119:9; John 15:3).

It is compared to bread, or food for our souls (Job 23:12). It is bread for the hungry, milk for babes, strong meat for men, and honey to sweeten the lives of those who experience bitterness in this world. The Book of God is compared to both fire to melt, warm, and comfort and a hammer to break (Jeremiah 23:29). It is the sword of the Spirit (Ephesians 6:17; Hebrews 4:12). It is called good seed which is sown by the preaching of the gospel (Luke 8:11; Ecclesiastes 11:6; Psalm 126:6).

> The thoughts of man are lies,
> The Word of God is true.
> To bow to that is to be wise;
> Then hear, and fear, and do.

The law of the LORD is perfect, converting the soul: the testimony of the LORD is sure, making wise the simple. The statutes of the LORD are right, rejoicing the heart: the commandment of the LORD is pure, enlightening the eyes. The fear of the LORD is clean, enduring for ever: the judgments of the LORD are true and righteous altogether. More to be desired are they than gold, yea, than much fine gold: sweeter also than honey and the honeycomb' (Psalm 19:7-10).

'In the beginning God created the heaven and the earth'.
(Genesis 1:1)

Chapter 3

God Is

The Bible makes no attempt to prove the existence of God. It never occurred to any prophet or apostle to prove that God is. All the inspired writers presupposed an awareness of God's Being among all men. I make that same assumption. All attempts to prove the existence of God are as redundant as it would be for a man to try to prove that light is light, fire is fire, ice is cold, or heat is hot.

The words which head this page are a simple and forthright declaration of the fact that God is. The existence of God is confirmed by many, many things but, as John L. Dagg puts it, the Bible is 'The Volume of Revelation, a light emanating from the Father of lights, and is, of itself, an independent proof of his existence'. While heaven and earth, day and night, speak for God, we do not depend upon natural things for our knowledge of him. Instead, we look to the Bible. Here God speaks for himself. Creation never contradicts, but always confirms what is revealed in the Bible. Yet, we must never build our faith upon natural things. So we will begin and end our study of God's Being with the Bible, and make no appeal to any other source for the proof of his existence. We begin where the Bible begins in Genesis 1:1. – 'In the beginning God created the heaven and the earth'. The Bible begins with the announcement of the fact that God is and that he is the sovereign Creator of all things.

The Being or existence of God is the foundation of everything.

> The Being of God is the foundation of all religion; for if
> there is no God, religion is a vain thing; and it matters not
> neither what we believe, nor what we do; since there is no
> superior Being to whom we are accountable for either faith
> or practice. (John Gill)

When we come to the study of God, we come to the most
transcendent theme that can ever occupy the minds of men. The
Being of God is a subject as inexhaustible as it is incomprehensible,
a theme that is delightful, profitable, and blessed beyond measure.

The Bible tells us that God's Being, his existence, and certain
aspects of his nature are made known to men in several ways.

The physical universe

Read Psalm 19:1-6 and Romans 1:18-20. God has never left
himself without a witness. Every human being who has ever enjoyed
the privilege of living upon God's earth with sanity and reason has
seen and heard God's testimony of his own existence in creation
and providence. This is what Paul and Barnabas told the heathen at
Lystra who worshipped them as gods (Acts 14:15-16).

Three things are revealed to all men in creation which cannot be
denied. The Book of God declares that all men know these three
things about God; (1) God is (2) God is wise (3) God is almighty.

Throughout history wherever human beings have been found
they have demonstrated a knowledge of these three things. This
natural knowledge is inadequate and is always perverted because of
man's depravity; but all men know that God is, that he is wise, and
that he is almighty, because all men live as his creatures upon the
earth he created, where his voice is heard every day and every night.

Creation is not the only source of light possessed by all men.
The scriptures also tell us that all men are aware of God's Being,
because he has stamped his image upon man's soul and written his
law in his conscience (Romans 2:14-15).

The conscience of man

Man is by nature, by the stroke of his Creator, a religious being. Every human being lives with an irrepressible God consciousness. Every man's conscience proclaims loudly that God is, that he is almighty, that he is holy, and that he will punish sin.

According to the first chapter of Romans, all men by nature 'hold the truth of God in unrighteousness'. That is to say, they hold it down, suppress it, and try to deny it; but they cannot escape it. They will by training and education become either professed atheists or base idolaters. That is the best that training and education can do, apart from the grace of God. Civilization has never turned barbarians into Christians. It only turns them into clothed barbarians who can read and write. This God consciousness has all men convinced of three things. No matter how they try to suppress it, all men know that God is omnipotent and holy, that they are sinful and in need of a sin atoning sacrifice, and that they possess immortal souls which must meet the holy Lord God in judgment.

The light of nature, this God consciousness, renders all men without excuse, but brings none to a saving knowledge of God. The Holy Spirit tells us (Romans 1:18-20) that this knowledge of God by creation and conscience renders all men without excuse; but it never leads to or gives repentance and faith. It reveals 'the wrath of God', but never the grace of God. The witnesses of God in nature do not constitute gospel light, but only a basis for judgment and condemnation.

Men are without excuse because they will not obey the light of God in creation. They never have, never will, and never can do so, because all men are depraved, perverted, and spiritually dead. Therefore, they take the knowledge of God that they have and pervert it, heaping upon themselves even greater condemnation (Romans 1:18-32).

As you read Romans 1:18-32, be sure to note the order of man's degeneracy. It is written for our learning. This is the way of man when left to himself. First, he suppresses the truth of God. Then, he changes the truth of God into a lie and makes images of God to suit his own ideas of God. Idolatry is followed by utter uncleanness, vile affections, moral perversity, and the universal acceptance of them.

Because all men are dead in trespasses and in sins, perverse and depraved at heart, it takes more than the light of nature given to and stamped upon men by creation to bring them to the knowledge of God. Therefore, the Lord God reveals himself and makes himself known to his creatures by his written Word.

The Bible

Read Psalm 19:7-11 and 2 Timothy 3:16-17. Blessed beyond comprehension are those men and women who are privileged of God to have his Word delivered to them. If we had nothing else except the written Word of God our blessedness would be incalculable; but there is a blessedness even greater than this. God graciously sends his messengers to his elect, making himself known to chosen, redeemed sinners by the preaching of the gospel (Romans 10:9-17). He establishes gospel churches in which he meets with and speaks to sinners and allows himself to be worshipped by men (Matthew 18:20). Added to that is this great, great boon of grace, God almighty then allows saved sinners to be the instruments by which he makes himself known to other chosen sinners. No wonder Paul spoke as he did to the church at Rome as one who was a debtor to all men, who owed it to all men, to preach the gospel to them (Romans 1:14-17). Every saved sinner ought to have the same attitude. We are honour bound, in payment of a debt, to carry the good news of the grace and knowledge of God to perishing men.

Yet, in the purpose and pleasure of God, there is necessity for more knowledge still. It is not enough merely to have the light of creation, and of God consciousness, and even the light of the written Word of God. The knowledge of God by which sinners are saved and have eternal life comes by the revelation and knowledge of God in Christ (John 1:1-3, 14, 16-18; 17:3; Hebrews 1:1-3).

The incarnate Word

The Lord Jesus Christ is the incarnate Word of whom the written Word speaks. It is utterly impossible for sinners to know God apart from God's revelation of himself in the Person and work of Jesus Christ, his dear Son. It is in, by, and through Christ that we have the complete revelation of God. He is the sum of all God's purposes, the fulfilment of all the types and pictures of holy scripture, and the message of all the prophets. In Christ all the fulness of God resides. In him is the expression and revelation of all God's Being. If we want to know who God is, what God is, what God has done, and what God requires of men, if we want to know the way to God, we must look to and study the words, works, ways, and person of the Lord Jesus Christ (John 14:6; 9).

Herein lies the necessity for the preaching of the gospel. The scriptures cannot be known, and Christ cannot be known, except through the preaching of the gospel (1 Peter 1:23-25; Romans 10:13-17). Yet, the mere preaching of the gospel will never communicate a saving knowledge of God to lost sinners. The only way sinners can know God is by the gift and operation of God the Holy Spirit in the new birth, by the gift of faith (Hebrews 11:1-6; Ephesians 2:8-9).

The experience of faith

The only way we can know God is to believe him; and the only way we can believe him is for God himself to give us faith in Christ. Faith in Christ is the gift and operation of God in us, created in and bestowed upon chosen, redeemed sinners in regeneration by the irresistible power and grace of His Spirit (Ephesians 2:8; Philippians 1:29; Colossians 2:12). This gift of faith is communicated to and wrought in God's elect through the instrumentality of gospel preaching (1 Corinthians 1:18-24). With this gift of faith, every believer is given the abiding unction of the Spirit by which we are given grace through the Word of God to know all things spiritual (1 Corinthians 2:12-16; 1 John 2:20-27).

It is a sad, sad proof of human depravity that men everywhere deny or disregard the existence of God. We read in the Book of God of the fool who cries, 'no God', of nations that 'forget God', and of individuals who do not have God in all their thoughts. Such people, while they cannot convince themselves that there is no God, so despise him that they want nothing to do with him. They say, 'Depart from us. We desire not the knowledge of your ways'. There is only one cure for this sad, cursed condition. The only effectual cure for men's souls is the new birth (John 3:3-7).

Yet, even in the thoughts of regenerate men and women, even among those who are true believers, sometimes horribly sinful questions and doubts arise concerning the existence of God. These are things with which Satan harasses and seeks to destroy God's elect. For such harassing thoughts the only cure is grace. The remedy for such wicked thoughts is the diligent study of God's Word and works, asking him to graciously apply them to your heart. Carefully mark the hand of God's providence in everything. Prayerfully and confidently acknowledge God in all your ways. Walk humbly with God, seeking and bowing to his will in all things. 'If we habitually walk with God, we shall not doubt his existence' (John L. Dagg).

Let us ever remember our God and walk before him and with him in the humility of faith. 'Trust in the Lord with all thine heart; and lean not unto thine own understanding. In all thy ways acknowledge him, and he shall direct thy paths. Be not wise in thine own eyes: fear the LORD, and depart from evil. It shall be health to thy navel, and marrow to thy bones. Honour the LORD with thy substance, and with the first fruits of all thine increase: So shall thy barns be filled with plenty, and thy presses shall burst out with new wine' (Proverbs 3:5-10).

'For there are three that bear record in heaven, the Father, the Word, and the Holy Ghost: and these three are one'.
(1 John 5:7)

Chapter 4

The Unfathomable Mystery of the Trinity

What do we know about the biblical doctrine of the Trinity? Do we have a comfortable, crisp understanding of the doctrine of the Trinity as it is set forth in the Word of God? I think it is safe to assume that most people who profess to believe the doctrine of the Trinity would be hard pressed to show from the scriptures why they believe it.

Without question, clear, biblical instruction is needed. Multitudes fall prey to the many heretical cults (and they are all heretical cults) which deny the doctrine of the Trinity and the eternal deity of our Lord Jesus Christ. In these days of unity at any price, denominations, churches, and preachers who deny these essential facts are even embraced as Christian by many. Such compromise is both unbiblical and intolerable.

We worship one God in the Trinity, or Tri-Unity of his sacred Persons (Father, Son, and Holy Spirit), and adore each as the God of all grace by whom we are saved. It must be acknowledged that it is an utter impossibility for sinful mortals to understand, much less explain, the mystery of the holy Trinity. No mortal can comprehend the being of the infinite God. The doctrine of holy Trinity is, indeed, an unfathomable mystery.

Critics, sceptics, and infidels arrogantly boast that they will not believe anything that they cannot understand and explain; but their boast is not true. They would not think of denying that the sun shines, though few, if any, can explain or understand why and how. The fact is we live in a world full of things we cannot or do not personally understand. Yet, we never question them. I do not understand how a brown cow can eat green grass and give white milk that makes yellow butter; but I drink the milk and eat the butter.

Nothing is more confusing to scientists than the complexity of humanity. Neither the biologist nor the psychologist can grasp the mystery of what a man is. They tell us, in their folly, that we are the highest form of animal life. Yet, they cannot find an animal anywhere like a man. Why? Because man is not an animal. He is the only creature in the universe made in the image of God. That makes humanity an unfathomable mystery. The Word of God speaks of man as a trichotomy, a being of three parts. Unlike the animals around us, we are all material, rational, and spiritual beings. Each of us possesses a material body, a rational mind, and an immaterial or spiritual soul.

We are, in one sense, a unity, a personality. Yet, in another sense, we are a plurality, a tri-unity, or a trinity. How do we put all that together in one person? I cannot answer that question; but I know it is so. No one will ever be able to adequately explain the complex mystery of humanity. All we can do is watch and observe.

If that is true with regard to humanity, how much more so must it be true when we think about the infinite God! We cannot understand or explain even the works of God. We certainly cannot understand his Being! I make no pretence of being able to explain the Trinity. I cannot explain what I do not understand. Someone once said, 'That man is a fool who denies the doctrine of the Trinity; and he is equally a fool who tries to explain it'. My only object in this study is to show that the Word of God teaches this doctrine and that it is a doctrine full of comfort and encouragement.

A Bible doctrine

The Bible clearly and unmistakably teaches the doctrine of the Trinity. This is not a matter of guesswork. It is not a point of theological speculation or conjecture. 1 John 5:7 specifically and clearly states the doctrine of the Trinity. 'There are three that bear record in heaven, the Father, the Word, and the Holy Ghost: and these three are one'. Certainly, this is not the only place where the doctrine is taught. Throughout the scriptures, God reveals himself as a triune Being, one in three and three in one. All are equal in all things and co-eternal.

When we say we believe in the Trinity of the divine Persons, we do not mean that there are three equal, but separate Gods. We do not mean that there is one God manifest in three personalities. We mean that we worship one God in three divine Persons: Father, Son, and Holy Spirit. The Divine Trinity is the union of these three Persons in one Godhead, so that all three are one God as to substance, but three Persons as to individuality. 'In the nature of the one God', wrote A. H. Strong, 'there are three eternal distinctions which are represented to us under the figure of three Persons, and these three are equal'.

Is this or is it not the doctrine of the Bible? That is the only thing that matters. Search the scriptures and see for yourself that the Word of God clearly teaches the doctrine.

The Trinity is a doctrine found in the Old Testament scriptures as well as the New. In the self-disclosure, or self-revelation, of God in the Old Testament, the Lord our God is always represented as one God, but always as one God with plural Persons within the

Godhead (Deuteronomy 6:4; Genesis 1:1-2, 26). The Old Testament scriptures constantly point us to the three Persons of the Godhead. We are often confronted with God the Father, the Spirit of the Lord, and the many pre-incarnate appearances of Christ as the Angel of the Lord.

One of the most common Hebrew words used for God is the word El. You find it in a thousand combinations in the Old Testament. The plural form of the word El is Elohim. This is the word used in Genesis one. W. A. Criswell has powerfully demonstrated the significance of the way these words are used.

> In the first chapter of Genesis, that word Elohim is used thirty-two times. In the books of Moses, Elohim is used more than five hundred times. In the Old Testament scriptures, Elohim is used more than five thousand times. In all thirty-two times in the first chapter of Genesis, in all the more than five hundred times in the writings of Moses, and in all the more than five thousand times in the Old Testament, without exception, Elohim is used with a singular verb. Elohim, plural, referring to the majesty and abounding marvel and mystery of God, appears with a singular verb.

The implication of that fact is obvious. The Lord our God, the triune God, is one God; and this triune God is the one true and living God. There is no other God.

The New Testament clearly and emphatically declares the doctrine of the Trinity. No effort is made in the Word of God to prove the doctrine. It is simply stated as a matter of fact, a fact commonly received and believed by all who were numbered among the saints. It is presented almost casually ...

– in connection with the incarnation (Matthew 1:20-23).
– in connection with our Lord's baptism (Matthew 3:15-17).
– in connection with the great commission (Matthew 28:19-20).

– in connection with the Saviour's promise to send the Holy Spirit another Comforter exactly like Himself (John 14:16).
– in connection with the apostolic benedictions (2 Corinthians 13:14).

The New Testament declares that God the Father is God (Romans 1:7), God the Son is God (Hebrews 1:8), and God the Holy Spirit is God (Acts 5:3-4). Yet, 'The LORD our God is one LORD'. The doctrine of the Trinity runs through all the New Testament (Luke 1:35; John 14:26; 15:26; Galatians 4:6; Ephesians 1:17; 2:18; 3:14-16; 4:4-7; 5:18-20; 6:17-23; 1 Peter 1:2; Jude 20-21; Revelation 1:4-6). Without question, the doctrine of the Trinity is a Bible doctrine. Someone accurately stated:

> The Father is all the fulness of the Godhead invisible (John 1:18); the Son is all the fulness of the Godhead manifested (John 1:14-18); the Spirit is all the fulness of God acting immediately upon the creature (1 Corinthians 2:9-10).

I confess my inability to produce a single argument drawn from nature or logic to prove the doctrine of the Trinity. It is a mystery filled with such grandeur that it defies comprehension by finite minds. But our faith does not stand upon nature and logic. Our faith stands upon the Word of God alone. All Christians believe the doctrine of the Trinity because it is revealed in holy scripture; and I see it clearly because I believe it.

A gospel doctrine

All three Persons in the Godhead are equally gracious. This is one of the many great gospel truths the Holy Spirit shows us in the first chapter of Ephesians. As the three Persons of the eternal Godhead are equal in Divinity, but distinct in personality, so all three of the Divine Persons are equal in grace, but distinct in the operations of grace.

God the Father is set before us as the Fountain of all grace (Ephesians 1:3-6). It was God the Father who, in the covenant of grace, proposed redemption, devised the plan, and chose the people whom he would save by his almighty grace. He found a way whereby his banished ones could be brought back to him and never expelled from his presence. Then, in the fulness of time, he sent his Son to be the Medium or Mediator of grace to his chosen (Galatians 4:4-6).

God the Son, the Lord Jesus Christ, is the channel of all grace (Ephesians 1:7-12). All grace comes to sinners through Christ the Mediator. In this chapter Paul tells us fourteen times that everything God requires of sinners, does for sinners, and gives to sinners is in Christ. Apart from Christ there is no grace! God will not deal with man, but by Christ. Man cannot deal with God, but by Christ. Christ is the Revelation of God, the incarnation of God, and the only way to God.

Are we chosen of God? We are chosen in Christ. Are we blessed of God? We are blessed in Christ. Are we predestinated by God? We are predestinated to be conformed to the image of Christ. Are we adopted as the children of God? We are adopted in Christ. Are we accepted of God? We are accepted in Christ. Are we redeemed by God? We are redeemed in Christ. Are we forgiven by God? We are forgiven in Christ. Are we justified before God? We are justified in Christ. Are we sanctified by God? We are sanctified in Christ. Do we know God? We know him in Christ. Do we have an inheritance from God? We have it in Christ. Are we called of God? We are called in Christ.

Do you see this? All grace comes to chosen sinners through Christ. There is no other way the grace of God can reach a sinner. Let no rejecter of God's Son imagine that he shall be the beneficiary of God's grace. It is the work of Christ upon the cross which has brought grace and justice together in the salvation of sinners. It is through his blood, only through the blood of the cross that 'mercy and truth are met together; righteousness and peace have kissed each other' (Psalm 85:10). Blissfully lost in the contemplation of God's matchless grace in Christ, John Bunyan penned the following rapturous words ...

> O Thou Son of the Blessed! Grace stripped Thee of thy glory. Grace brought Thee down from heaven. Grace made Thee bear such burdens of sin, such burdens of curse as are unspeakable. Grace was in Thy heart. Grace came bubbling up from Thy bleeding side. Grace was in Thy tears. Grace was in Thy prayers. Grace streamed from Thy thorn-crowned brow! Grace came forth with the nails that pierced Thee, with the thorns that pricked Thee! Oh, here are unsearchable riches of grace! Grace to make sinners happy! Grace to make angels wonder! Grace to make devils astonished!

The Fountain of all grace is God the Father. The medium of all grace is God the Son. God the Holy Spirit is the Administrator of all grace (Ephesians 1:13-14). It is God the Holy Spirit who effactually applies the blood of Christ to chosen, redeemed sinners. He regenerates the dead by omnipotent power (John 6:63). He calls the redeemed with irresistible grace (Psalm 65:4; 110:3; John 16:8-11). He gives faith to the chosen by almighty operations of grace (Ephesians 2:1-9; Colossians 2:12). He seals God's elect unto everlasting glory.

Redemption was effectually accomplished for God's elect by Christ at Calvary; and it is effectually applied to all the redeemed by God the Holy Spirit in effectual calling (Hebrews 9:12-14). Without the sovereign, gracious operations of God the Holy Spirit in conversion no sinner would ever become the beneficiary of grace. He takes the things of Christ and shows them to his people. He quickens those the Father chose, reclaims those the Son redeemed, and leads to the Good Shepherd every one of those lost sheep for whom the Good Shepherd laid down his life (John 10:11). 'He conquers the stoutest hearts and cleanses the foulest spiritual leper.

He opens the sin-blinded eyes and unstops the sin-closed ears. The blessed Holy Spirit reveals the grace of the Father and applies the grace of the Son' (C. D. Cole)

All three Persons in the Godhead are equally gracious; and all three must be equally praised. In fact, whenever the three Persons of the Holy Trinity are presented together in the scriptures, it is always in connection with redemption, grace, and salvation. I have not found an exception.

> Praise God from whom all blessings flow!
> Praise Him all creatures here below!
> Praise Him above, ye heavenly hosts!
> Praise Father, Son, and Holy Ghost!

Sometimes God the Father is presented alone, as when he stood upon Mount Sinai, clothed with thunder and lightning, delivering the law to Moses. So terrible was his presence that the very mountain shook in the prospect of God's awesome judgment (Exodus 20:18).

Sometimes God the Son appears alone, as when he appears in his glorious second advent. Then men and women who have despised and rejected him will cry for the mountains to fall upon them and pray in terror that they might be saved from 'the wrath of the Lamb' (Revelation 6:14).

When God the Holy Spirit is represented alone, the consequences are the same. Those who blaspheme him, committing that sin which can never be forgiven, are reserved as reprobates unto everlasting judgment (Matthew 12:31-32). Whenever one Person in the Trinity is presented alone, the result is judgment.

However, when all three of the Divine Persons are set before us together, the consequence is always mercy, grace, redemption, and salvation (Ephesians 1:3-14; Revelation 1:4-6). In other words, – The whole Being of God, in all his attributes, in all his glory, in the Trinity of his Persons is set for the everlasting salvation of his elect (Jeremiah 32:41; Romans 8:28-32).

An inspiring doctrine

No doctrine in the Bible more forcibly inspires unity among true believers than the doctrine of the Trinity. This is not some abstract point of theological speculation, or some profitless point of doctrinal refinement. This is a subject so far above our comprehension that it should inspire our deepest reverence and humility, as well as the most circumspect consecration and unity.

In our baptism, you and I have publicly avowed our consecration to our God (Romans 6:4-6). Being baptized in the name of the Father, and of the Son, and of the Holy Spirit, we publicly declared our consecration and commitment to obey the will of the Father, live for the glory of the Son, and submit to the leadership of the Holy Spirit.

Let every thought about the holy Trinity stimulate in us a desire that we may be one even as God the Father, God the Son, and God the Holy Spirit are one (John 17:20-22). 'Who can think of the Father, the Son, and the Holy Spirit as one – one in nature, one in love, one in purpose – and not hope for the day when the intercessory prayer of Christ will be answered in the union of all his followers?' (J. M. Pendleton)

All true believers should earnestly devote themselves, as the sons and daughters of the triune God, to unity. Oh, that God's saints on earth might truly be one in purpose – seeking the glory of God, one in labour – serving the cause of Christ, and one in the love of Christ (Philippians 2:2-5).

As the children of God in this world, for Christ's sake (Ephesians 4:32-5:1), for his glory, believers must learn by the grace of God to be patient with one another, to highly esteem one another, to forgive one another, to be forbearing with one another, and to give deference to one another. Soon, we shall be one in glory (John 17:22; Ephesians 4:1-6).

'They that know thy name will put their trust in thee: for thou, LORD, hast not forsaken them that seek thee'.
(Psalm 9:10)

Chapter 5

The Names of the Lord

Throughout the Word of God names were given to children that had special meaning and significance. Sometimes a person's name would be changed or a name would be ascribed to him, either by God or by someone else, indicating radical change of life. Here are some examples: Adam means 'red earth', indicating his being created by God from the dust of the earth. Jacob means 'cheat, supplanter'; but God changed his name to Israel, which means 'prince with God'. Moses means 'drawn forth'. He was so named because Pharaoh's daughter drew him out of the water. In the Bible, the name given to a person said something about that person.

The same thing is true concerning the names of the Lord our God. However, no single word in human language is sufficient to serve as a name for him. Therefore, there are several words or names by which he has made himself known. The names applied to God in scripture describe his glorious character, reveal his great attributes, and display his redemptive purpose. In this chapter we will look at the names by which God reveals himself in the holy scriptures and their meaning. There are ten specific names ascribed to our God in holy scripture.

1. The first revelation of God is found in Genesis 1:1 'In the beginning God created the heaven and the earth'. The name of God given there is '**ELOHIM**'. 'Elohim' means 'to worship'. This is the name of our God. He is THE WORSHIPPED ONE. He is the only object of true worship, praise, adoration, and trust. The word 'Elohim' is given in the plural, though it refers to One God. The significance is obvious. We worship One God who is three distinct Persons in One glorious Being; Father, Son, and Holy Spirit (1 John 5:7).

2. Another name of God is '**EL**' or '**ELI**'. In Genesis 12:7-8 the Lord appeared to Abraham, and made a covenant with him. Abraham built an altar there and called the place 'Beth-El', which means 'the house of God'. This is the word our Lord used, when he cried, 'Eli, Eli, lama sa-bach-tha-na?' that is to say, 'My God, my God, why hast thou forsaken me?' (Matthew 27:46). This name, 'El', means 'strong or mighty God'. It is expressive of the power of God.

3. Next, God reveals himself under the name '**ELIOM**' in Genesis 14:18-22. 'Eliom' means ' the most high God'. It is expressive of God's supremacy and majesty. Our Lord Jesus, of whom Melchizedek was at least a type, (if not Christ himself in one of his many pre-incarnate manifestations) is called 'the Son of the Highest' (Luke 1:32). Eliom is the high and lofty One who inhabits eternity.

4. God also revealed himself to Abraham by the name '**SHADDAI**', which we translate 'Almighty' (Genesis 17:1). 'Shaddai' means 'God all-sufficient'. It expresses more than the power of God alone. It expresses the power and sufficiency of God to bestow his grace and fulfil his promises. El-Shaddai is God able to save, able to do his will, able to shower his blessings upon his people.

5. In 1 Samuel 1:9-11, we see Hannah calling upon '**THE LORD OF HOSTS**' in her deep distress. 'The Lord of Sabaoth' (Isaiah 6:3; James 5:4) is our God. This name is expressive of God's sovereign dominion and power over all his creatures. The Lord of Hosts has 'his way in the armies of heaven and among the inhabitants of the earth; and none can stay his hand, or say unto him, what doest thou?'

> Did we in our own strength confide,
> Our striving would be loosing,
> Were not the right Man on our side,
> The Man of God's own choosing.
> Dost ask who that may be?
> Christ Jesus, it is He—
> Lord Sabaoth His name,
> From age to age the same—
> And He must win the battle!

6. In Genesis 15:2, Abraham called upon God by the name '**ADONAI**', to give him the promised covenant seed. 'Adonai' means 'the Cause', or 'the Support'. Most certainly, Adonai is a suitable name for our God. He is the original cause of all things (Romans 11:36). Our God supports and maintains all things (Hebrews 1:3); and he upholds his saints with the right hand of his righteousness (Isaiah 41:10).

7. In Exodus 3:13-14, the Lord appeared to Moses as '**EJEH**', which means 'I Am that I Am'. 'Ejeh' refers to the immutability of our God and Saviour (Malachi 3:6; Hebrews 13:8). With our God there is no variableness, neither shadow of turning. He is eternally the same (Malachi 3:6; Hebrews 13:8; James 1:17). 'I Am' is God who changes not.

8. In the New Testament, the word by which our God is most often revealed is '**LORD**', the Greek words translated Lord are 'Kurios' and 'Despotes' (2 Peter 2:1). 'Lord' simply means, God who is

sovereign. It refers to God's dominion, power, authority, and right of ownership over all things. This is the word commonly used to describe Christ our Mediator King (Acts 10:36; 1 Corinthians 8:6; Ephesians 4:4). When this particular word is applied to men it is often translated 'master' or 'sir', and used as a title of respect. When it is applied to Christ, it implies his dominion and authority as Lord over all things. Yet, it also implies the willing surrender of all believers to him as their Lord (Luke 14:25-33). Christ is the sovereign despot of all men (2 Peter 2:1). He is our Lord (John 20:28).

9. The word translated 'GOD' in the New Testament is 'Theos'. 'Theos', God, is one who is holy, who sees all things and knows all things, and disposes of all things. God who is light is perfectly holy. He sees all things with perfect clarity. He disposes of all things as he will.

These nine names of God tell us that God is infinite, eternal, almighty, self-existent, self-sufficient, ineffably glorious and holy. This great God is a God to be feared, worshipped, and obeyed. He is a consuming fire, unapproachably glorious in holiness. Let me have nothing to do with this God; 'who only hath immortality dwelling in light, which no man can approach unto, whom no man hath seen, nor can see!' I am a frail, fickle man of sinful flesh. Should I ever meet this great, majestic, glorious, and holy God, should I ever be required to stand in his presence, his sovereign power would consume me more quickly than dry grass in a blazing furnace.

Is there then no hope for sinners? Is there not a daysman or mediator to stand between us and God? Is there not One with holy hands and a pure heart who has never lifted up his soul unto vanity, who can approach God in our stead, and stand before him to plead our cause? Indeed there is! Blessed be God, there is a Substitute, who is himself God! He is constantly revealed under a tenth name of God throughout the scriptures.

10. God's glorious redemptive name is '**JEHOVAH**'. The word 'Jehovah' means 'Saviour' or 'Deliverer' (Exodus 6:3). God in Christ is God mighty to save. 'Jehovah', essentially means 'to be'. Our Lord Jesus Christ declares that he is the One 'which is, which was, and which is to come' (Revelation 1:4). He is the eternal God of salvation, redemption, and deliverance.

'This glorious and fearful name, THE LORD THY GOD' (Deuteronomy 28:58) is not to be taken in vain, used in common speech, or spoken with any levity. 'Thou shalt not take the name of the Lord thy God in vain; for the Lord will not hold him guiltless who taketh his name in vain' (Exodus 20:7).

He that sent redemption to his people and commanded his covenant forever is to be reverenced by us. 'Holy and reverend is his name' (Psalm 111:9). Let us ever extol, honour, praise, and magnify the name of the Lord our God. 'I will praise thee, O Lord my God, with all my heart: and I will glorify thy name for evermore. For great is thy mercy toward me: and thou hast delivered my soul from the lowest hell' (Psalm 86:12-13).

'Not unto us, O Lord, not unto us, but unto thy name give glory, for thy mercy, and for thy truth's sake' (Psalm 115:1).

'And they that know thy name will put their trust in thee: for thou, LORD, hast not forsaken them that seek thee'. (Psalm 9:10)

Chapter 6

Jehovah – God's Covenant, Redemptive Name

'Jehovah' is God's most famous name. It is the name of him who alone is the necessary and self-existent Being. The name, Jehovah, implies God's eternality. It comes from a root word which signifies 'to be'. Jehovah is God who is, who was, and who is to come (Revelation 1:4). This is God's personal, proper, incommunicable name. 'That men may know that thou, whose name alone is JEHOVAH, art the most high over all the earth' (Psalm 83:18). The other names of God are sometimes applied to creatures, but Jehovah is used exclusively of the true and living God.

In his book, *The Divine Inspiration of the Bible*, A. W. Pink gives the following, instructive comments showing the distinct use of God's names 'Elohim' and 'Jehovah'.

The names Elohim and Jehovah are found on the pages of the Old Testament several thousand times, but they are never employed loosely or used alternately. Each of these names has a definite significance and scope, and were we to substitute the one for the other the beauty and perfection of a multitude of passages would be destroyed. To illustrate: the word God occurs all through Genesis 1, but 'Lord God' in Genesis 2. Were these two Divine titles reversed here, a flaw and blemish would be the consequences. 'God' is the creatorial title, whereas 'Lord' implies covenant relationship and shows God's dealings with His own people. Hence, in Genesis 1, 'God' is used, and in Genesis 2, 'Lord God' is employed, and all through the remainder of the Old Testament these two Divine titles are used discriminately and in harmony with the meaning of first mention. One or two examples must suffice. 'And they went in unto Noah into the ark, two and two of all flesh, wherein is the breath of life. And they that went in, went in male and female of all flesh, as God (Elohim) had commanded him'. 'God' because it was the Creator commanding with respect to His creatures, as such; but in the remainder of the same verse, we read, 'and the Lord (Jehovah) shut him in' (Genesis 7:15,16), because God's action here toward Noah was based upon covenant relationship. When going forth to meet Goliath David said 'This day will the Lord (Jehovah) deliver thee into mine hand (because David was in covenant relationship with him); and I will smite thee, and take thine head from thee; and I will give the carcases of the host of the Philistines this day unto the fowls of the air, and to the wild beasts of the earth; that all the earth (which was not in covenant relationship with Him) may know that there is a God (Elohim) in Israel. And all this assembly (which were in covenant relationship with him) shall know that the Lord (Jehovah) saveth not with sword and spear: for the battle is the Lord's, and he will give you into our hands' (1 Samuel 17:46,47). Once more: 'And it came to pass, when the captains of the chariots saw Jehoshaphat, that they said, It

is the king of Israel. Therefore they compassed about him
to fight: but Jehoshaphat cried out, and the Lord (Jehovah)
helped him; and God (Elohim) moved them to depart from
him' (2 Chronicles 18:31). And thus it is all through the Old
Testament.

The name Jehovah is frequently used as a compound with other
words to set forth some specific aspect of God's character and work
in meeting the needs of his elect.

There are fourteen distinct usages of these 'Jehovah' titles in the
Old Testament.

1. JEHOVAH-JIREH – 'The Lord will provide'. 'And Abraham
called the name of that place Jehovah-jireh: as it is said to this day,
In the mount of the Lord it shall be seen' (Genesis 22:14).
2. JEHOVAH-RAPHA – 'The Lord that healeth thee'. 'And said, If
thou wilt diligently hearken to the voice of the Lord thy God, and
wilt do that which is right in his sight, and wilt give ear to his
commandments, and keep all his statutes, I will put none of these
diseases upon thee, which I have brought upon the Egyptians: for I
am the Lord that healeth thee' (Exodus 15:26).
3. JEHOVAH-NISSI – 'The Lord our Banner'. 'And Moses built
an altar, and called the name of it Jehovah-nissi' (Exodus 17:15).
4. JEHOVAH-M'KADDESH – 'The Lord which doth sanctify you'.
'Speak thou also unto the children of Israel, saying, Verily my
sabbaths ye shall keep: for it is a sign between me and you throughout
your generations; that ye may know that I am the Lord that doth
sanctify you' (Exodus 31:13); 'And ye shall keep my statutes, and
do them: I am the Lord which sanctify you' (Leviticus 20:8).
5. JEHOVAH-RA-AH – 'The Lord my Shepherd'. 'The Lord is my
shepherd; I shall not want' (Psalm 23:1).
6. JEHOVAH-HOSEENU – 'The Lord our Maker'. 'O come, let
us worship and bow down: let us kneel before the Lord our maker'
(Psalm 95:6).

7. JEHOVAH-ELOHEENU – 'The Lord our God'. 'Exalt ye the Lord our God, and worship at his footstool; for he is holy ... He spake unto them in the cloudy pillar: they kept his testimonies, and the ordinance that he gave them. Thou answeredst them, O Lord our God: thou wast a God that forgavest them, though thou tookest vengeance of their inventions' (Psalm 99:5,7,8).

8. JEHOVAH-ELOHEKA – 'The Lord thy God'. 'I am the Lord thy God, which have brought thee out of the land of Egypt, out of the house of bondage: ... Thou shalt not bow down thyself to them, nor serve them: for I the Lord thy God am a jealous God, visiting the iniquity of the fathers upon the children unto the third and fourth generation of them that hate me ... Thou shalt not take the name of the Lord thy God in vain; for the LORD will not hold him guiltless that taketh his name in vain' (Exodus 20:2, 5, 7).

9. JEHOVAH-ELOHAY – 'The Lord my God'. 'And ye shall flee to the valley of the mountains; for the valley of the mountains shall reach unto Azal: yea, ye shall flee, like as ye fled from before the earthquake in the days of Uzziah king of Judah: and the Lord my God shall come, and all the saints with thee' (Zechariah 14:5).

10. JEHOVAH-SHALOM – 'The Lord our Peace'. 'Then Gideon built an altar there unto the Lord, and called it Jehovah-shalom: unto this day it is yet in Ophrah of the Abiezrites' (Judges 6:24).

11. JEHOVAH-TSEBAHOTH – 'The Lord of Hosts'. 'And this man went up out of his city yearly to worship and to sacrifice unto the LORD of hosts in Shiloh. And the two sons of Eli, Hophni and Phinehas, the priests of the Lord, were there' (1 Samuel 1:3); 'And as Esaias said before, Except the Lord of Sabaoth had left us a seed, we had been as Sodoma, and been made like unto Gomorrha' (Romans 9:29); 'Behold, the hire of the labourers who have reaped down your fields, which is of you kept back by fraud, crieth: and the cries of them which have reaped are entered into the ears of the Lord of sabaoth' (James 5:4).

12. JEHOVAH-HELEYON – 'The Lord Most High'. 'I will praise the Lord according to his righteousness: and will sing praise to the

name of the LORD most high' (Psalm 7:17); 'For the Lord most high is terrible; he is a great King over all the earth' (Psalm 47:2); 'For thou, Lord, art high above all the earth: thou art exalted far above all gods' (Psalm 97:9).

13. JEHOVAH-TSIDKEENU – 'The Lord our Righteousness'. 'In his days Judah shall be saved, and Israel shall dwell safely: and this is his name whereby he shall be called, THE LORD OUR RIGHTEOUSNESS' (Jeremiah 23:6); 'In those days shall Judah be saved, and Jerusalem shall dwell safely: and this is the name wherewith she shall be called, The Lord our righteousness' (Jeremiah 33:16).

14. JEHOVAH-SHAMMAH – 'The Lord is there'. 'It was round about eighteen thousand measures: and the name of the city from that day shall be, The Lord is there' (Ezekiel 48:35).

'And this is life eternal, that they might know thee the only true God, and Jesus Christ, whom thou hast sent'. (John 17:3)

Chapter 7

The Attributes of God

There is no possibility of salvation, no possibility of eternal life, no possibility of true Christianity apart from knowing God in his true character, as he is revealed in holy scripture. Therefore, it is of utmost importance that we have some knowledge and understanding of the Divine character, that we know the attributes of God's Being, the perfections of his nature. A proper, biblical knowledge of God's attributes is essential to saving faith. That person who claims to believe God, but has no idea what his character is, is deluded with a false faith. Our Lord Jesus tells us plainly, 'And this is life eternal, that they might know thee the only true God, and Jesus Christ, whom thou hast sent'. A knowledge of God's character, his attributes, lies at the very foundation of true religion.

Knowledge essential to faith

It is impossible to trust and love God until we know who he is, until we know the character of his Being. Indeed, it is impossible for us to know our need of such a Saviour as Christ is until we have some concept of the infinitely holy character of God. We may be terrified by the fear of wrath to come and of eternal judgment, and we may be delighted by the hope of escaping the wrath of God in hell through Christ; but that is not salvation. Jesus Christ is not a fire-escape from hell. He is the revelation of and way to the living God. Eternal life, true Christianity, true salvation is a knowledge of God as God, faith in God as God, and love for God as God.

Yet, our Lord Jesus tells us that 'God is Spirit'. Because God is Spirit, he cannot be known by natural senses and abilities. He can be known by us only as he is pleased to reveal himself to us in his Word and works, through the mediation of our Lord Jesus Christ (John 1:1-3, 14-18).

What are God's attributes?

The attributes of God are the perfections of his nature, the characteristics of his Being as God. God's attributes are those traits of character essential to Divinity. As we look at the attributes of God revealed in the scriptures, remember that if even one of these attributes did not belong to him, he would not and could not be God. These are the things which are essential to Godhood.

Theologians have many ways of classifying the Divine attributes. Some have classified them as communicable and incommunicable. Communicable attributes are those which are communicated to rational creatures (angels and men). They would be wisdom, power, righteousness, love, and mercy. Incommunicable attributes are attributes belonging to God alone, such as infinity, immutability, omnipotence, omniscience, and omnipresence.

Others have attempted to classify the attributes of God as natural and moral. They would, for example, say that infinity, eternality, and omnipotence are among God's natural attributes, and that holiness, justice, and truth are moral attributes.

There are other ideas put forth by men to classify God's attributes; but the Bible never attempts to do so. When trying to understand the character of our God, we must recognize that this is a subject so majestically sublime that it is simply inappropriate to attempt to analyse God and divide his nature into parts like a psychologist dissects the psyche of a man. Instead, we must look at the glorious attributes of our God with the reverent wonder of simplicity. I will give a brief sketch of God's attributes with numerous scripture texts illustrating them. Look up each text, read it in its context, and bask your soul in the contemplation of God's glorious Being. Here are thirteen of those attributes which are essential to God's Being. The list could be much longer; but some of God's attributes can be viewed together, simply because they are intimately connected. For example: justice demands veracity, omnipresence demands infinity, and goodness demands love.

1. Self existence – God almighty is Life in himself, independent and underived. His Being is inexhaustible (Psalm 36:9; Isaiah 41:4; John 5:26; Acts 17:24-25; Romans 11:35-36; Genesis 1:1; Exodus 3:14).

2. Spirituality – God is Spirit. He is not just *a* spirit. He is Spirit. He has no body or parts like we do. He is the pure, underived, eternal Spirit (Genesis 1:2; Deuteronomy 4:15-19; Psalm 139:7; Isaiah 60:1; Ezekiel 37:14; 39:29; Joel 2:28-29; John 4:24; Acts 17:28; Romans 8:9; 13:1; 1 Corinthians 2:11; 2 Corinthians 3:17; Philippians 3:3; Hebrews 12:9).

3. Unity – Though there are three Persons in the Godhead, these three are One and this triune God is the only God there is (Exodus 20:3; Deuteronomy 4:35, 39; 6:4; 1 Samuel 2:2; 2 Samuel 7:22; 1 Kings 8:60; 2 Kings 19:15; Nehemiah 9:6; Psalm 86:10; Isaiah 44:6-8; 45:22; Jeremiah 10:10; Joel 2:27; Zechariah 14:9; Mark 12:29; John 17:3; Romans 1:21-23; 1 Corinthians 8:4-6; Galatians 3:20; Ephesians 4:6; 1 Timothy 2:5; 1 John 5:7).

4. Eternity – God's eternality means that he always is, that he is unlimited by time. He is the eternal 'I AM' (Genesis 21:33; Exodus 15:18; Deuteronomy 32:40; 1 Chronicles 16:36; Nehemiah 9:5; Psalm 90:1-4; Isaiah 44:6; 48:12; 57:15; Jeremiah 10:10; Lamentations 5:19; Daniel 4:3, 34; Micah 4:7; Habakkuk 1:12;

Romans 1:20; 16:26; 1 Timothy 1:17; Hebrews 1:10-12; 2 Peter 3:8; Revelation 4:8-10).

5. Immutability – God is unchanging and unchangeable. When the scriptures declare that God changes not, we are taught that though he changes all things, nothing moves or changes him. In his Being and in his purpose, God is unchangeable. That is our security (Exodus 3:15; Numbers 23:19; 1 Samuel 15:29; Psalm 33:11; Proverbs 19:21; Ecclesiastes 3:14; Isaiah 14:24; Ezekiel 24:14; Malachi 3:6; Romans 11:29; Hebrews 6:17-18; James 1:17).

6. Omnipresence – God is unlimited by space. He is everywhere present, in all the fulness of his being at all times. It means that he is immanent, that he fills all things with his Being and comprehends all things in his Being (Genesis 28:15-16; Deuteronomy 4:39; Joshua 2:11; 1 Kings 8:27; Psalm 139:7-10; Proverbs 15:3, 11; Isaiah 66:1; Jeremiah 23:23-24; Amos 9:2-4, 6; Acts 7:48-49; 17:27-28; Ephesians 1:23).

7. Omniscience – God knows all things absolutely and at all times. God's omniscience must not be confused with his foreknowledge. Omniscience is an attribute of God's Being. Foreknowledge is an act of his grace (Genesis 18:18-19; 25:23; Exodus 3:19; Deuteronomy 31:21; 1 Samuel 2:3; 1 Kings 8:39; 2 Kings 8:10, 13; 1 Chronicles 28:9; Psalm 94:9, 11; 139:1-16; 147:4-5; Proverbs 15:3, 11; Isaiah 29:15-16; 40:28; Jeremiah 1:4-5; 16:17; Ezekiel 11:5; Daniel 2:22, 28; Hosea 7:2; Amos 4:13; Nahum 1:7; Zechariah 4:10; Matthew 6:4, 6, 8, 18; Luke 16:15; Acts 15:8, 18; Romans 8:27, 29; 1 Corinthians 3:20; 2 Timothy 2:19; Hebrews 4:13; 1 Peter 1:2; 1 John 3:20).

8. Wisdom – God is all wise. He always accomplishes the best designs by the best possible means (Psalm 104:24; Proverbs 3:19; Isaiah 28:29; Jeremiah 10:12; Daniel 2:20-21; Romans 11:33-36; 1 Corinthians 1:24-25, 30; 2:6-7; Ephesians 3:10; Colossians 2:2-3).

9. Omnipotence – God is all-powerful, almighty. In the truest sense nothing is impossible with him. His will, his work, his purpose, is irresistible; because God is omnipotent (Genesis 1:1; 17:1; 18:14;

Exodus 15:7; Deuteronomy 3:24; 32:39; 1 Samuel 14:6; 1 Chronicles 16:25; 2 Chronicles 20:6; Job 40:2, 9; 42:2; Psalm 33:9; 135:6; Isaiah 40:12-15; Jeremiah 32:17; Ezekiel 10:5; Daniel 3:17; 4:35; Amos 4:13; 5:8; Zechariah 12:1; Matthew 19:26; Mark 10:27; Luke 1:37; 18:27; Romans 1:20; Ephesians 1:19; 3:20; Colossians 1:16, 17; Revelation 15:3; 19:6).

10. Holiness – God is absolute moral purity. He can neither sin nor tolerate sin. All that God is, is holy. He cannot do anything, be anything, associate with, or accept anything short of absolute, perfect holiness. R. L. Dabney wrote, God's 'holiness is the collective and consummate glory of his nature'. A. A. Hodge said, 'Infinite, moral perfection is the crown of his Godhead; holiness is the total glory thus crowned'. (Exodus 15:11; Leviticus 11:44-45; 20:26; Deuteronomy 32:4; Joshua 24:19; 1 Samuel 2:2; 2 Samuel 22:31; Ezra 9:15; Psalm 5:4; 111:9; 145:17; Isaiah 6:3; 43:14-15; Jeremiah 23:29; Ezekiel 39:7; Daniel 9:7, 14; Habakkuk 1:13; Zechariah 8:8; Malachi 2:17; Matthew 5:48; Luke 1:49; John 17:11; James 1:13; 1 Peter 1:15-16; 1 John 1:5; 3:3; Revelation 4:8; 15:3-4).

11. Justice – God is just and always demands justice. He demands righteousness from all his creatures and always deals righteously toward them, upon the grounds of absolute, strict justice. God never does anything except that which is just and right (Genesis 18:23-32; Exodus 20:5-6; Deuteronomy 7:9-10; 10:17-18; 24:16; 2 Chronicles 19:7; Nehemiah 9:23; Psalm 9:8, 16; 89:14; Proverbs 24:12; Isaiah 9:7; 45:21; Jeremiah 17:10; 32:19; Lamentations 1:18; Ezekiel 18:1-32; 33:18-20; Daniel 9:7, 14; Nahum 1:3; Malachi 3:5; Luke 12:47-48; Acts 10:34-35; 17:31; Romans 3:24-26; Galatians 2:6; 6:7-8; Ephesians 6:8-9; Colossians 3:25; Hebrews 6:10; 1 Peter 1:17; 2 Peter 2:9; 1 John 1:9; Jude 14-15; Revelation 16:17).

12. Goodness – God's goodness includes his benevolence, love, mercy, grace, long-suffering, patience, forbearance, and kindness (Genesis 19:16; Exodus 34:6-7; Numbers 14:18; Deuteronomy 4:31; 7:7-8; Judges 2:18; 1 Kings 8:23; 2 Kings 13:23; 1 Chronicles 16:34;

2 Chronicles 30:9; Nehemiah 9:17, 31; Psalm 23:1-6; 25:8-10; 86:5, 15; Proverbs 22:23; Isaiah 63:9; Jeremiah 3:12; 31:3; Lamentations 3:22-23; Ezekiel 33:11; Daniel 9:9; Hosea 11:1-4, 8, 9; Joel 2:13; Jonah 4:2, 10, 11; Micah 7:18-20; Nahum 1:7; Ephesians 3:17; Zechariah 9:17; Malachi 1:2; Matthew 5:45; 19:17; Luke 1:50; 6:36; John 3:16; Acts 14:17; Romans 2:4; 5:8; 8:38-39; 2 Corinthians 1:3; 13:11; Ephesians 2:4, 7; 2 Thessalonians 2:16; Titus 2:11; 3:4-5; James 5:11; 1 Peter 1:3; 2 Peter 3:9; 1 John 3:1; 4:7-10, 16).

13. Faithfulness – The Lord our God is absolutely trustworthy, dependable, and true in all things. His decrees are sure. His promises are certain. His words will never fail. We may safely trust him in all things, with all things, and at all times. (Exodus 34:6; Numbers 23:19; Deuteronomy 4:31; 31:7, 9; Joshua 21:43-45; 23:14; 1 Samuel 15:29; 2 Samuel 7:28; 1 Kings 8:24, 56; Psalm 105:8; 119:89-90; Isaiah 25:1; 49:7; Jeremiah 4:28; Lamentations 3:23; Ezekiel 12:25; 16:60, 62; Daniel 9:4; Micah 7:20; Luke 18:7-8; John 3:33; Romans 3:4; 15:8; 1 Corinthians 1:9; 10:13; 2 Corinthians 1:20; 1 Thessalonians 5:24; 2 Thessalonians 3:3; 2 Timothy 2:13; Titus 1:2; Hebrews 6:18; 10:23; 1 Peter 4:19; 2 Peter 3:9, 13; 2 Peter 3: 4, 8; 1 John 1:9; Revelation 15:3).

How does God reveal his attributes to us?

We see some of our God's great attributes in creation. Everything our eyes see, our ears hear, or our hands handle, in heaven and earth is filled with the glory of the Lord. Even the unbelieving and the heathen have God's attributes sufficiently revealed to them to render them utterly without excuse (Romans 1:19-20).

The Lord's attributes are revealed to us in his Word. Even before the fall, in innocence, Adam and Eve were ruled by the Word of God, by his revealed will; and God's revelation of himself is the revelation of his attributes.

The attributes of God are somewhat revealed in the character even of fallen men, who are created in the image of God. Without question, the image of God in man is terribly effaced since the fall;

but man still reflects his Creator. The law of God is stamped in the hearts of all. Man is so much a reflection of God, even in his fallen state, that those who abuse, malign, or murder their neighbours incur the wrath of God in doing so (Genesis 9:6; James 3:9).

Certainly, we see the attributes of our God in the Lord Jesus Christ, our great and glorious Redeemer, the incarnate God (John 1:14; Colossians 2:9). Though our Lord Jesus veiled his glorious attributes as God, emptying himself of any display of his dazzling, essential glory as God, still, Godhood beamed forth and radiated from him while he walked on this earth as a man. Now, the exalted Christ is worthy as a man to receive all the honour of his Divine attributes as it is heaped upon him in his glory (Revelation 5:12).

The law of God, in great measure, displays the attributes of his Being. The precepts of the law are a mirror in which we see the reflection of God's perfections. Each commandment is an expression of his nature. The book of the law reveals what God loves and what he hates, what he approves of and what he despises, thus revealing in some measure what his character is. Still, in all these things (creation, law, man, even the incarnation), as Job puts it, we see only 'parts of his ways' (Job 26:14).

The only total, full, complete revelation of God's glory as God, the only full display of his glorious attributes is the gospel of our great and glorious Saviour, the Lord Jesus Christ. The only place in this world where God is fully revealed is in the sin-atoning sacrifice of Christ at Calvary for the salvation of God's elect. With regard to all the other manifestations of God's glory, it must be said, 'No man hath seen God at any time. The only begotten Son, who is in the bosom of the Father, he hath declared him'. It is only in the death of Christ as our Substitute that every attribute of God's Being meets and is revealed in perfect harmony.

I do not suggest for a moment that God's attributes ever conflict with one another. They do not. But everywhere else, they appear to conflict. We see many displays of righteousness, justice, and truth, and of mercy, love, and grace. But only in our glorious Christ do we see them all displayed fully and perfectly (Psalm 85:9-13).

We see justice in the flood, and mercy in the ark. We see justice in Sodom's destruction, and mercy in Lot's deliverance. We see justice in the slaying of the firstborn, and mercy in the salvation of Israel. We see mercy in the parting of the sea, and justice overflowing Pharaoh's army. We see justice in the fires of hell, and mercy in the glories of heaven. But only in the crucified Son of God, slain as our Substitute for the saving of our souls, do we see mercy and justice, peace and truth shining forth brilliantly unto the glory of God (Romans 3:24-26). This is the glory of the gospel. It reveals the glory of God in the face of Jesus Christ (2 Corinthians 4:6).

'If ye then, being evil, know how to give good gifts unto your children: how much more shall your heavenly Father give the Holy Spirit to them that ask him?'
(Luke 11:13)

Chapter 8

Our Heavenly Father

'Your heavenly Father', what a delightful name for our God this is. The Lord Jesus Christ teaches us that his Father is our Father. He who is the God and Father of our Lord Jesus Christ is our heavenly Father. Do not fail to observe the fact that each of the three Divine Persons is mentioned in this one sentence. God the Son, our Lord Jesus Christ, is speaking about God the Father sending God the Spirit to his elect. 'If ye then, being evil, know how to give good gifts unto your children: how much more shall your heavenly Father give the Holy Spirit to them that ask him?'

We have seen already the clarity with which the scriptures teach the doctrine of the Trinity. The doctrine of the Trinity, though plainly and unmistakably revealed in the Word of God, is a doctrine far beyond the reach of our puny brains. Precisely because it is such a magnificent doctrine, it is a doctrine about which confusion abounds. This is nothing new. Throughout the history of the church, heretics have denied the doctrine of the Trinity. Many of those heretics who openly deny or craftily pervert the doctrine of the Trinity are embraced by many as brethren in Christ!

There are some among the papists who would include the virgin Mary (a sinner saved by grace just like we are) in the Godhead. Mormons and Russellites (Jehovah's Witnesses) deny the eternal Deity of our Lord Jesus Christ. Others of differing sects of heretics deny the doctrine of the Trinity and teach that the names Father, Son, and Holy Spirit are only varying representations of the one God. Some go so far in their abominations as to teach that when sinners are saved by the grace of God, they themselves become divine!

I have no interest in trying to answer all the questions and objections raised by such heretics against the doctrine of the Trinity. But I do want to help you to know what God has revealed about himself in his Word. If we would understand anything at all about the distinct works of the Father, the Son, and the Holy Spirit, we must not fail to recognize that each of the three Divine Persons in the eternal Godhead is a separate, distinct Person from the others. The Father is not the Son or the Spirit. The Son is not the Father or the Spirit. The Spirit is not the Son or the Father. Each is distinct from the other. Yet, the Lord our God is one (Deuteronomy 6:4; Zechariah 14:9; Mark 12:29; Ephesians 4:5; 1 John 5:7).

There are some works ascribed to all three of the Divine Persons, because the Father, the Son, and the Spirit are one God. Yet, there are some works ascribed specifically to each of the Divine Persons alone, because each is a distinct Person within the eternal Godhead. In this chapter we will meditate upon the distinct works of God our heavenly Father. There are certain works distinctly ascribed to God the Father in holy scripture which cause believing hearts to adore him and rejoice to look up to heaven and call him, 'our heavenly Father'.

We commonly speak of the first, second, and third Persons of the Trinity. We call God the Father the first Person, God the Son the second Person, and God the Spirit the third Person. Some ignorantly imagine this to mean that God the Father is the primary Person in the Godhead and the Son and the Spirit are secondary Gods. That is not the case at all. The three Persons of the Holy Trinity are in all things equal to and co-existent with one another. This division (first, second, and third persons) is made simply because our puny brains must have some order in which to think of the infinite God. Let me show you fifteen things that God the Father, our heavenly Father, has done, is doing, and shall hereafter do for his chosen people.

1. Our heavenly Father is the eternal Father of the eternal Son (John 1:14).

I will say no more about this great mystery than is plainly revealed in the Word of God. As the Lord Jesus Christ is the only begotten of the Father from everlasting to everlasting, full of grace and truth, so God the Father is the Father of the Son from eternity. There never was a time when the Son began to be the Son or the Father began to be the Father. Yet, Christ is the eternally begotten Son of the eternally begetting Father. We know no more about the subject than that; and even that is too profound a mystery for us to comprehend. I do not pretend to understand it; but I often contemplate it with utter amazement.

2. We understand and rejoice in the fact that our heavenly Father created the heavens and the earth and all that dwell therein (Hebrews 1:1-2).

The creation of all things is ascribed to God the Father. He is here described as creating the worlds by his Son, the Lord Jesus Christ. That does not mean that the Son was the mere instrument by whom the Father created all things, but that the Father and the Son together are the co-efficient cause and Creator of all things.

3. Our hearts rejoice to know that it is our heavenly Father who dictates and rules all the affairs of providence (Romans 11:33-36; Isaiah 46:9-11; Daniel 4:35).

He who is the Captain of the ship of time, he who sits at the helm of the ship and steers the course of all things, according to the map of his own sovereign purpose, to their appointed destiny, is our heavenly Father. Sometimes we have nothing but this to fall back on. But when a person can fall back on this, 'My Father did this', he needs nothing else to fall back on! With confident hearts, in the face of the most tragic of events, believers can and should say, with old Eli, 'It is the Lord: let him do what seemeth him good' (1 Samuel 3:18).

4. Not only does our heavenly Father rule all things in providence, he does it according to his own eternal purpose of grace in sovereign predestination.

Do not be afraid of, or ashamed of, the Bible doctrine of predestination. He who predestinated all things is God, our heavenly Father. He did it from eternity. He did it for the salvation of his elect sons and daughters. He will never alter his purpose or turn away from the people of his love, for whom he predestined all things (Ephesians 1:11; Romans 8:28-31).

5. God's eternal purpose of grace in predestination, and his execution of that purpose in providence, is according to our heavenly Father's sovereign choice of his people unto salvation in Christ, before the world began, in eternal election (Ephesians 1:3-6; 2 Thessalonians 2:13-14; 1 Peter 1:2).

Here again is a display of the distinct Persons within the Godhead. The Father chose us to salvation in the Son and through the sanctification of the Spirit to the obtaining of the glory of Christ.

6. Not only did the Father choose to save us, it was our heavenly Father who found a way to save us that is altogether consistent with and honouring to his own glorious holiness, justice, and truth.

Love chose us; but justice demanded satisfaction. Mercy resolved to spare us; but truth said, 'The soul that sinneth, it shall die'. Grace cried, 'Forgive'; but holiness insisted, 'Without holiness, no man shall see the Lord. It must be perfect to be accepted'. Our Heavenly Father looked upon his darling Son (who was willing to live as a man and die as a Substitute for us), and the Father himself willing to sacrifice his dear Son for us, looked upon his chosen and said,

Eureka – 'Deliver him from going down to the pit: I have found a ransom' (Job 33:24; Psalm 89:19-29).

> Love found a way to redeem my soul,
> Love found a way that could make me whole;
> Love sent my Lord to the cross of shame,
> Love found a way, – O praise His name!

7. Our heavenly Father entered into a covenant with his Son on our behalf for the saving of our souls.

In Hebrews 13:20, this covenant is called 'the everlasting covenant'. Frequently, it is called 'the new covenant'. It is a covenant made in eternity between God the Father, God the Son, and God the Holy Spirit; but it was made for us. Insofar as the benefits and blessings of it to us are concerned, it is an unconditional covenant. The Lord God said, 'I will love them freely ... I will be their God; and they shall be my people'. This everlasting covenant of grace is a sure covenant, a covenant which infallibly secured and guaranteed to God's elect all the blessings of salvation and eternal life in Christ (Jeremiah 31:3, 31-34; 32:38-40; 2 Samuel 23:5).

The only condition to the covenant and the blessings of grace and salvation promised in it was the obedience of the Son of God as our Substitute unto death (Hebrews 13:20). Be sure you understand that there was never the slightest possibility of failure on his part. He was willing to obey. He was able to obey. He did obey his Father's will even unto death, even unto the shedding of his blood, the blood of the everlasting covenant.

8. Having found a ransom for our souls, our heavenly Father gave his chosen people into the hands of his Son, as sheep into the hands of a shepherd, and trusted him with the salvation of our souls and the glory of his own great name (John 6:39; Ephesians 1:12-13).

If God the Father has trusted his glory to his dear Son as our Substitute and Saviour and trusted the salvation of our souls to his hands, we can and should trust him with our immortal souls and with all that concerns us. If the Father trusted him, he is a trustworthy Saviour.

9. Moreover, our heavenly Father has adopted us into his family as the sons of God from eternity (1 John 3:1-2; Galatians 4:6-7).

John Gill wrote, 'This is a privilege that exceeds all others; it is more to be a son than to be a saint; angels are saints, but not sons, they are servants; it is more to be a child of God, than to be redeemed, pardoned, and justified; it is great grace to redeem from slavery, to pardon criminals, and justify the ungodly; but it is another and an higher act of grace to make them sons; and which makes them infinitely more honourable, than to be the sons and daughters of the greatest potentate upon earth; yea, gives them an honour which Adam had not in innocence, nor the angels in heaven, who though sons by creation, yet not by adoption'.

10. Having chosen and adopted us, our heavenly Father accepted us in Christ from eternity (Ephesians 1:3-6).

Be sure you do not fail to grasp the teaching of holy scripture regarding the matter of the believer's acceptance before God. Our acceptance is in Christ. Our acceptance is from everlasting to everlasting. Our acceptance is absolute and unconditional. Our acceptance means that God the Father, our heavenly Father, looks upon us in Christ as perfect in him, and has done so from eternity. He declares, 'It must be perfect to be accepted!'

11. Being 'accepted in the beloved', our heavenly Father has blessed us with all spiritual blessings in Christ from eternity and has promised to bless us forever for Christ's sake (Ephesians 1:3; 2 Timothy 1:9).

The Lord God commanded Aaron, his high priest, to bless his people symbolically (Numbers 6:23) because he had sworn from eternity, for Christ's sake, saying, 'I will bless them' (Numbers 6:27).

12. If you want to get some idea of just how great his blessings are, try to get hold of this fact. Our heavenly Father has given his own dear Son for us and to us (2 Corinthians 9:15; Isaiah 49:8; John 3:16; Romans 5:8; 8:32; 1 John 4:9-10).

The Father gave us his Son in promise before the world began. He gave us his Son in the fulness of time in the incarnation to fulfil all righteousness for us. Our God gave us his Son as a sin-atoning Sacrifice and Substitute at Calvary. Our heavenly Father gave us his Son in regeneration, forming his Son in us by the power of his Holy Spirit. And he will give us his Son in resurrection glory when he brings us into heaven.

13. Our heavenly Father gives his Spirit to all his elect.

He does not give his Spirit to some of his elect and withhold his Spirit from others. The Father gives the Spirit to all the chosen and to all the redeemed according to his covenant promise and upon the basis of Christ's intercession (Galatians 3:13-14; John 14:16; 16:8-15). The Holy Spirit is given to every chosen, redeemed sinner as a Sanctifier, Convincer, Comforter, Strengthener, Teacher, Enlightener, Illuminator, Guide, and Seal.

14. Our heavenly Father graciously and effectually teaches chosen sinners, causing us to come to Christ for salvation and life (John 6:44-45; Titus 2:11-14).

He teaches us his will and his way as we seek it for his glory (Proverbs 3:5-6).

15. It is God, our heavenly Father who keeps us in the way of life and grace by his omnipotent, sovereign power (1 Peter 1:5).

How we ought to rejoice to know that our final salvation, our perseverance and preservation, depend not upon our strength, but his, not upon our faithfulness, but his, not upon our resolve, but his (Ecclesiastes 3:14; Philippians 1:6; 1 Thessalonians 5:24).

> He will keep me 'til the river
> Rolls its waters at my feet.
> Then he'll bear me safely over,
> Where my Saviour I shall meet!

What a privilege is ours to be the sons and daughters of God almighty! To lift our hearts to heaven, beholding God upon his throne,

and say, 'Our Father, which art in heaven, hallowed be thy name!'
'For ye have not received the spirit of bondage again to fear; but ye
have received the Spirit of adoption, whereby we cry, Abba, Father.
The Spirit itself beareth witness with our spirit, that we are the
children of God: And if children, then heirs; heirs of God, and joint-
heirs with Christ; if so be that we suffer with him, that we may be
also glorified together' (Romans 8:15-17).

'For many deceivers are entered into the world, who confess not that Jesus Christ is come in the flesh. This is a deceiver and an antichrist. Look to yourselves, that we lose not those things which we have wrought, but that we receive a full reward. Whosoever transgresseth, and abideth not in the doctrine of Christ, hath not God. He that abideth in the doctrine of Christ, he hath both the Father and the Son. If there come any unto you, and bring not this doctrine, receive him not into your house, neither bid him God speed: For he that biddeth him God speed is partaker of his evil deeds.'
(2 John 7-11)

Chapter 9

'The Doctrine of Christ'

Without question, 2 John 7-11 speaks specifically of those who deny the incarnation as being antichrist. However, John's statement is not to be interpreted as merely meaning that those who deny the fact of the incarnation are antichrist. He is telling us that all preachers, teachers, and religious leaders who deny the eternal deity and godhead of Christ, the necessity of his incarnation to save fallen men, the efficacy of his redemptive work as the incarnate God, and the glory of his exaltation and dominion as the God-man are deceivers and antichrists. In other words, all who teach any doctrine which in any way perverts the gospel of God's free, sovereign, effectual, and irresistible grace in Christ are deceivers and are antichrists. We are to have nothing to do with them.

However, my purpose in this chapter is to demonstrate the fact that the doctrine of Christ and the doctrine of the Bible are synonymous. The teaching of holy scripture is Christ. I do not mean to say only that the teachings of the Bible are the teachings of Christ, though that is certainly true. I mean that all the teachings of God's Word are Christ himself. He is the Truth of whom the scriptures speak. Christ is the living Word of whom the written word speaks. All the doctrines, all the teachings of holy scripture are designed of God to reveal and exalt God's dear Son, our Saviour, and to lead us to faith in him.

That which separates the truth from a mere religion is that the truth concerns a person, the Lord Jesus Christ. That may appear to some to be a trite and worn out phrase, but it is true that salvation is a Person, not a doctrine. The importance of this distinction cannot be overstated. There are many who find fault with insistence upon this point. I am constantly told, 'That is an over simplification. You cannot preach the Bible without preaching doctrine; and you cannot always preach Christ and the gospel if you faithfully expound the Word of God'.

The first part of that objection is true. We cannot preach the Bible without preaching doctrine. I make no apology for preaching and teaching doctrine, or for being a doctrinal preacher. The word doctrine simply means teaching. Certainly you cannot teach without teaching. To teach is to indoctrinate. It would be impossible to preach the person and work of Christ without preaching doctrine. Yet, it is quite easy to preach doctrine and never preach Christ. However, I take strong exception to the notion that 'you cannot always preach Christ and the gospel if you faithfully expound the Word of God'.

To preach all the counsel of God is to preach the gospel. It is to preach Jesus Christ and him crucified. I repeat, the message of scripture is Jesus Christ himself (Luke 24:27, 44-46; John 1:45; 5:39; Acts 10:43). What Paul said to the Ephesian elders (Acts 20:27) and what he wrote to the saints at Corinth (1 Corinthians 1:23; 2:2) are different ways of stating the same thing. Christ crucified is all the counsel of God. This fact is demonstrated in the book of Acts. In that inspired history of the church's earliest years, the words preach, preached, and preaching are used thirty-seven times. Every time they are used, the subject preached was a person – the Lord Jesus Christ. 'The apostles' doctrine' was not a creed, but a person (Acts 5:42).

Truth is in some ways like a jigsaw puzzle. A jigsaw puzzle is made of many parts, each one important. The puzzle could not be complete if any individual part were missing. Yet, we all realize that the value of such a puzzle does not lie in the individual pieces, but in the image that is made when all these pieces are joined together in their proper relationship. Even though an unassembled jigsaw puzzle contains the very same materials and pieces as an assembled one, there is a great difference between the two. The assembled puzzle gives us an image, a picture to enjoy. An unassembled puzzle is just a box of cardboard pieces.

The Word of God is similar: It is made of many parts, each one important. Yet the value of these parts lies not in themselves, but in the image they create when assembled through the preaching of the gospel. All the doctrines of the scriptures are pieces of a divine puzzle which, when assembled, provide us with an image of the Lord Jesus. One may emphasize the various individual pieces of this puzzle, and become quite expert in them, and never see the image which they were designed to create.

Our Saviour said to the Pharisees, 'Search the scriptures; for in them ye think ye have eternal life: and they are they which testify of me'. The Pharisees were expert in the pieces but utterly ignorant of the image they made. I fear that most preachers and Bible teachers in our day are very much like the Pharisees. Like ignorant babies playing with the pieces of a jigsaw puzzle, they play with and are greatly consumed in playing with the pieces of holy scripture. If someone stands up and plainly preaches the gospel, plainly sets forth Jesus Christ and him crucified, like babies with a puzzle, they start pulling out the pieces.

Those who preach, but do not preach Christ, those who teach from the Bible, but do not teach the gospel, do not understand the Word of God at all. That doctrine which does not have Christ crucified for its beginning, middle, and end is false doctrine. Be sure you understand the words of Peter in 1 Peter chapter one. The Word of God has not been preached unless the gospel has been preached, unless the gospel of Christ has been preached (1 Peter 1:23-25).

Every man sent of God to preach the gospel is in total agreement with every other man sent of God to preach the gospel, insofar as the message they preach is concerned. They all see eye to eye in this matter (Isaiah 52:7-8). 'For we preach not ourselves, but Christ Jesus the Lord'. When the scriptures speak of 'preaching Christ', this is what they mean:

– All preaching is to be done with the purpose of revealing Christ and making him known, so that chosen sinners may see him, believe on him, and worship him. The goal of all the apostles and their successors has been to make Christ known in truth.

– To that end, preaching Christ means we must view all scripture as a revelation of Him and interpret it according to that rule, not being satisfied with the mere pieces of truth, but determined to learn and declare how each piece fits into the puzzle.

This understanding of scripture and this kind of preaching will help us in seven distinct ways.

1. Preaching Christ will deliver us from becoming a mere religious movement

Someone once said that all organizations go through three stages: 'the man (who founded it), the movement (an organization that carries on under the momentum the man generated), and the monument (a dead organization which may bear the name of the founder but has little or no connection to him or his vision)'. Lutheranism bears the name of its founder, but few Lutherans adhere to Martin Luther's doctrine. Presbyterianism is associated with John

Calvin; but few Presbyterians rejoice in Calvin's doctrine. Preachers in most Protestant and Baptist churches use the names of C. H. Spurgeon and John Bunyan; but few preach the gospel those faithful men proclaimed.

The only thing that preserves the church from such a fate is that 'the man', (in this case, the Man, Christ Jesus) is continually revealing Himself from generation to generation. This revelation is accomplished through the preaching of Christ. When Christ is preached, the Spirit of God takes those things of Christ, shows them to his elect and a new generation is joined to Christ. When Christ is preached, we are never dependant upon the momentum of one generation to carry the work of the gospel into the next generation. When Christ is preached, every generation is a brand new work, full of the vitality and energy of the Man who founds it, the Lord Jesus Christ.

2. Preaching Christ will deliver preachers and those who hear them from dry and lifeless sermons

No doubt the goats will not be satisfied with what they hear, but we are not concerned with them. The sheep find the preaching of Christ to be 'green pastures' and 'still waters'. Christ is their bread, and the preaching of Christ is the bread coming down from heaven to nourish their souls. When Christ is the preacher's Subject and Message he never needs to figure out a way to make his messages more exciting, clever, or appealing to those who hear them. The message of Christ is as clever and exciting as any sheep could desire. We simply should not concern ourselves with what goats think about our preaching.

Preaching Christ is the best, indeed, the only way to purify the church. Gospel preaching reveals who the sheep are and purifies the church. Everywhere I go, I find that among religious people the two major concerns are the morality of the sheep and the purity of the church. This is revealed in the attention they give to the work of church discipline. The scriptures, however, teach that the preaching of Christ will accomplish this work very well. The preaching of

Christ provides the content and motivation of godliness (Ephesians 4:17-24). Ungodliness is contrary to the truth of Christ. Where Christ is preached, growth in grace is the result!

Preaching Christ will purify the church by removing from its ranks those professed believers who do not truly love the Lord Jesus (Corinthians 1:18). Our Lord was referring to this matter in his parables when he told us plainly that we do not have the ability to distinguish between sheep and goats, between wheat and tares, or good fish and bad. Therefore, we are to leave them alone and leave the separation of the one from the other to him.

Those who do not know Christ will, in time, grow weary of hearing him preached and leave. People will not long endure the preaching of what is foolishness to them. The surest way to maintain a herd of goats in a congregation is to preach Christless doctrine to them. 'Knowledge puffeth up', and Christless doctrine, no matter how true it may be, puffs men up with a sense of knowledge. Even the goats can tolerate true doctrine if their knowing it gives them an occasion for pride. But, knowing the truth through the revelation of Christ leaves no room for pride, only a sense of gratitude that the truth has been revealed. In this way, the preaching of Christ purifies the church. More correctly, by the preaching of Christ, Christ purifies his church.

3. Preaching Christ has the promise of Divine accomplishment (Isaiah 55:11)

The word that goes forth out of God's mouth is Jesus Christ, called by John, 'the Word' (John 1:1). Isaiah 55:11 refers primarily to the coming of Christ in the flesh, teaching us that whatever purpose God intended in the sending of Christ was accomplished; and when Christ returned to God, he did so, not as a failure, but as a champion who had fully accomplished all the work given him to do.

The Word that goes forth may properly be expanded to also include the preaching of Christ which is, indeed, a sending of Jesus Christ. Every time Christ is preached, God has a purpose in it, and that purpose shall be accomplished.

4. Preaching Christ helps to protect the preacher from pride and the hearers from idolatry

Those who hear the preaching of Christ will love and respect the man who preaches to them; but they will worship Christ. Those who preach Christ will rejoice in the results that are obtained by it, but will glorify Christ for those results. Far too often preachers and religious leaders talk and act as though the works wrought through them were wrought by them, as though it were Calvin and Luther who brought about the reformation, as if Spurgeon filled the tabernacle. If there could be any sadness in glory, it must be found among those faithful men of the past whose names are now revered as though they accomplished anything. If these men were to return to earth, they would be appalled at the churches and colleges raised in their names. Any work done by any man ought to die with the man and will. Let us preach the work of him who never dies and pray that he will be pleased to work through us.

5. Preaching Christ is the only message that will do sinners any good (1 Corinthians 1:21)

'It pleased God by the foolishness of preaching to save them that believe'. The word translated 'preaching' puts the emphasis on the content of what is preached. The 'foolishness' that is preached is Christ or 'the cross', the doctrine of Christ crucified. Christ is what sinners need. If they will not have him, there is nothing else good to give them. Consequently, there is no value in giving them something else. I say to all who preach the gospel, 'Pour on the coal! Preach the sovereign, unchangeable Christ to sinners. Flood them with the "truth as it is in Jesus" until they either shout "crucify him" or "my Lord and my God".'

6. Preaching Christ glorifies him who alone deserves all praise, honour, and glory

Dare a preacher aim for less? I pray for the salvation of sinners through my preaching, but, whatever may come of sinners, may Christ be honoured and glorified by what comes from my lips. Does not every God-called preacher feel the same? Does not every believer feel the same with regard to his testimony of the truth. God grant it be so. Therefore, we preach and teach Christ. I pray that God will give me the grace to deny every fleshy temptation to preach anything else. I know this, the man who follows this pattern until it seems utterly absurd and absolute foolishness to proud flesh, and only that man, has entered into that which is the power and wisdom of God.

God helping me, this is the determination of my heart and my solemn promise to all who hear me preach or who read what I may be enabled of God to write. I am 'determined not to know anything among you, save Jesus Christ, and him crucified ... God forbid that I should glory, save in the cross of our Lord Jesus Christ, by whom the world is crucified unto me, and I unto the world ... So, as much as in me is, I am ready to preach the gospel ... For I am not ashamed of the gospel of Christ: for it is the power of God unto salvation to every one that believeth; to the Jew first, and also to the Greek. For therein is the righteousness of God revealed from faith to faith: as it is written, The just shall live by faith'.

'And she shall bring forth a son, and thou shalt call his name JESUS: for he shall save his people from their sins.'
(Matthew 1:21)

Chapter 10

The Son of God Our Saviour

There is one word in the Bible which in itself forms an entire library, one word which is the sum and substance of the entire Bible, one word which comprises all truth. That word is 'Christ'. He is the uncreated, living, eternal Word, whom to know is life eternal.

When chosen, redeemed sinners are brought out of darkness into light by the irresistible, regenerating grace and power of God the Holy Spirit, when Christ is revealed in the chosen vessels of mercy, when they become savingly acquainted with the divine Word, they are 'made wise unto salvation through faith which is in Christ Jesus'. (2 Timothy 3:15). As we are led by the Spirit in the life of faith, enabled by his grace to live upon, walk with, and rejoice in the glorious Person and finished salvation of the Lord Jesus Christ, we are brought into what the Apostle Paul describes as – 'All the riches of the full assurance of understanding, to the acknowledgement of the mystery of God, and of the Father, and of Christ; in whom are hid all the treasures of wisdom and knowledge' (Colossians 2:2-3).

Our Lord's own statements with regard to this 'mystery of God', the mystery of the perfect unity and oneness of the Persons in the eternal Godhead are crystal clear (John 10:30; 14:7-11). It is stated concisely, but emphatically, in 1 John 5:7, – 'There are three that bear record in heaven, the Father, the Word, and the Holy Ghost: and these three are one'. The scriptures also plainly state these facts, – The revelation of the Holy Trinity is found in Christ alone. Christ, and Christ alone, is the visible Jehovah. The invisible God is seen and known only in him who is 'the image of the invisible God' (John 1:18; Colossians 2:9).

Robert Hawker wrote, 'Our most glorious Christ, being the only visible Jehovah, is the sole Executor, Administrator, and efficient Source of all the works and ways of God, as revealed to the church in all the departments of nature, providence, grace, and glory. And as his person is the only visible Jehovah, so his obedience is the only means of recovery from the Adam-fall and transgression' (Acts 4:12).

It is never written in scripture that if a person believes in God, or if he believes in the Holy Spirit, he is saved. It is written throughout the Word of God, 'Believe on the Lord Jesus Christ, and thou shalt be saved' (Acts 16:31). The fact is – No one believes God and no one has the Spirit of God, except those sinners who believe on the Lord Jesus Christ as he is revealed in the scriptures as the Saviour of his people. As the all-glorious Christ is alone the embodiment and revelation of God, he is also the only Saviour of sinners.

In Matthew 1:21 we have the words of the angel of the Lord to Joseph concerning the incarnation, birth, and work of the Son of God, our Lord Jesus Christ. 'And she shall bring forth a Son, and thou shalt call his name JESUS: for he shall save his people from their sins'.

Why did Christ come?

It is reasonable for anyone who reads or hears that the Son of God assumed human flesh and came into the world as a man to want to know why. Why did the Son of God come into this world? The angel's revelation to Joseph is unmistakable: – God the Son came into this world for a specific purpose, to do a specific thing, on a specific mission. He came to save 'his people from their sins'. This was the Father's will which he came to perform (Hebrews 10:5-14; John 6:39). This was the stipulation of the covenant which he came to fulfil (Hebrews 13:20; Isaiah 49:8). This was the commandment of God which he came to obey (John 10:16-18).

My mind is lost in wonder and admiration when I think of the fact of Christ's coming into this world. Is it not astonishing to you that the Son of God would become the Son of Man. That he who created all things would become the woman's Seed. That he who is Lord of all would take upon himself the form of a servant to be despised and rejected of men, a man of sorrows and acquainted with grief. That in the fulness of time he might die the painful, shameful, ignominious death of the cross in the place of guilty sinners? These things utterly astonish me. I say with Paul, 'Great is the mystery of godliness; God was manifest in the flesh' (2 Corinthians 8:9; 9:15).

Who is this Jesus?

You have heard about Jesus all your life. Perhaps you think, 'Everyone knows who Jesus Christ is'. That is a mistake. The fact is, very few people in this world know who the Lord Jesus Christ is. The Christ that is worshipped in the average church is nothing but an idolatrous figment of man's imagination, an idol, a false god carved from one of the trees in the dark forest of man's depraved mind. Our Lord himself warned us of these days, saying, 'There shall arise false Christs, and false prophets, and shall show great signs and wonders; insomuch that, if it were possible, they shall deceive the very elect'. So when men come to you and say, 'Lo, here is Christ, or there; believe it not' (Matthew 24:24, 23).

That makes this question very important: – Who is this Jesus? Who is the Christ of the Bible? We must know, trust, and worship this Christ, if I would know God and be accepted of him (John 17:3). If we trust a false Christ, no matter how sincere we are, we are lost, under the delusion of Satan. Allow me to show you from the scriptures who this Jesus is, of whom it is written, 'He shall save his people from their sins'.

This Jesus is the Son of God. When the Bible speaks of Jesus Christ as the Son of God, it is declaring to us that Jesus Christ is God the eternal Son, the second Person of the Holy Trinity (1 John 5:7), in every way equal with the Father and the Spirit. We who believe are the sons of God by adoption. Christ is the Son of God by nature.

To say that he is the Son of God is to declare that this Man, whose name is Jesus, is himself God over all, blessed forever. He is not just a god, a likeness of God, or a creature of God. Jesus Christ is God manifest in the flesh (John 1:1-3). All the attributes of divinity belong to him. He is the Creator of all things, the Sustainer of all things, the Ruler of all things, and the Disposer of all things. Jesus Christ is the Revelation of God (John 1:18).

If Jesus Christ is not God, if he is anything less than almighty God, we have no Saviour. He is an impostor, a fake, a charlatan. None but God could make atonement for our sins. That man who was born at Bethlehem, who died upon the cross, who rose again the third day, and now sits upon the throne of heaven is God (Colossians 2:9).

This Jesus, who is God almighty, is the sinner's Substitute. He is the Daysman, the Surety, the Representative, the Mediator, the Substitute by whose obedience sinners are reconciled to God, without whom we could never be accepted of God.

The key to understanding the Book of God is to understand the gospel doctrine of substitution. When I say that Jesus Christ is the sinner's Substitute, I mean that he stood before God as the Substitute for his people before the world began as the Lamb slain (Revelation 13:8). He is our eternal Mediator in whom we were from everlasting blessed with all spiritual blessings (Ephesians 1:3). The Lord Jesus

Christ is the Surety of the everlasting covenant in whom God's elect were given grace and salvation before time began (2 Timothy 1:9). He lived in obedience to God as our Substitute in this world to fulfil all righteousness on our behalf (Romans 5:19). He died under the wrath of God as the Substitute in the place of his people upon the cross (Galatians 3:13; 2 Corinthians 5:21). He intercedes for us today as an advocate in heaven (1 John 2:1-2) as our Substitute before the throne of grace (1 John 2:1-2). And he will stand before God in the last day as our Substitute at the bar of justice as the ground of our eternal salvation (Jeremiah 23:6).

Be sure you understand this. If Jesus Christ is indeed God (and he is!), then all that he has undertaken to do as our Substitute must be effectually and completely accomplished by his own omnipotent arm.

Those whom he came to redeem are redeemed. Those whom he undertook to justify are justified. All those whom he undertook to save must be saved. It is written, 'He shall save his people from their sins'. 'He shall not fail' (Isaiah 42:4). This Jesus, the Christ of the Bible, who is Almighty God, is the Saviour of his people. Christ alone is our Saviour. He is our complete salvation (1 Corinthians 1:30; Colossians 2:10). This Christ is the effectual Saviour of his people.

Furthermore, this Jesus, who is God, in order that he might save his people, is the sovereign monarch of the universe (John 17:2). Without question, he is the Monarch of all things by virtue of his eternal Godhead. Yet, he has been given this place of dominion as a man, as the reward of his obedience to God as our Mediator (Acts 5:31; Romans 14:9).

Do you understand who Jesus Christ is? He is the Son of God. He is the sinner's only, all-sufficient, effectual Substitute. He is the Saviour of his people. The Lord Jesus Christ is the sovereign Monarch of the universe. If the Christ you worship is not this Christ, your Christ is a false Christ, nothing but the idolatrous figment of your imagination.

Who are his people?

Who are those people the Bible says Christ shall save? Those people he came to save were his people long before he came to save them. The angel said, 'He shall save his people'. He did not say, 'He shall save those who shall be his people'. Whoever his people are, they were his people before he saved them; and they were his people before he came to save them (Psalm 110:3; John 10:16).

All men naturally think that Christ came to save everyone in the world. All men think that Christ died for everyone in the world. That is not the doctrine of the scriptures. What does the Word of God say? This is our standard. If a man does not speak according to the words of holy scripture, it is because there is no light in him. Those who declare that Christ died to save everybody in the world do not have one ray of spiritual light in them. To teach such a doctrine is to deny the very deity of Christ.

I realize that many object to such dogmatism. Many who would not hesitate to say that those liberals are complete heretics who deny Christ's incarnation, his virgin birth, his perfect holiness, his vicarious atonement, or his resurrection from the dead, object vehemently to saying the same thing about those who deny the glorious efficacy of his atonement. I make no apology for such a declaration. Christ's sin-atoning work is the very heart of the gospel. To deny the efficacy of his sacrifice is to deny he is God. He cannot be God if he fails to do what he came to do (Isaiah 42:4), if his love can be changed to wrath (Malachi 3:6), if his blood does not fully satisfy divine justice and effectually redeem every sinner for whom it was shed (Isaiah 53:9-12; Romans 3:24-26; Hebrews 9:12).

The Son of God did not come to save all people. He came to save his people, his peculiar people. Who are his people? They are his seed (Isaiah 53:10-12). They are his sheep (John 10:11, 15, 26). They are his chosen Bride, the Church (Ephesians 5:25-27). They are his elect (Ephesians 1:3-7). His people are those whom God the Father chose in him before the foundation of the world, whom he loved with an everlasting love, whom he predestinated unto the adoption of children by Jesus Christ to himself according to the good pleasure of his will (Romans 8:28-31).

These are the people for whom the Son of God lived, died, and rose again. Those who teach that he came to save all men, that he lived, died, and rose again for all men blaspheme God in the doctrine they preach. Their doctrine makes the love of God a useless, helpless, fickle passion, the justice of God a mockery, the immutability of God a meaningless notion, and the will of God insignificant.

How does Christ save?

How does the Lord Jesus Christ save his people? Whoever his people are, they shall be saved from their sins. That fact cannot be disputed. It is Christ who saves us. We do not save ourselves, or contribute anything in the work of salvation (1 Corinthians 4:7). How does he do it? Here are three distinct and distinguishing works of grace by which Christ saves his people from their sins.

1. Redemption – He has saved us from the penalty of our sins by the particular, effectual redemption of our souls from the curse of God's holy law (2 Corinthians 5:21). This is 'how' Christ died for our sins according to the scriptures (1 Corinthians 15:3). He died in the room and stead of God's elect as a voluntary, vicarious, victorious sin-atoning sacrifice (Hebrews 10:5-14; Isaiah 53:4-6; John 10:16-18; Hebrews 1:1-3; 9:12, 26).

2. Regeneration – Christ saves his people from the power of their sins by the power of his Spirit in sovereign, effectual regeneration (John 5:25; Ephesians 2:1-5 Psalm 65:4). As he raised Lazarus from the dead, so he raises his people from spiritual death to spiritual life by the omnipotence of his saving grace (John 5:25). The Lord Jesus saves his people from their sins by making his people righteous before God. In justification, the righteous obedience of Christ is imputed to us, just as our sins were imputed to him (2 Corinthians 5:21). In sanctification, his righteous nature is imparted to us (Galatians 5:22-23; 2 Peter 1:4; 1 John 3:5-10).

3. Resurrection – The Son of God shall save his people from the presence and the consequences of their sins in the resurrection of the just (John 5:28; 1 Thessalonians 4:13-18). There shall be a resurrection of the just and of the unjust. The wicked shall be raised to suffer the consequences of their sins; but the righteous shall be raised to be forever freed from the consequences of sins.

Upon what grounds may a sinner have confidence that he is one of 'his people'? There is one answer, and only one, to that question. If you trust the Christ of God as your only Lord and Saviour, you are one of 'his people'. He chose you. He redeemed you. He has called you and given you the gift of eternal life (1 John 5:9-13).

'And I will pray the Father, and he shall give you another Comforter, that he may abide with you for ever; Even the Spirit of truth; whom the world cannot receive, because it seeth him not, neither knoweth him: but ye know him; for he dwelleth with you, and shall be in you.'
(John 14:16-17)

Chapter 11

The Person and Work of God The Holy Spirit

As God the Son is the gift of the Father to his elect, God the Holy Spirit is the ascension gift of the enthroned Christ to his church and kingdom in this gospel age. He is described as our Comforter, the Promise of the Father, and the Blessing of Abraham (John 14:16-17; 1 Thessalonians 4:7-8; Acts 1:4-5; Galatians 3:13-14). In the capacity of his office, the Holy Spirit is distinctly set before us in the New Testament as the gift of God to his church and people through the mediation of the Lord Jesus Christ, our exalted Lord and King.

In this day of religious confusion in which men and women have substituted sentimentality and sensationalism for substantial gospel truth, in this day when almost everyone confuses emotionalism with worship, there is much need for clear, biblical instruction with regard to the Person and work of God the Holy Spirit. In this chapter, I

want to show you six things from the Word of God about the Person
and work of the Holy Spirit.

**1. The Holy Spirit is himself God, the third person of the holy
Trinity, in all things equal with the Father and the Son**

He is named as one with the Father and the Son, both in the
Apostolic benediction and in the inspired definition of the Trinity
given by the Apostle John (2 Corinthians 13:14; 1 John 5:7). Far
too often men and women think of the Holy Spirit as a great force,
a mighty influence for good, or an emanation of God. Let us never
dishonour him by such low thoughts. We cannot lie to an emanation,
as Ananias and Sapphira lied to the Holy Ghost. We cannot grieve
a force, as believers are said to grieve the Holy Spirit by unkindnesses
done to one another. We cannot blaspheme an influence, as all those
do who wilfully turn away from Christ and his gospel in rebellion
and obstinate unbelief. The Holy Spirit is God.

**2. The work of the Holy Spirit is as necessary for the salvation
of God's elect as the works of the Father and the Son**

Far too often we think of the covenant of grace as a covenant
made between the Father and the Son. It was not. It was a covenant
made between the Father, the Son, and the Spirit. God the Father
elected us unto salvation (Ephesians 1:3-6; 2 Thessalonians 2:13-
14). He chose us, adopted us, blessed us, and predestinated us unto
heavenly glory. We rejoice in that. Without election no one could
ever have been saved. However, the Father's election, by itself, could
never save a sinner. We also had to be redeemed.

God the Son, the Lord Jesus Christ, volunteered to redeem us
and became our Substitute (Ephesians 1:7-12; Hebrews 7:22). As
Judah spoke to Israel his father for Benjamin (Genesis 43:9) and
became surety for him, so our Lord Jesus Christ spoke for God's
elect and became our Surety in the covenant of grace before the
world began, assuming total responsibility for the everlasting
salvation of our souls. The Father trusted the Son with our souls
(John 6:39; 10:29; 17:9 Ephesians 1:12). They struck hands, as it

were, and the covenant was set in motion. Then, in the fulness of time, Christ redeemed his elect. He bought us with his own precious blood. The Lord Jesus Christ brought in an everlasting righteousness by his obedience to God as a man, satisfied the justice of God by his death upon the cursed tree, and obtained eternal redemption for all God's elect (Hebrews 9:12).

Yet, redemption alone could never bring a sinner to God. Something else must be done. Redemption is a work of God wrought for us. Redemption changed our standing; but it did not change us. Though chosen in eternal election and redeemed by Christ's effectual atonement, we could never be saved, we could never enter into heaven until something was done in us, until grace actually changed us. Redemption alone is not enough. It is written, 'Ye must be born again!'

That is the work of God the Holy Spirit (John 3:5-7; 6:63; Ephesians 2:1-5). God the Spirit agreed to effectually apply the blood of Christ to every chosen, redeemed sinner, create each one new in Christ, give them faith, and seal to them all the blessings of the covenant. That is exactly what he has done for us (Ephesians 1:13-14). In order for any sinner to be saved: – God must first choose to save him. That is election. Then God must put away his sin and justify him. That is redemption. Then God must sanctify him. That is regeneration.

3. The advent of the Holy Spirit on the day of Pentecost was a once for all, never to be repeated, climactic event

There is much confusion about what happened on the day of Pentecost in Acts chapter two. The charismatic movement, with its emphasis on works, free will, tongues, visions, and miracles, is one of the horrible evils of divine judgment upon this generation (2 Thessalonians 2:7-10). The revivalist theology of modern religion, with its emphasis on decisionism, works and free will, upon euphoric feelings and experiences in temporary spasms of religious convulsion, is a reflection of the same divine judgment (2 Thessalonians 2:7-12).

Believers know that these things are the workings of antichrist and not of Christ. Yet, those who pretend to have the Holy Spirit and those apostolic gifts by which Christ's ministry was announced and confirmed in the book of Acts, point to the day of Pentecost in Acts 2 as proof that their doctrine, claims, and experiences are biblical. What really happened on that momentous day?

The day of Pentecost in Acts 2 signalled the advent of the Holy Spirit. As the virgin birth was the advent of the Son of God in his office capacity as our Substitute and Redeemer, so the day of Pentecost and the events recorded in Acts 2 signalled the advent of the Holy Spirit in the capacity of his office as the Comforter and Sanctifier of God's elect. Yes, the Holy Spirit was in the world before, even as the Son of God was in the world and working in the world before his advent. But now the Holy Spirit has come in his office capacity to fulfil his part in the covenant of grace.

> At Pentecost the Holy Spirit came as He had never come before. Something then transpired which inaugurated a new era for the world, a new power for righteousness, a new basis for fellowship. On that day, the fearing Peter was transformed into the intrepid evangelist. On that day, the new wine of Christianity burst the old bottles of Judaism, and the Word went forth in a multiplicity of Gentile tongues. (A. W. Pink)

On that remarkable day, three thousand souls were regenerated and converted to Christ by the power of the Holy Spirit. What happened on that day? Four things specifically …

First, on that day the Lord Jesus Christ baptized his church, his kingdom, his body into the Holy Spirit as had been promised by John the Baptist (Mark 1:8). This was the inaugural gift of King Jesus to his church. When he ascended on high and began his rule as our Redeemer-King, he immersed his kingdom into the realm of the Spirit. There are seven references in the New Testament to this baptism 'in the Holy Spirit' (Matthew 3:11; Mark 1:8; Luke 3:16; John 1:33; Acts 1:5; 11:16; 1 Corinthians 12:13).

In each of these places where we are told of baptism 'with the Spirit', the word 'with' would be better translated 'in'. As a person who is baptized with water has been dipped in water, so one who has been baptized with the Holy Spirit has been immersed in the Spirit. The Person who did the baptizing is the Lord Jesus Christ. The people baptized are the church of God. The element into which the church was baptized is the Holy Spirit. When reading these references to baptism with the Holy Spirit, we should always read them as speaking of baptism in the Spirit.[1]

The first five of these references were prophetic, spoken in anticipation of Pentecost. Acts 11:15-17 looks back to what had happened at Pentecost. When the Gentiles in Cornelius' household experienced the same thing the believing Jews experienced at Pentecost, Peter remembered the promise of Christ and said, 'This is the same thing!' It was confirmed to him that the gift of the Spirit was to the Gentiles, too (Acts 11:17).

1 Corinthians 12:13[2] also refers back to Pentecost. In Christ, by the Spirit of God, all true believers are one. All racial, social, cultural

---

[1] If the word should be translated 'in' instead of 'with', why is it translated 'with'? One answer to that question is obvious. The translators of our Authorized Version were all ministers in the Church of England. They were all working under orders of the King. As such, they laboured hard to make room for some mode of baptism other than immersion. Not only did they refuse to translate the word baptize, (Baptize is a transliteration, not a translation of the Greek word baptidzo. A translation would be 'dip, plunge, or immerse'.), but they also translated the word 'in' (en) as 'with' almost every time it is used in the New Testament in connection with baptism.

[2] The context of 1 Corinthians 12:13 demands that we understand this statement as referring to the water baptism of the believer. Our baptism speaks both of our identification and union with Christ as our Substitute and of our identification and union with his people in the life of the Spirit.

barriers have been broken down (Colossians 3:11; Ephesians 2:13-22). Every truly regenerate person has been baptized in the Holy Spirit, not when he is born again, not when he is baptized in water, but at the day of Pentecost when Christ immersed his church into the realm of the Spirit. When a person is born again, he is born into that body, that family, that church which was baptized in the Spirit on the day of Pentecost.

Second, on the day of Pentecost the promise of the Father was fulfilled (Acts 1:4-5; Galatians 3:13-14). This promise of the Father was an unconditional promise of covenant grace. Baptism in the Holy Spirit was not dependent upon the will, works, worth, or spirituality of the people, but upon the faithfulness of God. That which took place on the day of Pentecost was not a possibility, but an absolute certainty.

As all of God's elect were redeemed by Christ at one time, so, too, all were baptized by Christ into the Spirit at one time. As we now receive and experience the benefits of redemption day by day, so, too, we receive and experience the benefits of this baptism day by day. But the baptism itself will never be repeated. There is no need. There is no more need of another Pentecost than there is of another Passover. Once redeemed, forever redeemed! Once baptized in the Spirit, forever baptized in the Spirit!

Third, this great advent of the Spirit fulfilled the Old Testament type set forth in the Feast of Pentecost (Exodus 34:22; Deuteronomy 16:10; Leviticus 23:15). The crucifixion of Christ took place on the day of atonement, when the paschal lamb was to be slaughtered, because that is what the passover represented. The out-pouring of the Holy Spirit took place on the day of Pentecost, because this is what Pentecost represented. The Feast of Pentecost was at the beginning of the harvest season when wheat was harvested. On the day of Pentecost, Israel was required to present two loaves to God called, 'The first fruits unto the Lord'. These loaves represented the first fruits of Christ's atonement. That is exactly what believers are (James 1:18). The first wave loaf represented the ingathering of

God's elect from among the Jews (Acts 2 – three thousand in one day). The second wave loaf represented God's elect gathered from among the Gentiles (Acts 10).

Fourth, this mighty outpouring of the Holy Spirit at Pentecost also fulfilled the typical Shekinah (Numbers 9:15-22; 2 Chronicles 7:1-3). As the glory of the Lord led the children of Israel, so the Spirit of God leads us through this world. As the glory of the Lord protected Israel, so the Holy Spirit now protects God's elect. As the glory of the Lord filled the temple in Solomon's day, so the Spirit of God fills and abides with the church, the temple of God, in this day of the Prince of Peace (1 Corinthians 3:16-17).

Let us ever seek, by the grace of God, to be taught by the Spirit, led by the Spirit (Romans 8:14), filled with the Spirit (Ephesians 5:18), and to walk in the Spirit (Galatians 5:17-23). But we do not seek the baptism of the Spirit. We have that if we are born of God.

4. The works of the Holy Spirit, in general, are fourfold

I use the word 'general' only for lack of a better word. There is nothing general about these four works of supernatural, divine power which are ascribed to the Holy Spirit. Creation is a work in which God the Holy Spirit participates with the Father and the Son (Genesis 1:2). 'The Spirit of the Lord hath made me, and the breath of the Almighty hath given me life' (Job 33:4).

Providence, like creation, is a work of God the Holy Spirit. 'Who hath directed the Spirit of the Lord, or being his counsellor hath taught him? With whom took he counsel?' (Isaiah 40:13-14). It is the Spirit of God who turns the king's heart whithersoever he will.

Inspiration is the work of the Spirit (2 Timothy 3:16; 2 Peter 1:21). The Book of God is his Book. He inspired it. Every word was written, every sentence was formed, and the order in which the whole Book was written was by his supernatural, unerring, infallible direction. Though many instruments were used to write the Book, God the Holy Spirit is its only Author.

The incarnation and virgin birth of Christ are works attributed to the Holy Spirit (Matthew 1:20; Hebrews 10:5). The holy human body and soul of Christ was created by the Holy Spirit in the womb of the virgin Mary. It was God the Holy Spirit who prepared a body for our Saviour in which he could both obey the law of God and satisfy its justice by the sacrifice of himself as our Substitute.

5. It is by the sovereign, irresistible work of God the Holy Spirit that lost sinners are born again and brought into a living union of faith with Christ (Psalm 65:4; 110:3; John 6:63)

Regeneration, the new birth, is his work (John 3:3-8). It is the Spirit of life who gives life to dead sinners. The revelation of Christ is the Spirit's work (John 16:13-14; 2 Corinthians 4:6). We know Christ only as God the Holy Spirit makes him known to us and in us. We know the things of God only as he makes them known (1 Corinthians 2:10-14). Chosen, redeemed sinners are convinced of their sin, of righteousness established by Christ, and judgment finished by his blood atonement, only by the almighty, efficacious grace of the Spirit of God (John 16:8-11).

Effectual calling is the work of his omnipotent, irresistible grace (1 Thessalonians 1:4-5). As David sent Ziba to 'fetch' Mephibosheth, so the Lord Jesus Christ, our King, sends his Spirit, at the appointed time of love, to 'fetch' the objects of his covenant love to himself. The fact that they are all by nature unwilling to be fetched is no difficulty with him. He is not just an influencer. He is God the Holy Spirit. He makes the chosen willing in the day of his power and causes them to come home to Christ (Psalm 65:4; 110:3). He converts those whom he calls and effectually gives them faith in Christ by the operations of his omnipotent grace (Ephesians 2:8-9; Colossians 2:12).

6. It is by the work of God the Holy Spirit that the believer's life is ordered and protected, and preserved in this world unto eternal glory

Believers are people who have been born again and live in the realm of the Spirit, the realm of faith (Romans 8:5-9). God lives in us and we live in God. God the Holy Spirit takes up residence in every believer permanently from the moment of regeneration. He dwells in every believer forever. He works in every believer continually. He is the sanctifying power in every believer's life. He is the earnest of our inheritance and gives us the assurance of salvation (Romans 8:16; 2 Corinthians 1:22; Ephesians 1:14). The Holy Spirit is the Comforter, the Teacher, the Illuminator, the Unction of God's saints in this world (John 14:16-18; 1 Corinthians 2:9-12; Ephesians 1:17; 1 John 2:20, 27). He leads the believer in obedience and service to Christ (Romans 8:14; Galatians 5:16; Acts 8:27, 29; Hebrews 8:10). The Holy Spirit calls, qualifies, and equips men for special service in the kingdom of God (Acts 13:2-4). He distributes spiritual gifts in the body of Christ as he will (1 Corinthians 12:4-11). He gives us the power and grace to do what we are called of God to do (Acts 1:8; 1 Corinthians 2:4; 1 Thessalonians 1:5).

The Spirit of grace produces in every believer the fruit of grace (Galatians 5:22-25). They are the produce of his grace, not of our works. It is the Spirit who teaches us to pray according to the will of God (2 Samuel 7:27; Romans 8:26-27; Galatians 4:6). The Holy Spirit directs the believer's heart in worship (John 4:23-24; Philippians 3:3). In the last day, God the Holy Spirit will be the agent of Christ (Romans 8:11-23) in the resurrection of our bodies (the second resurrection), as he has been in the resurrection of our souls (the first resurrection – Revelation 20:6).

'In whom also we have obtained an inheritance, being predestinated according to the purpose of him who worketh all things after the counsel of his own will:'
(Ephesians 1:11) [also: Romans 8:29-30 & Ephesians 1:5]

Chapter 12

Predestination

God almighty, the one true and living God, the God of the Bible, is a God of purpose; sovereign, eternal, unalterable purpose. Everything that comes to pass in time is brought to pass by the hand of our God, 'According to the eternal purpose which he purposed in Christ Jesus our Lord' (Ephesians 3:11). This eternal purpose of God is what we call, in Bible terms, predestination. 'Predestination is the decree of God whereby he hath for his own glory foreordained whatever comes to pass.' (Charles Buck)

A Bible doctrine
There is absolutely no question about the fact that the Word of God teaches the doctrine of predestination. It is taught throughout the scriptures and clearly stated in numerous passages of Inspiration (Matthew 25:34; Romans 8:29, 30; Ephesians 1:3, 6, 11; 2 Timothy 1:9-10; 2 Thessalonians 2:13; 1 Peter 1:1-2; John 6:37; 17:2-24; Revelation 13:8; 17:8; Daniel 4:35; 1 Thessalonians 5:9; Matthew 11:26; Exodus 4:21; Proverbs 16:4; Acts 2:23; 4:28; 13:48; Romans 9:11; Ephesians 3:11).

The basis of our faith is the Word of God, and the Word of God alone. We do not believe the doctrine of predestination because it is a logical and reasonable part of a theological system, though it is both logical and reasonable. We do not believe this doctrine, or any other doctrine for that matter, simply because it has been upheld and maintained by true believers throughout the ages of Christianity, though it cannot be denied that Christians have always taught God's sovereign predestination. This is a doctrine the Church of God has always maintained. Yet, neither logic nor history is the basis of our faith. The basis of our faith is the Word of God alone. We believe this doctrine, rejoice in it, and preach it from the housetops because it is plainly taught in holy scripture. The fact that predestination is a Bible doctrine simply cannot be disputed. The only question to be answered is this: What does the Bible teach about predestination?

Misrepresentations

This is a doctrine which is often deliberately misrepresented by those who oppose it and ignorantly misrepresented by those who try to defend it. In fact, it is hard to say whether this doctrine has suffered more in the camp of its enemies or in the camp of its friends. So we will begin this chapter by identifying four common misrepresentations of divine predestination.

First, the Bible does not teach that impersonal, stoic philosophy which says, 'Whatever will be will be'. That sort of philosophical fatalism attempts to remove from man all responsibility for his actions and for his condition in life. We do not for a moment believe that a man is the master of his own destiny. Yet, the scriptures make every person responsible for his own soul. Our eternal destiny is our own responsibility.

Second, the Word of God does not teach that religious fatalism which says, 'The elect will be saved, no matter what'. We believe and rejoice in the Bible doctrine of election. It is impossible to believe the Book of God and not believe in election. However, the Word of God never suggests, or even allows the possibility that, 'The elect will be saved no matter what'. The scriptures plainly declare that no one will ever be saved who does not hear the gospel (Romans 10:17), believe on the Lord Jesus Christ (Mark 16:15-16), acknowledge and confess his sin (1 John 1:9), repent of his sins (Luke 13:5), and persevere in the faith (Matthew 10:22). God has predestinated the use of specific means for the accomplishment of his purposes. The use of those means is as necessary and as certain as the end itself.

Third, the Word of God nowhere teaches that God has arbitrarily predestinated some to go to heaven and some to go to hell. The all-wise God never does anything arbitrarily. He has a wise and good purpose for everything he does and everything he purposed from eternity. The everlasting condemnation of the reprobate was as much a part of God's decree as the salvation of the elect (Proverbs 16:4; 1 Peter 2:8; Jude 4). The Bible speaks as plainly about 'the vessels of wrath fitted to destruction', as it does about 'the vessels of mercy, which he had afore prepared unto glory' (Romans 9:21-24). However, we must never fail to recognize that God's predestination, while securing the salvation of the elect by God's hand alone, leaves the responsibility for every sinner's damnation upon his own shoulders. The elect, the vessels of mercy, are prepared for glory by God's free grace in Christ; whereas the reprobate, the vessels of wrath, are fitted to destruction by their own sin and wilful unbelief. Salvation is always set before us in the Bible as being God's doing and God's work alone. Damnation is always set before us in the Bible as being man's fault and man's work alone.

Fourth, divine predestination is not based upon God's foreknowledge. Predestination is not God's foreknowledge of what would come to pass, but his purpose and determination of what must come to pass. It is not the result of what God knew man would do. Rather, predestination is what he determined he would do. The fact is, nothing could be absolutely foreknown that was not absolutely predetermined. That which is foreknown must have been foreordained. God knew the end of all things from the beginning, because he had predestinated the end from the beginning (Isaiah 14:24, 26, 27; 46:9-11).

The doctrine of scripture

Essentially the doctrine of divine predestination is this: Before the world began, God sovereignly predestinated all his elect to be conformed to the image of his dear Son, the Lord Jesus Christ, which he accomplishes in time by his sovereign, irresistible, immutable grace, and foreordained all things necessary to accomplish that great goal in the way which is most honouring to himself.

Eternal predestination is God's sovereign work. Carefully observe the language of scripture. 'He also did predestinate'. 'He' is the original cause of all things. 'He' is the source of salvation. Everything springs from him. It is written, 'All things are of God' (2 Corinthians 5:18; Romans 11:36).

Specifically, predestination is God's eternal purpose of grace toward his elect. It is God's determination to save his elect. It is his determination of the everlasting destiny of chosen sinners before the world began. Without question, God's sovereign purpose and absolute decree included all things, all people, and all events, in heaven, earth, and hell. However, the revealed object of predestination is the salvation of the chosen. Divine predestination is absolutely free, sovereign, and unconditional. This work of God was finished before the world began. Predestination was an immutable, unalterable work of God's free grace in Christ. God's predestination is his gracious purpose to save specific sinners, his purpose founded upon and arising from his everlasting love (Jeremiah 31:3; Romans 8:29-30; Ephesians 1:3-5; 2 Timothy 1:9-10).

Salvation is accomplished by the irresistible power of God's grace, according to the sovereign purpose of God in his eternal decree, through the merits of Christ's blood and righteousness as the sinners' Substitute. Salvation is not the result of man's will, but of God's. It is not the sinner's will that brings him to Christ, but God's will. God's will is not ruled by, or subject to, man's will. Man's will is ruled by and subject to God's will (John 1:12-13; Romans 9:16).

Salvation is God's work. It is accomplished by God's sovereign, deliberate purpose. It is a work which the Lord God almighty purposed to accomplish from eternity. The means, or method, by which he would accomplish this glorious work was devised and resolved upon from eternity in the everlasting covenant of grace and counsel of peace. This is God's purpose. In eternal mercy, he determined to save a people for the glory of his own great name by the substitutionary sacrifice of his dear Son (Job 33:24; Psalm 89:19; Romans 3:24-26; 5:8; 2 Corinthians 5:21).

The death of Christ at Calvary was no accident, or afterthought with God. Our Lord Jesus Christ went to the cross to accomplish our salvation by his death as our Substitute, according to his Father's own determinate counsel (Luke 22:22; Acts 2:23; 4:28). It was God almighty who determined the time, place, and circumstances of Christ's birth. It was God alone who determined the time and instrument of his Son's betrayal. It was God the Father who determined the time, place, and circumstances of his Son's execution at the hands of wicked men. And it was God who determined what the results of his Son's sacrificial death upon the cross would be. The Father resolved from eternity to save chosen sinners by the sin-atoning death of his own darling Son (Isaiah 53:10-11).

All of this the Lord God resolved upon and predestinated for his own glory in the salvation of his elect. He chose to save sinners by the sacrifice of Christ, through the power of his grace, without any aid or assistance from them, for the glory of his own great name (Psalm 106:8; Ephesians 1:6, 12, 14; 1 Corinthians 1:30-31).

Whatever predestination affords, brings to pass, and accomplishes is for God's elect. Read the scriptures. Predestination concerns God's chosen. It secures their salvation, their preservation, and their glory. Predestination is much, much more than an abstract theory of theological speculation. Predestination is one of the most practical, blessed, and glorious doctrines revealed in holy scripture.

Predestination does not keep anyone out of heaven. People often look upon predestination as a frightful monster which stands at the gate of heaven and arbitrarily shuts multitudes out, saying, 'No, you cannot come in, you cannot be saved, no matter how much you want to be, because you were not chosen and predestinated to salvation'. Nothing could be further from the truth. God's work of predestination is what opens the gates of heaven.

Any sinner who is lost at last and goes to hell will do so as the result of deliberate action on his part. If anyone goes to hell, it will be his own fault. If men refuse to walk in the light God has given them, that is their fault. And when they are cast into hell, they will acknowledge the justice of God in casting them into hell. Reprobation is always presented to us in the Word of God as a judicial act. Judgment is an act of justice. It is something God does in justice in response to man's sin. God sends blindness because men and women choose not to see. He sends hardness of heart to those who harden their hearts against him. He sends men to hell because they will not bow to his Son (2 Thessalonians 2:10-11; Matthew 23:37-38).

Be sure you understand this. If anyone goes to hell, it is his own fault alone. He has no one to blame but himself. But if anyone is saved, it will be God's doing alone, the result of deliberate effort on God's part. We will have no one to thank and praise for it but God. God's salvation began in eternal predestination. Without predestination we would all be damned forever. Predestination is the guarantee of salvation for God's elect.

God almighty predestinated all things for the everlasting salvation of his elect and the glory of his name. In other words, all that comes to pass in time was purposed by God in eternity, purposed for our souls' everlasting good and God's everlasting praise (Romans 8:28-30; Ephesians 1:11-12).

The object

The object of our God in predestination is that we should be conformed to the image of his own dear Son. The one thing God almighty is determined to accomplish in us by his purpose, his providence, his power, and his grace is an exact likeness to the Lord Jesus Christ (Romans 8:29; Ephesians 1:4). God predestinated us to be conformed to the image of his Son. I cannot imagine anyone being upset with that fact, except those who yet hate God and his Son.

Through the sin and fall of our father Adam, we all became sinners. We lost God's image in which we were created, and forfeited life, communion, fellowship, and acceptance with him forever (Romans 5:12). Yet, God's purpose was not overthrown when Adam sinned. It was executed exactly according to his sovereign will and infinite wisdom (1 Corinthians 15:21-22). God almighty was determined from the beginning to glorify himself in his creation, by rescuing a multitude which no man can number from Adam's fall and restoring them to his image perfectly, forever through another representative man, the God-man, Christ Jesus.

God looked upon his Son from eternity with such joy and delight that he said, I will have an innumerable multitude of sons and daughters just like him. Thus when predestination has done its work, every chosen sinner will be exactly conformed to the image of God's dear Son, 'holy and without blame' before God himself.

Believers are being conformed to Christ in his nature. He is begotten of God and so are we. We are conformed to Christ in his relationship. He is the Son of God; and we are the sons and daughters of the almighty (1 John 3:1). We must also be conformed to Christ in his experience. Like Christ, we must learn obedience through the things we suffer. Like him, we must endure abuse from men. Like our Master, we must suffer the attacks of Satan. Like Christ, we must struggle against temptation and sin. We must be conformed to Christ in his character. Like him, we must be consecrated to God. Like him, we must live by God's Word. Like him, we must seek our Father's will. Like him, we must be loving, kind, and tender toward one another. Because God purposed it, we must at last be conformed to the image of Christ in his glory. Salvation, when it is finished, will be perfect and complete, communion with, consecration to, and conformity to the Lord Jesus Christ forever. This salvation, from start to finish, is accomplished by God, according to his own sovereign purpose of grace in predestination. God predestinated from eternity who will be saved, the means by which he would save them, the time of their salvation, all the events and circumstances necessary for and leading to their salvation, the place where he would save his chosen, their place in glory, and everything required to bring us safely home.

For Christ's sake

The ultimate end of God in predestination, as in all other things, is the exaltation and glory of our Lord Jesus Christ. God has determined to glorify himself in glorifying his glorious Son. He has predestinated his elect unto the adoption of sons, that Jesus Christ his eternal, only-begotten Son, might be the firstborn among many brethren (Romans 8:28-30; 11:33-36; Colossians 1:16-18).

Predestination gives Christ the pre-eminence, because Christ is the centre of God's decrees. He is the Head of a new, elect race. He is the centre and glory of heaven. Predestination gives Christ pleasure, because his delights were with the sons of men before time began. Now he has a race of men in whom and with whom he delights. He loves them; and they all love him. This was the joy set before him, for which he endured the cross, despising the shame. This is the reward of his labour. Predestination gives Christ praise. God has arranged things so that all the population of heaven will owe everything to Christ, so that everyone in glory land will chant Immanuel's praise forever, and Immanuel's praise alone.

This is the glorious doctrine of predestination in which we rejoice. It is a most profitable doctrine. It destroys every basis of human pride. It exalts the glory of Christ and the grace of God. It gives us a purpose in evangelism. It gives us a sure hope before God (2 Samuel 23:5). It puts us at peace with God's providence. It opens the doors of heaven to sinners and guarantees that some shall enter therein. It shuts us up to God for everything (Jeremiah 9:23-24).

'Whatsoever the LORD pleased, that did he in heaven, and in earth, in the seas, and all deep places.'
(Psalm 135:6)

Chapter 13

The Sovereignty of God

With the words above the Psalmist David both declares God's absolute, universal sovereignty and calls upon us to trust, worship, and praise him because he is the sovereign God of the universe. The very foundation of our confidence and faith in our God is his sovereignty. Were he not sovereign, absolutely, universally sovereign, we could not trust him implicitly, believe his promises, or depend upon him to fulfil his Word. Only an absolute sovereign can be trusted absolutely. We can and should trust our God implicitly because he is sovereign. Nothing is more delightful to the hearts of God's children than the fact of his great and glorious sovereignty. Under the most adverse circumstances, in the most severe troubles, and when enduring the most heavy trials, we rejoice to know that our God has sovereignly ordained our afflictions, that he sovereignly overrules them, and that he sovereignly sanctifies them to our good and his own glory.

A matter of great joy

Every believer rejoices in the sovereignty of God. God's saints rejoice to hear him say, 'Is it not lawful for me to do what I will with mine own?' (Matthew 20:15). Nothing in this world is more comforting to the believer's heart than the knowledge of the fact that 'Our God is in the heavens: he hath done whatsoever he hath pleased' (Psalm 115:3). Yet, in this day of religious darkness and confusion, there is no truth of holy scripture for which we must more earnestly contend than God's dominion over all creation, his sovereignty over all the works of his hands, the supremacy of his throne and his right to sit upon it. We rejoice in God's sovereignty. Yet, there is nothing revealed in the Bible that is more despised by worldlings and self-righteous religionists.

Natural, unregenerate, unbelieving men and women are happy enough to have God everywhere, except upon the throne of total, universal sovereignty. They are happy to have God in his workshop, creating the world and naming the stars. They are glad to have God in the hospital to heal the sick. They are pleased to have God in times of trouble to calm the raging seas of life. They are delighted to have God in the funeral parlour to ease them throught pain and sorrow. But God upon his throne is, to the unregenerate man, the most contemptible thing in the world. Any man who dares to preach that it is God's right to do what he will with his own, to dispose of his creatures as he sees fit, and save whom he will, will be hissed at, despised, and cursed by this religious generation. Still, it is God upon the throne that we love, trust, and worship. And it is God upon the throne that we preach.

Sovereignty or idolatry

God's sovereignty is so basic and fundamental that it is impossible to understand any doctrine taught in the Bible until we recognize and have some understanding of the fact that God is sovereign. A God who is not sovereign is as much a contradiction as a God who is not holy, eternal, and immutable. A God who is not sovereign is no God at all. If the god you worship is not totally sovereign, you are a pagan, and your religion is idolatry. You would be just as well off worshipping a statue of Mary, a totem pole, a spider, or the devil himself as to worship a god who lacks total sovereignty over all things.

In one of his letters to the learned and scholarly Erasmus, Martin Luther said, 'Your thoughts of God are too human'. No doubt Erasmus resented the remark for it exposed the heart of his heretical theology. Yet it exposes the heart of all false religion. I lay this charge against the preachers and theologians of our day, and against the people who hear them, follow them, and support them. Their thoughts of God are too human. I know the seriousness of what I have written, but it must be stated with emphatic clarity. The God of the Bible is utterly unknown to most of this religious generation.

God's charge against apostate Israel was, 'Thou thoughtest that I was altogether such an one as thyself' (Psalm 50:21), and that is his indictment against the religious world of our day. Men today imagine that God is moved by sentiment, rather than by the determination of his sovereign will. They talk about omnipotence, but imagine that it is such an idle fiction that Satan can thwart the power of God. They think that if God has a plan, it must, like the plans of men, be subject to constant change. They tell us that whatever power God does possess must be limited, lest he violate man's free will and make him a machine. The grace of God is thought by most people to be nothing but a helpless, frustrated desire of God to save men. The precious sin-atoning blood of Christ is thought by most to be a waste, shed in vain for many. The invincible, saving power of the Holy Spirit is reduced by most to a gentle offer of grace which men may easily resist. All such thoughts about God are the blasphemies of idolaters.

The god of this generation no more resembles the sovereign Lord of heaven and earth than a flickering candle resembles the noon-day sun. The god of modern religion is nothing but an idol, the invention of men, a figment of man's imagination. Pagans in the dark ages used to carve their gods out of wood and stone and overlay them with silver and gold. Today, in these much darker days, pagans inside the church carve their god out of their own depraved imaginations. In reality, the religionists of our day are atheists, for there is no possible alternative between a God who is absolutely sovereign and no God at all. A god whose will can be resisted, whose purpose can be frustrated, whose power can be thwarted, whose grace can be nullified, whose work can be overturned, has no title to Deity. Such a god is not a fit object of worship. Such a puny, pigmy god merits nothing but contempt.

When I say that God is sovereign, I am simply declaring that God is God. He is the most High, Lord of heaven and earth, overall, blessed forever. He is subject to none. He is influenced by none. God is absolutely independent of and sovereign over all his creatures. He does as he pleases, only as he pleases, and always as he pleases. None can thwart him. None can resist him. None can change him. None can stop him. None can hinder him. He declares, 'My counsel shall stand, and I will do all my pleasure' (Isaiah 46:10). 'He doeth according to his will in the army of heaven, and among the inhabitants of the earth, and none can stay his hand, or say unto him, What doest thou?' (Daniel 4:35). Divine sovereignty means that God sits upon the throne of universal dominion, directing all things, ruling all things, and working all things 'after the counsel of his own will' (Ephesians 1:11).

This is a subject about which hundreds of books have been written, and yet 'the half hath not been told'. Divine sovereignty is not some isolated doctrine, taught in a few verses of scripture. It is revealed, literally, upon every page of Inspiration. In this study, we will consider just five things which manifestly and irrefutably reveal the sovereignty of God: (1) predestination, (2) creation, (3) providence, (4) salvation, and (5) spiritual gifts.

Predestination

God's sovereignty is irrefutably revealed in the eternal predestination of all things. Does the Bible teach predestination? Of course it does! Anyone who attempts to deny that it does is either totally ignorant of the Word of God, or a liar. God chose some men and women in eternity to be the objects of his saving grace and predestinated those elect ones to be conformed to the image of his dear Son (Romans 8:28-29). Before the world began God sovereignly determined that he would save some, who they would be, and when he would save them. Having determined these things, our great God infallibly secured his eternal purpose of grace by sovereign predestination.

Yes, God predestinated from eternity everything that comes to pass in time to secure the salvation of his elect. That is the plainly stated doctrine of holy scripture (Ephesians 1:3-6, 11; Romans 11:36). It is written, 'All things are of God' (2 Corinthians 5:18). 'The Lord hath made all things for himself' (Proverbs 16:4). Eternal election marked the house into which God's saving grace must come. Eternal predestination marked the path upon which grace must come. Sovereign providence led grace down the path to the house at the appointed time of love.

Creation

No one can reasonably deny the revelation of God's sovereignty in his marvellous work of creation (Genesis 1:1; Revelation 4:11). Nothing moved God to create, except his own sovereign will. What could move him when there was nothing but God himself? Truly, 'the heavens declare the glory of God' (Psalm 19:1-4). God created the heavens and the earth as a stage upon which to work out his purpose of grace (Psalm 8:1-9). He created the angelic host to be ministering spirits to those who shall be the heirs of salvation (Hebrews 1:14). God created the sun, the moon, and the stars for the benefit of his elect. He created all plants and animals to provide food, comfort, and pleasure for man. At last, God created man in his own image and after his own likeness that he might show forth the glory of his grace in man. Adam was created in the image of Christ, our eternal Surety and Substitute (Romans 5:12-21). He was created in conditional holiness. In God's wise, holy and good purpose of grace, Adam was permitted to fall and we all fell in him that we might be raised to life again in Christ, the second Adam.

Providence

We see God's sovereignty in all the works of his daily providence (Romans 8:28; 11:36). In divine providence, God almighty sovereignly accomplishes his eternal purpose of grace in predestination. The Holy Spirit showed John a beautiful picture of this recorded in the book of Revelation. He saw the Lord Jesus Christ as our Mediator, the Lamb of God, taking the book of God's purpose, opening the book, and fulfilling all that was written in it in all the world (Revelation 5:1-10; 10:1-11). He who is God our Saviour, the Lord Jesus Christ, rules all things in providence by the book of God's predestination.

God's sovereign rule of providence extends to all his creatures. Inanimate matter, irrational creatures, all things in this world perform their Maker's bidding. It was by the will of our God that the waters of the Red Sea divided (Exodus 14). By his word the earth opened up her mouth to swallow his enemies (Numbers 14). When he willed it, the sun stood still (Joshua 10) and went backward ten degrees on the sundial of Ahaz. Once, he even made an axe head float. Ravens carried food to his prophet (1 Kings 17). Lions were tamed by God's decree for his servant Daniel. He made the fire refuse to burn his faithful servants when they were cast into the fiery furnace. All things come to pass, or not, at his pleasure.

God's rule of providence extends even to the thoughts, and wills, and actions, and words, even of wicked men. He kept Abimelech from adultery with Sarah. He kept the Canaanites from desiring the possessions of Israel when his people went to worship him (read Exodus 34:23-24). The hearts of all men, their thoughts, intents, and passions, are in the hands of our God (Proverbs 21:1). Shimei was sent of God to curse David. Even the wrath of man shall praise him, and the remainder of wrath, that which he chooses not to use for his praise, he restrains (Psalm 76:10).

The object of God's providence, the object of God in all that he does, or allows to be done, is threefold. It is for the salvation of his elect, the eternal, spiritual good of all his people, and the glory of his great name. Here is a resting place for every believer's troubled heart. Neither Satan, the demons of hell, nor men, nor sickness, nor war, nor pestilence, nor the whirlwind is beyond the reach of God's sovereign throne (Matthew 10:30). Blessed be God, 'Our times are in his hand!'

Salvation

God's indisputable sovereignty is conspicuously revealed in the salvation of sinners by his almighty grace (Romans 9:8-24). God chose to save some, but not all. He gave Christ to die for some, but not all. He sends his gospel to some, but not all. He gives his Spirit to some, but not all. He causes some to hear his voice, but not all. He saves some who seek him, but not all. He saved the woman with the issue of blood but not the rich young ruler, the one leper but not the nine, the publican but not the Pharisee. 'Salvation is of the Lord!' He planned it. He purchased it. He performs it. He preserves it. He perfects it. He shall have all the praise for it.

Spiritual Gifts

God's sovereignty is also conspicuously revealed in the various spiritual gifts he bestows upon his people (1 Corinthians 12:14, 18, 28-29). He sees to it that his church has everything she needs to carry out the work he has for her to do. We need missionaries, and pastors too. We need preachers; and deacons, as well. We need faithful witnesses; and we need the prayers of God's saints. We need workers; and we need givers. We need some to do great things; and some to do small things. In a word, we need Marthas and Marys, Johns and Jameses, Peters and Pauls, Lydias and Lucases. God gives each when they are needed and where they are needed for the accomplishment of his will. Let each child of God covet earnestly the best gift, the gift of love one for another. If we have that, we will serve God and his people well, using all other gifts accordingly.

'Our God is in the heavens. He hath done (and is doing) whatsoever he hath pleased'. Let us, therefore, believe him confidently, walk with him in peace, submit to him cheerfully, serve him faithfully, and honour him supremely.

'(For *the children* being not yet born, neither having done any good or evil, that the purpose of God according to election might stand, not of works, but of him that calleth;)' (Romans 9:11)

Chapter 14

'The Purpose of God'

We believe, according to the scriptures, that the Lord our God is a God of purpose, absolute and unalterable purpose, a God whose purpose must and shall be accomplished. Before the world was made, before time began, almighty God sovereignly purposed all that comes to pass. Everything that is, has been, and shall hereafter be was purposed by God from eternity. Everything in the universe is moving toward the predestined end of God's eternal purpose with absolute, precision and accuracy. Everything that comes to pass in time was purposed by our God in eternity. Look into the Word of God and see if this is true. 'To the law and to the testimony: if they speak not according to this word, it is because there is no light in them'.

Consider the following five texts of scripture:

– Romans 8:28 'And we know that all things work together for good to them that love God, to them who are the called according to his purpose'.

– Romans 9:11 Here Paul tells us that God chose Jacob in everlasting love and rejected Esau in everlasting hatred, and that he revealed this fact to the boys' parents '... the children being not yet born, neither having done any good or evil, that the purpose of God according to election might stand, not of works, but of him that calleth'.

– Ephesians 1:11 'In whom also we have obtained an inheritance, being predestinated according to the purpose of him who worketh all things after the counsel of his own will'.

– Ephesians 3:11 Paul explains here that he preached the gospel to the Gentiles, even the unsearchable riches of Christ, that the manifold wisdom of God revealed in the gospel of Christ might be made known to all men ... 'According to the eternal purpose which he purposed in Christ Jesus our Lord'.

– 2 Timothy 1:9 'Who hath saved us, and called us with an holy calling, not according to our works, but according to his own purpose and grace, which was given us in Christ Jesus before the world began'.

These texts from the Word of God tell us five distinct facts about the purpose of God. (1) The purpose of God is eternal. (2) The purpose of God includes all things (Isaiah 45:7; Romans 11:36). (3) The purpose of God has for its particular and peculiar design the spiritual and eternal benefit of God's elect. Everything God has purposed is for the ultimate, spiritual, and eternal blessedness of his covenant people. (4) The purpose of God is immutable and sure. 'What God does', wrote A. H. Strong, 'he always purposed to do'. That which comes to pass in time is exactly what God purposed from eternity. The Lord God declares, 'My counsel shall stand, and I will do all my pleasure' (Isaiah 46:10). And (5) in its ultimate end,

God's purpose will accomplish the eternal salvation of his elect and the glory of his own great name.

We rejoice to know that our God is a God of purpose and that his purpose has been, is, and ever shall be accomplished everywhere, in all things, and at all times. Yet, we are often confused and frustrated because we do not presently see what God's purpose is. How often have you said to yourself, 'If I could only see what the Lord's purpose is in this trial, it would make it more bearable'.

I have searched the scriptures and have found seven things, which God has purposed, seven things which must come to pass. We are going to look at several passages of scripture in this study. The key word in each text is the word 'must'. These seven things must, of a certainty, come to pass. These things must come to pass, because God has purposed that they shall come to pass.

1. The Son of Man must suffer and die upon the cross

This is the matter of primary importance so we will look at it first. The death of our Lord Jesus Christ was not an accident. It is not something that came to pass as the result of man's free will, or because the Jews would not allow Jesus to be their king. The death of Christ was a necessity. It was something that must be accomplished. He said so (Luke 9:22).

Why? Why must the Lord Jesus Christ, the holy, sinless Son of God, the perfect Son of Man, the God-man, suffer and die upon the cursed tree? Why must the Lord of glory lay down his life as a sin-atoning sacrifice at Calvary?

Christ had to die at Jerusalem because God purposed it from eternity (Acts 2:23; 4:28). Our Saviour had to die at Jerusalem two thousand years ago in order to fulfil his covenant engagements as our everlasting Surety. The Son of God voluntarily took upon himself the responsibility of our redemption from eternity. He freely laid down his life for us at Calvary. Yet, having voluntarily agreed to become our Surety, he had to lay down his life for us. His honour and faithfulness demanded it (Genesis 43:8-9; John 10:18).

If he would fulfil all the types and prophecies of the Old Testament scriptures, our Redeemer had to die as a slaughtered, sin-atoning sacrifice in the place of his people, uplifted upon the cursed tree (Acts 13:29; Psalm 22:6-8, 16, 18; 34:20; Exodus 12:46; Psalm 69:21; Isaiah 50:6; 53:3-6, 10-12; Zechariah 12:10; Isaiah 45:21-22; John 3:14-17; Romans 3:24-26).

It is only through the death of the God-man, our most glorious Christ, that it is possible for our God to be 'a just God and a Saviour'. Only by the sacrifice of Christ could the righteousness of God be revealed. Only by his death as our Substitute is the sin of man exposed and condemned. The justice of God could be satisfied by no other means (Hebrews 10:1-14). Only by his blood could the people of God be forgiven of all sin and justified (Hebrews 9:22). The mercy, love, and grace of God is revealed and manifest to sinners only by the cross of Christ (Romans 5:6-8).

However, the death of Christ alone is not sufficient to save us. Something else must be done.

2. In order to save us from our sins the Lord Jesus Christ must rise from the dead

A dead Christ could never save anyone. A dead Christ could never be of any value to either God or man. A dead Christ might be a good example; but he could never be a mighty Saviour. It was when the crucified Christ arose from the dead that the foundation of our faith was fixed (John 20:9).

It was his resurrection that demonstrated, in an undeniable manner, that our Redeemer is the Son of God (Romans 1:1-4). The resurrection of Christ assures us that our sins have been put away and justice has been satisfied (Romans 4:25; Hebrews 9:12). The greatest apologetic for Christianity in this world is the empty tomb. The resurrection of our Lord is the sure evidence of his power and ability to save every sinner who comes to God by him (Romans 8:31-34; Hebrews 7:25).

Here is the third thing that must come to pass because God has purposed it.

3. The gospel of the grace of God, the glorious gospel of the glorious Christ, must be preached in all the world

In Mark 13:10 we are told that, prior to the second advent of our Lord Jesus Christ, the gospel of the grace and glory of God in him must be heralded throughout the whole world. There are three reasons why it must be so: (1) To declare to all men the glorious accomplishments of the Son of God as our Redeemer, (2) For the salvation of God's elect out of every nation, kindred, tribe, and tongue, and (3) To leave the reprobate, the unbelieving, without excuse.

4. Once this gospel has been declared in all the world, and before Christ comes again, all God's elect must be saved

God allows the world to stand, and allows it to stand only, because he has a people in this world whom he is determined to save. Because he is 'longsuffering to us', the world is not yet destroyed (2 Peter 3:9). Our Lord has not yet come in final judgment, because he has not yet saved all his people (John 10:16; Isaiah 65:8).

The scriptures are abundantly clear in asserting that all God's elect shall be saved. Not one of Christ's sheep shall perish. Every sinner redeemed by blood shall be saved by grace and crowned with glory. The purpose of God demands it. The law of God demands it. Justice satisfied cannot punish those for whom it has been satisfied. The satisfaction of Christ demands it. Were one of those for whom he died to perish under the wrath of God, the Lord Jesus could never see of the travail of his soul and be satisfied (Isaiah 53:11).

Christ must come, at the appointed time of love to seek his lost sheep (John 4:4). Before they can enter into the kingdom of heaven, every chosen, redeemed sinner must be born again (John 3:3-8). They must come to God through Christ, believing that he is, and that he is the Rewarder of them who diligently seek him (Hebrews 11:6). Their wills must be broken by almighty grace (John 3:30). They must learn to worship God in Spirit and in truth (John 4:23-24). These things are matters of certainty, because the cross of our Lord Jesus Christ shall never be shown to have failed.

5. The Lord Jesus Christ must reign as King

Read 1 Corinthians 15:24-28 and rejoice. Our all glorious Christ, the Son of God, is the sovereign Ruler and King of the universe. We must either bow to his dominion or perish as his enemies. There are no other options. Repent or perish! Turn or burn! Bow or be damned! Either way, 'He must reign!' He does reign!

– For the salvation of his people (John 17:1-3).
– Because he earned the right (Romans 14:9; Philippians 2:9-11).
– Because none can stop him!

6. The bodies of God's elect must be raised from the grave

Once God's elect have all been saved by his grace, and all the purposes of God have been accomplished in this time world, the Lord Jesus Christ must come again in power and great glory to gather his elect unto himself in resurrection glory (1 Corinthians 15:51-58). Oh, yes, Christ must come again! Our Redeemer shall come again to raise his saints, destroy his enemies, create all things new, and reign gloriously forever (Job 19:25-27).

7. According to the eternal purpose of God, everyone must stand before the Lord Jesus Christ in judgment

When at last everything which was purposed by our God from eternity has been accomplished, you and I are going to meet God in judgment (2 Corinthians 5:10-11; Acts 17:31). When you stand before Christ your God, before the august majesty of his great white throne in judgment, how will you fair? Let every child of God take comfort in this fact: The purpose of God shall stand. Our God will do all his pleasure. If any read these lines who are yet rebels against King Jesus, I call you to repentance. Bow to him now. The King of glory has once more given you his terms of peace – SURRENDER!

'... he hath made with me an everlasting covenant, ordered in all *things*, and sure: for *this is* all my salvation, and all *my* desire ... '
(2 Samuel 23:1-5)

Chapter 15

The Everlasting Covenant

There is a hush in the city of Jerusalem, a quiet stir in the king's palace. The people are anxious and fearful. The king is on his bed. His brow is wet with a cold sweat. His pulse is weak. His palms are clammy. David the king, the great and good monarch of Israel, is dying. He has reigned as king for forty years. He has led Israel in battle after battle, from conquest to conquest. He has ruled the land in righteousness and justice in the fear of God.

For forty years David had led the chosen nation both in civil righteousness and in spiritual devotion. He was both God's king and God's prophet; but now he was dying. What would become of the kingdom of Israel when Israel's king was gone? David had led them in the way of truth and righteousness. He had spoken to them, in the name of God, that which was the very Word of God. Would the nation ever hear from God again? David's family and friends were gathered around his bed, anxious to hear his last words. The people were gathered in the palace halls and in the streets of the city, anxious for any word from their beloved king. 'Now these be the last words of David'. These are the last words of David, the son of Jesse, the man after God's own heart. What will he say?

First, he describes himself (2 Samuel 23:1). 'David, the son of Jesse'. Jesse named his son well. David means 'loving'. But when he spoke of himself, David made no reference to the meaning of his name. He thought only of his humble background. This man whom God made to be the king of Israel was nothing but a poor, plain, ordinary shepherd boy. 'The man who was raised up on high, the anointed of the God of Jacob' (1 Samuel 16:1-12). God chose David to be king in the stead of Saul. God chose David instead of his brothers; and David never got over the wonder of God's electing love (Psalm 65:4; 2 Samuel 6:21). 'The sweet psalmist of Israel', this man was not only God's king and God's prophet, he was an inspired hymn writer. His blessed, sweet psalms were the hymnbook of the Old Testament church. They are always the most worn pages in an old saint's Bible, because they express in words the deepest, most constant struggles of our souls.

Second, in verses 2 and 3, David describes his God, the Lord our God, in the Trinity, or tri-unity of his sacred persons (1 John 5:7): 'The Spirit of the Lord' who is, The Holy Spirit, 'The God of Israel' who is, God the Father, and 'The Rock of Israel' who is, God the Son, our Lord Jesus Christ.

Third, David describes his Psalms and prophecies (v. 2). 'The spirit of the LORD spake by me, and his word was in my tongue'. His compositions were not merely his, but God's. They did not originate with him, but with God. He wrote only that which God the Holy Spirit dictated to him and directed his pen to write (2 Timothy 3:16; 2 Peter 1:21). Without question, every word he wrote in the Sacred Volume was his, an exact expression of his thoughts, emotions, and experiences. Yet, every word he wrote was the

Revelation of God to men, the very Word of God, as completely the Word of God as if no man had part in it.

Fourth, David describes his rule (vv. 3-4). 'The God of Israel said, the Rock of Israel spake to me, He that ruleth over men must be just, ruling in the fear of God. And he shall be as the light of the morning, when the sun riseth, even a morning without clouds; as the tender grass springing out of the earth by clear shining after rain'. These verses, are a declaration by David of his faithfulness as God's servant. He is saying, 'I have fought a good fight, I have finished my course, I have kept the faith'. What a way to leave this world!

Fifth, in verses 3 and 4, David also describes his great Son, the Lord Jesus Christ. Prophetically, these words refer to and describe the Son of God, our Saviour, great David's greater Son.

Then, in verse 5, the sweet singer of Israel declares his dying hope and comfort. Here, the man after God's own heart gives us the pillow of consolation upon which he laid his dying head. 'Although my house be not so with God; yet he hath made with me an everlasting covenant, ordered in all things, and sure: for this is all my salvation, and all my desire, although he make it not to grow'. As he laid on his dying bed, this saved sinner found comfort and hope in God's everlasting covenant of grace. So, too, may all who trust the Lord Jesus Christ, the Mediator and Surety of the covenant.

David's sigh

As the man of God lay upon his death bed, looking within himself and looking around upon his family and friends, he remembers many, many things that caused him sorrow and pain. He sighed, 'Although my house be not so with God'. He makes this concession, and it must be made by us all. So long as we live in this world, in this body of flesh, things are never altogether right with God's saint. Nothing here is really as we wish it to be.

The words 'my house' may be properly applied to four things. Perhaps David was saying 'my kingdom', my nation is not so with

God. A king's house is his kingdom. Certainly the nation of Israel was not as David desired it to be. Though David ruled in the fear of God, his people did not walk in the fear of God. Because she forgot God, the kingdom of Israel was a tottering kingdom and ready to fall. Godly men lament a godless nation.

By the words 'my house', David may have been referring, at least in a typical way, to the church of God. David's house (the nation of Israel) was typical of the church. The Church of God in this world is ever a house in need of repair.

The words 'my house' certainly refer to David's physical family. His heart was heavy because many in his household were without grace, life, and faith. Few in his family knew and worshipped his God. His wife, Michal, despised his God. His son, Amnon raped his own sister (2 Samuel 13:19-29). Absalom murdered Amnon, publicly shamed his father, tried to kill him, sought to overthrow the kingdom of God, and died a rebel's death in his revolt against God (2 Samuel 18:33). Only Abigail, Bathsheba, and Solomon appear to have known God.

Without question, when David says, 'Although my house be not so with God', he is talking about himself, his own life in this sinful estate, in this body of flesh. Though God did not remember his sins, David could not forget them. Even on his death bed, this saint of God speaks as one whose heart breaks with repentance. David knew and acknowledged his sin. Repentance is a lifelong business. David continued repenting until he left this world. I am sure, he had some specific things on his heart, as he was about to leave this world, which caused him enormous grief: his vengeance against Nabal (1 Samuel 25), his behaviour before Achish (1 Samuel 21:13), the matter of Uriah the Hittite (2 Samuel 11 and 12), his mourning over Absalom (2 Samuel 19:1-8), and the numbering of Israel, for which 70,000 died (2 Samuel 24:1-14).

David found no comfort in himself. His 'good works' gave him no reason for joy, but only grief and sorrow. His comfort was found in his God, his Saviour, and the covenant of grace made and executed on his behalf. Let all who are wise learn the obvious lessons taught us by this lamentation and sigh from the heart of that man who was the man after God's own heart. They are crystal clear.

1. Grace does not run in bloodlines, only corruption (John 1:12-13; Romans 8:11-16).
2. The afflictions of God's people, both personal and domestic, are the fruits of God's covenant grace, not indications of his wrath or displeasure (Psalm 89:30-34). They are not for our destruction, but for our good (2 Corinthians 4:17-5:1).
3. The sins of a faithful man's family are not an indication of evil in him or a bar to his usefulness.
4. The sins of a believer do not destroy his hope, haunt him with fear in the hour of death, or rob him of his everlasting inheritance in Christ (Psalm 32:1-5; Romans 4:8).

David's solace
'Yet, he hath made with me an everlasting covenant, ordered in all things and sure'. David knew something about covenant mercy, covenant promises and obligations, and covenant blessings. He had made a covenant with Jonathan. When the time came, he performed his oath to Jonathan upon Mephibosheth. When David looked on Mephibosheth, when he did something for Mephibosheth, he saw Jonathan. Here he says, that is what God has done for me. When God does something for us, he does it for Christ. When God looks on us, he sees Christ. When God hears us, he hears Christ. When God accepts us, he accepts Christ. This passage is talking about God's everlasting covenant of grace and salvation, that covenant made on behalf of chosen sinners before the world began.

This is not the covenant of works that God made with Adam, which he broke and we broke in him (Romans 5:12-18). This is not the covenant of circumcision which God made with Abraham, for that was for the Jews only and was forever abolished by God's own word (Galatians 5:2, 4). This is not that legal, Sinai covenant that

God made with Israel through his servant Moses. That legal covenant has been abolished by him (Hebrews 8:6-7). The law of God was not abolished; but the covenant of the law was, the curse of the law was, the constraint of the law was, and the condemnation of the law was. It is written, 'Ye are not under law, but under grace'. 'We are dead to the law'. 'Christ is the end of the law!'

The covenant of which David spoke, the covenant that comforted his heart and soul in the hour of death, is the covenant of grace, and peace, and life (Isaiah 54:10; Malachi 2:5). This is a covenant of pure, free grace (Psalm 89:19-35; Jeremiah 31:31-34; 32:38-40). It is a covenant made with God's elect in our covenant Surety, the Lord Jesus Christ, the Son of God (Hebrews 7:22; Psalm 89:19). It is an everlasting covenant, without beginning and without end (Proverbs 8:23-31). It is a well ordered covenant. Whatever the covenant required, it also provided and supplied (Ephesians 1:3-14; 2 Timothy 1:9). It is a sure covenant. It's mercies are 'the sure mercies of David' (Isaiah 55:3). That is to say, they are sure to all who are heirs of the covenant. Covenant mercies are sure to all God's elect, all the redeemed, all the called, all who believe the gospel. And this is an immutable covenant (Psalm 89:30-37).

David's salvation

David says concerning God's covenant, 'This is all my salvation'. There is much more implied in those words than can be dealt with in this brief study; but I want to simply state some things that, when understood, will thrill your soul and fill your heart with wonder and praise to God for his amazing grace.

Christ our Surety, with whom the covenant was made for us, is 'all our salvation'. 'Mine eyes have seen thy salvation' (1 Corinthians 1:30). There is a definite sense in which our salvation was complete when the covenant was made in eternity. The scriptures state this plainly (Romans 8:29-30; 2 Timothy 1:9). All God's elect were from eternity blessed with all the blessings of grace and salvation in Christ the Lamb, our Surety, slain from the foundation of the world

(Ephesians 1:3-6). All our salvation springs from, is determined by, and depends upon this glorious covenant (Jeremiah 32:38-40). This covenant, the covenant of grace, being fulfilled by Christ, is the believer's title to heaven (Revelation 13:8).

Not long before he died, John Gill wrote a letter to his nephew, stating exactly what David did in 2 Samuel 23:5 on his death bed. Gill wrote,

> I depend wholly and alone upon the free, sovereign, eternal, unchangeable love of God, the firm and everlasting covenant of grace, and my interest in the persons of the sacred Trinity, for my whole salvation; and not upon any righteousness of my own; nor anything in me, or done by me under the influences of the Holy Spirit; not upon any services of mine, which I have been assisted to perform for the good of the church do I depend, but upon my interest in the persons of the Trinity; the free grace of God, and the blessings of grace streaming to me through the blood and righteousness of Christ, as the ground of my hope. These are no new things to me, but what I have been long acquainted with; what I can live and die by. I apprehend that I shall not be long here, but this you may tell to any of my friends.

Then, just before he died, Gill said, to one of his friends standing by his bed, 'I have nothing to make me uneasy', and quoted one verse of a hymn, written by Isaac Watts, in honour of that Redeemer whom he loved, trusted, and served ...

> He raised me from the depths of sin,
> – The gates of gaping hell,
> And fixed my standing more secure,
> Than 'twas before I fell.

David's satisfaction

He said, concerning this covenant, 'This is all my salvation, and all my desire, although he make it not to grow'. Look at his last words first. 'Although he make it not to grow', means, 'although I do not yet see the covenant fulfilled and manifest in me, I am fully confident that God will fulfil his word of grace'.

'This covenant', David says, 'is all my desire'. Matthew Henry wrote, 'Let me have an interest in this covenant and the promises of it, and I have enough. I desire no more'. John Gill said, 'It is the desire of every (believer), who knows anything of the covenant of grace and the scheme of salvation by it, to be saved this way, by and through the covenant of grace, and not of works'. All who believe on the Son of God are heirs to this everlasting covenant of grace of which David spoke with joy on his dying bed. Read Ephesians 1:3-14 one more time, and rejoice and give thanks to God for that covenant grace which is ours in Christ, by which we are saved.

All who are heirs of this covenant are elected by God's sovereign grace, loved of God with an everlasting love, adopted as his sons, redeemed by the precious blood of Christ, forgiven of all sin, accepted in the Beloved, justified from all things, sanctified, heirs of God, joint-heirs with Christ, sealed by his Spirit, and forever one with Christ himself! The gospel of God's everlasting, covenant grace proclaims a Saviour in whom is everything you need forever.

My God, the cov'nant of Thy love,
  Abides forever sure;
And in its matchless grace I feel,
  My happiness secure.

What, though my house be not with Thee,
  As nature could desire!
To nobler joys than nature gives,
  Thy servants all aspire.

Since Thou, the everlasting God,
  My Father art become;
Jesus my Guardian and my Friend,
  And heaven my final home,

I welcome all Thy sov'reign will,
  For all that will is love;
And when I know not what Thou dost,
  I'll wait the light above.

Thy cov'nant the last accent claims,
  Of this poor, faltering tongue,
And that shall the first notes employ,
  Of my celestial song.

                      Philip Doddridge

'Although my house be not so with God; yet he hath made with me an everlasting covenant, ordered in all things, and sure: for this is all my salvation, and all my desire, although he make it not to grow'.
(2 Samuel 23:5)

Chapter 16

The Character of the Covenant

It is needful for us to understand the teaching of holy scripture regarding the covenant of grace so that we may find the same strength, comfort, and satisfaction in it that David did when he was dying. 'These be the last words of David, the sweet psalmist of Israel ... Although my house be not so with God; yet he hath made with me an everlasting covenant, ordered in all things and sure: for this is all my salvation, and all my desire, although he make it not to grow'. Happy is the man who can, from his heart, speak with such confidence of God's covenant!

An agreement

The covenant of grace is a compact, an agreement, a contract between the three persons of the Holy Trinity concerning the salvation of God's elect. The words translated 'covenant' in the Old and New

Testaments give a broad meaning to the term 'covenant'. The Old Testament word 'covenant' means, 'to create, to choose, and to dispose of'. In the covenant of grace God the Father, Son, and Holy Spirit, having created a scheme of grace, chose a people, and disposed of all things in sovereign predestination to accomplish the salvation of those chosen.

The New Testament word for 'covenant' is sometimes translated 'testament' and sometimes 'covenant'. It is the word we would use when describing a person's will. It means 'to appoint' and 'to dispose'. In the covenant of grace, the Triune God appointed the people he would save to the obtaining of eternal salvation, appointed Christ to be our Saviour, and disposed all things to secure the accomplishment of his covenant purpose.

The covenant of grace is called by various names in the Word of God. We sometimes call it the 'covenant of grace', because all grace flows to us from this covenant (Ephesians 1:3-14). Sometimes we call it the 'covenant of redemption', because it is the covenant by which our redemption was secured; but in the Word of God it is called by four specific names.

1. A covenant of peace (Isaiah 54:10, Ezekiel 37:26; Malachi 2:5) – In this covenant God set down the terms of peace and reconciliation; and Christ (the Surety of the Covenant) agreed to them.
2. A covenant of life (Malachi 2:5) – It contains in it the promise of life which God, who cannot lie, made to Christ as the Representative of his people before the world began.
3. A new covenant (Jeremiah 31:31) – It is called 'a new covenant' in the sense that it is newly revealed in the gospel, and in the sense that it is constantly new and never grows old.
4. An everlasting covenant (Hebrews 13:20) – The covenant of grace is an eternal covenant. It was made in eternity. It deals with eternal matters; and it shall stand throughout eternity. It is a covenant that can never be broken. Not one promise of the covenant shall fall to the ground.

2 Samuel 23:5 shows us a threefold character of the covenant of grace. There are more characteristics to the covenant than these three; but staying with this one text, we are given three aspects of the covenant of grace that gave comfort to a ransomed sinner's heart as he anticipated meeting God face to face.

Everlasting

The covenant of grace is an everlasting covenant. David said, 'He hath made with me an everlasting covenant'. When he speaks of God making a covenant with him, David is talking about God doing so representatively. He made his covenant with Christ our federal head and representative, the Surety of the covenant (Hebrews 7:22). When the Lord God promises to make a covenant with repentant sinners, the meaning is, 'I will manifest my covenant to you' (Isaiah 55:3). An everlasting covenant could only be made with one who is everlasting. That means it was made with Christ in eternity and is manifest to God's elect in time.

Nothing can be more comforting and delightful than the knowledge of the fact that the covenant of grace and all the blessings of grace are from everlasting to everlasting. This is a covenant that bears the date of eternity upon it, a covenant that shall continue to eternity. It is the everlasting covenant.

It springs from the everlasting love of God for his elect. 'God hath loved his people with an everlasting love; not only with a love that shall abide forever; but with a love which was from all eternity' (John Gill). Read Jeremiah 31:3, John 17:23-24, and Psalm 89:2-4.

The Lord Jesus Christ, the Son of God, is the Mediator of this everlasting covenant of grace. As such, he was set up from everlasting, from the beginning, before ever the earth was (Hebrews 7:22; 8:6; Proverbs 8:11-13). The promise of the covenant, the promise of eternal life to all the elect, was made with Christ the Mediator before the world was made (Titus 1:2). The salvation secured by the covenant was given to God's elect in their Surety from eternity (2 Timothy 1:9; Romans 8:29-30). All the blessings of the covenant were freely bestowed upon God's chosen in Christ, God's Son, our Covenant Head, before the world began (Ephesians 1:3).

As this covenant of grace is from everlasting, so it is to everlasting. It is written, 'God hath commanded his covenant forever; Holy and Reverend is his name' (Psalm 111:9). That simply means that God has ordained and established his covenant so that it will continue forever. Nothing shall ever be able to subvert it, or make it null and void. No matter what is done to his elect, no matter what is done by them, God will not break his covenant, nor alter the thing that has gone out of his lips. When we sin, he chastens us; yet his lovingkindness will he not take from us, nor suffer his faithfulness to fail (Psalm 89:30-35). Though we provoke him, yet his lovingkindness shall not depart from us, neither shall the covenant of grace be removed. The covenant of grace is an everlasting covenant. It will never wax old. It will never fail. It will never be replaced (Hebrews 8:13; 10:9). It lasts forever!

Ordered

Not only is it an everlasting covenant; it is a well ordered covenant, 'ordered in all things'. That simply means that everything in the covenant is ordered and orderly, being designed by God to fulfil a specific purpose, or purposes. It is 'ordered in all things' to advance the glory of the triune God.

– God the Father for his purpose of grace (Ephesians 1:3-6).
– God the Son for his purchase of grace (Ephesians 1:7-12).
– God the Spirit for his performance of grace (Ephesians 1:13-14).

This covenant of grace is 'ordered in all things' for the security and salvation of God's elect. All the elect were trusted to and put in the hands of Christ, our Surety, (John 6:37-40; Ephesians 1:13; John 10:29-30), who alone is able to keep us, save us, and present us faultless before the presence of the divine glory. The covenant is ordered and filled with all spiritual blessings, all grace, and all things pertaining to life and godliness. In a word, all things needful for our salvation here and our eternal glory hereafter are ordered by God in the covenant from everlasting.

In the everlasting covenant of grace everything regarding the grace of God was ordered, fixed, and established from eternity, irrevocably and immutably ordered and established by God himself. In the covenant of grace it was eternally settled who would be saved (John 15:16; Ephesians 1:4-5; 2 Thessalonians 2:13). It was also settled and fixed who the Author of eternal salvation must be, none other than the Son of God himself (Psalm 89:19; 1 John 4:10). The method of God's grace, the method by which God would save his people was also settled and fixed from eternity. God arranged the salvation of his people in such a way that he can be both 'a just God and a Saviour' (Isaiah 45:21). He purposed that righteousness be established and redemption accomplished by Christ (Ephesians 1:6), that regeneration and faith be granted to chosen, redeemed sinners by the almighty power and effectual grace of the Holy Spirit (2 Thessalonians 2:13-14), and that all grace be communicated to the chosen through the preaching of the gospel (2 Thessalonians 2:14; Romans 10:17) and the prayer of faith (Ezekiel 36:37).

Moreover, all the blessings of grace were provided and settled, predestinated and bestowed upon God's elect in Christ in this everlasting covenant (Ephesians 1:3; Romans 8:28-30; 2 Timothy 1:9). Before the worlds were made, every chosen sinner was adopted by an eternal adoption, redeemed with an eternal redemption, forgiven by an eternal forgiveness, justified in an eternal justification, sanctified in an eternal sanctification, blessed with an eternal heirship, and glorified in an eternal glorification.

Sure

The covenant of grace is an everlasting covenant, ordered in all things; and thirdly, David declares that this everlasting covenant of grace, with all its blessings and promises, is a sure thing, 'ordered in all things and sure'. It is sure to Christ our Covenant Surety (Isaiah 53:11-12). 'He shall (not might, wants to, or hopes to, but 'shall') see his seed'. 'The pleasure of the Lord shall prosper in his hand'. (John 17:4-5). It is sure to all for whom the covenant was made. All the promises of the covenant are yea and amen in Christ. All the blessings of the covenant are 'the sure mercies of David' (Christ). Here are three things that make the covenant a sure thing.

1. It is founded upon the Word of God, who cannot lie.
2. It is ratified by the blood of Christ, who cannot fail.
3. It is sealed by the Spirit of God, whose seal cannot be broken.

This covenant of grace all blessing secures;
    Believers rejoice! For all things are yours!
And God from his purpose shall never remove,
    But love thee, and bless thee, and rest in his love!

John Kent

'I delight to do thy will, O my God: yea, thy law is within my heart'.
(Psalm 40:8)

Chapter 17

The Will of God

The words recorded in Psalm 40:8 find their ultimate and perfect fulfilment in the Lord Jesus Christ. God the Spirit tells us this in Hebrews 10:7-9. How we rejoice to know that Christ, the God-man, our Substitute, has fulfilled all the will of God for us! By his obedience to God in our stead, the Lord Jesus Christ obtained eternal redemption for God's elect. His obedience to God is our righteousness. His blood is our atonement for sin. We are complete in Christ; and we are accepted in him, because he delighted to do the will of God as our Substitute.

Yet, the words of the fortieth Psalm were also David's words. They express the desire, ambition, and driving force of every believer's heart. 'I delight to do thy will, O God'. All who are born of God bear this distinct mark of grace in the likeness of Christ. Believers in their inmost souls delight to do the will of God. Our joy and happiness is not merely in receiving good from God, but in rendering active service to God. We desire to obey and serve our heavenly Father in all things and do his will at all times, not reluctantly, but cheerfully. God's will is our joy and delight.

More than that, we delight to see God's will done in and by others, too. Our heart's prayer is, 'Our Father which art in heaven, Hallowed be thy name. Thy kingdom come. Thy will be done in earth, as it is in heaven' (Matthew 6:9-10). God the Holy Spirit has taught every believer in the world to pray with Christ, 'Thy will be done'.

Were it possible to gather all the desires, ambitions, aspirations, goals, and prayers of all God's saints in heaven and earth into one expression, it would be this: 'Thy will be done'. Every believer delights to do the will of God! When the believing heart cries, 'I delight to do thy will, O God', the meaning is: My heavenly Father, my God, in my heart of hearts, from the depths of my inmost soul, I delight to fulfil your will of purpose, to satisfy your will of pleasure, and to obey your will of precept.

We know that our heavenly Father, the God of the Bible, is a God 'who worketh all things after the counsel of his own will' (Ephesians 1:11). All who know him delight to do his will in all things. It is not my purpose in this study to answer the objections which men raise against the sovereignty of God in the exercise of his will. If your heart is yet in rebellion to God, no words of mine can change you. You must bow to Christ. You must surrender to his dominion as Lord. My purpose is simply to instruct, comfort, and encourage God's saints in seeking, doing, and submitting to the will of God. In order to dispel confusion about this subject and to help you who delight to do God's will, I will make three statements and answer two questions.

1. It is the duty and responsibility of all men, women, and children to obey the will of God revealed in his precepts

The Bible reveals God's will to be made up of three parts, his precept, his pleasure, and his purpose. His *precept* is that which he requires and commands of his creatures. As a wise and loving Father demands obedience from his children, so God demands obedience from all rational creatures. God's *pleasure* is that in which he delights and that of which he approves. As a father delights in a child's willing obedience to his parents, so the Lord God takes pleasure in the willing obedience of his children. He accepts us and what we endeavour to do for him, through Christ, and takes pleasure in our efforts to honour and serve him. God's *purpose* is that which he is determined to accomplish.

These three things never contradict each other. They are never at odds. They are always in perfect harmony. They are, together, the will of God. Let's look at them one at a time, beginning with God's will of precept. This is his revealed will, that which he requires of men, that which he commands us to do.

When a person in authority expresses his will to those under his authority, his revealed will is to them a law, a command, a precept, which they are responsible to obey. That which God has revealed to be his will and pleasure is to us a precept, a law, a command which we are responsible to obey. God's will of command, or precept, made known to us, is our rule of duty (Ecclesiastes 12:13; Exodus 20; Romans 2:12-15, 18). In the day of judgment God will judge every man by that which has been revealed to him. No one will be held accountable except for that knowledge of God's will that is within his reach.

The moral requirements of God's law are revealed to all men by the light of nature. The tables of the law are inscribed upon every man's conscience by the finger of God, our Creator (Romans 2:12-15). All men by nature, even the most heathen, barbaric tribesmen of ancient cultures, know that God is and that he requires man to love him supremely and love his neighbour as himself. It is man's unceasing violation of the law of God written upon his heart that floods his soul with a sense of naked guilt before God, though he does not know him.

God revealed his will upon Sinai in the giving of the law, summarized in what we call the Ten Commandments (Exodus 20:1-

17; Romans 13:8-9; Ephesians 6:2). The Decalogue, that which is commonly referred to as the moral law, reveals what God requires of all men in their relations to God and to one another. Though in Christ we are free from the yoke of the law's rule and its curse, these requirements are never altered.

The ceremonial law given to the nation of Israel was God's revealed will concerning worship in the Old Testament. It began when God commanded Israel to observe the passover (Exodus 12) and ended when Christ our Passover was sacrificed for us, when the handwriting of the ordinances was nailed to the cross (1 Corinthians 5:7; Colossians 2:14).

Since Christ has come and fulfilled all the requirements and types of the moral and ceremonial law, the revealed will of God to all men is the gospel of Christ (1 John 3:23). No man is able to fulfil the righteousness of God revealed in the law. Christ therefore fulfilled the law in the place of chosen sinners. The righteousness of the law is fulfilled in us through faith in him (Romans 8:2-4; 3:31). This is the only way in which sinners can fulfil God's holy law. We look to Christ alone for both righteousness and satisfaction (1 Corinthians 1:30).

This is what God requires and commands of all men 'Believe on the Lord Jesus Christ' (1 John 3:23). Faith in Christ is the revealed will of God. This is God's precept. All men are responsible to obey it (John 3:36). In this sense, every believer says, 'I delight to do thy will, O God'.

2. It is the desire of every believer to obey the will of God's holy pleasure

A loving child wants to do more than merely avoid his father's disapproval. He seeks to know and do that which is his father's pleasure. A loving wife wants more than to do just what her husband requires. She wants to please her husband in all things. And the believer wants something indescribably greater than to avoid the wrath of God. He wants to do the will of God. He wants to do that which gives pleasure, satisfaction, and delight to his heavenly Father. We do not and cannot add anything to God's infinite pleasure. Still, believing sinners earnestly seek to do what pleases him. Do we not? Do you seek to do the will of your heavenly Father's pleasure?

There are some things revealed in the Bible that please God (Micah 6:6-8). Though we recognize our utter inability to do so, believers do endeavour to walk humbly before God, dealing with men in uprightness (justice), mercy, and love, following the example of Christ our Lord (1 Corinthians 4:7; Ephesians 5:18-21; Philippians 2:1-4; Ephesians 4:32-5:1). There are also some things revealed in the scriptures that are displeasing and grievous to our Lord (Ephesians 4:17-5:1). While acknowledging, with broken hearts, that every lust and abomination known to man resides in our depraved hearts (1 John 1:9), we studiously seek to avoid the evils of our flesh. This is my constant prayer. I hope it is yours: My Father, grant me grace that I not dishonour your name or offend in thought, word, or deed. Give me grace that I may not offend your children, bring reproach upon the name of your dear Son or the gospel of your free grace in him, or grieve your Holy Spirit.

Still, every heaven born soul is fully aware of the fact that the only way sinful men and women can please God is by faith in Christ (Hebrews 11:5-6). God is pleased with his Son, only with his Son. God is pleased with us in his Son, only in his Son (Matthew 17:5; Ephesians 1:6). Yet, our God is pleased with our feeble efforts to please him for his Son's sake (1 Peter 2:5). In this sense too, regarding the will of God's holy pleasure, we say, 'I delight to do thy will, O God'. We delight to trust Christ as our only, all-sufficient Substitute and Saviour.

3. We are assured in the Bible that all things obey the secret will of God's eternal purpose

Read Deuteronomy 29:29. Moses certainly does not there suggest that we can know nothing about divine predestination, or that God does not intend us to study the subject. The only thing Moses is telling us is this – We do not know what God has predestined and what must come to pass. However, we do know what God requires of us; and that is our duty.

It is a clearly revealed fact that the Lord our God has purposed, decreed, and predestinated all things that have ever come to pass and all things that ever shall come to pass, without exception (Psalm 115:3; 135:6; Isaiah 46:10; Daniel 4:35; Acts 2:23; 4:27-28; 13:48; Romans 8:28-30; 9:15-18; 2 Corinthians 5:18; Ephesians 1:11). In this sense, everything that is, has been, or shall be is the will of God. God is absolutely sovereign in directing the affairs of the universe. His will of purpose includes all things, evil as well as good, sin as well as salvation, error as well as truth. Furthermore, God's will of purpose is always, perfectly accomplished in and by all things. That is not a secret thing, but a revealed thing.

With regard to God's will of purpose, we must understand that God wills whatever he does in providence (Job 23:13; Ephesians 1:11). God acts voluntarily in all that he does. He is never compelled to do anything. Creatures do not force the hand of the Creator. The clay does not mould the potter. The potter moulds the clay. God does in providence whatever he willed to do from eternity (Acts 15:18). Nothing comes to pass in time except that which God purposed in eternity. Nothing purposed by our God in eternity fails to come to pass in time. If God could will, desire, or purpose to do anything that he failed to accomplish, he would not be omnipotent. God's will of purpose includes all things (Psalm 76:10; Proverbs 16:4).

C. D. Cole stated this doctrine of scripture very clearly – God's 'will includes whatsoever comes to pass. Hence, everything that comes to pass is providential and not accidental so far as God is concerned. He worketh all things after the counsel of his own will (Ephesians 1:11)'. He goes on to explain, 'The will of God includes the wicked actions of sinful men, but does not take away their blameworthiness. We may not see how this can be, but the scriptures declare it and we should believe it. The scriptures were not written to confirm our reasoning, but rather to correct it. On the day of Pentecost Peter said, concerning Jesus, 'Him being delivered by the determinate counsel (will) and foreknowledge of God, ye have taken, and by wicked hands have crucified and slain' (Acts 2:23). And on a later occasion he said that Herod and Pilate, the Gentiles and the people of Israel were gathered together "For to do whatsoever thy hand and thy counsel (will) determined (Greek – predestinated) to be done" (Acts 4:27-28). We may not be able to see how God can will or determine a sin without becoming the author of sin, but the fact remains that the greatest of all sins, the slaying of the Son of God, was divinely ordained'.

The will of God, his eternal purpose of predestination, is in every way consistent with the character of his Being. It is his eternal will. It is his immutable will. It is his sovereign will. It is his unconditional will. It is his effectual will. It is his wise and holy will. God's will, his purpose of grace, is the cause of our salvation (John 1:11-13; Romans 8:28-30; James 1:18).

Because depraved rebels are ever bent upon perverting the things of God, a few words of caution regarding the will of God's purpose are needful. The sovereignty of God's purpose does not destroy man's responsibility, or even his will. Man's sin has put his will in bondage to sin, not God's purpose. The universality of God's purpose does not make God the author of sin. God is not the author of sin; but he is the author of the good which he accomplishes by overruling sin. God does not bear the blame for our ruin by the sin and fall of our father Adam; but he does get all the credit and praise for our recovery by his grace. He does not bear the blame for man's hatred toward and crucifixion of his Son; but he does receive all praise, honour, and glory as the author of that redemption accomplished by his Son's death in the place of his people.

It must also be stated emphatically that the immutability of God's purpose does not imply that God made some only to damn them. He did make all men only to save some men for the glory of his own great name; and believing hearts rejoice to praise his sovereign wisdom and grace. When we hear God say regarding all things, 'I will do all my pleasure', we rejoice to bow before him and say, 'Thy will be done', 'I delight to do thy will, O God'.

Thy will, not mine, O Lord,
However dark it be;
O lead me by Thine own right hand,
Choose out my path for me.
I dare not choose my lot;
I would not if I might;
Choose Thou for me, O Lord my God,
So shall I walk aright.

Take Thou my cup, and it
With joy or sorrow fill;
As ever best to Thee may seem,
Choose Thou my good and ill.
Not mine, not mine the choice
In things both great and small;
Be Thou my guide, my guard, my strength,
My wisdom, and my all.

                                           Horatius Bonar

4. Is it possible for a believer to miss or be out of the will of God?

Without question, insofar as God's revealed will, his precept, and his pleasure is concerned, a believer can miss, disobey, and be out of the will of God. Any act of sin, unbelief, or disobedience, and act, movement, or decision, made contrary to the direction of the Holy Spirit is, in that sense, out of God's will. The thing which David did in the matter of Uriah 'displeased the Lord' (2 Samuel 11:27). Yet, God's purpose was accomplished. Our Redeemer came into the world through the union of David and Bathsheba. Elimelech was out of God's will of pleasure and precept in going down to Obed-Edom; but his disobedience was overruled by God to accomplish his will of purpose and predestination for the salvation of his elect.

Let it be understood and emphatically clear that no one, and no action performed by anyone, is ever out of the will of God's purpose! 'He worketh all things after the counsel of his own will'. God's purpose is always accomplished, even when we are disobedient to his revealed will. That fact does not lessen our responsibility to any degree; but it does give us reason to adore and worship our God, whose purpose is ever wise and good. Even when it is contrary to our will, our choice, and our actions, believers still declare, honestly, 'I delight to do thy will, O God'.

5. How can we know the will of God?

No one can determine what God's will is for you, except you. Paul said, 'I conferred not with flesh and blood'. If we seek to find God's will for us by the counsel of other men, we are sure to miss it. God reveals his will to those who seek it in three ways: (1) By his Word, (2) By his Spirit, and (3) By his providence. He will reveal his will to all who truly seek his will in faith (Proverbs 3:5-6). Let this be our prayer – 'Thy will be done!' Let this be our determination – 'I delight to do thy will, O God'. Let this be our attitude – 'It is the Lord, let him do what he will'.

Chapter 18

'Things Which Become Sound Doctrine'

When I was trying to raise my daughter, as she grew from a little girl into a young lady, I frequently suggested that she do this or that, or not to do this or that, and always found one argument sufficient to persuade her willing compliance. I would say, 'Sweetheart, that just is not becoming a young lady'. She always wanted to be and to appear to be a young lady. Therefore, she chose not to speak, dress, and act in a manner unbecoming a young lady.

The Holy Spirit uses similar reasoning with us. When believers are given directions for their conduct and behaviour in the New Testament, the basis of and motive for compliance is that there are some things becoming to the gospel and some unbecoming. Paul told the saints at Ephesus not to live like their neighbours in fornication, uncleanness, and covetousness. Instead, he urged them to live 'as becometh saints' (Ephesians 5:3). If we profess to be saints, we ought to live 'as becometh saints'. In Philippians 1:27, the Apostle urges us to so order our lives as to 'let our conversation be as it becometh godliness'. Then, in Titus chapter two, the inspired Apostle instructed Titus and all who preach and teach in the kingdom of God to speak those 'things which become sound doctrine'.

The study of Bible doctrine should always be practical and applicable to our lives day by day. As I was preparing this chapter, I received a letter from a young man that reminded me just how needful such instruction is. It was, I think, the most horribly astonishing letter I have ever received. To make it worse, it was written by a preacher, a young man I have been trying to help, a young man who, I hoped and thought, was seeking the glory of God and trying to faithfully serve him by preaching the gospel of Christ. The following is a small portion of his letter. I include it here because it reveals a shocking, alarming perversion of the gospel of God's free and sovereign grace in Christ which must be denounced.

'My goal is not to preach Christ or even serve him. My goal is to follow my joy ... I want to enjoy myself as much as possible. I don't even want to do what is right as much as I want to do whatever I wish ... I am free! I am a child, not a slave. God did not die for me so that I would tend his garden and do his dishes. He did not need a slave, but he desired a son. I am that ... His beloved son and to me he says, "with you I am well pleased". This is what my Lord did for me. He set me free, not in order that I turn and serve him, but be truly free. I can quit the ministry any week and surf the rest of my life and never pick up a Bible or preach again and he will still be pleased with me, because of what his Son did on the cross.

'So I take the freedom and run with it. I will follow my joy until he calls me home ... I do not try to resist sin. I just live ... I follow my joy and tremble and trust that God really is sovereign and that he really will have his way with me ... I am like a dog that digs up gardens and jumps fences and follows his instincts wherever they lead ... I do not want to be cautious ... I do not ever want to ask myself, "Is this glorifying to my Lord?" That will kill me. I trust that he will glorify himself through me, if it pleases him to do so and meanwhile I am going to chase that tennis ball.'

I truly hope that the man who wrote those words is insane, because unless he is insane, unless he has simply lost his mind, the man who wrote those words is utterly void of the knowledge of the grace of God in Christ. As Paul said to the Ephesians when they were tempted to embrace the licentious antinomianism of pagan Gentile religion, I said to him, as I urged him to both quit trying to preach and seek Christ, lest he perish forever – 'Ye have not so learned Christ' (Ephesians 5:20).

Titus 2:1-15

In Titus 2:1-15, God the Holy Spirit tells all God-called preachers and teachers exactly how to lead and instruct God's saints in the gospel of Christ and the doctrines of it. He tells us plainly that the gospel of the grace of God teaches all to whom it is revealed that salvation is by grace alone; and that the grace of God teaches us how to live in this world for the glory of God. These are 'things which become sound doctrine'.

The adornment of grace

In verses 1-10 Paul tells both the man who preaches the gospel and the people who hear it and believe it how to adorn the gospel. He tells us how to behave ourselves so that we may 'adorn the doctrine of God our Saviour in all things' (v. 10).

This is both our personal responsibility and our privilege. I hope it is our desire. We are to 'adorn the doctrine of God our Saviour in all things'. That is to say, we are to set forth in our lives as well as in our doctrine the beauty, glory, and attractiveness of the gospel of Christ. If we hope to persuade men and women to believe the gospel we preach, we must show them, by our lives (not by a show of religion, but by the way we live), the beauty of the gospel. If we would honour Christ and his gospel in the eyes of men, we must have our lives regulated and governed by the gospel.

All who preach in the name of God are responsible to adorn the gospel by faithfully preaching it. 'But speak thou the things which become sound doctrine' (v. 1). Every preacher has a mandate from God. The preacher's mandate is always the same. All who are sent of God as his messengers to eternity bound men and women are sent to preach the gospel, to constantly declare those 'things which become sound doctrine' (2 Timothy 4:1-5). The doctrine we are to preach is the doctrine of grace, which is the doctrine of Christ. Those things which become sound doctrine are those things that are consistent with and honouring to the gospel (divine sovereignty, – effectual, substitutionary atonement, – salvation by grace alone, through faith alone, in Christ alone).

Gospel preachers are responsible to pointedly apply the gospel to the daily affairs and responsibilities of men and women in this world. It is every pastor's responsibility to faithfully teach people how to live in this world for the glory of Christ, applying the Word of God to every area of life. It is the responsibility of God's saints to obey the gospel, applying it personally to every area of their lives.

I realize that many people prefer to ignore this fact, but it is a fact nonetheless – God almighty does interfere with people's lives. If the God of glory is pleased to open the windows of heaven and drop his saving grace into a sinner's heart, he will take over. He insists on it. Christ will either be Lord of all or he will not receive you at all. This is what Paul teaches in verses 2-10. He has a word here for everyone who professes faith in Christ.

Verse 2 – 'That the aged men be sober, grave, temperate, sound in faith, in charity, in patience'.
Verses 3-4 – 'The aged women likewise, that they be in behaviour as becometh holiness, not false accusers, not given to much wine, teachers of good things; … That they may teach the young women to be sober, to love their husbands, to love their children' (vv. 3-4).
Verse 5 – 'To be discreet, chaste, keepers at home, good, obedient to their own husbands, that the word of God be not blasphemed'.

Verse 6 – 'Young men likewise exhort to be sober minded'.

Verses 7-8 – To pastors he writes, 'In all things showing thyself a pattern of good works: in doctrine showing uncorruptness, gravity, sincerity, … Sound speech, that cannot be condemned; that he that is of the contrary part may be ashamed, having no evil thing to say of you'.

Verses 9-10 – 'Exhort servants (employees) to be obedient unto their own masters, and to please them well in all things; not answering again; … Not purloining, but showing all good fidelity; that they may adorn the doctrine of God our Saviour in all things'.

The Holy Spirit here calls all who believe the gospel of the grace of God to adorn it, to show forth the beauty and grace of the gospel in all things for the glory of God (1 Corinthians 10:31). If we are indeed born of God, if we truly are believers, if we have really experienced the grace of God, we know that grace teaches us so to live.

The work of grace

Verse 11 – 'For the grace of God that bringeth salvation hath appeared to all men'. As Paul uses the term here, 'the grace of God' refers to 'the doctrine of God our Saviour'. 'The grace of God' in this verse means 'the gospel of the grace of God'. The gospel we preach, 'the doctrine of God our Saviour', is the gospel of 'the grace of God'.

The doctrine of the gospel is the message of grace. The message of the gospel is not free will, but free grace. It is not works, but grace. It is not grace and works, but grace alone (Galatians 5:2,4). Grace is the origin of the gospel. Grace is the message of the gospel. Grace is conveyed by the gospel (1 John 1:1; 1 Peter 1:23-25). Grace is the rule of the gospel (Romans 6:12-14; 2 Corinthians 5:14-15).

This gospel, the grace of God, brings salvation. Salvation is by God's operations of grace, that is, it is an act of free and sovereign grace, grace that is almighty and irresistible. However, in this context, 'the grace of God' is used as a synonym for 'the gospel of God'. The Holy Spirit is telling us that the gospel is the means by which salvation is brought to and worked out in chosen, redeemed sinners. The gospel of the grace of God shows us the way of salvation – faith in Christ. It proclaims the person and work of Christ, who is salvation. It is the announcement of salvation accomplished by Christ (John 19:30; Hebrews 9:12).

The gospel of the grace of God is the means by which God the Holy Spirit brings salvation to elect sinners (Romans 10:13-17). There is no spiritual life, no faith in Christ, and no salvation given to sinners without the gospel (Romans 1:15-17; 1 Corinthians 1:21; 1 Peter 1:23-25; James 1:18).

This gospel of the grace of God has appeared unto all men. Certainly, Paul does not mean for us to understand that every person in the world has heard the gospel. Obviously that is not so. There are people in every part of the world (in Paul's day and in ours), many of them who have never heard the gospel. Paul is simply telling us that the gospel has been and is preached freely to all men and women, people of every rank, race, and region (Romans 16:25-26).

God has his elect among all people. It is our responsibility to preach the gospel to all men (Matthew 28:19-20). The gospel we preach brings salvation to all who believe. 'It is the power of God unto salvation to everyone that believeth' (Romans 1:16).

The teaching of grace

Verse 12 – 'Teaching us that, denying ungodliness and worldly lusts, we should live soberly, righteously, and godly, in this present world'. Whenever the gospel of the grace of God comes into a sinner's heart by the life-giving, regenerating power and grace of God the Holy Spirit, it effectually teaches him some things. It teaches us to whom we must look for eternal life (Isaiah 45:22).

The gospel teaches us what we must believe (Galatians 1:6-9). It teaches us how to live in this world. The gospel is not given for intellectual speculation, but for practical direction. It is given for our eternal salvation and for the ordering of our lives. It tells us plainly what we are to do and what we are not to do. It tells us what to follow and what to shun.

The grace of God effectually teaches saved sinners to deny ungodliness and worldly lusts. The gospel teaches us to say 'No' to unbelief and the neglect of God, his Word, his worship, and his will. It also teaches us to say 'No' to worldly lusts, sensuality, covetousness, ambition, and the desire for recognition and praise.

The grace of God also teaches people to live right. With respect to ourselves, the gospel teaches us to live soberly. With respect to others, it teaches us to live righteously. With respect to our God, it teaches us to live godly (1 Corinthians 6:19-20; Romans 12:1-2).

The expectation of grace

Verse 13 – 'Looking for that blessed hope, and the glorious appearing of the great God and our Saviour Jesus Christ'. Paul does not tell us to set dates or even speculate about when the time of our Lord's coming may be. He does not tell us to look for signs of the end time, or even to think about when the end time may be. Grace teaches us to look for Christ himself, and to do so standing upon the tiptoe of faith and expectation. Grace gives us a good, well-grounded hope, a hope that breeds expectation, anticipation, and desire.

There is one common and blessed hope for all believers. There is not one hope for one group and another hope for another group. We all have the same hope, upon the same grounds, a glorious, blessed hope, a hope that no eye has seen, no ear has heard, and no mind has imagined.

The basis of our hope is grace, free grace through Christ, our crucified Substitute (Ephesians 1:18). The thing hoped for is glory. It is the design of the gospel to set our hearts upon the hope laid up for us with Christ in heaven, not upon the things of this world (Matthew 6:33; Colossians 3:1-4).

Fade, fade each earthly joy, Jesus is mine.
Break every tender tie, Jesus is mine!
Dark is this wilderness,
Earth has no resting place.
Jesus alone can bless. Jesus is mine!

Farewell, mortality – Jesus is mine!
Welcome, eternity – Jesus is mine!
Welcome, oh loved and blest!
Welcome sweet scenes of rest!
Welcome my Saviour's breast! Jesus is mine!

Our hope of eternal glory with Christ, if we trust him, is a well-grounded hope. Our Father promised it (Titus 1:2). Our Saviour purchased it (Hebrews 9:12). Our Representative possesses it (Hebrews 6:20). We have the earnest of it (Ephesians 1:14). In Christ we are worthy of it (Colossians 1:12).

Our blessedness will be attained when Christ, who is our hope, appears. Notice how Paul describes our Saviour. It seems that he was not able to find words worthy of him. Jesus Christ is 'the great God'. He is the great God 'and our Saviour'. Soon, this great God, who is our Saviour, 'shall appear'. Then, we also shall appear with him in glory. This is the expectation of grace (1 John 3:1-3).

The motivation of grace

As we have seen, the Holy Spirit calls for us to 'adorn the doctrine of God our Saviour' in every aspect of our lives. How will he induce us to obey his admonition? How will he persuade us? How will he motivate us? He does not threaten us with the terrors of the law, or entice us with promises of reward. (God's saints are not mercenaries!) Rather, the Lord God urges us to honour him by the declaration of his bountiful, free, immutable grace in Christ.

Verse 14 – 'Who gave himself for us, that he might redeem us from all iniquity, and purify unto himself a peculiar people, zealous of good works'. Christ gave himself for us that he might redeem and deliver us from all iniquity, from all sin and all the consequences of it. He died for us that he might, by his blood and by his grace, 'purify unto himself a peculiar people, zealous of good works'. Yes, God's saints are, indeed, a 'peculiar'[1] people. We are loved with a peculiar love (Jeremiah 31:3), objects of God's peculiar favour (Romans 8:28), blessed with peculiar blessings (Ephesians 1:3), supplied with peculiar provisions (Philippians 4:19), and separated from the world by peculiar grace (1 Corinthians 4:7).

Christ's peculiar people are made, by the grace of God, to be 'zealous of good works'. God the Father ordained that we should walk in good works (Ephesians 2:10). God the Son redeemed us that we should walk in good works. God the Holy Spirit effectually teaches every chosen, ransomed sinner to be zealous of good works.

Verse 15 – 'These things speak, and exhort, and rebuke with all authority. Let no man despise thee'. This is Paul's admonition to Titus; and the admonition of God the Holy Spirit to every gospel preacher. 'These things speak'. God's servants are to preach both the doctrine and the duties of grace, 'and exhort', pressing these matters with earnestness. Faithful pastors must also 'rebuke', or reprove all who neglect, oppose, contradict, and deny these things, these doctrines and duties of grace. It is the preacher's responsibility to go about the business of preaching the gospel 'with all authority' as one who speaks in God's name, with God's authority, with God's approval. Then, the Holy Spirit adds, 'let no man despise thee'. Those who preach and teach the Word of God must take great care that they give no one reason to despise them. Yet they must have no regard for the opinions of disobedient men. Paul shows us by his own example what he means in 1 Corinthians 4:1-3.

---

[1] The word 'peculiar' means 'distinctively excellent, valuable, and honourable'. We are Christ's portion, the lot of his inheritance, the jewels of his crown, his fulness (Ephesians 1:23), his peculiar people.

'In the beginning God created the heaven and the earth'.
(Genesis 1:1-31)

Chapter 19

Creation

It is not my intention in these studies give you a course in systematic theology. In fact, I do not believe we should attempt to systematize the teachings of holy scripture. As soon as we try to set divine revelation in human order, or mould the Word of God to any human system, our doctrine becomes corrupt and erroneous. Why? Because the only way anyone can fit the scriptures into a human system is by forcing the scriptures to bow to his system. We dare not treat the Word of God so contemptuously. We must always bow to the scriptures. Whenever the Word of God contradicts our doctrine, we must discard our doctrine, not the Word of God. Lest there should be any implied systematization of the scriptures, I am deliberately avoiding a systematic order in these studies.

The subject of this chapter is creation. I am aware of the fact that most studies in Bible doctrine move from the existence and attributes of God to the decrees of God. Without question, as we have already seen, the decrees of God are from everlasting. However, God's sovereign decrees are revealed to us in the scriptures much later than his wondrous work of creation. We will, therefore, consider the teaching of scripture regarding creation, before looking into the wonders of grace in our election unto salvation.

The fact is, creation is a very instructive picture of God's wondrous works of grace in salvation. In 2 Corinthians 5:17 the Apostle Paul tells us, 'If any man be in Christ, he is a new creature'. The work of God in the new creation of grace is beautifully symbolized in the creation of the world. As the creation of the world was the work of God alone, so the making of men and women new creatures in Christ is the work of God alone.

The creation of the world

'In the beginning God created the heaven and the earth' (v. 1). Thus opens the Word of God with a bare statement of fact. 'In the beginning God created the heaven and the earth'. That is all we are told concerning the original creation. No argument is given to prove the existence of God. Instead, his existence is simply affirmed as a fact to be believed. Nothing is given to gratify the curious minds of men. How long did it take for God to create the world? We are not told. How old is this world? We are not told. We are simply told, 'In the beginning God created'. The truth of God is simply stated as a fact to be received and understood by unquestioning faith.

'In the beginning God' – This is the foundation of all truth. All true theology, all true religion begins with this statement. All human religion and philosophy begin with man and work up to God. The scriptures begin with God and work down to man.

If we are to understand anything, we must begin with God. This is most especially true in the matter of salvation. It is impossible to understand salvation unless we begin with God. In the Garden of Eden, Adam sinned and brought in death. But God was not taken by surprise. In the beginning, before ever the world was created, in anticipation of the fall, God provided his Son as 'the Lamb slain from the foundation of the world' (Revelation 13:8), 'who verily was foreordained before the foundation of the world' (1 Peter 1:20).

In the new creation the sinner who is saved by grace repents, believes on the Lord Jesus Christ and walks with him in the newness of life. But it began with God. In the beginning God chose us in Christ (Ephesians 1:4) and predestined us to be his children (Ephesians 1:5). 'We love him, because he first loved us' (1 John 4:19). Everything begins with God. Understand that and you will not stray far from the truth.

The book of Genesis is the book of beginnings. In fact, the word 'genesis' means 'beginning'. Someone said, 'The book of Genesis is the seed plot of the Bible'. It contains in seed form all the great doctrines and truths revealed more fully in the rest of the volume. In the fifty chapters of this first book of Moses, ...

God is revealed – He is revealed as the creator-God, the covenant-keeping God, and the almighty God, 'the Most High, Possessor of heaven and earth'. From the opening verse hints are given concerning the blessed trinity, the plurality of Persons in the Godhead 'God said, Let us make man' (v. 26). The creation of the world was a work that involved all three Persons in the Holy Trinity, Father, Son, and Holy Ghost, even as the works of redemption and providence involve all three of the divine Persons (Ephesians 1:3-14).

The origin and character of man is set forth – First, we see him as God's creature, then as a fallen sinner, then as one brought back to God, finding grace in his sight, walking with God, and made the friend of God.

Satan's devices are exposed – The arch-enemy of our souls, the tempter, the deceiver, seeks to ruin men by calling into question the Word of God, casting doubt upon the goodness of God, and raising suspicions about the veracity of God.

God's sovereign election is exhibited – God approves of Abel and rejects Cain. Noah is chosen as the object of God's grace. It is written, 'Noah found grace in the eyes of the Lord'. God chooses Abram and passes by his idolatrous neighbours. God chooses Isaac and rejects Ishmael. God loves Jacob and hates Esau.

Salvation in Christ is typically displayed – Our fallen parents, Adam and Eve, were sought and found by grace and clothed with the skins of innocent victims. In order to clothe the fallen pair, blood must be shed, innocent victims had to die in the place of the guilty. As those innocent animals were slain for Adam and Eve, so the Lord Jesus Christ was slain for sinners that we might be robed forever in his perfect righteousness.

Justification by faith is revealed – Abraham believed God and it was counted unto him for righteousness. Faith, by believing God's testimony concerning his Son, receives righteousness, the very righteousness of God in Christ.

The believer's security is beautifully displayed – As the Lord brought Noah and his family into the ark and shut them in, so every believer, being brought into Christ by almighty grace, is shut in him, sealed, preserved and kept secure by the power of God. 'They shall never perish' (John 10:28).

In addition to these things, the incarnation of Christ is prophesied. The substitutionary death of Christ is portrayed. The resurrection and exaltation of Christ is symbolized. The priesthood of Christ is anticipated. All the blessings of Christ upon the Israel of God are declared. Genesis is the book of Beginnings.

In this book of beginnings, as in all the scriptures, everything speaks of Christ – Christ is the Tree of Life in the midst of the Garden of God. Christ is the promised Seed of the woman, who crushed the serpent's head. Christ is the Lamb whose blood was represented in Abel's sacrifice. Christ is the One whom Enoch believed, by whom he pleased God. Christ is the Ark by which sinners are saved from the flood of God's wrath. Christ is the Seed of promise who came from Abraham's loins, in whom all the nations of the earth are blessed. Christ is the Lamb of sacrifice whom God provided to die in the place of his chosen. Christ is the Ladder Jacob saw, by whom the blessings of God come down to men, and by whom men ascend up to God. Christ is that Priest after the order of Melchisedec, by whom God's elect are blessed. Christ is our Joseph, ruling over all things, in whom are all things, from whom all things come. Christ is the Surety portrayed in Judah. Christ is the Lawgiver prophesied by Jacob. In the book of Beginnings 'Christ is All, and in all'.

Do not imagine that I have strayed from my subject. We must know him. It does not matter what we believe about the creation of the universe, if we do not know him who is Creator and Lord of all. Christ is the beginning of the creation of God. All things were made by him and for him. He is before all things. He is in all things. By him all things consist. All things point to him. Both the creation and the new creation begin with Christ.

We must know the Lord Jesus Christ. He is the One who made all things in the beginning. He is the One who declares, 'Behold, I make all things new' (Revelation 21:5).

'In the beginning God created the heaven and the earth' – The creation was a reflection of the Creator

In verse 2 we read that the earth became 'without form and void'. It certainly was not created that way (Read Isaiah 45:18). In its pristine beauty, the earth was perfect beyond imagination. There were no groans of suffering, no darkness of iniquity, no worms of corruption, or shades of night. God reigned supreme, without rival. Then something happened. 'The earth' became 'without form and void; and darkness was upon the face of the deep'.

The ruin and confusion of God's creation

This ruin is described in verse two. 'And the earth was without form, and void; and darkness was upon the face of the deep. And the Spirit of God moved upon the face of the waters'.

The word 'was' in verse 2 really should be translated 'became' (Strong's Concordance). God did not create the world in a state of confusion. Between verses one and two, some terrible catastrophe took place. Many think the catastrophe was the fall of Satan or

Lucifer (Isaiah 14:12-17; Ezekiel 28:14-18). However, the scriptures do not specifically tell us that this was the time of Satan's fall; and it is best not to guess. The only thing clearly presented is the fact that something happened by which the earth 'became without form and void'. Whatever the catastrophe was, it left the earth 'without form and void', a desolate, uninhabitable, ruined mass of confusion[1].

We read in Exodus 20:11, 'In six days the Lord made heaven and earth, the sea, and all that in them is'. There is a difference between 'creating' and 'making'. In Genesis 1:1, God created the world out of nothing. In Genesis 1:2, 'the earth became without form and void; and darkness was upon the face of the deep'. In Genesis 1:3-31, God made the earth in six days, forming it and fashioning it out of that which he had created. A. W. Pink wrote ...

> Out of the chaos was brought the 'cosmos', which signifies order, arrangement, beauty. Out of the waters emerged the earth. A scene of desolation, darkness, and death, was transformed into one of light, life, and fertility, so that at the end all was pronounced, 'very good'.

As this is a picture of the world's history, it is also a picture of man's history. In the beginning of time, on the sixth day, God created man. What a creature he was, created in the image and likeness of

---

[1] I have no interest in trying to answer the quibbles of godless scientists and evolutionary philosophers. Perhaps the Lord God created the earth with all the markings of an aged, mature earth, as he did Adam specifically to confuse unbelieving men. Yet, if it could be irrefutably established that the earth were many thousands, or even millions of years old, that would be no contradiction to the Scriptures. We have no indication of how long an interval there was between the creation of the world, as it is stated in verse one and the ruin of the world, as it is described in verse two. It is certainly wide enough to embrace all the prehistoric ages that may have existed! However, all that took place from Genesis 1:3-31 transpired in six twenty-four hour days, less than six thousand years ago.

God, gloriously reflecting the very character of God. God himself said man was 'very good'. He had no sinful heredity behind him, no sinful principle within him, no sinful stain upon him, and no sinful environment around him. Man and woman walked together with God in the bliss of perfection, contentment and mutual delight. Man was delighted with God and God was delighted with man.

Then, there was a catastrophe. It is described in Genesis 3. Sin dared to raise its horrid head against God. Man defied God's right to be God. Sin entered into the world, and death by sin. Man died. He was separated from God. The earth was cursed. It began to bring forth thorns and thistles. God's creature became without form and void. The dark slime of the serpent corrupted the race of mankind. This great catastrophe, the fall, is verified in hearts of all Adam's descendants. Man is fallen (Ecclesiastes 7:20, 29), alienated from God (Ephesians 4:18), depraved (Jeremiah 17:9), and spiritually dead (Romans 5:12). Genesis 1:2 describes the condition of fallen man. Like the earth after the catastrophe, so man after Adam's fall is in a state of disorder.

It is a state of confusion 'The earth became without form'. Nothing was in harmony with God. Nothing was right. Fallen man is out of kilter. Nothing in him is in harmony with God. Nothing in him is right or good.

It is a state of emptiness 'The earth was void', utterly empty, incapable of life and fruitfulness. So, too, man without Christ is spiritually void, empty and barren, incapable of life and fruitfulness toward God. Fallen man can meet no conditions or requirements of any kind. If he is recovered from the ruins of the fall, he must be recovered by a work of God.

It is a state of darkness 'Darkness was upon the face of the deep'. To be lost is to be under the power of darkness, to be under the rule of Satan, the prince of darkness. There is not one ray of spiritual light in man by nature. Fallen man has no spiritual light, knowledge, or understanding.

The restoration of God's creation

Genesis 1:2-31 describe the restoration of God's creation. The order followed by God in restoring the physical creation is the same order followed by God in the new creation, in the restoration of fallen man by his almighty grace. The work of God in the restoration of his creation corresponds exactly to the experience of a believer. Here are seven works performed by God in the restoration of his creation which picture his work of grace in the believer.

1. 'And the Spirit of God moved upon the face of the waters' (v. 2)

The earth, no doubt, moved in its orbit and rotated upon its own axis, but its motions could not mend it. It had to be moved upon by the Spirit of God. Otherwise, it would forever remain 'without form and void'. Even so, regeneration is not accomplished by the works of man or the emotions of the heart, but by the working of God the Holy Spirit. The new birth is not an evolution, but a creation. 'It is not of him that willeth, nor of him that runneth, but of God that sheweth mercy' (Romans 9:16). 'It is the Spirit that quickeneth; the flesh profiteth nothing' (John 6:63). The new birth is not accomplished by man's movement toward God, but by God's movement upon the heart of man.

2. 'And God said, Let there be light; and there was light' (v. 3)

If the Spirit of God moves upon a man it is by the Word of God. No less than ten times in this chapter we read these words, 'And God said'. God does not work apart from his Word. Without question, God could have refashioned and restored the earth without speaking a word; but he did not choose to do so. His purposes were worked out and his counsels were fulfilled by his Word. Light came and was produced by the Word of God. These two things are inseparably joined together: (1) The ministry of the Holy Spirit and (2) the ministry of the Word of God. The Word of God, the gospel of Christ, is the power of God (Romans 1:16; 1 Peter 1:23-25), and the source of spiritual light (2 Corinthians 4:6). The Word of God, the gospel, is the seed of life (James 1:18; 1 Peter 1:23-25), the means by which life and faith are conveyed to the soul (Romans 10:17). The gospel, the Word of God, is God's ordained means of grace and salvation (1 Corinthians 1:23; 1 Timothy 4:16).

3. 'And God divided the light from the darkness' (v. 4)

As God separated the light from the darkness in the old creation, so he separates the light from the darkness in the new creation. 'Ye are the children of the light, and the children of the day: we are not of the night, nor of darkness' (1 Thessalonians 5:5). The Word of God, by the power of the Holy Spirit working in the new man, divides between the soul and the spirit, separates the spiritual from the carnal (2 Corinthians 6:14-18). This is true both in doctrine and in life. Those who are born of God know light from darkness; and they walk in the light as he is in the light (1 John 1:5-7).

4. 'And God said, Let the earth bring forth fruit' (v. 11)

Where there is the work of the Spirit, the Word of God and the light of grace, there will be fruit unto God (Galatians 5:22-23). This fruit is the result of a condition, not an effort. It is the result of what we are, not of what we do. The fruit of Christ in us is Christ likeness. Those who are born of God bear fruit after his kind; as the seed within bears fruit after its kind on the earth. Apples produce apples. Grapes produce grapes. Grace produces grace. The grace of God moulds and controls a believer's character and conduct.

5. 'And God said, Let there be lights in the firmament of heaven to give light upon the earth' (vv. 14-15)

The lights must be above the earth if they are to shine upon it. Those who are born of God have been raised above the earth. They 'are the light of the world' (Matthew 5:14). As the moon reflects the light of the sun, believers reflect the light of Christ in this world (Matthew 5:16). Good works are the only lights by which the world sees Christ in his people. Therefore we are admonished to be careful to maintain them (Ephesians 2:10; Titus 3:8). We are saved by grace. Works have nothing to do with salvation. But salvation always produces good works.

6. 'God created man in his own image' (v. 27)

Here is the climax of the Creator's power. God made man in his own likeness. He made him out of the soil of the earth, even the earth which had become 'without form and void!' Here is a work even greater than that. In the new creation, the God of all grace creates sinners new in Christ (2 Corinthians 5:17; Galatians 6:15; Colossians 3:10). God takes men and women who are utterly 'without form and void' spiritually and makes them (by his great works of redemption, regeneration, and resurrection) exact replicas of his dear Son.

7. God blessed the man he had made and gave him dominion over all his creation (vv. 28-31)

All who are born of God are blessed of God (Ephesians 1:3). 'All things are yours, for ye are Christ's, and Christ is God's'. One day soon God shall put all things under our feet even as he has put all things under the feet of his dear Son (Hebrews 2:6-9; Romans 16:20). Then the purpose of God shall be fulfilled. Then God shall be 'all in all'.

Until we are one with Christ, we are out of harmony with God's creation. If you are yet without Christ, come to him now. Believe on the Lord Jesus Christ. Come, enter into that blessed sabbath of faith portrayed in Genesis 2:1-3'.Thus the heavens and the earth were finished, and all the host of them. 'And on the seventh day God ended his work which he had made; and he rested on the seventh day from all his work which he had made. And God blessed the seventh day, and sanctified it: because that in it he had rested from all his work which God created and made'. Cease from your works as God did from his, and trust, rest in the Lord Jesus Christ as your only, all-sufficient Saviour. If you do, you are a new creation in Christ!

'And God said, Let us make man in our image, after our likeness: and let them have dominion over the fish of the sea, and over the fowl of the air, and over the cattle, and over all the earth, and over every creeping thing that creepeth upon the earth. So God created man in his own image, in the image of God created he him; male and female created he them. And God blessed them, and God said unto them, Be fruitful, and multiply, and replenish the earth, and subdue it: and have dominion over the fish of the sea, and over the fowl of the air, and over every living thing that moveth upon the earth'.
(Genesis 1:26-28)

Chapter 20

The Creation of Man

Solomon understood that all the problems of men in this world are owing to the sin and fall of our father Adam. Original sin is the origin of all evil, sorrow, and death in this world (Ecclesiastes 7:20, 29). God created our father Adam morally upright and righteous, in the image of Christ; but Adam sinned and, sinning, plunged all the human race into sin and spiritual death, under the curse of God's holy law. In this chapter, we will see the original state in which our father Adam, as the head of all the human race, was created, the circumstances in which he lived, and the terrible sin and crime by which our race was plunged into spiritual death and made subject to eternal death and the wrath of God.

The creation of man

Genesis 1:26-28 speaks of a consultation made between the three Persons of the holy Trinity in which God the Father said to God the Son and God the Spirit, 'Let us make man in our image, after our likeness'. Then, on the sixth day of creation, as the crowning work of his hands, the Lord God 'formed man of the dust of the ground, and breathed into his nostrils the breath of life; and man became a living soul' (Genesis 2:7).

Throughout the ages there have been some who have taught that there was another race of men created by God prior to Adam. This pre-adamite doctrine has been maintained for many reasons. Today, in some circles it is even taught as a justification for some form of racism. If you are exposed to such doctrine, do not allow the arguments given in defence of this error to have any effect upon you. The scriptures speak plainly about Adam and describe him as 'the first man Adam' (1 Corinthians 15:45). That one statement is sufficient to lay to rest all arguments given to support the pre-adamite error.

I cannot add anything to all that has been said and written about the creation of man. I simply want to remind you of those things obviously revealed in the Word of God. I hope you will be led, in the consideration of these things, to worship, trust, and adore your Creator. As we consider the things taught in holy scripture about the origin of man, we should stand in awe of God, declaring with David, 'I will praise thee; for I am fearfully and wonderfully made: marvellous are thy works; and that my soul knoweth right well' (Psalm 139:14).

In his original state man was created, body, soul, and spirit, in the image of God[1]. Without question, that means many, many things. It certainly includes the fact that man was created with intellect,

---

[1] The fact that man was created in the image of God places special sanctity upon all human life. 'Whoso sheddeth man's blood, by man shall his blood be shed: for in the image of God made he man' (Genesis 9:6).

emotion, and will. It certainly includes the fact that man was given dominion over all creatures in the earth and over the earth itself. Without question, it also includes the fact that man, as he was created by God, was given a living, undying, immortal soul.

Man's physical uprightness reflects the image of Christ, our God, Mediator, and Creator. Others debate the issue, but I have no doubt at all that it certainly includes, though it is not limited to, the erect posture of man's body. Man's erect body is one of many things which distinguish him from four-footed animals. I am fully aware that God is not a physical Being. 'God is Spirit'. He does not have physical parts or a physical body. However, our Lord Jesus Christ, who alone is said to be 'the Image of the invisible God', does possess a physical body. When God said, 'Let us make man in our image', he certainly had in mind the physical as well as moral image of the incarnate God who would come into the world in the fulness of time. In other words, the first Adam was made in the image of the last Adam.

John Gill observed that by the erectness of his body, 'Man is fitted and directed to look upward to the heavens, to contemplate them, and the glory of God displayed in them; and even to look up to God above them, to worship and adore him, to praise him for mercies received, and to pray to him for what are wanted'. Gill went on to say that the uprightness of our bodies, 'Instructs men to set their affections not on things on earth, but on things in heaven. Indeed, it is natural for every man, whether in any great distress, or when favoured with an unexpected blessing, and when he receives tidings that surprise him, whether of good or bad things, to turn his face upwards. In the Greek language man has his name, anthropos, from turning and looking upwards'.

Man was created in the image of God morally. I mean by that that our father Adam, in his original creation was righteous. He was created with an uprightness and rectitude of character, holy and righteous. 'God made man upright' (Ecclesiastes 7:29). Adam was free from all error, weaknesses, and mistakes of character as well as free from all sin. He was perfect. His will was biased toward God. His affections flowed out to his Creator. His thoughts were pure. His deeds were holy. There was no sin in him, no propensity toward sin, and no inclination to sin. 'This righteousness of his', Gill said, 'was natural, and not personal and acquired. It was not obtained by the exercise of his free will. It was lost, not got, that way'.

Adam was created in the image of God typically, too. The first Adam was created by God to be a type, picture, and representative of the last Adam, our Lord Jesus Christ. The first man was a picture of the second man (1 Corinthians 15:45-47). As we were lost by the work, sinful work and disobedience, of the first Adam, so we are saved by the righteous work and obedience of the second Adam (1 Corinthians 15:21-22; Romans 5:12, 18-21).

The coronation of man

Read Psalm 8:1-9, and see how God has crowned man with a dignity surpassing all other creatures. Man was originally created in the image of God; and, as man was the crowning work of God in creation, God crowned him above all his creatures. This is a subject worthy of much more attention than I can give it at this time; but here are a few things which will display the high honour God placed upon man, exalting him above all his creatures.

The Lord God planted the Garden of Eden for man (Genesis 2:8). No one has any idea where Eden was; but it was a perfect spot for the perfect man whom God had made. God gave Adam everything he needed in the Garden of Eden to support and maintain his life (Genesis 2:9-10). The tree of life was a type and picture of Christ, the Tree of Life in the midst of the Paradise of God (Proverbs 3:8; Revelation 2:7; 22:2). That tree was filled with fruit to sustain Adam in life. It was God's gift to him and represented the fact that his life was from God, maintained by God, and depended upon God. Thus, even in his daily meals, Adam lived by faith in God and worshipped him.

There was also a river in the Garden with four heads, by which both the Garden and all the earth were watered. This river symbolized life, vitality, and refreshment. It was typical and representative of Christ, the gospel of God's free grace in him, the Spirit of God, the Word of God, and the everlasting love of God, all of which are represented to us in the scriptures under the symbol of water (Psalm 46:4; John 7:37-39; Revelation 22:1). The gospel of Christ and the doctrines of it, like this river, go forth out of Zion to water the earth, making it fruitful everywhere. The Spirit of God, like a mighty river, flows with living waters of grace to all who believe on the Lord Jesus Christ. Christ himself is a river, a fountain opened for cleansing from sin. The everlasting love of God toward his elect is a pure river of the water of life, flowing to sinners through all the earth. It is a river with four blessed heads, or branches: (1) Sovereign Election, (2) Effectual Redemption, (3) Irresistible Grace, and (4) Eternal Life (Romans 8:29-30).

Adam was placed in the Garden to dress it and keep it (Genesis 2:15). There was no toil or fatigue involved in the work. Adam's worship of God had as much to do with tending the Garden as it did with walking with the Lord in the cool of the day. Even in innocence, man was not without work. Even the angels of God have work to do by which they serve him. They are ministering spirits sent forth to minister to God's elect. The work Adam was given was the most honourable work imaginable. He was God's gardener!

God gave Adam dominion over all his creation. He made Adam king over everything (Genesis 1:28) and gave everything in the earth to him to use and enjoy as he saw fit for the glory of God (Genesis 1:29-30). Then he brought every living creature to Adam to be named by him (Genesis 2:19). What a brilliant man Adam must have been. Even Plato was overwhelmed by the brilliance of that mind that gave names to all things, saying that it must have been more than human.

Then the Lord God made an helpmeet for Adam (Genesis 2:21-25). Adam was formed first, then Eve. They were not equal partners in a self-gratifying relationship. They were a man and woman, husband and wife, living together in love for God and one another. Their relationship is a beautiful picture of Christ and his church. As Adam was put into a deep sleep for Eve's creation, so Christ was slain for the life of his church. As Eve was taken from Adam's side, so the church is born from the wounded side of the second Adam. As Eve was created for Adam, not Adam for Eve, so the church exists for Christ. As Eve was to be obedient to Adam in all things, so the church is to be obedient to Christ in all things. As Adam was in all things responsible for Eve, so in all things Christ is responsible for his church. As Adam willingly became sin and died under the wrath of God because of his love for Eve, so Christ willingly became sin and died under the wrath of God because of his love for us. As Adam by his disobedience brought Eve into death and condemnation, so Christ, by his obedience brought his church into life and blessedness.

The covenant with man

Genesis 2:16-17 reveals a covenant God made with Adam. We know that this commandment given to Adam by God was a covenant because God says so in Hosea 6:7 where he speaks of Adam's sin as the transgression of his covenant. This covenant made with Adam was a covenant of works. It was a covenant sanctioned by the promise of life and the threat of death. The only thing God required of Adam was perfect, personal, perpetual obedience. The covenant was soon broken by Adam. In this covenant, Adam was God's appointed substitute, federal head and representative of all men. It is in this sense that Adam was a type and figure of him that was to come (Romans 5:12-14).

The breaking of this covenant did not take God by surprise. He said to Adam, 'In the day thou eatest thereof', (not if you eat thereof, but when), thou shalt surely die'. The sin and fall of Adam was typical of and made way for the coming of the second man, the Lord from heaven, the Lord Jesus Christ and the new covenant of grace in him (Psalm 76:10). The breaking of this covenant, Adam's disobedience to God, led to the sin, corruption, and death of the whole human race.

The corruption of man

Adam's transgression of God's covenant was the ruin of our race. The scriptures teach, emphatically and constantly, that which is commonly referred to as the doctrine of original sin. That is to say, – All men and women became sinners when Adam sinned and are born as sinners, in a state of utter and total depravity (Psalm 51:5; Romans 5:12), going astray from God from the womb, 'speaking lies' (Psalm 58:3), with hearts which are 'deceitful above all things and desperately wicked' (Jeremiah 17:9).

The conversion of man

The fall of the first Adam made room for the obedience of the last Adam. Adam's sin made necessary Christ's righteousness. Our ruin by Adam made room for our redemption, resurrection, and restoration by Christ. After Adam and Eve sinned, the Lord God came seeking the fallen pair (Genesis 3:9). God himself preached the gospel to the guilty couple (Genesis 3:15). Before he drove them from the Garden, God made a sacrifice for Adam and Eve and clothed them with the skins of an innocent victim (Genesis 3:21). This is exactly what God did for us in the sacrifice of his dear Son upon the cursed tree (Isaiah 53:10-11; 2 Corinthians 5:21; 1 Peter 3:18).

'And the LORD God took the man, and put him into the garden of Eden to dress it and to keep it. And the LORD God commanded the man, saying, Of every tree of the garden thou mayest freely eat: But of the tree of the knowledge of good and evil, thou shalt not eat of it: for in the day that thou eatest thereof thou shalt surely die'.
(Genesis 2:15-17)

Chapter 21

God's Covenant with Adam

When the Lord God placed Adam in the Garden of Eden, he made a covenant with our father Adam, as the federal head and representative of all men, a covenant which Adam broke, by which he plunged the human race into sin and death and placed us all under the curse of God's holy law. This is what is spoken of in Genesis 2:15-17.

The covenant with Adam

God governs all rational creatures by law. This is what is often referred to as 'God's moral government of the world'. The Lord God gave a law to his angels, a law which some obeyed and others broke. The angels who kept their first estate were confirmed forever in a state of obedience. Those who kept not their first estate were plunged into everlasting destruction and misery by their disobedience.

God also gave a law to Adam. This law was given to him in the form of a covenant, with a revealed threat of death, destruction, and misery if it was disobeyed and an implied promise of life if it was obeyed. In this covenant which God made with Adam, Adam was, by Divine appointment, made to be the representative of the entire human race.

We know that the commandment given to Adam (Genesis 2:15-17) by God was a covenant because God says so (Hosea 6:7). This covenant made with Adam was a covenant of works. The covenant was given as a trial, a test of man's obedience to the will of God. As long as Adam complied with this Divine law, he displayed reverence for, submission to, and faith in the Lord his God as his rightful Master and King.

This was a covenant sanctioned by the promise of life and the threat of death. The only thing God required of Adam was perfect, personal, perpetual obedience. If Adam had obeyed God, his obedience would have secured for him a continued life of innocence. In making that statement, I grant that it is something implied, rather than clearly revealed, in the text.

However, the implication is obvious, as long as Adam did not break the law, he would continue in life. However, we are not to infer from that that Adam would have gained eternal life by his obedience to this command.

I stress this fact because many preachers and theologians of great reputation teach that if Adam had obeyed the terms of this covenant for a specified length of time, he would have won for himself and all men eternal life. That is neither stated nor implied in the scriptures. The life Adam would have gained would have been the life he had as a creature, an innocent, natural life upon the earth; but no more.

Here are five reasons why I say Adam could never have attained eternal life in the Garden.

1. Eternal life was promised to God's elect in the covenant of grace made with Christ long before this (Ephesians 1:3; 2 Timothy 1:1; Titus 1:2; 1 John 5:10).

2. Eternal life is the free gift of God's grace in Christ the Mediator, through the merit and virtue of his blood, and by the knowledge of him (John 10:10, 28; 17:3; Romans 6:23).

3. If eternal life could have been won by Adam's obedience, then eternal life would have been gained by works, not by the grace and gift of God. Eternal life is nothing less or more than the consummation of salvation in everlasting glory with Christ; and this, the scriptures everywhere declare, is the work and gift of God's free grace alone (Romans 6:23; Ephesians 2:8-9).

4. Life and immortality are brought to light by the gospel of Christ, not by Adam, Abraham, or Moses (2 Timothy 1:9-10).

5. There is no proportion between the best works of man, not even in his state of innocence and sinlessness, and eternal life.

The other sanction of the covenant God made with Adam was death. God said, 'In the day thou eatest thereof, thou shalt surely die'. It has been suggested that that sentence might be better translated, 'In the day thou eatest thereof, dying, thou shalt die'. The death threatened upon Adam and executed upon men as the result of sin is a threefold death.

1. Physical death – Physical, corporal death is the separation of the soul from the body, the returning of ashes to ashes and dust to dust (Genesis 3:19). As soon as Adam sinned, he was stripped of immortality. The seeds of corruption and death were put in him. He became subject to sicknesses, diseases, and miseries, which are the forerunners of death. As soon as he sinned, man began to die. 'The wages of sin is death', physical death.

2. Spiritual death – Spiritual death is the separation of the soul from God, alienation from the life of God, banishment from communion with God, deformation of the image of God in man, corruption and defilement in every moral, mental, and emotional faculty, spiritual impotency, and a disinclination to all that is holy, good, and spiritual. Thus man is born, dead in trespasses and sins, in a state of enmity against God (Ephesians 2:1-3; Romans 8:6-7). 'The wages of sin is death', spiritual death.

3. Eternal death – Eternal death is the separation of the soul and body from God and good forever. It is the everlasting banishment of man from light, life, liberty, and love in the presence of God. Eternal death is everlasting darkness, everlasting destruction, everlasting dismay.

Eternal death is everlasting hell, whatever that is! It is not annihilation, but torment. It is not a cessation of being or of consciousness, but a cessation of blessedness and peace.

Adam broke the covenant. We are not told how long he lived in that state of innocence in which he was created. However, it appears that it was not for very long. Adam and Eve were sinners before they were parents.

In this covenant, Adam was God's appointed substitute, federal head and representative of all men. It is in this sense that he was a type and figure of him that was to come (Romans 5:14). Nothing happened when Eve sinned. The covenant was not made with Eve, Eve was not the one responsible.

Adam was the covenant head and representative even of Eve; just as he was the covenant head and representative of the entire race. This is, itself, a sign of hope. If we were lost by a representative, there is hope that we might be saved by a representative (Romans 5:17-19).

The breaking of this covenant did not take God by surprise. Ever remember that nothing is out of God's control or outside God's purpose. He said to Adam, 'In the day thou eatest thereof', (not if you eat, but when), 'thou shalt surely die'.

The sin and fall of Adam was typical of and made way for the coming of the second man, the Lord from heaven, the Lord Jesus Christ and the new covenant of grace in him (Psalm 76:10). Yet, the breaking of this covenant, Adam's disobedience to God led to the sin, corruption, and death of the whole human race.

The spiritual death of man

All men and women became sinners when Adam sinned and are born as sinners, totally depraved and corrupt in all our faculties. All the children of men, since the sin and fall of Adam, are estranged from the womb and go astray, as soon as they are born, speaking lies. There are no exceptions. Like the aborted infant described in Ezekiel 16, we are all born dead, polluted in our own blood, cast off, and utterly helpless. Like the bones in the prophet's vision, all the human race is, by nature as an army long ago slain. None of those slain can ever come to life again, but by the power and grace of God the Holy Spirit. Like Lazarus in the tomb, all human beings are by nature spiritually dead.

The gospel preached in Eden

The fall of the first Adam made room for the obedience of the last Adam. Adam's sin made necessary Christ's righteousness. Our ruin by Adam made room for our redemption, resurrection, and restoration by Christ. As soon as they sinned, Adam and Eve were made aware of their nakedness before God. They were pricked in their consciences with guilt. They immediately began the religion of fallen man, the religion of works and self-righteousness, by which man attempts to hide his sin from God. Such religion will never give a sinner real peace. Though they were wearing their fig leaves, when God came to them, Adam and Eve hid themselves from the Lord. If they were to be saved, they must be saved by grace alone, altogether by a work of God.

As we saw in the preceding study, after Adam and Eve sinned, the Lord came seeking the fallen pair (Genesis 3:9). The Lord God himself preached the gospel to the guilty couple (Genesis 3:15). Before he drove them from the Garden, God made a sacrifice for Adam and Eve and clothed them with the skins of an innocent victim (Genesis 3:21). And that is exactly what God did for us in the sacrifice of his dear Son upon the cursed tree (2 Corinthians 5:21; Galatians 3:13).

Adam and Eve believed God. You might wonder, 'Where is that found?' You will remember that Adam named his wife 'Woman', because she was taken out of his side. But in Genesis 3:20, after hearing and observing all that the Lord said and did, Adam gave her a new name. He called her 'Eve', because she would be the mother of all living. Adam believed that though he must die physically, he would live to have sons and daughters and that Eve would as well. He believed that God had not only forgiven their sins through the life and death of a Substitute man, but that that man would be born of Eve, through whom all who live before God shall live. That is why Eve, exclaimed with joy when Cain was born, 'I have gotten a man (The Man!) from the Lord!'

The Lord Jesus Christ is that Man, that Man who is God, by whom the serpent's head has been crushed, through whose blood sinners are forgiven, with whose righteousness all who believe are clothed. Thus, in the very beginning of things, even in the sin and fall of our father Adam, we have a picture, a promise, and a testimony from God of his free, saving grace in Christ (1 John 5:9-13, 20).

'Wherefore, as by one man sin entered into the world, and death by sin; and so death passed upon all men, for that all have sinned: ... Therefore as by the offence of one judgment came upon all men to condemnation; even so by the righteousness of one the free gift came upon all men unto justification of life. For as by one man's disobedience many were made sinners, so by the obedience of one shall many be made righteous. Moreover the law entered, that the offence might abound. But where sin abounded, grace did much more abound: That as sin hath reigned unto death, even so might grace reign through righteousness unto eternal life by Jesus Christ our Lord'. (Romans 5:12-21)

Chapter 22

The Sin and Fall of Our Father Adam

The Apostle Paul, writing by Divine inspiration, draws a very instructive parallel between the first Adam and the last Adam, between the first representative man (Adam) and the second representative man (the Lord Jesus Christ, 'The Lord from heaven'). Five things are revealed in this last half of Romans chapter five which need to be clearly understood.

1. Sin and death entered into this world and were passed upon all the human race by the sin and fall of one representative man, our father Adam (v. 12).
2. In his act of disobedience and the penalty of death he incurred as our representative, Adam was a type and figure of our Lord Jesus Christ, who was ordained of God to come into this world as the Saviour of a chosen race (v. 14).

184 Basic Bible Doctrine

3. God's elect are made righteous and granted life and salvation in Christ in exactly the same way as we all became sinners, died, and became subject to eternal damnation in Adam, – by the doing and dying of that representative man, who is himself God, the Lord Jesus Christ (vv. 15, 17-19).

4. The Lord God, in his sovereign wisdom, goodness, and grace, ordained and permitted the entrance of sin into the world by Adam's disobedience so that he might magnify his name and the glory of his grace in the salvation of his elect by Christ, so that in the very place where sin abounded grace might super-abound (vv. 16, 20).

5. The purpose of God was not, to any degree, frustrated, but perfectly fulfilled in the sin and fall of our father Adam (v. 21).

The law God gave to Adam and the covenant he made with him as our representative were broken shortly after Adam and Eve were placed in the Garden. Though he was created in the image of God, in a state of innocence, integrity, and righteousness, by an act of wilful disobedience and sin, Adam fell from that lofty state of righteousness and life into a state of sin and death; and we all (all the human race) fell in him.

As we seek to understand what happened in the Garden, I want to answer three questions. The questions are simple. The answers are revealed with utmost clarity in the Word of God. Yet, the answers to these three questions are some of the most controversial and profound things revealed in holy scripture.

Who sinned?

The Word of God declares that both Adam and Eve, the first man and the first woman, sinned against God, first Eve, then Adam (1 Timothy 2:13-14). Eve was first in the transgression (Genesis 3:1-6). She was beguiled and deceived by the old serpent, the devil. He persuaded her to eat of the forbidden fruit. However, it was by Adam's sin that sin and death entered the world and plunged all the human race into sin and death, under the wrath of God.

God's covenant was not made with Eve. It was made with Adam. I do not minimize the fact that Eve personally transgressed God's law and his covenant; but she was not the covenant head and representative of the race. When she ate the forbidden fruit, nothing happened. But when Adam, with his eyes wide open, took the fruit in defiance of God, immediately, the human race was corrupted by sin and plunged into spiritual darkness and death, under the wrath of God (Genesis 3:6-7).

Adam was Eve's federal head and representative in exactly the same way as he was our federal head and representative. I stress this because it is very important. God arranged it so that the entire human race would stand or fall by the obedience or disobedience of one representative man. He did that because he had purposed that all his elect would be recovered from Adam's fall by the obedience of one man, the God-man, his darling Son, our Lord Jesus Christ (1 Corinthians 15:21-22).

In his act of sin, by which we were all made sinners, in his spiritual death, by which death passed upon all men, our father Adam was, by Divine appointment, a type and figure of our Lord Jesus Christ. This is not merely a matter of theological reasoning. These are the words of God the Holy Spirit. Adam was 'the figure of him that was to come' (Romans 5:14).

Adam's transgression was a horrible, treasonous act of rebellion against the Lord God. He knew exactly what the consequences of Eve's sin would be. She had sinned. Therefore, she must die. Adam, therefore, with his eyes wide open, in a fit of fury against his Creator, snatched the fruit from Eve's hands and wilfully plunged himself into death, under the curse of God.

How does this typify and portray our Lord Jesus Christ? As Adam loved Eve, so Christ loved his bride, the Church. Because of his love for Eve, rather than be separated from her forever, Adam chose to become what she was, to become a sinner with her. Even so, the Lord Jesus Christ, because of his great love for us, rather than be separated from his people forever, chose to become one of us and to be made sin for us. When Adam took that forbidden fruit, he knew full well that the result would be his own death under the terrible wrath of almighty God; he willingly chose that death because of his love for Eve. So, too, the Son of God, because of his great love for us, chose to become sin for us, knowing that when he was made to be sin he must also suffer all the wrath of God and be banished from his Father as a cursed thing, as our Substitute.

There are, however, two great disparities between the first Adam and the last Adam. (1) When Adam chose sin and death for Eve's sake, it was an act of the highest and greatest possible rebellion and disobedience. When the Lord Jesus chose sin and death for us, it was an act of the highest and greatest possible love and obedience to God. (2) Adam's disobedience brought ruin, judgment, and death. Christ's obedience brought righteousness, life, and salvation.

Thus it has come to pass exactly as the Lord God purposed from eternity that where sin abounded grace did much more abound; and as sin reigned unto death, so grace now reigns through righteousness unto eternal life by our Lord Jesus Christ!

How could a perfect man, created in the image and likeness of God, commit such a crime?

That is a fair, honest, and reasonable question. I have asked it many, many times when contemplating the sin and fall of Adam. How could a man, so wise, so knowledgeable, so holy, just, and good, a man created in the very image and likeness of God commit such a violent, treasonous act as this?

We know that the Lord God did not cause Adam to sin. It seems abhorrent that I should have to even make such a statement as that. But those who despise our God and the gospel of his grace, despising the fact of his absolute sovereignty in all things, falsely accuse us of making God the author of sin. Nothing could be further from the truth. God did not make Adam sin. He forbade it. He resented it. He was displeased with it to the highest degree. James declares, 'God cannot be tempted with evil, neither tempteth he any man'.

However, the sin and fall of Adam did not take God almighty by surprise. Considering this matter with reverence and sobriety as we read the Word of God, certain things simply must be acknowledged by anyone familiar with the character of God and the plain statements of scripture.

God almighty could easily have prevented Adam's sin and fall had he been pleased to do so. He who kept Abimelech from sinning with Sarah, kept Laban and Esau from hurting Jacob, and kept Balaam from cursing Israel could easily have kept Adam from sinning in the Garden. Had it been his will to do so, God who kept Satan from destroying Job could have simply commanded the devil to leave Adam and Eve alone.

Without question, it must also be acknowledged that God, who 'worketh after the counsel of his own will', foreordained, and predestined the sin and fall of Adam. I know, some people squirm at this; but either God was in control here, or he was not. Either he had his way, or someone else had their way. Either God's purpose stood, or it fell to the ground. What does the Bible say? The Bible says, 'all things are of God' (Isaiah 14:24, 26; 46:9-10; Lamentations 3:37; Romans 8:28; 11:36). Nothing is done, or can be done, that God does not will and purpose to be done. The Word of God tells us plainly that the suffering and death of Christ to redeem us from sin and deliver us from the fall was ordained before the foundation of the world (Acts 2:23; 4:28; 1 Peter 2:20). If our deliverance was foreordained, the fall from which we are delivered was so foreordained.

It cannot be denied that this thing came to pass because God permitted it. I do not mean by that that God simply allowed it, or suffered it to come to pass without interference, or that he stood by as a spectator; but that he permitted it in the sense that he wisely and graciously planned it and willed it, though he did not in any way coerce Adam to sin.

John Gill stated the matter well when he wrote, 'God permitted or suffered Adam to sin and fall, which permission was not a bare permission or sufferance. God was not an idle spectator of this affair. The permission was voluntary, wise, holy, powerful, and efficacious, according to the unchangeable counsel of his will. He willed, and he did not will the sin of Adam, in different respects. He did not will it as an evil, but as what he would overrule for good, a great good. He willed it not as sin, but as a means of glorifying his grace and mercy, justice and holiness'.

Satan, with great craftiness and subtlety, used that which was dearest and most pleasing to Adam to destroy him. The old serpent enticed Eve, and thus arranged for Eve to become Adam's snare. Adam chose to rebel and sin, therefore he rebelled and sinned. That is the long and short of the matter. Adam sinned with the full consent of his will, without any force upon him.

With purpose, forethought, and determination, he took the forbidden fruit. Never did a hungry man eat bread or a thirsty man drink water with greater eagerness than Adam had when he took the forbidden fruit.

What are the consequences of Adam's iniquity, transgression and sin?

Read Romans chapter five again. Three answers to this question are given in verses 12, 18, 19, 20, and 21.

1. When Adam sinned, we all sinned in him representatively, and we all became sinners (v. 12). Adam's sin was legally charged and imputed to all the human race. 'All have sinned'. Adam's sinful, depraved nature is passed to all his descendants by natural generation.
2. Death and the sentence of death passed upon all men, because 'all have sinned'. 'The wages of sin is death'. When Adam sinned, we all died spiritually. We are all dying physically. We are all subject to eternal death.
3. In verses 18-21, the Holy Spirit tells us that the sin and fall of our father Adam, as it prefigured it, also made a way for the display

of God's glorious, super-abounding grace in and through the Lord Jesus Christ.

Had there been no fall, there would have been no recovery. Had there been no ruin, there would have been no redemption. Had there been no sin, there would have been no Saviour. Had there been no Saviour, there would have been no such anthems as these ...

> There is a fountain filled with blood,
> Drawn from Immanuel's veins;
> And sinners plunged beneath that flood,
> Lose all their guilty stains! (John Newton)

> Amazing grace! How sweet the sound!
> That saved a wretch like me!
> I once was lost, but now am found,
> Was blind, but now I see! (William Cowper)

'Unto him that loved us, and washed us from our sins in his own blood, And hath made us kings and priests unto God and his Father; to him be glory and dominion for ever and ever. Amen. Thou art worthy to take the book, and to open the seals thereof: for thou wast slain, and hast redeemed us to God by thy blood out of every kindred, and tongue, and people, and nation; And hast made us unto our God kings and priests: and we shall reign on the earth'. (Revelation 1:5,6; 5:9,10)

When we consider the sin and fall of our father Adam, and the consequences of it, we ought to bow before the throne of our great God in worshipful reverence, and say, with the apostle Paul, 'O the depth of the riches both of the wisdom and knowledge of God! How unsearchable are his judgments, and his ways past finding out! For who hath known the mind of the Lord? or who hath been his counsellor? Or who hath first given to him, and it shall be recompensed unto him again? For of him, and through him, and to him, are all things: to whom be glory for ever. Amen'.

'In Adam all die'.
(1 Corinthians 15:22)

Chapter 23

Spiritual Death

Here are four words which reveal what happened when our father Adam sinned in the garden. These four words must be understood. They are necessary. They are vital. Until these four simple words are understood there is no understanding of anything else taught in the Bible. The words are, 'In Adam all die'.

When God gave his law to Adam, the sanction of the law was death: physical death, spiritual (moral) death, and eternal death. 'The wages of sin is death!' As soon as Adam sinned, he and all his posterity became mortals, stripped of immortality of body which God had given him in creation, and became subject to and infested with all the corruptions of sickness, disease, and death; and a spiritual, moral death seized his being, a spiritual, moral corruption and death which is passed upon all men, generation after generation. 'In Adam all die'.

Because of Adam's sin, and our sinning in him, the understanding of man is darkened. His mind and conscience are defiled. We are filled with inordinate affections. Our wills, by nature, are biased toward everything that is evil. We have a natural taste and relish for sin. Indeed, until regenerated and saved by the grace of God, all the sons and daughters of Adam are to every good work lifeless and reprobate. Everyone by nature is born in a state of spiritual death, being dead in trespasses and in sins. This is the language used by the Holy Spirit to describe man's lost condition – 'In Adam all die' (Romans 5:12; Ephesians 2:1-3).

As we were all born sinners, in a state and condition of spiritual death, we were all also born 'children of wrath', under the curse of God's holy law and subject to eternal death. Eternal death is the just wage and retribution paid to sin by God. Eternal death is the wrath of God revealed against all unrighteousness. It is that which shall forever torment the children of disobedience, unless we are saved from it by the obedience and death of the Son of God, the Lord Jesus Christ, the last Adam.

This eternal death is the curse which Zechariah saw in his vision, as a flying roll flying over the whole earth, by which all the wicked are cut off forever (Zechariah 5:1-3). God's elect are saved from this universal curse, because (and only because) Christ has redeemed us from the curse of the law and delivered us from the wrath to come. He is made of God unto us both righteousness and redemption; and we are now made righteous in him.

The result of Adam's sin

Spiritual death is the result of Adam's sin as our representative and substitute in the Garden. It is the result of our sin in him.

In Romans 5, the Holy Spirit uses four distinct words to describe what Adam did in the garden of Eden. In verse 12, it is called 'sin'. In fact, in the Greek text, it is twice referred to there as 'the sin'. It is called 'the sin' because it was the first sin and because it is the fountain of all sin. In verse 14, it is called a 'transgression'. The Apostle John tells us that every sin is a transgression of the law (1 John 3:14). Adam's sin, and our sin in him, was a transgression of that law which God made with Adam as our representative (Genesis

2:17). In Romans 5:19, it is called 'disobedience'. It was an act of wilful disobedience to the revealed will of God. Then, in Romans 5:15-20, the Apostle uses the word 'offence' four times to describe Adam's sin, because sin is abhorrently offensive to the holy Lord God. This word, 'offence', conveys the idea of a fall.

That is why we refer to Adam's sin as 'The Fall'. It was the offence, or the fall, by which Adam and the entire human race represented by him fell from a state of honour, integrity, righteousness, life, and happiness into a state of dishonour, sin, unrighteousness, death, and misery.

Though Adam's sin is represented to us as the simple act of eating that fruit which he was forbidden by God to eat, his act of sin was much more complex than most imagine. He sinned against light and knowledge, when he was in full power to have resisted temptation. Adam's sin was the height of ingratitude to God his Maker. It was an affront to God in the highest degree. It was an act of wilful unbelief, making God a liar, rejecting the truthfulness of his word. It was an act of intolerable pride, an affectation, pretence, and assumption of deity, of equality with God. It was an act of unparalleled selfishness by which Adam displayed a total disregard, lack of concern for, or even thought of affection or care for God, his creation, or any of the human race, with whose souls he had been entrusted. We flinch from acknowledging it, but the fact is, all acts of sin have these three elements in them. Every act of sin is an act of wilful unbelief, intolerable pride, and horrible selfishness.

Adam's sin included all aspects of sin. His one transgression was a total, complete breach of God's holy law. The laws of God, according to James 2:10, are so intertwined that he that 'offends in one point is guilty of all'. One of the old writers said, 'Adam, at one clap, broke both tables of the law, and all the commandments of God'.

Adam's one act of rebellion, sin, and disobedience was a transgression of each of the commandments (Exodus 20:1-17). He chose another god when he followed the devil. He idolized and deified his own belly. He made his belly (his lusts) his god. He took the name of God in vain when he believed him not. He kept not the rest and estate wherein God had set him, thus violating, breaking, and disregarding the sabbath day. He dishonoured his Father which was in heaven. Therefore his days were not long in that land which the Lord his God had given him. He murdered, in the most horrible massacre of all history, himself and all his posterity. He committed spiritual fornication and adultery. He went whoring after other gods. Like Achan, he stole that which God forbade; and his robbery is that which troubles all Israel and the whole world. He bore witness against God when he believed not his word. He coveted and his covetousness cost him his life, and brought death upon all his family.

It is this death, this spiritual death, which is the result of Adam's sin, which Paul speaks of when he says, 'In Adam all die'.

Total depravity

Spiritual death is the total spiritual, moral corruption, and defilement of human nature. The Word of God gives us only a very brief account of what happened to Adam after the fall. Perhaps that is because he was very quickly recovered from it by the grace of God, who brought him to life, repentance, and faith by his irresistible power, and gave him a higher, nobler standing in Christ than he had before he fell.

Immediately after the fall, God sought Adam out, called him by his grace, and promised a Saviour, the Seed of the woman, by whom he and all elect sinners would be recovered from all sin. Because these things happened so quickly after the fall, we are not informed about all the mischief, misery, and madness Adam experienced as a result of his sin in spiritual death. However, some of the sad effects of the fall are clearly revealed in the Word of God. Here are seven things involved in the spiritual death of the human race, seven sad consequences of Adam's sin.

1. Corruption

The first sad consequence of Adam's fall upon himself and us is the utter corruption and depravity of the entire human race. As soon as he sinned, man who was made upright became unrighteous, filled with unrighteousness, and wickedness, and every abomination. Therefore, the Apostle tells us, 'There is none righteous, no not one'. This corruption of nature was signified by nakedness (Genesis 3:7).

This was more than a physical nakedness. Adam and Eve were physically naked before the fall. This is a nakedness of their souls before God, a nakedness which came upon them by their sin. This nakedness of soul is our lack of righteousness, our lack of clothing before God. The nakedness of their bodies became now an emblem of corruption and guilt before God.

As Adam immediately tried, by the works of his hands, to cover his nakedness, so every man and woman, since we became sinners, is utterly self-righteous by nature. Every sinner goes about to establish his own righteousness, and refuses to submit to the righteousness of God in Christ, until God strips him of his imaginary righteousness and exposes his naked corruption. 'It is as natural to man', wrote John Gill, 'to be self-righteous as to be sinful'. Yet, all that men do to attain righteousness by their own works is of no more significance than Adam's fig leaves. Nothing can cover us from the sight of Divine justice, nothing can shelter us from the stormy winds of Divine wrath, nothing can justify us in the sight of God, nothing can entitle us to eternal life, except the blood and righteousness of the Son of God. The first consequence of sin, the first thing involved in spiritual death is corruption.

2. Guilt

The second aspect of spiritual death is guilt. It was a guilt of conscience that made Adam and Eve perceive their nakedness. Guilt is the universal consequence of sin. Guilt is not something imposed by society. Guilt is the imposition of God upon the consciences of sinners. The consciousness of guilt causes shame. It causes men and women, like Adam and Eve, to hide themselves from God. Sometimes, guilt becomes altogether intolerable. It will drive impenitent sinners to utter insanity. Yet, even that is better than having a conscience so seared that it no longer accuses and condemns for sin. That sinner whose conscience is utterly seared is reprobate and damned, even while he lives.

3. Fear

A third thing involved in spiritual death, a third consequence of sin, is fear, the slavish fear and dread of God. There is in every man by nature a fearful looking for of judgment and righteous indignation, even in the most brazen of sinners. Adam said to God, 'I was afraid, because I was naked; and I hid myself'.

He hid himself, but to no purpose. There is no fleeing from the presence of God. Darkness and light are the same to him. How silly it was for Adam to try to hide behind the shade of a tree from the all-seeing eye of the omniscient God! Yet this is exactly what all men try to do (Amos 9:2-3). Even when judgment comes, men and women will still try to hide from God. When their fig leaves of self-righteousness are torn away, they will try to hide in the rocks and mountains. So utterly devoid of life and light is fallen man that even the great white throne judgment will do nothing to change his nature (Matthew 7:22-23; Revelation 6:15-17).

4. Ignorance

Corruption, guilt, and fear are common traits of spiritual death. Another characteristic of spiritual death is ignorance, spiritual ignorance. The natural man does not understand anything spiritual (John 3:3; Romans 3:11; 1 Corinthians 2:14). No man by nature knows or can know God the Father, his Son Christ Jesus, or the Spirit of grace. No man knows, or can know by any natural power, the way of life, salvation, and peace. The natural man, no matter how religious and well trained, can never even see, much less enter into, the kingdom of God (John 3:3-7).

Spiritually speaking, all men and women are more ignorant than brute beasts. Man is like a wild ass's colt by nature in his rebellion, but far more ignorant. Even the ass knows his master's crib. Man by nature is like the ox, strongly plowing the fields of iniquity, but again more ignorant. Even the ox knows his owner. Even wild birds know the time of their coming and going; but no man knows the Lord God, or his ways, either of grace or of judgment. Therefore, as the horse rushes to battle, so man rushes on in sin to judgment and to hell (Job 11:12; Isaiah 1:3; Jeremiah 8:6-7).

5. Banishment

The fifth thing involved in spiritual death is banishment, banishment from God, banishment from good, banishment from life (Genesis 3:24). This banishment was, as John Gill put it, 'an emblem of that alienation from God, from the life of God, and communion with him, which sin has produced, and which has set man at a distance from God. Hence Christ suffered to bring his people near unto him; and by his blood they that were afar off were made nigh unto God'.

6. Condemnation

Spiritual death involves condemnation. As soon as Adam and Eve became sinners they were brought under the curse and condemnation of God's holy law. Not only shall fallen man be cursed and condemned forever in hell, he is cursed and condemned even now, universally cursed. Everything he is and everything he does is cursed. Even the plowing of the wicked is an abomination to the Lord (Genesis 3:16-19; Deuteronomy 25:15-18).

7. Inability

In addition to all these things, corruption, guilt, fear, ignorance, banishment, and condemnation must be added inability. Man's spiritual death and total depravity has brought him into a state and condition of utter and total helplessness and inability. There is nothing a man can do to change his condition. He has neither the will nor the ability to alter his condition.

There is in fallen humanity a general corruption and depravity of all the powers and faculties of the soul, which are all immersed in sin, and full of it. All the members of the body are willingly yielded as instruments of unrighteousness. There is in us all a propensity and proneness to all that is sinful, an inordinate desire after the lusts of the flesh and of fulfilling them. We all by nature serve our lusts and pleasures. We serve our lusts as our highest pleasures by nature, because we are all by nature lovers of sinful pleasures more than lovers of God.

There is, also, a terrible disinclination to all that is good, and an utter aversion to it. We all hate good and love evil. Indeed, the carnal mind is enmity against God and all that is good.

Moreover, there is an impotency, an inability to do that which is good; hence man is represented as being without strength, having lost it, and become unable to do anything that is spiritually good. He can sin with a high hand and a willing heart; but no man can, of his own accord and by his own power, cease from sin, repent of sin, and believe on the Lord Jesus Christ.

Sin has brought the entire human race into a state of slavery to sin, Satan, and the world. This is what we commonly call the corruption and depravity of nature. This is the effect of the first sin of Adam. This is the proverbial 'Pandora's box' from whence have sprung all spiritual maladies and bodily diseases. All the disasters, distresses, mischief, and calamities, that are, or have been in the world, are the result of sin.

Man's only hope

The only hope of salvation and deliverance from this state and condition of spiritual death is the free grace of God in Christ, the last Adam. 'For as in Adam all die, even so in Christ shall all be made alive' (1 Corinthians 15:22). As sin and death came by the doing and dying of the first representative man, Adam, so righteousness and life come to God's elect by the doing and dying of the second and last representative man, the Lord Jesus Christ, the second Adam (Psalm 69:1-4). Salvation comes to sinners by grace alone, by the free, sovereign, unconditional grace of God in Christ (1 Corinthians 1:30-31; Colossians 2:9-10). Here is the wisdom, grace, and goodness of God. He permitted the sin and fall of our father Adam, that we might be saved by the work of Christ, the last Adam, to the praise of the glory of his grace!

'The fool hath said in his heart, There is no God. They are corrupt, they have done abominable works, there is none that doeth good. The LORD looked down from heaven upon the children of men, to see if there were any that did understand, and seek God. They are all gone aside, they are all together become filthy: there is none that doeth good, no, not one'. (Psalm 14:1-3)

Chapter 24

Total Depravity

'The fool hath said in his heart, There is no God'. You will notice that the words 'there is' are italicized in the King James translation. That indicates that the words were added by the translators to make the passage read more smoothly. However, in this case, the added words are a detriment rather than a help. The text should not read, 'The fool hath said in his heart, There is no God', but simply, 'The fool hath said in his heart, No, God', or 'The fool hath said in his heart, No, to God'.

If David had said, 'The fool hath said in his heart, There is no God', that would be a direct contradiction of Paul's teaching in Romans 1 and 2. There the Apostle tells us plainly that there is no such thing as an atheist. There are many fools who would like to be atheists, and try to be. But all who claim to be atheists are liars. The

Apostle Paul, writing by Divine inspiration, tells us that all men are born with a God consciousness from which they can never escape.

Thus when David writes, 'The fool hath said in his heart, No, God', or 'No, to God', he is not suggesting that some men really are atheists. Not at all. David is telling us that all men are foolish rebels by nature, constantly shaking their fists in God's face and saying, 'No, God!' Read Psalm 14:1-3 again. You will see that what I have said about David's opening statement in the Psalm fits the context in which it is found. 'The fool hath said in his heart, No, God! They are corrupt, they have done abominable works, there is none that doeth good. The Lord looked down from heaven upon the children of men, to see if there were any that did understand, and seek God. They are all gone aside, they are all together become filthy: there is none that doeth good, no, not one'.

In these three verses, the Holy Spirit describes the character and condition of all human beings by nature since the fall of Adam. Here are seven facts about the entire human race.

1. All human beings are, by nature, rebellious fools, fools for their rebellion, for man's rebellion is against God almighty!
2. The whole human race is corrupt, abominable, and filthy before God.
3. We all became corrupt, abominable, and filthy at one time by Adam's one act of rebellion and treason against God.
4. We all, at one time, turned away from God. In the fall of our father Adam we wilfully, deliberately turned away from our God.
5. Because of Adam's sin and our sin in him, the entire human race has become totally ignorant of all things spiritual. 'There is none that understandeth!'
6. No one left to himself will ever truly seek the Lord. 'There is none that seeketh after God'. And,
7. No one has the ability to do anything that is good and acceptable before the holy Lord God. 'There is none that doeth good, no, not one'.

A Bible doctrine

Thus the Spirit of God tells us that man is, by nature, a totally depraved, helpless, perishing creature. Holy scripture teaches the doctrine of man's total depravity, from beginning to end, and teaches it so plainly that error concerning this doctrine is utterly inexcusable. We take our doctrine directly from the Word of God. I remind you again that the basis of our faith is the Word of God alone. We do not build our doctrine upon human opinion, reason, and logic, church tradition, historic creeds, confessions, and catechisms, or denominational history and tradition, but upon 'Thus saith the Lord'. All that we believe we believe because it is plainly stated in the Word of God. Does the Bible clearly and plainly teach that all the human race is totally depraved? I appeal to no authority except the Word of God. I want you to see and hear what God says in his holy Word about this subject.

– Genesis 6:5 'And God saw that the wickedness of man was great in the earth, and that every imagination of the thoughts of his heart was only evil continually'.
– Job 15:16 'How much more abominable and filthy is man, which drinketh iniquity like water?'
– Psalm 51:5 'Behold, I was shapen in iniquity, and in sin did my mother conceive me'.
– Psalm 58:3 'The wicked are estranged from the womb: they go astray as soon as they be born, speaking lies'.
– Isaiah 1:4-6 'Ah sinful nation, a people laden with iniquity, a seed of evildoers, children that are corrupters: they have forsaken the LORD, they have provoked the Holy One of Israel unto anger, they are gone away backward. Why should ye be stricken any more? Ye will revolt more and more: the whole head is sick, and the whole heart faint. From the sole of the foot even unto the head there is no soundness in it; but wounds, and bruises, and putrifying sores: they have not been closed, neither bound up, neither mollified with ointment'.

– Isaiah 53:6 'All we like sheep have gone astray; we have turned every one to his own way; and the LORD hath laid on him the iniquity of us all'.

– Jeremiah 13:23 'Can the Ethiopian change his skin, or the leopard his spots? then may ye also do good, that are accustomed to do evil'.

– Jeremiah 17:9 'The heart is deceitful above all things, and desperately wicked: who can know it?'

– Matthew 15:19-20 'For out of the heart proceed evil thoughts, murders, adulteries, fornications, thefts, false witness, blasphemies: These are the things which defile a man: but to eat with unwashen hands defileth not a man'.

– Romans 3:9-12 'What then? are we better than they? No, in no wise: for we have before proved both Jews and Gentiles, that they are all under sin; As it is written, There is none righteous, no, not one: There is none that understandeth, there is none that seeketh after God. They are all gone out of the way, they are together become unprofitable; there is none that doeth good, no, not one'.

– Romans 3:23 'For all have sinned, and come short of the glory of God'.

– Romans 5:12 'Wherefore, as by one man sin entered into the world, and death by sin; and so death passed upon all men, for that all have sinned'.

– 1 Corinthians 2:14 'But the natural man receiveth not the things of the Spirit of God: for they are foolishness unto him: neither can he know them, because they are spiritually discerned'.

– Ephesians 2:1-3 'And you hath he quickened, who were dead in trespasses and sins: Wherein in time past ye walked according to the course of this world, according to the prince of the power of the air, the spirit that now worketh in the children of disobedience: Among whom also we all had our conversation in times past in the lusts of our flesh, fulfilling the desires of the flesh and of the mind; and were by nature the children of wrath, even as others'.

– John 3:19 'And this is the condemnation, that light is come into the world, and men loved darkness rather than light, because their deeds were evil'.

These fifteen passages of holy scripture are but a very few of the many, many statements in God's Word about the total depravity of the entire human race. They stand without comment, declaring that all men are by nature totally depraved. To deny what these texts declare is to deny the Word of God. To argue against the doctrine of total depravity is to be found fighting against God himself.

This is the doctrine of holy scripture: All human beings are, since the fall of Adam, born in a state of total depravity, lost, corrupt at heart, condemned under the curse of God's holy law, and utterly incapable of removing that curse or changing their condition. In fact, as we shall see, man's depravity is so thorough and complete that he cannot even make any contribution toward removing the curse of the law, or changing his condition. Fallen man cannot even make a move toward God, much less bring himself back to God!

I want to be crystal clear in stating the doctrine of man's total depravity. Unless we have a clear understanding of man's utter depravity, we cannot have a clear understanding about any other gospel truth.

A fallen creature

Man, by nature, is a fallen creature (Ecclesiastes 7:29). When the Lord God created our father Adam, things were far, far different from the way they are now. God created Adam in perfect righteousness. He had no original sin. He had no inclination or bias toward sin. God placed Adam in a perfectly sinless environment in the garden.

By God's decree, Adam was the federal head and representative of the entire human race. God deals with all men in only two men: the first Adam and the last Adam (1 Corinthians 15:22, 45-49). When the Lord put Adam in the Garden, whatever Adam did would be imputed to all who are in him by nature. If Adam obeyed God, his righteous obedience would be confirmed and imputed to all his children. If Adam disobeyed God and broke the covenant, his sin would be imputed to all his children.

Our father, Adam, sinned against God, broke his covenant, and plunged himself and the entire human race into spiritual death, sin, and everlasting condemnation (Genesis 2:15-17; Romans 5:12-19). That is what we have seen in the last three chapters. Man by nature is a fallen creature. 'Wherefore, as by one man sin entered into the world, and death by sin; and so death passed upon all men, for that all have sinned'.

Biased toward evil

The Word of God plainly teaches us that all men, since the fall of Adam, are born with a decided bias toward evil, with an utter hatred of God (Mark 7:21-23; Romans 8:7). Sin is not a social disease. It is not something a man has to learn, or be taught. It is not something we catch from others. Sin is the inbred family disease of our race. It is a matter of the heart. Because our hearts are evil, we do evil. The evil tendencies of our hearts are guarded, restrained, and kept in check by many things. But the seeds of evil are in our hearts by nature. This is what our Lord tells us. All men, regardless of age, actions, or social standing, are vile, loathsome, and corrupt at heart. This must be evidently true to any reasonable man. History tells us that man is a depraved creature.

Who can read what men have done to men throughout history and even think about questioning the fact of man's depravity? Our daily newspapers tell us that man is depraved. Every newspaper in the world is a daily declaration of the fact that man is evil at heart. We see clear evidence of human depravity in our most darling children. What mother ever had to teach her child to lie, cheat, be selfish, or disobedient? Every man's conscience testifies of his depravity. Where is the man, or woman, who would want the world to know what he thinks? Every true believer has a constant painful reminder of human depravity in his own heart. Believers are a people who readily and painfully confess, 'In my flesh dwelleth no good thing!' Man is not good, but evil at heart. This world is what it is because man is what he is, sinful, depraved, and vile.

Utterly helpless

We are as utterly helpless as we are depraved. No one has the ability to save himself by his own works (Galatians 2:16). Loraine Boettner wrote: 'This doctrine of total inability, which declares that men are dead in sin, does not mean that all men are equally bad, nor that any man is as bad as he could be, nor that anyone is entirely destitute of virtue, nor that human nature is evil in itself ... What it does mean is that since the fall, man rests under the curse of sin, that he is actuated by wrong principles, and that he is wholly unable to love God or to do anything meriting salvation'.

It is impossible for anyone to be saved by works, because God demands perfection, and we cannot give it. God demands atonement, satisfaction for sin, but we cannot give it. We cannot change the principles of our heart. The very best that we do is marred by sin. Even in performing our best works, we are motivated and guided by the principles of a sinful heart, so that the very plowing of the wicked is an abomination to God, and our very righteousnesses are filthy rags in his sight. Even our holy things are full of evil (Proverbs 21:4; Isaiah 64:6; Exodus 28:38).

Incapable of faith

According to the plain statements of holy scripture, no one has the will or the ability to come to Christ by faith (John 5:40; 6:44). This is the real issue at hand. Modern day religion, for the most part, professes to believe in original sin and total depravity. Very few people openly teach that man can save himself by his own works. Yet, most people do teach that man by nature does have the ability to come to Christ and be saved, that he has the ability in himself, by his own free will, to believe on Christ.

By such teachings, they make salvation to rest ultimately upon man's free will. According to the commonly received heresy, man's free will makes the blood of Christ effectual, man's free will controls the operations of God, and man's free will determines who shall populate heaven.

The Bible declares that man is not only morally depraved and sinful, but that he is also spiritually impotent, unwilling and incapable of coming to Christ by faith. The Lord Jesus Christ says, 'Ye will not come to me, that ye might have life' (John 5:40). 'No man can come to me except the Father which hath sent me draw him' (John 6:44). He also declares that if the Father draws a man, that man will come to him; and he says, 'I will raise him up at the last day'.

In the scriptures the idea of 'coming to Christ', simply means believing on him. C. H. Spurgeon said, 'It is used to express those acts of the soul wherein, leaving at once our self-righteousness and our sins, we fly unto the Lord Jesus Christ, and receive his righteousness to be our covering and his blood to be our atonement'.

Today we are told that coming to Christ is the easiest thing in all the world. But here our Lord himself tells us that it is utterly and entirely impossible for any man to come to Christ, unless the Father draws him by effectual and irresistible grace. Man by nature is spiritually impotent, and helpless, utterly without strength. Indeed, man is altogether dead spiritually. Man's inability does not lie in any physical defect. Man's inability is not a lack of mental power. I am just as capable of believing on Christ mentally as I am of believing in Abraham Lincoln. The mind is just as capable of seeing the moral guilt of sin as it is of seeing the moral guilt of murder. Man's inability lies deep within his nature. A wolf cannot be domesticated and tamed into a trusted Peter. A loving mother cannot stab her nursing baby to death. She has no ability to do so, because it is contrary to her nature. Similarly, no man can ever come to Christ of his own accord, because of the obstinacy of the human will.

The Arminian, the will worshipper, cries, 'Any man can be saved who will'. That is certainly true. But it is not the issue. The issue is this: Are men ever found naturally willing to submit to the humbling terms of the gospel of Christ? The Son of God answers that question with an emphatic, 'No!' The human will is so desperately set on evil, so thoroughly depraved, so inclined toward evil, and so disinclined toward good, that without the powerful, supernatural, irresistible grace and call of God the Holy Spirit, no human being will ever come to Christ by faith.

No man will ever, of his own accord, come to Christ, because his understanding is darkened (John 3:3). He cannot see the exceeding evil of his own heart. He cannot see the strict justice of God's law. He cannot see the glory of electing grace. He cannot see the glory of our Lord's incarnation. He cannot see the glory of Christ's obedience unto righteousness. He cannot see the glory of Christ's substitutionary redemption. He cannot see the glory of Christ's intercession.

No man will ever, of his own accord, come to Christ, because his affections are corrupt. We love what we ought to hate. We hate what we ought to love. 'Men love darkness rather than light'.

No man will ever come to Christ of his own voluntary accord, without the power of God, because his conscience is depraved. Conscience may tell me that such and such a thing is wrong. But how wrong it is conscience does not know. The unenlightened conscience of man will never tell him that he deserves eternal damnation, that he must abhor himself, that he must have a perfect righteousness, or that he must have a perfect atonement.

It is true that men will not, and it is true that men cannot, by their own power, come to Christ, 'No man can come'. Man by nature is dead, spiritually dead. Certainly, if words mean anything, that means that man is without any spiritual power or ability whatsoever. If it is true that the Holy Spirit only gives me a *will* to come to Christ, and that the *power* to come is mine, then certainly I would have a right to share in the glory of my salvation.

Because man is guilty of sin, and because he sinfully refuses to believe on Christ, he remains under the wrath of God, and eternal damnation will be his just reward. But I cannot conclude this study with such a sad and gloomy picture. It is a terribly black scene that I have set before you. Man by nature is fallen. Our hearts are evil. Our works are evil. We are spiritually impotent. We are justly condemned. Yet, there is a bright ray of hope for such creatures as we are.

One hope

The only hope for fallen, guilty, depraved, helpless, and vile sinners, such as we are, is the free and sovereign grace of God in Christ. If salvation depends in any measure upon you or me, all hope is gone. But since it is entirely the work of God's free and sovereign grace in Christ, there is hope even for fallen, helpless sinners. God says, 'I will have mercy on whom I will have mercy, and I will have compassion on whom I will have compassion. So then it is not of him that willeth, nor of him that runneth, but of God that sheweth mercy' (Romans 9:15-16).

This is what God does for sinners by his sovereign, eternal grace. He chose to save a great multitude from Adam's fallen race. He determined to save his elect people by the sacrifice of his Son. He sent his Son into the world to accomplish eternal redemption for us. He sends his Spirit to regenerate his chosen people and effectually calls them to Christ in faith. He gives life to the dead. He convicts (convinces) chosen, redeemed sinners of sin pardoned, righteousness brought in, and judgment finished by the obedience and blood of Christ. He reveals Christ. He causes the awakened sinner, by the power of his irresistible grace, to come to Christ, saying, ...

> Could my tears forever flow,
> Could my zeal no respite know,
> All for sin could not atone,
> Thou must save and thou alone.
>
> Augustus Toplady

No man has any claim upon the grace of God. Any sinner who will come to Christ may freely come. All who come to Christ in true faith acknowledge most gladly that they were constrained to come. We who have been constrained by almighty, irresistible grace into the arms of Christ, do most gladly acknowledge and praise him for his matchless, free grace. The whole work of salvation, from start to finish, is due entirely to the grace of God.

All that I was, my sin, my guilt,
My death was all my own:
All that I am, I owe to Thee,
My gracious God, alone.

The evil of my former state,
Was mine, and only mine:
The good in which I now rejoice,
Is Thine, and only Thine.

The darkness of my former state,
The bondage – All was mine:
The light of life in which I walk,
The liberty is Thine.

The grace that made me feel my sin,
It taught me to believe:
Then, in believing, peace I found,
And now I live, I live!

All that I am, even here on earth,
All that I hope to be,
When Jesus comes, and glory dawns,
I owe it, Lord, to Thee!

In the light of these things, every believer rejoices to declare, 'By the grace of God I am what I am ... Not unto us, O Lord, not unto us, but unto thy name give glory, for thy mercy, and for thy truth's sake'. Amen.

'Knowing, brethren beloved, your election of God'.
(1 Thessalonians 1:4)

Chapter 25

Election

When the Apostle Paul wrote to the church at Thessalonica, he spoke confidently to God's saints there about the indisputable fact of their election. He said, 'Knowing, brethren beloved, your election of God'. Paul gave thanks to God for them, for their faith in Christ, for their love to one another, and for the other manifold blessings of God's grace upon them, because he knew that all these things must be traced to their election unto salvation by God.

This blessed, glorious, gospel doctrine of election is one of the most delightful doctrines of the gospel. Believers rejoice in it. In this study, we will simply go through the Word of God, observing the fact that the Bible teaches the doctrine of election, what the Bible teaches about election, and who God's elect people are. Because there is so much needless controversy among men about this subject, let me make three practical statements, by way of introduction, which I trust will help clarify some things for you.

1. Election is not the first thing to be learned

Precious, delightful, important as this doctrine is, it is not the first thing to be learned. We preach this doctrine without apology. I preach it everywhere I go. We teach it in our Sunday School classes, beginning with the toddlers. We are not, in the least bashful about proclaiming God's electing love. However, it is not our mission in this world to convince people that the doctrine of election is true. A person can go to hell believing election as well as he can go to hell denying it. Our mission is to get sinners to believe, trust, and come to the Lord Jesus Christ. Any sinner who bows to Christ as Lord will have no problem with the doctrine of election.

The first question to be settled in your heart and mind is not, 'Am I one of the elect?' It is impossible for anyone to determine that until the matter of first importance is settled. 'Do I trust the Lord Jesus Christ?' 'Am I a believer?' That is the matter of first importance. As I will show you in this study, if you trust the Son of God, if you, as a poor, helpless, guilty, bankrupt sinner, trust Christ alone as your Saviour and Lord, your faith in him is the proof of your election. The first thing to be learned is faith in Christ. Where faith is found in the heart, election is believed and loved.

2. God's sovereign election of some to salvation and eternal life in Christ is in no way inconsistent with the promises of God in the gospel

Let men say what they will, all the promises of God in Christ Jesus are yea and amen. You may not be able to see how election can be true and the promises of the gospel to sinners are also true; but they are.

Hear the promises God makes to sinners in the gospel. Come to Christ, whoever you are, believe on Christ, whatever you have done, trust the Son of God and these promises are yours!

– Matthew 11:28-30 'Come unto me, all ye that labour and are heavy laden, and I will give you rest. Take my yoke upon you, and learn of me; for I am meek and lowly in heart: and ye shall find rest unto your souls. For my yoke is easy, and my burden is light'.
– Mark 16:16 'He that believeth and is baptized shall be saved; but he that believeth not shall be damned'.

– John 3:36 'He that believeth on the Son hath everlasting life: and he that believeth not the Son shall not see life; but the wrath of God abideth on him'.

– John 6:37 'All that the Father giveth me shall come to me; and him that cometh to me I will in no wise cast out'.

– John 7:37-38 'In the last day, that great day of the feast, Jesus stood and cried, saying, If any man thirst, let him come unto me, and drink. He that believeth on me, as the scripture hath said, out of his belly shall flow rivers of living water'.

– Acts 16:31 'And they said, Believe on the Lord Jesus Christ, and thou shalt be saved, and thy house'.

– Romans 10:8-13 'But what saith it? The word is nigh thee, even in thy mouth, and in thy heart: that is, the word of faith, which we preach; That if thou shalt confess with thy mouth the Lord Jesus, and shalt believe in thine heart that God hath raised him from the dead, thou shalt be saved. For with the heart man believeth unto righteousness; and with the mouth confession is made unto salvation. For the scripture saith, Whosoever believeth on him shall not be ashamed. For there is no difference between the Jew and the Greek: for the same Lord over all is rich unto all that call upon him. For whosoever shall call upon the name of the Lord shall be saved'.

– Revelation 22:16-17 'I Jesus have sent mine angel to testify unto you these things in the churches. I am the root and the offspring of David, and the bright and morning star. And the Spirit and the bride say, Come. And let him that heareth say, Come. And let him that is athirst come. And whosoever will, let him take the water of life freely'.

3. God's election, this gospel doctrine of sovereign electing grace, does not, to any degree or in any way, remove or destroy your responsibility to obey the gospel

God commands all men, everywhere to repent (Acts 17:30). Our responsibility is not derived from the decree of God, but from the Word of God. We are not responsible for what God has purposed;

but we are responsible for what he has commanded. We are all responsible to be perfectly holy; we cannot do it. We are responsible to make complete atonement for our sins; but we cannot provide it. We are responsible to believe on and trust the Lord Jesus Christ as our only righteousness and our only redemption; we cannot even do that. We are, therefore, shut up to God's sovereign grace in Christ.

I want to show you from the Word of God that election is God's sovereign, eternal choice and purpose of grace toward his people in Christ, by which their salvation was secured and guaranteed before the world began. In order to accomplish that purpose, let me raise and answer three questions.

Does the Bible teach the doctrine of election?

The very first matter to be settled is this: does the Word of God teach the doctrine of election? If the Bible teaches it, believers bow to it, believe it, and rejoice in it. We do not have and do not want to have the option of believing what we want to believe. We believe God. If the Word of God teaches this doctrine, it matters not who opposes it, all believers bow to it. If God does not teach this doctrine in his Word, then we must reject it and denounce it, no matter who believes it, no matter who teaches it.

I ask only that you read the Word of God. Let God speak for himself. Let God be true, and every man a liar. This is the question – Does the Bible teach election? I will not attempt to show you this doctrine in the Old Testament, though it is written upon every page of it. Adam had two sons. God chose one and passed by the other. There were untold millions on the earth in Noah's day; but Noah alone found grace in the eyes of the Lord. Abraham had two sons. God chose one and passed by the other. God chose the nation of Israel to be his peculiar people, and passed by all the other nations of the world. God gave his law to Israel alone, sent his prophets (with rare exception) to Israel alone, and established his worship in Israel alone. It will suffice for us to begin in the book of Matthew and simply read some of what the New Testament says about election.

I have selected only those passages of scripture where the very words elect, elected, election, chosen, and ordained are used. I deliberately left out those numerous texts where the doctrine of election is only, by necessity, implied. In the following texts it is plainly stated by divine inspiration!

– Matthew 24:24 'For there shall arise false Christs, and false prophets, and shall show great signs and wonders; insomuch that, if it were possible, they shall deceive the very elect'.

– Matthew 24:31 'And he shall send his angels with a great sound of a trumpet, and they shall gather together his elect from the four winds, from one end of heaven to the other'.

– Mark 13:20 'And except that the Lord had shortened those days, no flesh should be saved: but for the elect's sake, whom he hath chosen, he hath shortened the days'.

– John 13:18 'I speak not of you all: I know whom I have chosen: but that the scripture may be fulfilled, He that eateth bread with me hath lifted up his heel against me'.

– John 15:16 'Ye have not chosen me, but I have chosen you, and ordained you, that ye should go and bring forth fruit, and that your fruit should remain: that whatsoever ye shall ask of the Father in my name, he may give it you'.

– Acts 13:48 'And when the Gentiles heard this, they were glad, and glorified the word of the Lord: and as many as were ordained to eternal life believed'.

– Romans 8:33 'Who shall lay any thing to the charge of God's elect? It is God that justifieth'.

– Romans 11:5 'Even so then at this present time also there is a remnant according to the election of grace'.

– Romans 11:7 'What then? Israel hath not obtained that which he seeketh for; but the election hath obtained it, and the rest were blinded'.

– Ephesians 1:4 'According as he hath chosen us in him before the foundation of the world, that we should be holy and without blame before him in love'.

– 1 Thessalonians 5:9 'For God hath not appointed us to wrath, but to obtain salvation by our Lord Jesus Christ'.

– 2 Thessalonians 2:13 'But we are bound to give thanks alway to God for you, brethren beloved of the Lord, because God hath from the beginning chosen you to salvation through sanctification of the Spirit and belief of the truth'.

– 1 Timothy 2:10 'Therefore I endure all things for the elect's sakes, that they may also obtain the salvation which is in Christ Jesus with eternal glory'.

– Titus 1:1 'Paul, a servant of God, and an apostle of Jesus Christ, according to the faith of God's elect, and the acknowledging of the truth which is after godliness'.

– 1 Peter 1:2 'Elect according to the foreknowledge of God the Father, through sanctification of the Spirit, unto obedience and sprinkling of the blood of Jesus Christ: Grace unto you, and peace, be multiplied'.

– 1 Peter 2:9 'But ye are a chosen generation, a royal priesthood, an holy nation, a peculiar people; that ye should show forth the praises of him who hath called you out of darkness into his marvellous light'.

– 1 Peter 5:13 'The church that is at Babylon, elected together with you, saluteth you; and so doth Marcus my son'.

The Word of God makes no attempt to explain how God can be righteous and just in showing mercy to whom he will, while passing by whom he will. Rather than answering such carping objections from unbelieving men, the Apostle Paul simply says, God does things this way because God has determined to do things this way.

– Romans 9:11-23 '(For the children being not yet born, neither having done any good or evil, that the purpose of God according to election might stand, not of works, but of him that calleth;) It was said unto her, The elder shall serve the younger. As it is written, Jacob have I loved, but Esau have I hated. What shall we say then? Is there unrighteousness with God? God forbid. For he saith to

Moses, I will have mercy on whom I will have mercy, and I will have compassion on whom I will have compassion. So then it is not of him that willeth, nor of him that runneth, but of God that sheweth mercy. For the scripture saith unto Pharaoh, Even for this same purpose have I raised thee up, that I might show my power in thee, and that my name might be declared throughout all the earth. Therefore hath he mercy on whom he will have mercy, and whom he will he hardeneth. Thou wilt say then unto me, Why doth he yet find fault? For who hath resisted his will? Nay but, O man, who art thou that repliest against God? Shall the thing formed say to him that formed it, Why hast thou made me thus? Hath not the potter power over the clay, of the same lump to make one vessel unto honour, and another unto dishonour? What if God, willing to show his wrath, and to make his power known, endured with much longsuffering the vessels of wrath fitted to destruction: And that he might make known the riches of his glory on the vessels of mercy, which he had afore prepared unto glory'.

The book of God teaches the glorious, gospel doctrine of election. No honest person can question that fact. Any who denies that the Bible teaches this doctrine is either totally ignorant of the Word of God or a liar. Either way, such a person has no business trying to teach others. As it is obvious that the scriptures teach this doctrine, the second question to be answered is this.

What does the Word of God teach about election?
Keep in mind the things we have already read in the Word of God. Here are eleven things expressly taught in the Word of God about election.
1. Election is 'in Christ'.
2. Election is 'unto salvation'.
3. Election is an act of God's pure, absolute, sovereignty.
4. Election took place in eternity.
5. The source and cause of election is God's love for his people.
6. God's election was an act of free, unconditional grace.

7. Election is God's personal choice of specific sinners to eternal life in Christ.

8. Election is irreversible.

9. Election is effectual.

10. Election is distinguishing (Isaiah 43:1-4).

11. Election is blessed, for it is the cause of all blessedness (Psalm 65:4; Ephesians 1:3-6; 1 Corinthians 4:7).

Now, go to 1 Thessalonians chapter one; and let me show you the answer to one final question.

Who are the elect?

No mere man can open and read the Lamb's Book of Life. No mortal can ever know who the elect are until they are regenerated and called by God the Holy Spirit. However, each of us can prove our own selves. We can make our calling and election sure. In 1 Thessalonians, the Apostle Paul, writing by Divine inspiration tells us that he knew these men and women in the Church there were elect, chosen of God, and precious by five distinct marks of grace upon them. If you are one of God's elect, these five marks are upon you. If I am one of the elect, these marks are upon me. Who are God's elect? Look into the Word of God and see. There is no guesswork here.

1. God's elect are people who hear the Gospel preached and receive the Gospel as it is preached in the power of God the Holy Spirit. The elect are those who are called by the effectual, irresistible power and grace of God the Holy Spirit (1 Thessalonians 1:5).

2. God's elect are those who follow Christ. Chosen sinners, when saved by the grace of God, are made disciples, followers of Christ, voluntary servants of King Jesus (1 Thessalonians 1:3, 6).

3. God's elect are a people who are committed to Christ and the gospel of his grace (1 Thessalonians 1:8).

4. God's elect experience repentance and conversion by the power of his grace. They turn from their idols to serve the living God (1 Thessalonians 1:9).

5. God's elect are waiting for Christ (1 Thessalonians 1:10).

'Behold, what manner of love the Father hath bestowed upon us, that we should be called the sons of God: therefore the world knoweth us not, because it knew him not'.
(1 John 3:1)

Chapter 26

Adoption

We rejoice to know that 'God is love!' Love is an attribute of his holy Being, without which he would not be God. We know that God is love because his love is revealed and made known by his deeds. Love is active. It is never dormant. Like fire, it must break out. It cannot be contained. It is known only when it is experienced, not by words, but by deeds. We know the love of God is that love that 'passeth knowledge'. Yet, God's love is revealed and made known by these six deeds of indescribable love.

The first act of God's love was our election in Christ (Deuteronomy 7:7-8). Election is not a hard doctrine. It is a delightful doctrine. Were it not for God's electing love toward sinners, there would be no salvation (Ephesians 1:4; 2 Thessalonians 2:13). We would never have come to know and love Christ had he not first loved us (John 15:16; 1 John 4:19).

The second act of God's love was our redemption by Christ (Romans 5:8; 1 John 3:16; 4:9-10). 'Greater love hath no man than this, that a man lay down his life for his friends!'

> This was compassion like a God,
> That when our Saviour knew –
> The price of pardon was his blood,
> His love he ne'er withdrew!

Because he loved us, the Son of God assumed our nature, assumed our sin, assumed our guilt and died under the wrath of God as our Substitute, to put away our sins. 'The Son of God loved me and gave himself for me!'

The third act by which God reveals his love to sinners is his effectual saving grace (Jeremiah 31:3). Those whom the triune God loved, the Father chose to save. Those whom the Father chose to save, the Son redeemed. And those whom the Son redeemed, the Holy Spirit will effectually call by his irresistible grace to life and faith in Christ. 'Blessed is the man whom thou choosest and causest to approach unto thee' (Psalm 65:4).

The love of God is revealed fourthly in the absolute preservation of his elect in a state of grace (John 10:28; Romans 8:39). Can you imagine one who is loved of God falling from a state of grace, perishing and suffering the wrath of God forever in hell? Such a notion is worse than nonsense, it is utter blasphemy! The love of God is without cause, without beginning, without condition, without change, and without end. It is free. It is discriminating. It is indestructible. It is everlasting.

Fifthly, God's love for his elect is seen in our Saviour's tender, providential care for us (John 11:35-36). Our God and Saviour really is touched with the feeling of our infirmities. We really are the apple of his eye.

But there is one act of love that goes beyond election, redemption, effectual calling, preservation, and providential care. Great and marvellous as those things are, there is one act of God that goes beyond them all. If the climax of God's love is our redemption by Christ, the apex of God's love is our adoption into the family of God (1 John 3:1-3). By birth, we are all sons of Adam, fallen, depraved and spiritually dead (Romans 5:12). By our deeds, we show ourselves to be children of the devil, sinful, deceitful, and wicked (John 8:44). By nature, we are all children of wrath (Ephesians 1:3), a people deserving the wrath of God. By grace, we who believe are the sons of God!

> Sons we are through God's election,
> Who in Jesus Christ believe;
> By eternal destination,
> Sovereign grace we here receive!
>
> Every fallen soul, by sinning,
> Merits everlasting pain;
> But Thy love, without beginning,
> Has restored Thy sons again.
>
> Pause, my soul, adore and wonder!
> Ask, 'Oh why such love to me?'
> Grace hath put me in the number
> Of the Saviour's family!

Election is the great fountain of grace. Redemption is the greatest mystery of grace. Adoption is the greatest privilege of grace. 'Behold, what manner of love the Father hath bestowed upon us, that we should be called the sons of God: therefore the world knoweth us not, because it knew him not'.

Why has God adopted us into his family?
No reason can be found in all the Bible for God's adoption of sinners into his family except his own free love and sovereign will

(Ephesians 1:4-5). Adoption is experienced and known in time; but it began in eternity. We were not adopted into the family of God when he gave us his Spirit, but when he chose us and accepted us in the Beloved. He gives us his Spirit in regenerating grace, not to make us sons of God, but because we are the sons of God (Galatians 4:1-7). The only distinction there is between the children of God and the children of wrath is the distinguishing love and grace of God (1 Corinthians 4:7); and this distinction was made by God in eternity.

By what power do sinners become the sons of God?

Were it not for the perversions of religious tradition, this question would be redundant. Man, by nature, is enmity against God. He cannot become one of the sons of God because he chooses to be. No preacher has any power to make men the sons of God. No church has power to make men the sons of God. We certainly cannot make ourselves children of God by works we perform or by the exercise of our wills (Romans 9:16). The only power that can translate a sinner from the family of nature into the family of grace (Jeremiah 3:19) is the power of God (John 1:12-13). Adoption is God's work, and God's work alone. No child of Adam shall ever become a child of God, but by the choice, power, and grace of God.

What is the method of God's adoption?

We must never suggest, or imply, or imagine that God must do anything, or that he must do anything in a specific way. God is totally free and sovereign. He can do whatever he is pleased to do, and he can do it however he is pleased to do it. However, God has revealed his method of grace in adoption in his Word. 'As many as received him, to them gave he power to become the sons of God, even to them that believe on his name: Which were born, not of blood, nor of the will of the flesh, nor of the will of man, but of God'. (John 1:12-13). Here John tells us three things about God's method of grace in adoption.

1. The Lord God drops the life of grace into a person's soul (v. 13). Those adopted by grace in eternity are 'born of God' at the appointed time of love. This work of grace, the new birth, is God's work. The adoption of grace differs from civil adoption. God gives his sons his name and his nature. This gracious gift of God is altogether the work of his free and sovereign grace in Christ. Grace does not run in any mere man's family bloodline. It is not a family heirloom, passed from one generation to the next. It does not come through our parents' 'blood'. Grace does not come to sinners by the will of friends and relatives, 'the will of the flesh', no matter how sincere, earnest, and zealous.

Neither does the grace of God come to sinners by their own will, 'the will of men, but of God'. Grace and salvation, all the blessings and privileges of adoption, come to chosen sinners according to God's purpose of predestination by his power.

2. As soon as God drops life into the soul, the regenerate sinner receives Christ, believing on his name. To believe on his name, the name of 'the Lord Jesus Christ', is to receive him as Lord (Master), Redeemer, and Saviour. It is to bow to him as my rightful Sovereign and trust him for all righteousness, sanctification, and redemption before God.

3. As soon as a sinner trusts Christ, God gives him the right, the power, the authority, the privilege of being his child. This power, authority, and right of sonship is the assurance of sonship conferred upon believing sinners by the Holy Spirit. That person who trusts Christ alone as Saviour and Lord knows that he has the right in Christ to speak to God almighty as his heavenly Father. Adoption is given to faith and faith is the evidence of adoption (Hebrews 11:1).

Why are the children of God so misunderstood and misrepresented by the people of this world?

If you are born of God, if you trust the Lord Jesus Christ, if you live in this world as a child of God, the men and women of the world will never be able to know you. You will be misunderstood and misrepresented. Your doctrine, your devotion to Christ, your desires to serve and honour him, are all things which mere worldlings find confusing. The reason for this misunderstanding is quite simple. – 'Therefore, the world knoweth us not, because it knew him not'.

What are the blessed privileges of adoption?

I have already told you that the greatest privilege of grace is adoption. Now, let me show you that that statement is true. Being the sons of God, ours is a blessedness beyond comparison.

1. We have an assured interest in God's infinite, everlasting love (John 17:23-26).
2. We have the Spirit of God (Romans 8:14-16; Galatians 4:6). God the Holy Spirit has been given to us, bequeathed and bestowed upon us by Christ our Lord. He has been given specifically to comfort us by teaching us the things of Christ, and as the pledge of our heavenly inheritance with Christ.
3. As the children of God, we have been brought into the discipline of our Father's house (Hebrews 12:5-11). Our heavenly Father's chastening rod is a blessing of grace by which he proves, strengthens, and purifies our faith, and by which he graciously weans us from this world.
4. Being the children of God, we are assured of our ultimate, perfect conformity to the image of Christ (Romans 8:29).
5. Our adoption into the family of God makes us the heirs of God and joint-heirs with Christ (Romans 8:16-17). Our inheritance is an inheritance of grace, an inheritance of pure, free grace in Christ. We were predestined to it (Ephesians 1:11). Christ has purchased it and claimed it for us (Ephesians 1:14; Hebrews 6:20). Grace has made us worthy of it (Colossians 3:12). It shall be glorious (Revelation 7:16-17).

'For the law having a shadow of good things to come, and not the very image of the things, can never with those sacrifices which they offered year by year continually make the comers thereunto perfect'.
(Hebrews 10:1)

Chapter 27

Five Old Testament Pictures
of Redemption

The only hope for fallen, guilty, depraved sinners is redemption, a redemption which includes atonement for sin, satisfaction for justice, and effectual deliverance from the guilt, power, dominion, and consequences of sin. Such redemption could be accomplished by only one Person, the Lord Jesus Christ, the Son of God, our Saviour. Not only could he alone do it, he has done it; and he has done it alone (Isaiah 63:5).

When we consider the doctrine of redemption, we have come to the most important of all gospel truths. In our day, men more quickly attack the doctrine of the cross than any other. They more vehemently deny the glorious efficacy of Christ's sin-atoning blood than they do any other doctrine. Multitudes who sing with Cowper ...

Dear dying Lamb, Thy precious blood
Shall never lose its power,
'Til all the ransomed Church of God
Be saved to sin no more,

... assert with absolute dogmatism that there is no real saving power and efficacy in Christ's blood; for they declare that multitudes are in hell today for whom Christ died.

In Hebrews 10:1, the Holy Spirit declares that the law given in the Old Testament scriptures had a shadow of good things to come. That is to say, God, in the Old Testament, under the types and shadows of the law, gave many pictures and prophecies of what he would do for and give to his people through his Son, the Lord Jesus Christ. Among those many 'good things to come' by Christ, none is more excellent and blessed than redemption.

I have often heard Pastor Henry Mahan say, 'Any man who cannot preach the gospel from the Old Testament, simply does not know the gospel'. He is right. The sacrifices offered to God in the Old Testament could never take away one sin. However, the law did have many instructive pictures, types, and shadows of our redemption by the blood of Christ.

Three words used for redemption

Our English word, 'redemption', comes from the Latin and means 'to buy again'. If we are to grasp the meaning of the word 'redemption', it will be needful for me to refer to some Greek words. In the Greek New Testament three words are commonly used in reference to our redemption by Christ.

1. AGORADZO – The basic meaning of agoradzo is 'to buy'. You and I who believe have been bought unto God from among men by the blood of Christ (Revelation 5:9), bought from the earth, from among the fallen sons of Adam (Revelation 14:3-4), and bought with the price of Christ's blood (1 Corinthians 6:19). The church of God has been bought, purchased with his own blood (Acts 20:28). 'Agoradzo' is the word you would use to describe the purchase of a house. If you buy a house, you take ownership of it as a piece of property; but you do not move it. You simply own it.

2. EKAGORADZO – This is a compound word. 'Ek' means 'out of', and 'agoradzo' means 'bought'. 'Ekagoradzo' means 'bought out of'. God's elect have been bought out of the hands of God's offended justice by the blood of Christ, which satisfied the justice of God for us (Galatians 3:13; 4:5). This is the word we would use if we were talking about redeeming an item from the pawn shop, or buying groceries, or purchasing a car, or any other item that is both purchased and delivered from the possession of one into the possession of another. 'Ekagoradzo' has the idea of deliverance by the payment of a price. As it is used in the Word of God, it refers to the deliverance of God's elect from the hands of his offended justice and the curse of his holy law by the price paid by Christ at Calvary, the price of his precious blood.

3. LUTROO – 'Lutroo' means 'to set free', or 'to loose'. It is the word that would be used to describe the deliverance of a slave, or a prisoner from bondage and captivity by paying a ransom price for him. So Peter tells us that we have been redeemed, not with silver or gold, the usual price of ransom, but with the precious blood of Christ (1 Peter 1:18). Our Lord Jesus declares that he came into the world to give his life a ransom price for many (Matthew 20:28).

We should keep these three words in mind whenever we think about the redemptive work of Christ: 'agoradzo' – to buy; 'ekagoradzo' – to buy out of; and 'lutroo' – to deliver by ransom. The Lord Jesus Christ bought his people from among the fallen sons of Adam, out of the hands of God's offended justice, and delivered us from our sins by the shedding of his precious blood. That is what redemption is. Anything less than that is not redemption. This is the work of redemption pictured for us in the Old Testament scriptures.

The redemption of Israel out of Egypt

The deliverance of the people of Israel out of Egypt was a very special and remarkable type of our redemption by Christ out of a far worse state of bondage than that of Egypt (Psalm 106:6-12). Israel was brought into Egyptian bondage by an act of sin, when Joseph's brothers sold him into slavery. Israel was redeemed by the hand of a man God raised up, Moses, the deliverer prophet who typified Christ (Acts 7:35). The price of redemption was the blood of the paschal lamb (Exodus 12:13). The power of their redemption was the omnipotent hand of God, a picture of regeneration and conversion by God's omnipotent grace (Exodus 14:13-14; 15:1-2, 16). This was a blood redemption, the redemption of a particular people, and an effectual redemption.

The atonement money paid by Israel

Exodus 30:11-16 describes redemption by atonement money. This numbering of the children of Israel and the atonement money they paid so that no plague came upon them, was typical of our ransom by Christ. None but Israelites were ransomed. A specific, numbered people were ransomed. The ransom price was the same for all. Those who were ransomed were preserved from any plague (Proverbs 12:21; Psalm 91:10).

The kinsman redeemer

The buying again of an Israelite who, by reason of great poverty had sold himself to another, by one of his near kinsman is another good, beautiful picture of our redemption by Christ (Leviticus 25:47-49). We have sold ourselves into bondage. We cannot redeem ourselves. No friend is able, or has the right, to redeem us. But there is a near Kinsman who is both able and willing to redeem, the Lord Jesus Christ (Hebrews 7:25).

Like Boaz, Ruth's kinsman redeemer, our Lord Jesus Christ as a man is our Near Kinsman. He is able to pay our debt. He willingly laid down his life to ransom us!

The deliverance of a debtor from prison

In ancient times a man in debt was liable to be arrested and cast into prison. There he would have to remain in bondage until his debt was paid, either by himself or another. That is what the Lord Jesus Christ has done for God's elect (Isaiah 49:8-10; 61:1-3; Philemon 18). Our sins are debts. They are debts which we can never pay. We are all, therefore, shut up in debtor's prison by nature. But Christ has paid our debt and set us free!

John Gill wrote,

Christ, as he has engaged to pay the debts of his people, has paid them, cleared the whole score, and blotted out the hand writing that was against them; in consequence of which is proclaimed, in the gospel, liberty to the captives, and the opening of the prison to them that are bound; and in the effectual calling Christ says 'to the prisoners', 'Go forth', opening the prison doors for them; and to them that sit in darkness, in the gloomy cells of the prison, 'show yourselves'; all which is done in virtue of the redemption price paid by Christ for his people.

The ransom of a slave

In the days of the Old Testament, godless men often took their slaves and threw them into deep pits at night. They would take them out of their pits only to perform slavish labour, or if a ransom price was paid for their deliverance. Christ has ransomed us and delivered us from slavery and corruption (Job 33:24; Psalm 40:2-3, Zechariah 9:11).

We are all slaves to sin and Satan by nature. Our old master, the devil, kept us ever in the deep, dark pit of darkness and night, until Christ came to deliver us. The Lord Jesus Christ delivered us from the slavery of Satan and the pit of darkness, corruption, and sin by the power of his omnipotent grace. The price he paid for the deliverance of our souls was his own precious blood.

Three lessons

These five pictures of redemption, drawn for us by the pen of inspiration, teach us these three things about redemption.

1. Sinners need a redeemer – As we have seen, sin as it is set forth in the scriptures is a pit of bondage, slavery, and condemnation from which no man can deliver himself (Psalm 130:1; 69:1-2).

2. Redemption is deliverance from sin by the blood of Christ – It is deliverance from the penalty of sin at the cross, from the dominion of sin in regeneration, from the reign of sin in these dying bodies, and from all the evil consequences of sin in resurrection glory.

3. Redemption is the unaided, unassisted, effectual work of Christ alone – 'Christ hath redeemed us!' Redemption is always spoken of as the effectual redemption of a particular people. It is never, not even once, portrayed as a failed effort.

'Yet it pleased the LORD to bruise him; he hath put him to grief: when thou shalt make his soul an offering for sin, he shall see his seed, he shall prolong his days, and the pleasure of the LORD shall prosper in his hand. He shall see of the travail of his soul, and shall be satisfied: by his knowledge shall my righteous servant justify many; for he shall bear their iniquities. Therefore will I divide him a portion with the great, and he shall divide the spoil with the strong; because he hath poured out his soul unto death: and he was numbered with the transgressors; and he bare the sin of many, and made intercession for the transgressors'.
(Isaiah 53:10-12)

Chapter 28

Effectual Atonement

What happened at Calvary? Did the Lord Jesus Christ redeem his people from all iniquity; or did he merely make men redeemable? Did he actually put away the sins of his people; or did he merely make it possible for men's sins to be put away? Did the Lamb of God reconcile his people to God; or did he merely make men reconcilable? Did he actually justify his people; or did he simply make it possible for men to be justified? Did he effectually secure the salvation of those for whom he died; or did he only make salvation a possibility for men? Did the incarnate Son of God actually make atonement for sin by the shedding of his blood; or did he just make a stab at it?

Isaiah 53 is a true, divinely inspired, prophetic description of the sin-atoning sacrifice of the Lord Jesus Christ and its results. The inspired prophet declared, 'He shall be satisfied'. 'He', the Son of God, our glorious Substitute, our great Sin Offering, our divine Saviour, the one who died in our place at Calvary, 'shall', without a doubt, without the possibility of hindrance, most assuredly, 'be satisfied', fully, completely, eternally satisfied! He was satisfied with the terms of redemption proposed to him as our Surety in the covenant of grace before the world was made. He is satisfied with his purchased possession, his bride the Church. He is satisfied with himself as a ransom price for the satisfaction of justice. He shall be satisfied with us, his redeemed ones. Without question, Isaiah's words describe a complete, effectual redemption accomplished by Jehovah's Righteous Servant, our Substitute and Saviour, the Lord Jesus Christ.

We trust an undefeated and undefeatable Saviour. It is written, 'He shall not fail!' The Son of God can never be frustrated in his purpose, defeated in his design, or hindered in his work. Christ was not conquered at Calvary. He conquered. He did not die as the helpless victim of circumstances. He died as the Lord of all things, the one who rules all circumstances. Nor will he be defeated in the end. 'He shall see of the travail of his soul and shall be satisfied!' The cross of our Lord Jesus Christ shall never be exposed as a failure.

The Lion of the tribe of Judah must prevail. The Word of God universally proclaims the infallible efficacy of Christ's atonement. That which the Son of God accomplished at Calvary was an effectual atonement for all the sins of God's elect, which were imputed to him. I want to show you from the Word of God the glorious, absolute, saving efficacy of Christ's atonement.

The subject matter before us is a matter of utmost concern. The one thing that characterizes every messenger of Satan is a denial of the efficacy of Christ's atonement. The one point of doctrine upon which all false prophets are agreed is this, they all deny that every soul for whom Christ died shall be saved. They may give lip service to Bible doctrine and Bible terms; but they deny the very foundation of the gospel, namely, substitution. The modern day prophets of Baal preach a redemption that redeems no one, an atonement that atones for nothing, and a salvation that saves no one. They preach possibility redemption, possibility atonement, possibility grace, and possibility salvation.

Today we are told that the sacrificial blood of the Lord Jesus Christ does not, in itself, secure the salvation of anyone; but that it only makes salvation possible for everyone. We are told that the blood of Christ becomes effectually operative by man's faith, by man deciding to believe on Jesus, by the act of man's great free will. Nonsense! Such doctrine is utter blasphemy and heresy! The notion of universal redemption is totally contrary to everything revealed in holy scripture.

In this study, we will confine ourselves to these three verses of holy scripture, looking at each verse line by line. This passage of holy scripture, in harmony with the entire volume of inspiration, talks not about a frustrated Christ, but a satisfied Christ. Christ is not our helper. He is our Saviour. He is not an accomplice in salvation, but the accomplisher of salvation.

'Yet, it pleased the LORD to bruise him; he hath put him to grief'

Our Saviour died by the hand of God, according to the will of God, for the glory of God. Though our Lord Jesus Christ 'knew no sin', the Lord God was pleased to bruise him in the place of sinners for sin. We recognize that our Redeemer was crucified by the hands of wicked men; but he was delivered into their hands by the will of God (Acts 2:23); and those wicked men did nothing but that which God himself had purposed and 'determined before to be done' (Acts 4:27-28).

The death of Christ was not an accident, or an after-thought. The death of Christ was in the mind and heart of God from everlasting (Revelation 13:8). The eye of faith looks beyond the malice of the Jews, the weakness of Pilate, and the Roman cross, and traces the death of Christ back to its original source, to the heart of God himself (Romans 5:8; 1 John 4:9-10).

The Lord Jesus Christ died according to the purpose, decree, and will of God (1 Peter 1:18-21; Acts 13:28-29). We do not, we dare not, impute to God the sin and guilt of the crime. Wicked men did exactly what they wanted to do. God did not force them to act as they did. But he did absolutely govern and control their actions and use them to accomplish his own purpose of grace toward his elect. Not a single action, circumstance, or pain involved in the Saviour's death came to pass except by the decree of God our Father. This is a foundation truth of holy scripture. Hold it firmly! God has written a book of sovereign and absolute predestination (Revelation 5:1).

> Chained to His throne a volume lies,
> With all the fates of men,
> With every angel's form and size,
> Drawn by the eternal pen.

Nothing escapes the will, purpose, decree, and power of God. Everything that comes to pass in time was ordained by God in eternity. You may be sure that God Almighty, who feeds the sparrows, clothes the lilies, and numbers the hairs of our heads, left nothing to chance or circumstance regarding the life and death of his dear Son.

The death of Christ is the very core of predestination. It is the centre and mainspring upon which God fashioned all his other purposes. It is the foundation upon which the structure of God's decrees was built. Jesus Christ is 'the Lamb slain before the foundation of the world', because 'it pleased the LORD to bruise him'. Long before there was a sinner, God provided a Saviour. Before the sheep went astray, God made Christ our Shepherd. Before we fell in the first Adam, we stood in the last Adam. Before ever we broke God's law, Christ was our ransom. Before we became polluted, Christ was our cleansing Fountain. Before we incurred the debt of sin, Christ stood as our Surety to pay our debt. Long before we were cursed by the law, Christ was our Redeemer. Before ever we died, Christ was our Resurrection and our Life!

The Son of God was sent into the world to die for us because the Lord God loved us with an everlasting love (Jeremiah 31:3; John 3:16; 13:1; 1 John 3:16; 4:9-10). God the Father loved us and sent his Son to be the propitiation for our sins. God the Son loved us and came to die in our place. 'He loved me and gave himself for me'. God the Holy Spirit loved us and formed the holy humanity of Christ in the womb of the virgin to be a sacrifice for our sins (Hebrews 10:5).

The Son of God, our Lord Jesus Christ, came into this world to die in order to accomplish his Father's will. In the fulness of time God the Father took his dear Son from his bosom and freely delivered him up for us all. 'Herein is love!' The offended Judge took his own holy Son, whom he loved dearly, and gave him up to suffer the pains of hell to accomplish the redemption of our souls, in order to save traitors and rebels who would never love him in return, except he create love in us.

Yet, the Lord Jesus was not a forced substitute. The Lord of Glory voluntarily laid down his life as our Substitute. 'It pleased the LORD to bruise him'; we must not forget that he is the Lord God who did the bruising as well as the one bruised. Christ was not a forced Surety but a willing one, a willing Servant, a willing Saviour, a willing Substitute, and a willing Sacrifice (Psalm 40:6-7; Proverbs 8:23-31; Isaiah 50:5-7; John 10:17; Hebrews 10:5-14; 12:2).

Still, the unutterable agony of Christ's death upon the cross was inflicted upon him by his Father's own hand. We read of the terrible agonies he endured in Psalm 22 as he hung upon the cross, suffering the wrath of God. Those woes were aggravated by the fact that it was the Father's hand that was turned upon his dear Son in wrath, and that at the very height of his obedience! 'It pleased the LORD to bruise him'. Oh, how he bruised him!

Our Saviour died a very violent death. His death could not be by natural causes. He died as our penal Substitute. As a penal Substitute, he had to die as a slain victim, as a sacrifice. Immanuel died a terribly painful death, tormented in body and in soul. He was

mercilessly beaten and barbarically crucified. He was forsaken by
his friends and mocked of men. He was made to be sin, and forsaken
by his Father. Why did he suffer so? Because justice must be satisfied
if redemption is to be accomplished. There was no other way for the
holy Lord God to be both 'a just God and a Saviour' (Isaiah 45:21).

Our Redeemer died a horribly ignominious, shameful death. He
'endured the cross, despising the shame'. He was slaughtered as a
shameful man, a common malefactor. He died in a shameful
condition, stripped naked before men and nailed to the cursed tree
as a cursed man. The Son of God died a specifically cursed death. It
is written, 'Cursed is everyone that hangeth on a tree'.

Our great Saviour died a slow, lingering death. Others gradually
grew weaker as they suffered. He was full of life to the end. Others
were given gall and myrrh to stupefy their senses. He was given
gall and vinegar to intensify his pains. In all his pains and agonies
there was none to help, not even a sympathetic soul to look upon
him with pity.

Because he loved us with an everlasting love, because he purposed
to save us for the glory of his own great name, because he was
resolved to be gracious to us, 'It pleased the LORD to bruise him;
he hath put him to grief!'

'When thou shalt make his soul an offering for sin'

Why did the Lord of glory endure such a death as this? The Lord
God bruised his Son and put him to grief upon the cursed tree because
he made 'his soul an offering for sin'. Christ died as he did, he had
to die as he did, so that he might be a suitable Substitute and Sin
Offering to God for his people. Here are four reasons for the
crucifixion, four reasons why the Lord Jesus Christ died the painful,
shameful, ignominious death of the cross.

1. Christ died the death of the cross because he must bear the curse
of the law in his death if he would save us (Galatians 3:13;
Deuteronomy 21:22-23).

2. The Lord Jesus died the horrid death of the cross to fulfil the Old Testament types as a sin offering. Those sacrifices were always lifted up upon an altar before God. The brazen serpent was lifted up on a pole. Even so, God's great sin offering, the true sin offering had to be lifted up (Numbers 19:9; John 3:13; 12:32).
3. Our Saviour died as he did upon the cursed tree to fulfil the Old Testament prophecies concerning his death (Psalm 22:16-17; Zechariah 12:10).
4. The Lord Jesus endured the death of the cross for us, as our Substitute, that God might be both just and the Justifier of all who trust him (Romans 3:24-26; Psalm 85:10-11; Proverbs 16:7; Isaiah 45:21).

God has no pleasure in the death of the wicked. Should all the world suffer the wrath of God forever in hell, justice could never be satisfied. Yet 'It pleased the LORD to bruise him'. By Christ's one great sacrifice for sin, the holy Lord God was pleased, his justice completely satisfied.

Beginning with the next sentence and going through the rest of the chapter, Isaiah shows us what the certain, just, and inevitable results of Christ's death must be. Do not ever think that the results of our Lord's death are uncertain. The Arminian, the freewiller must say, 'There are no sure and certain results of Christ's death. Everything is left to chance. Everything depends upon what man will do. Everything is determined by man's will'. Blasphemy! In these next lines God the Holy Spirit tells us exactly what the results of Christ's death must and shall be. 'He shall not fail!' Our Lord's death was not a gamble or a game of chance. He effectually accomplished all that he came here to do. Here we see the infallible efficacy of Christ's atonement.

'He shall see his seed'
We do not have to guess who his seed is. It is the generation that shall serve him (Psalm 22:30), the whole body of God's elect. He

sees them, all of them, justified, sanctified, and glorified (John 12:24, 32).

'He shall prolong his days'

That simply means that, once he had by his death fully satisfied the justice of God and put away the sins of his people, he was raised from the dead to declare in the most public, undeniable manner possible that all for whom he died are forever justified (Romans 4:25). Being raised from the dead, he was exalted and glorified to give eternal life to all his redeemed ones (John 17:2; Romans 14:9; Philippians 2:8-11).

'And the pleasure of the LORD shall prosper in his hand'

Pay attention to that word 'shall'. Everything that God wants done shall be done by the risen, exalted, glorified Christ. All the pleasure of God's eternal purpose is being and shall fully be accomplished by King Jesus (Revelation 10:1; Romans 8:28-31).

'He shall see of the travail of his soul, and shall be satisfied'

There is that word 'shall' again. Twice it is given in this sentence. The Holy Spirit intends for us to understand that there is absolutely no uncertainty about what the consequences of Christ's atonement are. As I said before, the cross of our Lord Jesus Christ shall never be exposed as a failure. This text is talking about a satisfied Saviour, not a frustrated assistant. When the Word of God talks about the satisfaction of Christ, it is talking about two things: Christ making satisfaction and Christ being satisfied. By his one offering for sin, our Redeemer has completely satisfied the law and justice of God (Galatians 3:13; 1 John 1:9). By his sin-atoning death, as our Substitute, our Saviour satisfied all types, shadows, and prophecies of the Old Testament scriptures.

The crucified Christ presented to sinners in the gospel satisfies all the demands of a guilty conscience, all the needs of a convicted sinner, and every new desire of a renewed heart (Hebrews 9:12-14;

1 Corinthians 1:30-31; Psalm 73:25-26; Philippians 3:7-14). The Son of God shall be satisfied with his ransomed people. Our Redeemer shall be satisfied with the results of his sin-atoning work as our Substitute. He shall be satisfied because they all shall be saved, satisfied because they shall be perfectly saved (Ephesians 5:25-27; Isaiah 62:5).

He was satisfied with his work when it was done. He is satisfied with the reward of his obedience, his exaltation and glory (Philippians 2:8-12). He is satisfied with his present position and work as our great High Priest (1 John 2:1-2). The Son of God shall be satisfied when he sees his seed, all his seed saved, completely saved (John 6:37-40), called by his Spirit, converted by his grace, and at last conformed to his image. He shall be satisfied in the day of the great and glorious resurrection (1 Corinthians 15:51-58). In the day of judgment he will say to all his ransom ones, 'Come ye, blessed, inherit the kingdom prepared for you from the foundation of the world'. In that great day, he will present all his ransomed ones before the presence of the glory of the triune God in perfect holiness, unblameable and unreproveable (1 Corinthians 15:24-28). Then, our Saviour shall be satisfied, in the marriage supper of the Lamb, with the everlasting blessedness of his people and the praise of his own great name (Revelation 4:11; 5:9-14).

Nothing will satisfy Christ short of the complete salvation of his people (Matthew 1:21). Nothing will satisfy the believer's heart short of perfect, complete conformity to Christ (Philippians 3:10). Both Christ and his saints shall be satisfied. I am certain this is the meaning of the phrase, 'He shall see of the travail of his soul, and shall be satisfied', because that is what the next phrase declares.

'By his knowledge shall my righteous servant justify many; for he shall bear their iniquities'

All the many whose iniquities Christ bore on the tree shall be (There's that word again – 'shall'.) justified, and they shall be justified by his knowledge. Perhaps that means by the knowledge of him; but I prefer to stick with our translation. Christ shall justify his elect according to his knowledge of the merits of his death and his knowledge of those for whom he died (John 10:14, 27-28).

'Therefore will I divide him a portion with the great and he shall divide the spoil with the strong; because he hath poured out his soul unto death: and he was numbered with the transgressors; and he bare the sin of many, and made intercession for the transgressors'

Here the prophet summarizes all that he has said concerning the glorious, infallible efficacy of Christ's redeeming work as our Substitute. Here is a declaration of Christ's exaltation and glory. 'Therefore will I divide him a portion with the great, and he shall divide the spoil with the strong'. Here are the reasons for his exaltation and glory. The Lord Jesus Christ is seated at the right hand of the majesty on high because his work is finished and his work was and is a complete success.

- 'He hath poured out his soul unto death!'
- 'He was numbered with the transgressors!'
- 'He bare the sin of many!'
- 'He made intercession for the transgressors!'

This he did 'not merely in a petitionery way, but by presenting himself, his blood, righteousness, and sacrifice, pleading the merits of these and calling for, in a way of justice and legal demand, all the blessings which were stipulated in the everlasting covenant, between him and the Father, to be given to his people in consequence of his sufferings and death' (John Gill).

The specific matter of our Saviour's intercession is given in John 17:9, 20-24. The Lord Jesus made intercession for us before the world began. He made intercession for us in the garden. He made intercession for us on the cross. He makes intercession for us today in heaven (1 John 2:1-2; Romans 8:33-34; Hebrews 7:24-25; 9:24). And our Redeemer's intercession is effectual. 'He shall not fail!'

'The Lord GOD hath opened mine ear, and I was not rebellious, neither turned away back. I gave my back to the smiters, and my cheeks to them that plucked off the hair: I hid not my face from shame and spitting. For the Lord GOD will help me; therefore shall I not be confounded: therefore have I set my face like a flint, and I know that I shall not be ashamed'. (Isaiah 50:5-7)

Chapter 29

The Free Obedience of Christ

Isaiah 53:10-12 describes the death of our Lord Jesus Christ as that which God the Father did to his Son when he made him to be sin for us. Isaiah 50:5-7 describes our Lord's sacrificial obedience unto death, even the death of the cross as our voluntary Surety and Substitute.

Like all the law of God given to Israel, the law regarding the bond slave in Exodus 21:1-6 was a messianic, prophetic law. It portrayed the work of our Lord Jesus Christ as Jehovah's righteous Servant. In the covenant of grace, before the worlds were made, the Son of God, our Saviour, became Jehovah's voluntary Servant that he might redeem and save his people by his free obedience to God as our Substitute. This is what the prophet describes in Isaiah 50:5-7.

A question
The death of our Lord Jesus Christ is the most wonderful, astounding, magnificent event in the history of the universe. Nothing

that is, has been, or shall hereafter be can be compared to it. Yet, as he was suffering the wrath of God, bearing the sins of his people, dying as the voluntary Substitute for guilty, hell-deserving, hell-bent sinners such as we are, we hear the Son of God expressing the most woeful, unexplainable lamentation imaginable. 'Is it nothing to you, all ye that pass by? behold, and see if there be any sorrow like unto my sorrow, which is done unto me, wherewith the LORD hath afflicted me in the day of his fierce anger' (Lamentations 1:12).

When I hear those words falling from the lips of the Son of God as he hangs upon the cursed tree, I simply cannot avoid asking, 'Of whom does the bleeding Lamb of God speak these words? To whom is the death of Christ meaningless and insignificant?'

Nothing in all the universe is more wonderful and magnificent in the eyes of God than the death of his dear Son. The Saviour himself declares, 'Therefore doth my Father love me, because I lay down my life!' The angels of heaven, like the cherubs facing the mercy-seat, ever look into the mystery and wonder of redemption by the blood of Christ with astonishment. God's servants, faithful gospel preachers, are so overwhelmed with the wonders of redemption and the glory of the Redeemer that they never cease to study, glory in, and preach the cross of our Lord Jesus Christ (Isaiah 6:1-6; Galatians 6:14; 1 Corinthians 2:2). Redeemed sinners on the earth cherish nothing, delight in nothing, marvel at nothing, like we do the death of our Lord Jesus Christ for us (Galatians 2:20; 1 John 3:16; 4:10). The ransomed in glory appear to think of nothing and speak of nothing except the dying love of the Lamb in the midst of the throne (Revelation 5:9-12). Hell itself looks upon the death of Christ as a wonderful, unexplainable, mysterious thing. I am certain that this is one thing that Satan himself did not understand: That Christ would triumph over him and crush his head by his death upon the cross. Else he would never have put it into the heart of Judas to betray the Master.

Yet, astonishing as it is to imagine, there are some to whom our darling Saviour speaks, as it were with astonishment, to whom his death is meaningless, insignificant, nothing. Who are these people to whom the death of Christ is nothing? Who is it that thinks little of the sin-atoning death of the Lord Jesus Christ? Our Lord is here addressing himself to everyone who passes by him, passes by his sacrifice, passes by his death as the sinners' Substitute. O unbelieving, Christless soul, it is you! O cold, calculating, heartless, preacher, you who pass by the crucified Christ and take to your lips meaningless, insignificant things (politics, social issues, denominational squabbles, religious history, traditions, etc.), it is you! Christ crucified is mundane, meaningless and insignificant only to unregenerate, unbelieving souls.

It is my heart's prayer that the death of our Lord Jesus Christ will be made the most important thing in all the world to you who read these lines. I pray that you and I may become totally consumed with the crucified Christ, that our hearts, our lives, every fibre of our souls may be constantly dominated by the death of Christ as our sin-atoning Saviour.

Our Lord Jesus Christ, of whom it is written, 'grace is poured into thy lips', declares plainly that his death at Calvary was the free, voluntary act of his own obedience to his Father's will, by which he won his Father's love as a man, as our Mediator and Surety. 'Therefore doth my Father love me, because I lay down my life, that I might take it again. No man taketh it from me, but I lay it down of myself. I have power to lay it down, and I have power to take it again. This commandment have I received of my Father'. (John 10:17-18).

The Father's commandment

In John 10, the Lord Jesus Christ speaks of himself not as God the eternal Son, but as the Good Shepherd, the Mediator, the Surety of his people. He says, 'This commandment have I received of my Father'. With those words he declares that his death as our Substitute was arranged by God before the world began (Psalm 40:7; Hebrews 10:7-10). The death of Christ was not accomplished by the arrangement of men, or by the arrangement of hell, but by the arrangement of the triune God (Acts 2:23; 1 Peter 1:18-20). The death of Christ at Calvary was accomplished by the arrangement of infinite love, through an eternal covenant, by the work of Divine providence (John 3:16; Romans 5:6-8; Hebrews 10:5-14).

Christ's obedience

The Lord Jesus Christ laid down his life voluntarily, as an act of free obedience to his Father. No man forced him to die. God the Father did not compel him to die, or take his life from him. Oh, No! Our Saviour died voluntarily, by his own will. His death was accomplished by his own will. 'He poured out his soul unto death'. It is true, as we have seen, 'it pleased the Father to bruise him'. The Father cried, 'Awake, O sword, against One that is my fellow. Smite the Shepherd'. But Christ took the cup of wrath in his own hands. The Son of God fell willingly upon the sword of justice. Our Saviour died by his own will. The Lord Jesus laid down his life for the satisfaction of justice. Our Saviour laid down his life as the Substitute for chosen sinners. The Son of God laid down his life for the glory of his Father. Our blessed Redeemer laid down his life because of his love for us. The Lord Jesus Christ laid down his life that he might take it again (Romans 14:9; Philippians 2:5-11).

The Father's love for the Son

Our Saviour says, 'Therefore doth my Father love me, because I lay down my life'. I know of nothing in heaven or earth so sweet to meditate upon and so impossible to explain as the Father's love for his darling, dying Son. The Father loved him for the loveliness of his Godhead. The Father loved him for the beauty of his holy humanity. The Father loved him because he laid down his life for us. The Father loved him as the glorious, saving, effectual Mediator of his people.

God himself never saw anything in all the world so lovely, so infinitely worthy of his love, admiration, and honour, as the death of his dear Son upon the cursed tree for his people. 'Herein is love!' Because of this great act of love, because of this great act of Christ's free obedience to the Father as our Surety, the Father has given his Son everything (Isaiah 53:4-12; John 3:35; 17:2).

Let us learn from the words and example of our Lord and Saviour that though a child of God may suffer greatly in this world, may often have to carry a heavy cross, and may often have the Father's face hidden from him, yet he is the darling object of his Father's love. Never did the Father more fully love his Son than when he was heaping upon him the fury of his wrath.

God honours those who honour his Son. The only way a sinner can honour the Son of God is to trust him. The only way of access to God is Christ. Our only worthiness of the Father's love and approval is Christ (John 17:22-26). Yet, in Christ, because of Christ, for Christ's sake, God loves us. God the Father gave his Son to die for us. God the Son laid down his life for us. God the Spirit now sprinkles us with the blood of Christ and declares us 'Redeemed'. 'Ye are not your own? For ye are bought with a price: therefore glorify God in your body, and in your spirit, which are God's'.

'All things are of God'.
(2 Corinthians 5:18)

Chapter 30

The Cause of Our Redemption by Christ

Writing to the saints at Corinth on the subject of redemption and salvation by Christ, the Apostle Paul tells us, 'All things are of God, who hath reconciled us to himself by Jesus Christ, and hath given to us the ministry of reconciliation'. As in all other aspects of salvation, our redemption by Christ is attributed to the Lord God alone. As we read the scriptures, we cannot avoid being confronted with the fact that in this matter of salvation nothing is ever ascribed to man, caused by man, or dependent upon man. But 'all things are of God'. That is the language of the Bible (Deuteronomy 7:6-9; Psalm 106:8; 115:1), and of all true faith (1 Corinthians 15:10).

What is the cause of our redemption? To find the answer to that question, we must look to the Word of God alone. The answer is not difficult to find. It is written out in plain, simple, constantly repeated words. The cause of our redemption by Christ is to be found in the Lord God himself, and in him alone. 'Salvation is of the Lord!'

The love of God

The redemption of our souls by the precious blood of our Lord Jesus Christ originates in, rises, and flows to us from the everlasting love of God for us. The holy Lord God so loved the world of his elect that he gave his Son so that we might have life through the merits of his sin-atoning blood (John 3:16; Romans 5:6-8; 1 John 3:16; 4:9-10, 19). The first cause of our redemption, the original source from whence it springs and flows, is the everlasting love of God for his elect. Indeed, this is the source and spring of every blessing of grace: election and adoption, regeneration and effectual calling, and redemption, justification, sanctification, preservation, and glorification (Ephesians 1:3-6).

The gift of Christ to be the Redeemer of his people flows from God's everlasting love. Christ was given to be a Redeemer before he was sent into the world to redeem us. When he was given for a covenant to the people, he was given in a covenant to be the Redeemer of them. This gift of Christ by the Father was the effect of his love. To this Christ himself ascribes it; 'God so loved the world (the world of his elect), that he gave his only begotten Son'.

God gave his Son to be our Redeemer long before he actually came into the world to redeem us. In those earliest days of time before the flood, Job knew the Son of God as his living Redeemer. All the Old Testament saints waited for Christ to come as the Lamb of God to redeem his people from their sins (Genesis 22:8). The mission of Christ in the fulness of time to be the propitiation for our sins, and to redeem us from them is given as a manifest, clear, and undoubted instance of his everlasting, free love for us. 'In this was manifested the love of God'. 'Herein is love'. John Gill wrote, 'God's not sparing his Son, but delivering him into the hands of justice and death, to die in the room and stead of sinners, while they were such, is a full demonstration and high commendation of his great love unto them'.

The grace of God

We trace our redemption by Christ to the free and sovereign grace of God in Christ. Whenever referring to the grace of God, I commonly use the adjectives free and sovereign to describe it, because few in these days of religious darkness and delusion understand that grace is of necessity both free and sovereign. It is the free grace of God, because grace if it is not altogether free is not grace. This is, like the love of God, unmerited, clear of all conditions, merit and motives in the creature (Romans 11:6). It is sovereign grace, because it is bestowed entirely according to the will of our great, Divine Benefactor (Romans 9:13-18).

The foundation and basis of our redemption by Christ is God's free and sovereign grace. We have been 'justified freely by his grace through the redemption that is in Christ Jesus: Whom God hath set forth to be a propitiation through faith in his blood, to declare his righteousness for the remission of sins that are past, through the forbearance of God; To declare, I say, at this time his righteousness: that he might be just, and the justifier of him which believeth in Jesus' (Romans 3:24-26).

That redemption that is in and by Christ is of free grace. The gift of Christ is a free grace gift (2 Corinthians 9:15). Our dear Saviour was sent and delivered up to death by the grace of God. It was 'by the grace of God he tasted death for every one', for everyone of the chosen, adopted sons of God (Hebrews 2:9). This cannot be attributed to any merit or worth in those for whom Christ died since we were without strength, ungodly wicked sinners, the chief of sinners, and enemies in our minds by wicked works. We do not contribute anything to the work of Christ in redemption, even by our faith. Our faith in Christ is the fruit and effect of redemption, not the cause. We receive the atonement by faith; but we do not make atonement by faith (Romans 5:10-11).

The mercy of God
We trace our redemption by Christ to the mercy of God. Mercy is the love and grace of God exercised toward and freely bestowed upon sinners. Mercy gives rise to redemption. God resolved to have mercy on sinful men, and determined to redeem and save them by the sacrifice of his own dear Son. It is through the tender mercy of our God that Christ, the Day Spring from on high, visited and redeemed his people, and so performed the mercy promised to his people (Luke 1:68, 69, 72, 78).

The scriptures declare that God saves us according to his mercy. Mercy, like justice and truth, is magnified in the redemption and salvation of God's elect by Christ. We delight to sing of the mercy of God and praise him, giving thanks to him for redeeming mercy (Titus 3:5; Psalm 107:1, 2; 136:23-24). It was by the love, grace, and mercy of our Father for chosen sinners that he determined to redeem us.

The purpose of God

Redemption is according to an eternal purpose of grace, which he has purposed in Christ before the world began (Romans 8:28-34; 2 Timothy 1:9-10; Ephesians 1:7-12). The Lord Jesus Christ, as the Lamb of God, was foreordained before the foundation of the world (1 Peter 1:18-20), to redeem us from our vain conversation, with his own precious blood. He was set forth, in the decrees and purposes of God, to be the propitiation for our sins. God the Father appointed his Son to be our Redeemer and Saviour and appointed us, not unto wrath (wrath which we fully deserve!), but to obtain salvation by him. The Lord Jesus Christ is that Lamb of sacrifice, slain in the mind, purpose, and decree of God, from the foundation of the world (Revelation 17:8) for the redemption of God's chosen vessels of mercy before prepared for glory.

The wisdom of God

Being moved by his love, grace, and mercy, moved by that which was found only in himself, to redeem and save his people, God in infinite wisdom found a ransom for his chosen in his own dear Son (Job 33:24). In Christ, the holy, just, and true God found a way to justify sinners, while fully maintaining his justice for the praise of the glory of his grace. In the everlasting covenant of grace and council of peace, the triune God 'abounded toward us in all wisdom and prudence'. So great and wise is God's purpose of grace in redemption that it is described as the revelation of 'the manifold wisdom of God' (Ephesians 1:7, 8; 3:10).

'And I will feed them that oppress thee with their own flesh; and they shall be drunken with their own blood, as with sweet wine: and all flesh shall know that I the LORD am thy Saviour and thy Redeemer, the mighty One of Jacob ... Thou shalt also suck the milk of the Gentiles, and shalt suck the breast of kings: and thou shalt know that I the LORD am thy Saviour and thy Redeemer, the mighty One of Jacob'.
(Isaiah 49:26 and 60:16)

Chapter 31

'Thy Saviour and Thy Redeemer'

In these two texts of scripture, the Lord our God, the Lord Jesus Christ, declares himself to be our God, our Saviour, and our Redeemer. He also declares that it is his intention and purpose to make himself known to his chosen, redeemed people as their God, Saviour, and Redeemer, and to ultimately cause all the world to behold him as our God, our Saviour, and our Redeemer.

In the course of these studies, we have seen from the Old Testament scriptures pictures of our redemption by Christ, the efficacy of his atonement, the freeness and voluntariness of his obedience unto death as our Redeemer, and the causes of our redemption by the Son of God. In these two passages, the great and glorious God, who created, rules, and disposes of all things exactly as he pleases, according to the good pleasure of his will, declares himself to be 'Thy Saviour and thy Redeemer'.

What could be more delightful and comforting? If he who is our Redeemer is indeed the Lord God Omnipotent, then it must be concluded that he will also be our Saviour. The blessed comfort and consolation of the gospel is that he who shed his blood at Calvary as our Redeemer will also be the Saviour of all the redeemed. Redemption would mean nothing if it did not carry with it the assurance of everlasting salvation. However, since redemption, in its very essence, carries the assurance of deliverance and salvation, when the Lord God would send a word of hope, comfort, and good cheer in the gospel, he declares himself to be our Redeemer (Isaiah 41:14; 44:24; 48:17; 54:8).

> Christ our Redeemer died on the cross,
> Died for His people, paid all their due!
> Sprinkled by grace with the blood of the Lamb,
> God now in justice must pass over you!
> Justice sees the blood! Justice sees the blood!
> Justice sees the blood!
> Now God must pass, must pass over you!

How did Christ become our Redeemer?

We have already seen the answer to this question in some measure. The Lord Jesus Christ, the Son of God, was appointed to the work of redemption by his Father, and he assented to it as our Surety in the covenant of grace before the world began. It was prophesied in the Old Testament that he would come to redeem his people from their sins; and numerous pictures and types of our redemption by him were given in the Old Testament scriptures. In the fulness of time he was made of a woman, made under the law, and sent to redeem them that were under the law. He did, by his own blood, enter in once into the holy place, having obtained eternal redemption for us. In Christ, all who believe have complete, eternal redemption through his blood and he is made of God unto us Redemption. So, when it is asked how Christ came to be our Redeemer, we must, according to the scriptures, trace it to God himself.

We trace our redemption by Christ to the everlasting love of God for his elect. The love, grace, and mercy of God the Father moved him to resolve upon redemption, appoint his Son to be our Redeemer, and call him to this great work (John 3:16; Romans 5:8; 1 John 4:9-10).

It was this same love, grace, and mercy toward us in the heart of the Son of God which moved him to accept the call and engage in the work. The love of Christ for his elect was in his heart from everlasting. It was a love of pleasure and delight for his people. Such was his love for us that he declares from eternity that his delights were with us (Proverbs 8:31). This love of Christ for his people showed itself in many acts of grace, and is most wondrously seen in our Saviour giving himself for his people to redeem us. Because he loved us, the Lord of glory gave himself an offering and a sacrifice for our sins. Because he loved us, he laid down his life for us (Titus 2:14; Ephesians 5:2,25; 1 John 3:16).

The love of Christ for us is a free, unmerited, undeserved, sovereign love. We did not even want his love, much less deserve it. He loved us freely and said, 'I will redeem them' (Isaiah 63:9; Hosea 13:14; 14:4).

Because of his great love for us, the Son of God voluntarily put himself into bondage as our Surety to redeem and save us. He is the Surety of that better covenant, established upon better promises, made on our behalf before the world began (Hebrews 7:22). Having entered into covenant engagements with the Father from everlasting, our Saviour considered himself to be and became Jehovah's bond slave (Isaiah 50:5-7). He considered himself under obligation to his Father to accomplish the great work of redemption. Therefore, he often spoke of it as something he must do (Matthew 16:21; 26:53-54; Mark 8:31; 9:12; Luke 22:37; John 3:14; 10:16-18; 12:34; 20:9). And that which he must do, because of his being bound by own honour and his own word, the Son of God will do (Proverbs 6:1-2).

Is the Lord Jesus Christ qualified to be our Redeemer?

Of course, to a believer, this question is redundant. Yet, it will
do our hearts good to meditate upon our Saviour's glorious fitness
to be our Redeemer. What a fit Redeemer he is! There is none fit to
redeem our souls but him. No animal sacrifices could redeem us.
No mere man could redeem us. No angel could redeem us. Not even
God, in his strict character as God could redeem us. Therefore,
Christ came to redeem us (Hebrews 10:1-14).

Christ's fitness for the work of redemption lies in the fact that he
is both God and man in one glorious person. It was the Son of God
that was sent to redeem us. He is of the same nature, and possesses
the same perfections and attributes as his Father. He is the brightness
of his Father's glory, and the express image of his person. This man
was and is in the form of God. Therefore, he thought it not robbery
to be equal with God.

Jesus Christ is God the Son, the second Person of the holy Trinity.
He is the true God, the great God. Therefore, he is fit to be the
Redeemer and Saviour of men. What a mighty redeemer he must
be! He is Jehovah, the Lord of hosts. That means that he is equal to
such a great work as this (Galatians 4:4; 1 John 5:20; Titus 2:13;
Jeremiah 50:34).

Our great Saviour and Redeemer is both God and man (Isaiah
9:6). He is the child born, as man, and the Son given, as a divine
person. He is Immanuel, God with us, God in our nature, God
manifest in the flesh. As such, as the God-man, the man who is
God, our Lord Jesus Christ is fit to be the Mediator between God
and man, the Umpire, the Daysman who can lay hands on both God
and man. He is fit to do the work required of a Redeemer of men, to
make reconciliation for the sins of his people, and to take care of all
things pertaining to the glory of God, his justice, and holiness.

As man he could be made, as he was made, under the law, and so
made capable of yielding obedience to it and bearing the penalty of
it. It was necessary that he do so if he would be the Surety and
Redeemer of God's elect. As man, he had blood to shed. It was with

this most precious blood he redeemed us unto God. As a man, he had a life to lay down, a sufficient ransom price for his people. As a man, the Son of God was capable of suffering all the wrath of God and dying in our room and stead, thereby making full satisfaction for us!

As God, he was zealously concerned for the glory of God in all the perfections of his nature. He secured the honour of all the divine attributes in the redemption which he wrought out and accomplished as our Substitute. As God, he put an infinite virtue into his blood. Divinity united to humanity in one glorious person made his sacrifice of himself a full and adequate ransom price for the purchase of his church and the redemption of our souls.

Our great Saviour's divinity gave support to his human nature under the load of sin as he suffered the wrath of God for us. His divinity was able to carry his humanity through the work, enabling him to endure the horrendous ordeal. Otherwise he could never have endured the cup of God's wrath and stood before his indignation until his indignation and wrath were satisfied.

As both God and man he had a right to redeem. As Lord of all, he had a right as well as power to redeem them that were his. As a man, our near kinsman, the right of redemption belonged to him. Therefore, he wears the name Goel, which signifies a redeemer and a near kinsman (Leviticus 25:47-49). No one could be so fit a Redeemer of the church as Christ, our near Kinsman, who is our head and our husband. Jesus Christ, the Son of God, the Son of Man, is our Boaz.

By what means did the Son of God accomplish our redemption?

Our redemption was accomplished, wrought out, and obtained by the precious blood of Christ by the sacrifice of his life, which was represented and present in that blood he shed so freely for the remission of our sins and the ransom of our souls. Let us ever thank God for the blood, the precious blood of Christ (Exodus 12:13; Ephesians 1:7; 1 Peter 1:18-20; Revelation 5:9).

It was deliberately shed blood. Had it been possible for his blood to have been spilt involuntarily, by accident, or by some outside force against his will, it would not have been a proper redemption price. It could not have answered for us as a payment to the justice of God. But it was purposefully and voluntarily shed, with our Master's full consent. Christ had the full control and disposal of his own life. He freely gave his life a ransom price for many; 'I lay down my life for the sheep', he said, as a ransom price for them; 'I lay it down of myself' (Matthew 20:28; John 10:15,18).

It was human blood, the blood of a man. That blood which was so freely shed for us was the same as the blood which flows in our veins. This, too, was necessary. We could not be redeemed with the blood of bulls and goats, which could never be an adequate price of redemption. Human blood must be shed for the atonement of men. Christ partook of the same flesh and blood with the children for whom he died. The only difference was this: His blood was not tainted with sin as ours is.

This was another requirement for our redemption. The ransom price had to be the blood of an innocent, perfectly righteous man. Much notice is given in scripture to the innocence, holiness, and righteousness of the Redeemer. He was holy in his nature and blameless in life. He knew no sin. He never committed any evil. He is the just and Holy One. He suffered and died the Just for the unjust. Great emphasis is laid upon this fact. The price with which men are redeemed is 'the precious blood of Christ, as of a Lamb without blemish and without spot' (1 Peter 1:18,19). If he had had any sin in him, he could not have been a redeemer from sin. His blood could not be the price of redemption. Yet there is more …

It was divine blood, the blood of a man who is God. It was necessary, if atonement was to be made and redemption accomplished for God's elect, that the blood shed also be the blood of One who is himself God as well as man. None but Christ ever made such a claim; and none but Christ meet this requirement. Therefore, we are told that God, who is Christ, 'purchased the church with his own blood' (Acts 20:28). It is the blood of Jesus Christ, God's Son, which cleanses us from all sin (1 John 1:7).

To whom was the ransom price for our redemption paid?

The ransom price was paid into the hands of God, whose justice was offended, whose law we broke, to God who is the lawgiver, to him who is able to save and to destroy, against whom all sin is committed, and who will by no means clear the guilty unless his justice is satisfied. He is the judge of all the earth, who must and will do right. Therefore, Christ is said 'to redeem' men 'unto God by his blood' (Revelation 5:9). The price of redemption, which is the blood of Christ, was paid unto God, whereby redemption from vindictive justice was obtained.

It was not paid into the hands of Satan, or any other enemy that had power over us. The power of Satan was only a usurped power. He had no legal right to hold us captives. Therefore the delivery of our souls out of his hand is by power and not by price. But the justice of God had a legal right to shut us up and detain us as prisoners, until satisfaction was given. Therefore, redemption from avenging justice, which is the redemption that is by Christ, is redemption by a price paid to divine justice for the ransom of his people. The Lord Jesus Christ, himself, is made of God unto us Redemption (1 Corinthians 1:30-31). He redeems and saves his elect by the ransom price of his own blood, the regenerating power of his grace, and the resurrection glory he shall accomplish for us and in us, and shall bestow upon us when he comes again.

'If there be therefore any consolation in Christ, if any comfort of love, if any fellowship of the Spirit, if any bowels and mercies, Fulfil ye my joy, that ye be like minded, having the same love, being of one accord, of one mind. Let nothing be done through strife or vainglory; but in lowliness of mind let each esteem other better than themselves. Look not every man on his own things, but every man also on the things of others. Let this mind be in you, which was also in Christ Jesus: Who, being in the form of God, thought it not robbery to be equal with God: But made himself of no reputation, and took upon him the form of a servant, and was made in the likeness of men: And being found in fashion as a man, he humbled himself, and became obedient unto death, even the death of the cross'. (Philippians 2:1-8)

Chapter 32

Why Did Christ Die?

Philippians chapter two is one of many passages of scripture in which we are exhorted and encouraged as believers to live in this world for the honour of God, serving and promoting one another's happiness and welfare. In this chapter the Apostle Paul urges us to seek and promote spiritual unity among God's saints, love and affection for one another, and humility and lowliness of mind. He urges us to exercise genuine care and concern for one another's happiness and welfare.

The basis of the Apostle's appeal is the grace of God toward us in and through the Lord Jesus Christ. Here and throughout the New Testament, believers are urged to godliness and obedience, not upon the basis of law, but upon the basis of grace. We are motivated and inspired, not by threats of punishment and promises of rewards, but by gratitude and love to God because of the mercy, love, and grace we have received and experienced in Christ.

Arguments for Christian unity

In the first verse of this chapter, Paul gives us four arguments for unity, peace, and love in the Church of God. If we belong to Christ, we ought to constantly strive for and promote unity and peace among God's elect. Indeed, if we truly belong to Christ, we do love one another; and we ought to walk in and build upon that love. Here are four reasons why we should do so.

1. 'If there be therefore any consolation in Christ' – The word 'consolation' means 'comfort' or 'confidence'. This is what Paul is saying: If we have any genuine ground of hope, comfort, and confidence in Christ, founded and based upon his person, his righteousness, his death, and his intercession as our Substitute and Advocate before God, then we ought to comfort one another and build one another up in the hope and confidence of the gospel.

2. 'If there be any comfort of love' – If we enjoy the comfort and strength of God's love, the everlasting love of the Father, the redeeming love of the Son, the regenerating love of the Spirit, and the brotherly love of grace, that love which is so pleasant and delightful, then we ought to give one another the strength and comfort of mutual love.

3. 'If any fellowship of the Spirit' – If we have been brought into fellowship with God and with one another by the Spirit of grace, then we should constantly strive to maintain and build upon that blessed fellowship.

4. 'If any bowels and mercies' – If we have any real depth of affection, if we have any real compassion and concern for Christ, his gospel, his glory, and one another, if our religion is real, if it is more than lip-service to God, let us show that love and concern to one another.

If these things are not in us, if they do not flow from our hearts to the hearts and lives of our brothers and sisters in Christ, if we do not truly love God's people, then our religion, our profession of faith, our doctrinal orthodoxy, and our moral uprightness is nothing but a vain show of hypocrisy. But if these things are in us, Paul says, 'Fulfil ye my joy, that ye be like minded, having the same love, being of one accord, of one mind' (v. 2). Let all the heirs of heaven, let all the children of God, let all believers in Christ, let all the family of God be like minded in all things. Some say that is expecting too much; but that is exactly what Paul is saying here. That is not expecting too much. Let us be like minded, of the same mind, of one accord in love, affection, and care, – in unity, harmony, and peace, – in mind, purpose, and desire. These things reveal the reality or hypocrisy of our faith. These are marks, fruits, and evidences of inward grace.

'Let nothing be done through strife or vainglory; but in lowliness of mind let each esteem other better than themselves' (v. 3). – Anything that is done through strife dishonours God. Anything that divides brethren is a reproach to Christ. Anything that is born of contention casts a slur upon the gospel of the grace of God. The source of strife, division, and conflict between brethren is always vain-glory, pride, self-seeking, self-serving, self-promoting pride (Proverbs 13:10). Let us, therefore, do nothing seeking recognition, honour, and praise. We should always look upon our brothers and sisters in Christ as being spiritually superior to ourselves, because in Christ they are perfect before God. Recognizing these things, we ought to willingly yield to the judgments, desires, pleasures, and rights of others.

'Look not every man on his own things, but every man also on the things of others' (v. 4). – That simply means that the way to promote this unity and peace, this fellowship and love is to look out for and look after one another and quit looking out for yourself. Do not seek your own praise. Seek someone else's praise. Do not promote yourself. Promote someone else. Do not be concerned about your own feelings. Be concerned about your brother's feelings and your sister's feelings.

Friendship and fellowship is a two way street; but we must be willing for it to be all one way, – willing to give and receive nothing in return, – willing to serve and not be served, – willing to care for others and to neither want nor have anyone to care for us. Why? Why should any man or woman be willing to so abase himself, or herself? Why should we set aside our own ambitions, feelings, desires, and preferences for the sake of others? Upon what grounds can anyone make such an appeal? The Holy Spirit gives us the answer to these questions in verses five through eight.

The mind of Christ

'Let this mind be in you', this loving, self-abasing, self-sacrificing mind, 'which was also in Christ Jesus': Our Lord thought not of himself, but of us. He served not himself, but us. He came not to be ministered unto but to minister and to give his life a ransom for us. Our great God and Saviour, the Lord Jesus Christ, 'Who, being in the form of God, thought it not robbery to be equal with God: But made himself of no reputation, and took upon him the form of a servant, and was made in the likeness of men: And being found in fashion as a man, he humbled himself, and became obedient unto death, even the death of the cross'.

This is what the Holy Spirit teaches us in these verses. If the Lord Jesus Christ so loved us, we ought, for Christ's sake, so to love one another (1 John 4:9-11; Romans 12:2; Ephesians 4:32-5:2). Because of his great love for us, that he might save us from our sins, ourselves, and the wrath of God, our all-glorious Lord Jesus Christ became obedient unto death, even the death of the cross.

God the Son willingly assumed our human nature. God's own dear Son, as a man, fulfilled all the requirements of God's law for his people. Then, having fulfilled all righteousness, the Son of God, our Lord Jesus Christ, died upon the cursed tree as the sinners' Substitute.

The purpose of Christ's death

Why did the Lord of Glory endure such great humiliation? Why did the Lord Jesus Christ die in the place of chosen sinners at Calvary? What was the object and purpose of his death? What did the Son of God have in mind, what did he hope to accomplish by dying upon the cursed tree in the place of his people?

Two things are certain. (1) Whatever Christ intended to accomplish in his death, in the act of dying and by the merit and virtue of his death, shall most assuredly be accomplished. Christ, who is himself almighty God, is an effectual Redeemer. It is written, 'He shall not fail' (Isaiah 42:4). And (2) the Word of God tells us plainly and exactly what the Son of God hoped and purposed to accomplish by his death. Here are seven things, plainly revealed in holy scripture, which the Lord Jesus Christ died to accomplish, seven revealed reasons for the death of God's dear Son upon the cursed tree.

1. Christ died that he might be Lord of the entire universe (Romans 14:9)

'For to this end Christ both died, and rose, and revived, that he might be Lord both of the dead and living'. The blessed gospel doctrine of particular, effectual redemption is plainly revealed throughout the scriptures. Christ died to redeem and save God's elect. He did not die to save those who perish in their sins. The Son of God did not lay down his life for those for whom he refused even to pray (John 17:9, 20). The priestly work of our Saviour cannot be divided. His sacrifice and his intercession are made for the same people.

Yet, there is a sense in which our Lord Jesus, as our Mediator, as the God-man, our Surety, bought the whole world and all who are in it (Matthew 13:44). As a man, our Mediator, bought the right to rule the whole world and all who are in it as a sovereign despot (John 17:2; 2 Peter 2:1). He bought the right to dispose of the whole world and all who are in it as a righteous judge (2 Thessalonians

1:6-10). And our Lord Jesus, as a man, bought the right to make all things new and to have the praise of all things (Revelation 21:5; Romans 8:23). By virtue of his death upon the cross, Christ the Man is Lord of all. He has all power over all flesh. He constantly exercises that power as the Sovereign Monarch of the universe to save his own elect (Psalm 2:8; Acts 2:36; John 17:2; Psalm 115:3; 135:6).

2. Christ died upon the cross, under the wrath of God, as our Substitute, so that God might be both just and the Justifier of all who believe on him unto life everlasting (Romans 3:19-28, 5:1)

It is not possible for any of us to justify ourselves by personal obedience to the law, because we are all sinners. It is not possible for God himself to justify us without the perfect fulfilment of the law's righteousness and the complete satisfaction of the law's justice by Christ. 'Shall not the Judge of all the earth do right?' Through the merits of Christ's obedience and death God is just and we are justified, made righteous in God's sight.

It was the specific object of Christ in his death to make all for whom he died righteous before God; and he did (2 Corinthians 5:21; Jeremiah 23:6). Since we who believe on the Son of God are justified without the works of the law, we have no grounds of boasting before God.

By faith in Christ, only by faith in Christ, we fulfil, honour, and satisfy the law of God (Romans 3:31). Thus, all who believe are justified freely by the grace of God through the redemption that is in Christ Jesus.

3. Christ died for us, as our Substitute, under the wrath of God, to put away our sins by the sacrifice of himself (Hebrews 9:24-26)

The Son of God was made to be sin for us (2 Corinthians 5:21). When he died, he put away our sins. Now, in him, God's elect have no sin. Our sins are removed from us as far as the east is from the west. The Lord God has cast them behind his back. Insofar as our heavenly Father is concerned, insofar as the law and justice of God are concerned, we have no sin (Numbers 23:21; 1 John 3:5, Romans8:38). H. G. Spafford described it well ...

> My sin, O the bliss of this glorious thought,
> My sin, not in part, but the whole,
> Is nailed to His cross, and I bear it no more,
> Praise the Lord! It is well with my soul!

4. The Lord Jesus Christ died upon the cursed tree, 'that he might bring us to God' (1 Peter 3:18)

'For Christ also hath once suffered for sins, the just for the unjust, that he might bring us to God, being put to death in the flesh, but quickened by the Spirit'. We were far off from God. Christ brought us nigh unto God. We were alienated from God. Christ reconciled us to God. We were enemies to God. Christ brought us peace with God. We were separated from God. Christ has given us access to God. We could never have come to God. Christ brought us to God, and will yet bring us unto God, and will at last present us holy, unblameable, and unreproveable in his sight, before the presence of his glory (Jude 24-25).

5. Christ 'gave himself for our sins, that he might deliver us from this present evil world, according to the will of God and our Father' (Galatians 1:4)

Our Saviour came down from heaven and died in our place at Calvary to deliver all his people from the evil kingdom of this world, the evil ways of this world, the evil things of this world, the evil religion of this world, and the evil end of this world. In the light of this fact, let us give all the more earnest heed to the inspired psalmist.

> Fret not thyself because of evildoers, neither be thou
> envious against the workers of iniquity. For they shall soon
> be cut down like the grass, and wither as the green herb.
> Trust in the LORD, and do good; so shalt thou dwell in

the land, and verily thou shalt be fed. Delight thyself also in the LORD; and he shall give thee the desires of thine heart. Commit thy way unto the LORD; trust also in him; and he shall bring it to pass. And he shall bring forth thy righteousness as the light, and thy judgment as the noonday. Rest in the LORD, and wait patiently for him: fret not thyself because of him who prospereth in his way, because of the man who bringeth wicked devices to pass. Cease from anger, and forsake wrath: fret not thyself in any wise to do evil. For evildoers shall be cut off: but those that wait upon the LORD, they shall inherit the earth (Psalm 37:1-9).

6. Christ 'gave himself for us, that he might redeem us from all iniquity, and purify unto himself a peculiar people, zealous of good works' (Titus 2:14)

Every word in this text is precious and full of instruction. Do not let a single syllable slip by your eyes unnoticed. The Son of God has redeemed us from all iniquity, its penalty, its dominion, and all its evil consequences. Christ purifies his people whom he has redeemed, as his peculiar, distinct people. He has purified our record in heaven (2 Corinthians 5:17). He gives every redeemed sinner a purified conscience by granting him faith in his blood and righteousness. He will purify us perfectly in the resurrection.

All who are redeemed by the blood of Christ and saved by his grace are his peculiar, distinct, special people; and they are zealous of good works. We belong to Christ as no one else. Every saved sinner is a blood bought, mercy sought, grace caught, Spirit taught, peculiar trophy of God's free, amazing grace in Christ.

All who are Christ's are zealous of good works. That does not mean that believers live in perfection, or even in anything that resembles perfection. It does mean that believers earnestly seek to do the will of God in all things, walking in love toward one another for the glory of him who loved us and gave himself for us.

7. Our most glorious Christ died for us that he might present us to his Father and our Father, before wondering worlds, in the beauty of perfect holiness, to the everlasting praise of the glory of his grace (Ephesians 5:25-27; Colossians 1:21-22; 1 Corinthians 15:24-28; Ephesians 2:7; Jude 24-25)

This, too, is the purpose of Christ in his death; and this, too, shall also be accomplished. These seven things are clearly set forth in the Word of God as the objects of his sin-atoning sacrifice. And, being the objects, the purposes for which he laid down his life, they shall be effectually accomplished by his grace and power. It is written, 'He shall not fail'!

The Lord Jesus Christ came into this world and laid down his life for us so that we, all his people, God's elect, the chosen sons and daughters of God almighty, might, through the merits of his precious, efficacious blood, receive and forever enjoy all the benefits and blessings of adoption in him (Galatians 4:4-5). Redemption, forgiveness, justification, regeneration, sanctification, preservation, and eternal glorification shall be the possession of every blood bought sinner forever to the praise of the triune God, because Christ died. Therefore, we confidently sing,

> Dear dying Lamb, Thy precious blood
> Shall never lose its power,
> 'Til all the ransomed Church of God
> Be saved to sin no more!

'Now unto him that is able to keep you from falling, and to present you faultless before the presence of his glory with exceeding joy, To the only wise God our Saviour, be glory and majesty, dominion and power, both now and for ever. Amen'.

'Even as the Son of man came not to be ministered unto, but to minister, and to give his life a ransom for many'. (Matthew 20:28)

Chapter 33

For Whom Did Christ Die?

Our all glorious Christ, the Son of God, effectually accomplished the redemption of his people by the sacrifice of himself at Calvary.

All men who claim to be Christians believe in and teach limited atonement. The Arminian, free will, works monger, who asserts that Christ died for all men, for those who perish in hell as well as those who are saved, limits the atonement of Christ contrary to scripture. They limit the merit and efficacy of Christ's blood and the atonement made by his blood, asserting that the blood of Christ must be supplemented by man's decision, man's faith, man's obedience, man's baptism, or something else performed by man.

We assert, according to the Word of God, that there is absolutely no limit to the merit and efficacy of Christ's blood and the atonement obtained and accomplished for God's elect by his blood. However, according to the Word of God, the atonement of Christ is limited in intent, scope, design, and purpose to God's elect. To suggest, imply, or teach, indeed, to believe that there are some in hell for whom the Lord Jesus Christ shed his blood and made atonement is to betray an idolater's heart and blaspheme the Son of God, denying his very godhead.

Many wonder why God's servants are so dogmatic regarding the gospel doctrine of particular, effectual redemption. Because this gospel doctrine is so divisive among religious people, and so commonly despised by those who do not know our God, it is the place where compromise is most prevalent. Yet, this is the very heart of the gospel. Either Christ redeemed his people or he failed in the work he came to do, and we are without hope. The blasphemy of universal redemption makes the Son of God a failure. The doctrine of universal, ineffectual redemption, of universal, ineffectual atonement is just as damning to the souls of men as any other doctrine which inherently denies our Saviour's divinity. These things make the doctrine of the atonement a matter of vital importance.

In this study, I want to answer this very important question from the Word of God: For whom did Christ die? We will begin in Matthew 20:28. This is what the Lord Jesus Christ himself says as he describes his mission in this world, 'The Son of man came not to be ministered unto, but to minister, and to give his life a ransom for many'.

Our Saviour here declares that there are indeed 'many' for whom he has given 'his life a ransom', a ransom price, the price of their redemption. They are described as 'many', not all, because these 'many' are a distinct and peculiar people. They are the 'many' who are ordained unto eternal life (Acts 13:48), the 'many' the Father has given to the Son (John 6:37-39), the 'many' whose sins he bore on the cross (1 Peter 2:24), the 'many' for whom his blood was shed for the remission of their sins (Matthew 26:28), the 'many' who are made righteous by his obedience (Romans 5:19), and the 'many' sons, he, the Captain of their salvation, brings to glory (Hebrews 2:10).

The objects of redemption, those for whom Christ died, for whom he made atonement by the shedding of his blood, for whom he obtained eternal redemption, are a special and distinct people. The scriptures declare that they are 'redeemed from the earth' (Revelation 14:3), from among all the other inhabitants of the earth. As explained in the very next verse, they are 'redeemed from among men' (Revelation 14:4). One end of Christ's redemption of them is, 'to purify to himself a peculiar people' (Titus 2:14).

The inspired writers seem to delight in using the pronoun 'us', when speaking of the death of Christ, and our redemption by it. Thus the objects of redemption are identified as a distinct, particular people. 'Christ died for us'. God 'delivered him up for us all'. Christ 'gave himself for us'. He did so 'that he might redeem us'. The saints around his throne sing unto the Lamb, 'Thou hast redeemed us unto God by thy blood'.

The scriptures everywhere teach limited atonement, particular, effectual redemption, accomplished and obtained for God's elect by the sin-atoning death of Christ as our Substitute. There is not a hint, suggestion, or implication of universal atonement anywhere in the Word of God. The Word of God tells us specifically and clearly who those sinners are for whom Christ died.

Do you wonder whether or not the Son of God died for you and obtained eternal redemption for you when he entered into heaven with his own blood? If so, you need only to read the book of God. Here are eight, plain, unmistakably clear answers, given in the book of God to the question: For whom did Christ die?

1. The Lord Jesus Christ died for every sinner in this world who is loved of God with an everlasting love

The objects of Christ's redemption and the objects of God's love are the same. Redemption flows from the love of God and Christ (John 3:16; Romans 5:8; 1 John 3:16; 1 John 4:10). This love from which redemption flows is much, much more than some imaginary, universal benevolence. It is much more than that general kindness shown in providence to all men as the creatures of God. This is a special and discriminating love. It is the special, saving favour which God bears to his own people alone as distinct from others. The Lord God declares, 'Jacob have I loved, but Esau have I hated'.

This special, redeeming love is that which Christ expressed in the sacrifice of himself towards his own that were in the world (John 13:1). All who are thus loved by Christ were redeemed by Christ. They are 'his' people, 'his' sheep, 'his' church. To suggest, or imply that Christ died for reprobate sinners, who are the objects of his just wrath and contempt, such as Esau, is utter nonsense.

2. Our all glorious Christ died for God's elect (Romans 8:30-34)

The objects of election and redemption are the same. 'Who shall lay anything to the charge of God's elect? It is Christ that died'. That bold challenge of faith makes sense only if you understand that Christ died for God's elect and infallibly secured their salvation by his death. The 'us all' for whom God delivered up his Son are the same as those whom he foreknew, and whom he predestinated; and whose calling, justification, and glorification were secured from eternity by God's sovereign purpose of grace toward them.

We see the same thing in Ephesians 1:4 and 7. The 'us' who are said to be chosen in Christ, before the foundation of the world, are the same as those who have redemption in him through his blood. Election and redemption are of equal extent. No more were redeemed by Christ at Calvary than were chosen in him before the foundation of the world.

God's elect are special to him above all people in the world. Special things belong to them which belong to no one else. Yet, we see that everything which is said to be true of the elect is also true of the redeemed. Therefore, we must conclude, according to the scriptures, that the elect and the redeemed are the very same people.

– Are the elect the beloved of the Lord? Does the act of election spring from love? Election presupposes love. So the redeemed are the beloved of God and Christ. Their redemption flows from love.

– Are the elect a people whom God has chosen for his peculiar treasure? The redeemed are purified by Christ to be a peculiar people to himself.

– Do the vessels of mercy, afore prepared for glory, consist of Jews and Gentiles alike? So Christ is the propitiation, not for the sins of the Jews only, or the Redeemer of the Jews only, but for the sins of the Gentile world also, the Redeemer of his people among the Gentiles.

– Are God's elect a great number, a multitude which no man can number out of all nations, kindred, peoples, and tongues? So Christ's redeemed ones are those he has redeemed unto God, out of every kindred, tongue, people, and nation.

– Is it true of the elect that they shall never perish, that they cannot be totally and finally deceived and perish? So, too, it is true of the ransomed of the Lord. They shall come to Zion with everlasting joy. Christ will never lose any part of the purchase of his blood.

3. Our great Saviour's sacrificial work as our sin-atoning Substitute, as our great High Priest was made for those for whom he undertook to be a Surety in the covenant of grace before the world began (Hebrews 7:22)

Those for whom Christ died, those who have been redeemed by his blood, are the same people as those for whom he became a Surety. He was made the Surety of the better testament, of the covenant of grace. As such, he became Surety for those, and for none but those, who had an interest in that covenant. In that great covenant the Son of God engaged himself to be our Surety and Redeemer.

This is very important. It is Christ's suretiship which is the ground and foundation of redemption. This is the reason why our sins, and the punishment of our sins were laid upon him, the reason why he bore and endured the wrath of God for our sins, and paid all our debts as his people. This is the reason why he redeemed us out of the hands of divine justice. The Son of God pledged himself to God the Father as a Surety, and laid himself under obligation to do all these things for us. He became responsible for us in all matters. But those for whom he did not become a Surety were not his responsibility. He was not obliged to pay their debts, or to suffer and die in their room and stead.

Christ's suretiship and redemption are of equal extent, and reach to the same objects; they are the Lord's Benjamins, the sons of his right hand, his beloved sons, that Christ, the antitype of Judah, became a surety for, and laid himself under obligation to bring them safe to glory, and present them to his divine Father. (John Gill)

4. Our almighty, all glorious Redeemer and Saviour died for those who are the people of God (Isaiah 53:8)

The objects of redemption are described by such words and characteristics as show them to be a special and distinct people. Particularly, those who are the objects of redemption are called the people of God and of Christ. 'For the transgressions of my people', says the Lord our God, 'was he stricken' by the rod of justice, to make satisfaction for our sins, and to redeem us from them.

When he was about to come and redeem us, Zacharias, the father of John the Baptist, at his birth said, 'Blessed be the Lord God of Israel! for he hath visited and redeemed his people'. He did so by sending Christ, the Dayspring from on high, as he called him. He visited his people in the flesh and redeemed them by his blood (Luke 1:68,78). Therefore, the angel that appeared to Joseph and instructed him to call the son who was to be born of his wife, Mary, by the name of Jesus, gave this reason, 'for he shall save his people from their sins' (Matthew 1:21).

Someone may say, 'All men are the people of God'. In a sense that is true, inasmuch as they are his creatures. Yet the scriptures expressly tell us that they are not all his redeemed people. Those who are redeemed by Christ are redeemed 'out of every people' (Revelation 5:9).

The redeemed are God's covenant people; of whom he says, 'They shall be my people, and I will be their God'. We are his portion and his inheritance, a people near and dear unto him. All God's elect are a people given to Christ, to be redeemed and saved by him; of whom it is written, 'Thy people shall be willing in the day of thy power'.

5. The Son of God laid down his life and died for those people who are specifically designated as his sheep (John 10:15, 26, 29)

The objects of redemption, those for whom Christ laid down his life a ransom price, are described as 'sheep'. They are the sheep of Christ, his special property as the Good Shepherd. They were given to him by his Father from eternity. These sheep are represented as being everlastingly distinct from others who are not his sheep.

The whole human race is divided into two groups: sheep and goats. Sheep never become goats. Goats never become sheep. We are all one or the other, either sheep or goats. Some of the sheep are saved. Some are lost. But all are safe. They are his sheep. Some are folded. Some are straying. But all are redeemed. They are his sheep. The Word of God tells us certain, specific things about these sheep, things which distinguish the sheep from the goats.

The sheep are known by Christ. He says, 'I know my sheep', not merely by his omniscience, as he knows all men; but he knows his sheep distinctly as his own. 'The Lord knows them that are his', from others. That is just another way of saying, Christ loves his sheep. He has knowledge of them and is joined with a distinct and special love for them. This knowledge and love is such as he has not for those to whom he will say in the last day, 'Depart from me: I know you not'.

The sheep know the shepherd, too. Christ is 'known' by his sheep, for whom he laid down his life. They all know him in his person, offices, and grace. Whereas there are multitudes who neither know the Father nor the Son. The sheep know the Shepherd's voice. That is to say, the sheep know the gospel of Christ, the joyful sound of grace, the glad tidings of redemption accomplished. Whereas the gospel is hid to them that are lost.

Those sheep for whom the Good Shepherd laid down his life, once they are called, hearing his voice, follow the Shepherd who died for them. They follow his Word, his example, and his Spirit. They imitate him in the exercise of grace, love, patience, and humility, and in the performance of every duty. As their Master symbolically fulfilled all righteousness, being buried in the waters of Jordan and rising again, so do the sheep. As the Shepherd kept the memorial feast of redemption accomplished, so do his sheep. It is written, regarding all the redeemed from among men; that they 'follow the Lamb whithersoever he goeth' (Revelation 14:4).

The sheep, being ransomed by the blood of Christ, 'shall never perish'. The goats, set on Christ's left hand, shall be forever cursed and cast into everlasting fire (Matthew 25:33, 34). The sheep shall be blessed forever They are forgiven, justified, sanctified, and sealed. 'They shall never perish'.

6. Our great, sin-atoning Substitute laid down his life and died for the children of God (John 11:52)

Redemption and adoption belong to the same people. According to the prophecy of Caiaphas, Christ was to die, not for the nation of the Jews only, but to 'gather together in one the children of God that were scattered abroad' throughout the Gentile world. Those who are predestinated to adoption by Christ are those who have redemption in him through his blood (Ephesians 1:5, 7).

This blessing of adoption, in the full enjoyment of it in resurrection glory, is called 'the redemption of the body'. The resurrection is called the redemption of our bodies, because redemption, insofar as the application of it is concerned, will not be complete until our very bodies are redeemed from all the consequences of Adam's fall (Romans 8:23; Ephesians 1:14; 4:30).

7. Our all glorious Redeemer died for and redeemed every sinner in this world who believes on him as Saviour and Lord

The fruit of redemption is the evidence of redemption; and faith in Christ is both the fruit and evidence of redemption. The children of God are a particular number of men, who are given of God to Christ, to be redeemed by him. They are the seed promised to him in covenant of grace, that he should see and enjoy, and with whom he shall be satisfied. These are the people of whom he is the everlasting Father. They are the people for whom and on whose account he became incarnate, 'took part of the same flesh and blood'. They are the many sons he shall bring to glory (Hebrews 2:10,13,14).

Not all men are the children of God. They, and only they, are the children of God who are openly and manifestly the children of God by faith, who believe in Christ. Their faith in Christ is owing to and the result of special grace and distinguishing love, a boon of mercy bestowed only upon those who are chosen, redeemed, and called of God (Romans 9:8; Galatians 3:26; John 1:12; 1 John 3:1). If you and I believe on the Son of God, our faith in him is the fruit and evidence of our redemption by him.

8. Our great and glorious Saviour died for, made atonement for, and redeemed his church, which is his bride and spouse, with his precious blood

The objects of redemption are the church and bride of Christ. It is the church which he loved and for which he gave himself as a sacrifice and ransom price. It is his beloved bride that he redeemed unto himself. It is the church he has purchased with his blood, even the general assembly, the church of the firstborn, whose names are written in heaven.

That church is the elect of God whose names are written in the Lamb's book of life (Ephesians 5:25; Acts 20:28). Of that church of which Christ is the head and husband, he is the Redeemer. 'Thy Maker is thine husband; and thy Redeemer the Holy One of Israel' (Isaiah 54:5).

This cannot be said of any denomination, or of all professing to be the church of Christ. The great whore of Babylon is not the spouse of Christ. Those who are drunk with the intoxicating wine of Babylon (Arminian, free will, works religion) do not belong to and have no part with this church which is the Bride of Christ. That church coming from Babel, our Redeemer calls a whore. The church, which is his Bride, he calls a chaste virgin. Though there may be 'threescore queens, and fourscore concubines' of Babylon's sort, yet, says Christ, 'my dove, my undefiled, is but one' (Song of Solomon 6:9). This is his Bride. This is his spouse.

Redemption is not universal and useless, but particular and effectual. Christ did not lay down his life and die for all in general, but for many in particular. If the redeemed are those who are the objects of God's special love and favour, then not all men are redeemed. There are some of whom it is written, 'He that made them, will not have mercy on them; and he that formed them, will show them no favour' (Isaiah 27:11). If the redeemed are the elect of God, and them only, then not all men are redeemed; for all are not chosen. 'The election hath obtained it and the rest are blinded' (Romans 11:7). If only those are redeemed for whom Christ became a Surety, then not all men are redeemed. Christ did not engage to pay the debts of all men. If the redeemed are the people of God and of Christ, then not all are redeemed. There are some on whom God writes a 'Loammi', saying, 'Ye are not my people; and I will not be your God' (Hosea 1:9). If the redeemed are the sheep of Christ, to whom he gives eternal life, then the goats, who will go into everlasting punishment, are not redeemed. If the redeemed are the children of God, and the church and spouse of Christ; then not all men are redeemed. 'For all men have not faith!'

'He that despised Moses' law died without mercy under two or three witnesses: Of how much sorer punishment, suppose ye, shall he be thought worthy, who hath trodden under foot the Son of God, and hath counted the blood of the covenant, wherewith he was sanctified, an unholy thing, and hath done despite unto the Spirit of grace?'
(Hebrews 10:28-29)

Chapter 34

The Blasphemies of Universal Atonement

In these two verses God the Holy Spirit declares that those who despise the gospel of God's free and sovereign grace in Christ shall, in the day of judgment, be worthy of much sorer and more severe punishment than those who despised the law of God given by the hand of Moses to the children of Israel.

There are many, many proper and very sober applications of this warning. Here God himself speaks of men who have 'trodden under foot the Son of God', have counted the blood of the Son of God, 'the blood of the covenant', an unholy thing, and have 'done despite unto the Spirit of grace'. I want you to see, from the Word of God, that those words very accurately describe the religion and the preachers of our day.

I have chosen my words deliberately and purposefully. I have chosen them, either by the Spirit of Christ or by the spirit of antichrist. I will leave that for others to decide; but there is no half-way-house between the two. This is the charge I make against the religion and the religious leaders of this apostate generation: All preachers of Arminian, free will, works religion; all preachers of the damning, blasphemous doctrine of universal atonement or universal redemption, that is to say, all who believe, teach, and preach that the Son of God died to redeem and save all human beings, even those who perish at last in hell under the wrath of God are guilty of this crime. They tread under their feet the blood of the Son of God, count the everlasting blood of the covenant an unholy thing, and do despite unto the Spirit of grace! There is not today, never has been, and never can be any doctrine in all the world more dishonouring to God, more blasphemous to the Lord Jesus Christ, more contrary to the Spirit of grace and to the Word of God, or more damning to the souls of men than the doctrine of universal atonement.

Be sure you understand me. I will not argue with anyone about terminology. When I use the terms *universal atonement* and *universal redemption*, this is what I mean. Universal atonement is the damning delusion of men, which teaches that the Lord Jesus Christ died to make atonement for the sins of all human beings without exception. It is the teaching that, by his blood, Christ merely made atonement possible for all, though he actually procured it for none. Universal redemption is that doctrine which says Christ shed his blood to redeem and save all people, that he made salvation possible for all and provided a way for all to be saved, though he did not actually secure and guarantee anyone's actual redemption and salvation by the shedding of his blood.

It is clearly the teaching of scripture that the Lord Jesus Christ actually and effectually redeemed and made atonement for every sinner for whom he died at Calvary. The death of Christ was not a gamble. Nothing was left to chance. He, by his sin-atoning blood, effectually and infallibly secured the everlasting salvation of God's elect.

Here is a list of indictments against every preacher and teacher of this blasphemous doctrine. I lay these fourteen charges against all who teach that the Lord Jesus Christ died for those who perish in hell under the wrath of God. These are serious, stern indictments. I do not make them lightly; I must make them. I am aware that many consider that the man who writes these lines and all those who believe them, are a bit hard-nosed about the doctrine of the gospel, a little too strict, a little too straight-laced, a little too dogmatic. However, if you will weigh the things here stated, and consider them in the light of holy scripture, I am confident that you will be convinced otherwise.

1. The teaching that Christ died to save all men makes man his own Saviour

If the Lord Jesus only made redemption possible, if he only rendered men saveable and put them in a saveable condition, if he only made it possible for man's sins to be put away, then any who are saved are saved, not because of what he did, but because of what they do. If they are justified, they must justify themselves by their own works. If they are made righteous, they must make themselves righteous by their own obedience. If they are to be born again, they must give themselves spiritual life by the exercise of their own will. If they are sanctified, they must sanctify themselves by their personal holiness. If they are preserved in life and grace, they must preserve and keep themselves.

The Word of God declares, in the plainest term possible, that the Lord Jesus Christ actually did put away the sins of his people and actually obtained eternal redemption for us by his blood (Hebrews 1:3; 9:12; 10:14).

2. The doctrine of universal atonement reduces the love of God to nothing

At first glance some would say, 'That cannot be right. The universal redemptionist says God loves everyone. You say God only loves the elect'. That is my point exactly. The Word of God highly commends the love of God displayed in the death of his Son and in our redemption by his blood. We rejoice to sing ...

> Could we with ink the oceans fill,
> And were the skies of parchment made,
> Were every stalk on earth a quill,
> And every man a scribe by trade –
> To write the love of God above,
> Would drain the oceans dry,
> Nor could the scroll contain the whole,
> Though stretched from sky to sky.

We delight in the love of God! But what kind of love is that which does not secure the salvation of its objects when it has the power to do so? If God loves all men alike, what does the love of God have to do with anyone's salvation? Absolutely nothing! But that is not the teaching of scripture.

The Word of God declares that those who are the objects of God's everlasting love and predestinating grace are also the objects of his effectual call and the possessors of his eternal inheritance (Jeremiah 31:3; Ephesians 1:4-11).

3. The notion of universal atonement is as blasphemous as it is unscriptural because it reduces the wisdom of God to foolishness

We worship and serve the all-wise, omniscient Lord God, wonderful in counsel and infinite in knowledge. But where is the wisdom of forming a plan for the salvation of a people whom he knew would never be saved? Where is the wisdom of God in sacrificing his darling Son for people who were already in hell when he made the sacrifice? That is not the wisdom of God Paul describes and glories in as he declares the everlasting purpose of God toward his elect in the Epistle to the Romans (Romans 8:28-39; 11:33-36).

4. Universal redemption is a denial of the justice of God

According to the Word of God redemption is primarily an act of divine justice. Read the scriptures for yourself, and you cannot fail to see this fact of divine revelation (Psalm 85:8-13; Proverbs 16:6; Isaiah 45:20-21; Romans 3:24-26). If Christ was punished for my sins and I must also bear the punishment for them, the justice of God is gone. In fact, the justice of God gives us as much hope as the grace of God. As hymnwriter Augustus Toplady puts it ...

> From whence this fear and unbelief?
> Has not the Father put to grief,
> His darling Son for me?
> And can the righteous Judge of men,
> Condemn me for that debt of sin,
> Charged to my great Surety?
>
> Complete atonement Christ has made,
> And to God's utmost justice paid,
> All that His people owed.
> Payment God cannot twice demand,
> First at my bleeding Surety's hand,
> And then again at mine!

5. Those who preach universal redemption blaspheme God in their preaching by reducing the omnipotence of almighty God to impotence weaker than the will of man

Isaiah declares that the Lord's arm is not short that it cannot save. But the Arminian tells us plainly that God cannot save multitudes for whom Christ died, though it is his will to do so, because they will not let him save them!

6. Those who preach universal atonement blaspheme God by asserting that the immutable God is, after all, fickle, mutable, and changeable

We are told that God loves all men now, while they live on the earth, but that he will cease to love them when they die and he will cast them into hell! Does that sound like God to you? Oh no! Our God changes not (Malachi 3:6; Job 23:13; James 1:17).

7. I lay the charge of blasphemy against all who teach that Christ died for all, even for those who perish in hell, because it robs God of his glory in salvation

The primary aim of the Triune God in saving sinners is his own great glory (Ephesians 1:3-14). But the Arminian, the free-willer, tells us that man has every reason to boast because it is he, not God, who makes him to differ from others. It is not God's will and God's work that makes the difference between men, but man's will and man's work.

8. Universal atonement is a blasphemous doctrine because it denies the satisfaction of Christ

Universal redemption denies that Christ, by his precious blood shed at Calvary, has satisfied anything. If those for whom he died yet perish themselves, then his death did not satisfy the Old Testament types, the words of the prophets (Isaiah 53:8-12; Daniel 9:24), or the requirements of God's holy law and justice.

9. Universal redemption is a blasphemous, damning heresy, for it affirms that there are multitudes in hell for whom the Lord Jesus Christ died in vain!

Did not the prophet declare, 'He shall see of the travail of his soul and be satisfied'? Did he not assert, 'He shall not fail'? The Son of God did not die in vain!

10. Universal redemption is a doctrine most clearly unscriptural and blasphemous inasmuch as it attempts to separate the priestly office and work of Christ, declaring that Christ sacrificed himself for and died in the place of a people for whom he refused to pray (John 17:9, 20)

What absurdity!

11. Universal atonement is a blasphemous doctrine in that it makes the cross of Christ a failure and asserts that he shall never see of the travail of his soul and be satisfied (Isaiah 53:10-11)

12. Universal redemption is as useless as it is blasphemous because it gives sinners no reason to look to, trust, and hope in Christ

The basis of our hope is redemption accomplished. 'Let Israel hope in the LORD: for with the LORD there is mercy, and with him is plenteous redemption' (Psalm 130:7) The Lord God sends his servants out to declare redemption accomplished, not redemption possible (Isaiah 40:1-2).

13. Universal atonement is as useless as it is blasphemous because it offers believers no reason to love, obey, and glorify Christ

If the Lord Jesus has done no more for his people than he has for the damned, if he loved the lost, prayed for the reprobate, tried to save the multitudes who perish in hell, and loved those who are forever cursed, why should anyone seek to live for him, serve him, and honour him. If it is the believer's will that has turned him to Christ, it seems to me that Christ should serve, honour, and glorify his people, that he is in debt to them, not them to him. Blasphemy! The Word of God makes the fact of our distinct redemption by Christ to be the motive and inspiration for our devotion to him (1 Corinthians 6:9-11, 20).

14. Above all else, I lay this charge against every preacher of universal redemption. He blasphemes God in that he declares that Lord Jesus Christ is a failure; a weak, frustrated, defeated failure, rather than the sovereign, effectual Saviour of his people

It is written, 'He shall (not might, may, or wants to, – but *shall*), save his people from their sins', and, blessed be his name, He shall.

'Wherefore also it is contained in the scripture, Behold, I lay in Sion a chief corner stone, elect, precious: and he that believeth on him shall not be confounded. Unto you therefore which believe he is precious: but unto them which be disobedient, the stone which the builders disallowed, the same is made the head of the corner, And a stone of stumbling, and a rock of offence, even to them which stumble at the word, being disobedient: whereunto also they were appointed'. (1 Peter 2:6-8)

Chapter 35

Stumbling Stones or Stair Steps?

We believe, according to the scriptures, that the Lord Jesus Christ accomplished the redemption of God's elect when he died as our Substitute under the wrath of God, that his blood paid our debt, satisfied the justice of God, and effectually put away our sins forever. We believe that all for whom Christ died shall be with him in glory. However, there are many who do not believe the testimony of scripture regarding the death of Christ. Rather than believing on him unto life everlasting, trusting Christ alone for redemption and righteousness, the vast majority of religious people in this world stumble over the gospel doctrine of the atonement and perish in their sins. As he is revealed in holy scripture, the Lord Jesus Christ is to reprobate, unbelieving, self-righteous men a stone of stumbling and a rock of offence. This is by divine arrangement.

God has so written his Word that reprobate men will get tripped up by it, and stumble over the scriptures as stumbling stones to hell. God has fixed it, so that those who are determined to cling to their own righteousness, who are determined not to submit themselves to the righteousness of God established by, revealed in, and found in Christ alone, will stumble over him and fall into hell. This is exactly what happened to those Jews described in Romans 9:31-33.

> But Israel, which followed after the law of righteousness, hath not attained to the law of righteousness. Wherefore? Because they sought it not by faith, but as it were by the works of the law. For they stumbled at that stumblingstone; As it is written, Behold, I lay in Sion a stumblingstone and rock of offence: and whosoever believeth on him shall not be ashamed.

Those very same scriptures, which, by the blessing of God the Holy Spirit, are as stair steps to God's elect, are stumbling stones to the reprobate and unbelieving.

In this study we will look at those texts of scripture which Arminians most commonly wrest to their own destruction. I have neither the desire nor the inclination to answer the cavils of blaspheming men and women against the Word of God. But I do want to help you who know and worship God to understand his Word and the wonders of his grace more fully. I also want to set forth the teachings of holy scripture with clarity, so that any who read these lines, who are yet without faith in Christ, may be brought by the Spirit of God to faith in our Saviour.

There is not even a hint of universal redemption in the Word of God. Read and interpreted contextually, there is not the slightest implication of the heretical doctrine that Christ died to redeem and save those who perish under the wrath of God in hell. Such doctrine is utter blasphemy. However, there are numerous texts of scripture which are often pointed to, quoted, twisted, and perverted by dishonest blasphemers, and those who are confused by their teaching, to refute the blessed gospel doctrine of distinguishing, particular, effectual redemption. Those scripture texts most often misinterpreted and perverted by men relating to the death of Christ and the atonement he made for God's elect by his blood may be lumped into three categories:

1. Those texts where the word 'all' is used to describe those for whom Christ died.
2. Those texts where the word 'world' is used to describe the people for whom Christ died. And,
3. Those texts which seem to suggest, in the minds of some, that some for whom Christ died might yet perish under the wrath of God.

We will examine these three groups of scripture texts, not to explain away the cavilling objections of those who despise the gospel, but to seek by the teaching of God the Holy Spirit the message of grace contained in them.

Sometimes, when we try to teach people the gospel, explaining passages like John 3:16 and 1 John 2:2, they respond by saying, 'All' means all and 'world' means world. When the Bible uses the word 'all', it means everyone, every human being, without exception. When the Bible uses the word 'world' it means everyone, every human being without exception'. But that simply is not the case. Indeed, the fact that that is not the case is obvious to anyone who cares to look.

For example, in Luke 2:1 we read, 'And it came to pass in those days, that there went out a decree from Caesar Augustus, that all the world should be taxed'. Obviously, the words 'all' and 'world' as they are used in this text refer to all within a specific, limited range, a specific group of people. They have absolutely no bearing upon or reference to you and me.

With that in mind, I want us to look at these three categories of scripture texts:

Scriptures where the word 'all' is used

Those texts of scripture where the word 'all' is used to describe those for whom Christ died *never* refer to all human beings without exception.

In John 1:7 we read, 'The same came for a witness, to bear witness of the Light, that all men through him might believe'. John the Baptist, like all true gospel preachers, was sent as a messenger from God to men, to preach the gospel to lost sinners, so that all who believe the message of redemption and grace in Christ might be saved. If God sent no preacher none could be saved, because faith comes by hearing and hearing by the Word of God. But John was not sent to everyone without exception. God never has sent his preachers to everyone without exception. There are many to whom God never sends a gospel preacher, some to whom God will not allow his servants to go, no matter how much they may desire to go (Acts 16:6-8). The word 'all', as it is used here, must mean all kinds of men, Jews and Gentiles, rich and poor, male and female, bond and free.

When the Lord Jesus said, 'I, if I be lifted up from the earth, will draw all men unto me' (John 12:32), he certainly was not referring to all in an absolute, universal sense. That is obvious from the facts that many were already in hell when he made that statement, and many never have the gospel preached to them. The word 'all' refers again to all kinds of men, not to all men universally.

'Therefore as by the offence of one judgment came upon all men to condemnation; even so by the righteousness of one the free gift came upon all men unto justification of life' (Romans 5:18). 'For as in Adam all die, even so in Christ shall all be made alive' (1 Corinthians 15:22). In these two passages, often quoted as proof texts for universal redemption, the Holy Spirit is declaring that all who were represented in Adam (the entire human race) died in him, and that all who are represented by the Lord Jesus Christ, the last Adam, are made alive by him. To suggest that the word 'all' in these verses means all in an absolute sense is to assert that all shall be saved without exception. Such an interpretation is a denial of the fact that some shall forever suffer the wrath of God.

In 2 Corinthians 5:14-15 we read, 'For the love of Christ constraineth us; because we thus judge, that if one died for all, then were all dead: And that he died for all, that they which live should not henceforth live unto themselves, but unto him which died for them, and rose again'.

The apostle here declares that all for whom Christ died, died with him. We were crucified with Christ (Galatians 2:20). The Son of God died for us that we might live unto God. It is the love of Christ, revealed and experienced in particular, effectual redemption, which motivates, compels, and constrains us in all things spiritual (1 Corinthians 6:9-11, 19-20). The 'all' for whom Christ died are the all who died with him at Calvary and live with him in grace, his sheep, his church, the many sons he shall bring to glory. All for whom the Lord of glory died, shall, as the sure result of his death, be made to live unto him by his grace.

1 Timothy 2:4-6 declares that the Lord God 'will have all men to be saved, and to come unto the knowledge of the truth. For there is one God, and one mediator between God and men, the man Christ Jesus; Who gave himself a ransom for all, to be testified in due time'. God is no respecter of persons. His grace does not come to anyone because of their earthly connections, family tree, or worldly position. The 'all' referred to means all sorts of men. God has his elect everywhere, in every rank of society. The Lord Jesus Christ gave himself a ransom for all God's elect, for whom he is the Mediator, for whom he makes mediation (John 17:9, 20). The objects of his priestly intercession and the objects of his priestly sacrifice are the same.

In 1 Timothy 4:10 we are told that the Lord our God is 'the Saviour of all men, specially of those that believe'. Our great and glorious God and Saviour is that One who is the Saviour of all men in the sense that it is he who preserves all men in life, providing all things necessary for life and maintaining life for and in all. In him we live, and move, and have our being. But he is 'specially' the Saviour of those who believe. He saves all in providence, to serve their ordained purpose for the saving of his own elect (Isaiah 43:1-5). The sons of Ham are kept in life for a while, that they might serve the sons of Shem and Japheth (2 Peter 3:9). It is not our believing that makes him our Saviour 'specially', but his being 'specially' our Saviour that makes us believe. Being our Saviour 'specially', the Lord God loved us with an everlasting love, chose us in eternal election, redeemed us with the precious blood of Christ, called us from death to life by the omnipotent power of his grace, gave us faith in Christ, preserves us in grace, and will bring us to glory in the end.

'For the grace of God that bringeth salvation hath appeared to all men, Teaching us that, denying ungodliness and worldly lusts, we should live soberly, righteously, and godly, in this present world' (Titus 2:11-12). This passage is often cited to refute the gospel doctrine of particular and effectual redemption; but that is precisely what it teaches. The grace of God has appeared to all men. That is to say, Christ has appeared to all men, or the gospel has appeared to all men. But the 'all men' to whom the grace of God has appeared must be understood in a relative sense. There are multitudes that have never even seen a Bible or heard the gospel. The grace of God has appeared to men in a general sense, and appears to all who hear the gospel. However, it comes effectually to those who are taught of God and converted by its power.

Hebrews 2:9 is cited by many who would deny the gospel, as a proof that Christ died for all men without exception. 'But we see Jesus, who was made a little lower than the angels for the suffering of death, crowned with glory and honour; that he by the grace of God should taste death for every man'. The word 'man' is not in the original. The verse ends with the word 'every'. The writer means for us to understand and rejoice in the fact that Christ tasted death for every one of those who are saved by his grace, as the context indicates: every son, every heir, every one of Abraham's seed, every one for whom the Son of God intercedes, every one he calls brother, every one in his church.

'The Lord is not slack concerning his promise, as some men count slackness; but is longsuffering to us-ward, not willing that any should perish, but that all should come to repentance' (2 Peter 3:9). There is no indication of universal redemption here. According to the context, the longsuffering of our God is 'to usward'; and his longsuffering 'is our salvation' (v. 15).

Scriptures where the word 'world' is used

Texts of scripture in which the word 'world' is used to describe those for whom Christ died do not contradict the plain revelation of the gospel. They do not teach the doctrine of universal redemption.

In John 1:9 we read, 'That was the true Light, which lighteth every man that cometh into the world'. That does not mean that he gives saving light to all. If he did, all would be saved. Christ is the Light of the world. He gives the light of creation and conscience to all men (Romans 1:18-20; 2:14-15). He gives the light of holy scripture and the light that comes by the preaching of the gospel to many. He gives the saving light of grace only to his elect.

When John the Baptist declared, 'Behold the Lamb of God, which taketh away the sin of the world' (John 1:29), he was not asserting that Christ takes away all the sins of all men throughout the world. If that were the case, none could ever be lost. Would God punish men for sin who have no sin? John was simply declaring what is declared throughout the New Testament. – The Lord Jesus Christ came to save and has effectually redeemed his people out of every nation in the world. He is not the Saviour and Redeemer of Jews only, but of God's elect among the Gentile nations as well (John 3:16; 4:42; 6:51; 2 Corinthians 5:19; 1 John 2:1-2; 4:14). Those meant by the world, which was reconciled to God by the blood of Christ, are the same as those whose sins God would not impute to them. It is the world of his elect, Jew and Gentile, black and white, bond and free, male and female.

Though saved by the grace of God, God's elect in this world are sinners still. The sweet, good news of the gospel is this: – When we sin we have an Advocate with the Father. Our sins, horrible as they are, can never change our standing before or relationship with God our Father because of who our Advocate is and what he has done. Our mighty Advocate with the Father is Jesus the Christ, the Righteous One. He is the justice satisfying, wrath consuming propitiation for our sins, for all the sins of God's elect in every age and throughout all the world.

Blessed be God, there is a Saviour! But there is only one Saviour for the whole world. Christ is the Way, the only Way. Christ is the Truth, the only Truth. Christ is the Life, the only Life. Christ is the Saviour, the only Saviour.

Scriptures which seem to many to suggest that some for whom Christ died might perish under the wrath of God

There are some passages of holy scripture which seem to suggest to many that some for whom Christ died might yet perish in hell under the wrath of God. Of course, that cannot be. God is just, righteous, and true. He cannot and will not violate his own character. He cannot send anyone to hell for whom his justice has already been satisfied by the sacrifice of his own darling Son.

Romans 14:15 is frequently cited to assert the absurd, that some will perish for whom the Son of God paid the ransom price at Calvary. 'If thy brother be grieved with thy meat, now walkest thou not charitably. Destroy not him with thy meat, for whom Christ died'. The word 'destroy' in this passage means to corrupt, mar, or defile. We must take great care not to use our liberty in Christ at the expense of corrupting the consciences of our weaker brethren for whom Christ died. If Christ died for you, it is a very small thing for me to refrain from any earthly pleasure for you. But what I do, while it may be of great harm to your present peace and stability, can never thwart the purpose of God, destroy the grace of God, or make the blood of Christ of none-effect.

1 Corinthians 8:11-12 must be interpreted in much the same way. 'And through thy knowledge shall the weak brother perish, for whom Christ died? But when ye sin so against the brethren, and wound their weak conscience, ye sin against Christ'.

I have not found a better, more sensible explanation of this text than that given by John Gill. He asserted that the word 'perish' here 'intends, not the perishing of his immortal soul; or of his perishing eternally in hell; which can never be the case of any for whom Christ died; for then the death of Christ would be so far in vain; and not be a security from condemnation; contrary to Romans 8:33'. If that were the case, the death of Christ could not be a full satisfaction to justice. Else, 'God must be unjust, to punish twice for the same offence'. Rather, the word 'perish' speaks of 'the perishing of his peace and comfort for a time; and is explained by 'defiling' and 'wounding' his conscience, and making him to 'offend', through the imprudent use of Christian liberty, in those who had stronger faith and greater knowledge (1 Corinthians 8:7,12,13). Every believer should take great care, therefore, not to offend his weaker brother or sister in Christ. They are 'as near and dear to Christ, since he died for him, as a stronger brother is'.

Many are outwardly sanctified by professed faith in Christ who have never been inwardly sanctified by the experience of grace. In time they forsake Christ and the gospel, bringing upon themselves even greater condemnation than they are under by nature. That is what Hebrews 10:29 declares: 'Of how much sorer punishment, suppose ye, shall he be thought worthy, who hath trodden under foot the Son of God, and hath counted the blood of the covenant, wherewith he was sanctified, an unholy thing, and hath done despite unto the Spirit of grace?'

2 Peter 2:1 is a remarkable declaration of Christ's absolute sovereignty over all men, not an admission of failure, frustration, and defeat on his part, as the Arminian would have us believe: 'But there were false prophets also among the people, even as there shall be false teachers among you, who privily shall bring in damnable

heresies, even denying the Lord that bought them, and bring upon themselves swift destruction'. The word 'Lord' in this verse would be better translated, and should be translated, 'despot'. The word 'bought' is not the word that means, 'to buy out of' or 'deliver'. Rather, it is the word that means, 'to purchase'.

If I were purchasing a house, I would use the word translated 'bought' in this passage. The house would be mine. I would take possession of it. But I would not move the house. If I went into the local pawnshop to redeem a treasured pocket watch I had previously pawned, the word used for redeem would be another word. It would be the word commonly translated 'redeem' in the New Testament, when speaking of the work of Christ at Calvary. It is a word which means, 'to deliver by the payment of a price'.

That is what the Son of God did as our God-man Mediator for his elect. He delivered us from the curse of the law and the wrath of God by the ransom price of his own life's blood. He did not deliver the reprobate or the false prophets described in 2 Peter 2:1. He did, however, as a man, as our God-man Mediator, purchase and take possession of them and of the entire world as a sovereign despot. As a man, he bought the right to rule over and dispose of all flesh, that he might give eternal life to God's elect (John 17:2; Romans 14:9; Philippians 2:9-11). He sold all that he had (2 Corinthians 8:9, and bought the field of God's creation, that he might get the treasure of God's jewels hidden in that field (Matthew 13:44).

It is a great pity that men and women will deliberately pervert and twist the Word of God, rather than acknowledge their total depravity and trust the work of Christ alone for acceptance with God. But we must not allow ourselves to get caught in the snare of debate with infidels. If we do, we rob ourselves of the joy of these holy things. Rather than trying to answer all the carping of reprobate men, let us simply take God at his word, rejoicing in the great and glorious gospel doctrine of particular, effectual redemption. Take these very texts, which are stumbling stones to the reprobate, and use them as stair steps to glory. From these verses we are taught:

1. Redemption by Christ is glorifying to all the character of God.
2. Redemption could never be accomplished or obtained in any other way.
3. Christ has obtained and holds redemption for all God's elect.
4. The redemption obtained by Christ is an eternal redemption.
5. All who believe on the Lord Jesus Christ, by the gift of his grace, through his Spirit, were redeemed by him at Calvary (Galatians 3:13-14).

'But we see Jesus, who was made a little lower than the angels for the suffering of death, crowned with glory and honour; that he by the grace of God should taste death for every man. For it became him, for whom are all things, and by whom are all things, in bringing many sons unto glory, to make the captain of their salvation perfect through sufferings'. (Hebrews 2:9-10)

Chapter 36

The Satisfaction of Christ

Without question, the most wondrous of all God's works is the work of redemption. When we attempt to consider what that work involved, we are lost in astonishment. When we think of the unutterable depths of shame and sorrow into which the Lord of glory entered to save us, we are awed and staggered. A. W. Pink wrote ...

> That the eternal Son of God should lay aside the robes of His ineffable glory and take upon Him the form of a servant, that the Ruler of heaven and earth should be 'made under the law' (Galatians 4:4), that the Creator of the universe should tabernacle in this world and ... 'have not where to lay His head' (Matthew 8:20), is something which no finite mind can comprehend; but where carnal reason fails us, God-given faith believes and worships.

Unfathomable agony

As we trace the path of our Saviour from the throne of life to the tomb of death and behold him who was rich, for our sakes, becoming poor, that we through his poverty might be made rich, we cannot fathom the depths of the wonders before us.

We know that every step in the path of our Redeemer's humiliation was ordained in the eternal purpose of God. Yet, it was a path of immeasurable sorrow, unutterable anguish, ceaseless ignominy, bitter hatred, and relentless persecution that, at last, brought the beloved Son of God, the Darling of heaven, to suffer the painful, shameful death of the cross! Who could ever have imagined such things as these?

Standing at the foot of the cross, as I behold the Holy One nailed to the cursed tree, covered with his own blood and the spit of an enraged mob, made to be sin, forsaken and cursed of God his Father, yet, realizing that this is the work of God's own hand, I am lost in astonishment! I am filled with reverence and awe (2 Corinthians 5:21; Galatians 3:13).

> Yonder – amazing sight! – I see,
> The incarnate Son of God.
> Expiring on the cursed tree,
> And weltering in His blood.
>
> Behold, a purple torrent run,
> Down from his hands and head.
> The crimson tide puts out the sun,
> His groans awake the dead.
>
> The trembling earth, the darkened sky,
> Proclaim the truth aloud;
> And with the amazed centurion, cry,
> 'This is the Son of God!'

Why?

Awed as I am with reverence for my crucified Lord, still there is a question that I cannot suppress, a question that reason and sound judgment cannot fail to ask. The question is just this: – Why? Why did the Son of God suffer such a death? Why did God so torment his beloved Son and kill him in such a horribly ignominious way?

Was it to save my soul? I know that he did so that I might live. He suffered, the Just for the unjust, that he might bring me to God. But was there no other way for the omnipotent God to save me? Was all this done to demonstrate the greatness of God's love to me? Indeed it was (Romans 5:8; 1 John 3:16; 4:9-10).

> Jesus, who left His throne on high,
> Left the bright realms of bliss,
> And came to earth to bleed and die,
> Was ever love like this?

But, surely, God could have revealed his love to me in some other way. Why did he slay his Son? What necessity was there for the Son of God to suffer and die upon the cursed tree?

Only one answer can be found to that question. The justice of God had to be satisfied. There was no necessity for God to save anyone. Salvation is altogether the free gift of his grace. But, having determined to save his elect from the ruins of fallen humanity, the only way God could save his people and forgive their sins was by the death of Christ. 'Without shedding of blood is no remission' (Hebrews 9:22). The justice of God had to be satisfied in order for God to save his people; and the only thing that could ever satisfy the justice of God is the blood of Christ.

Satisfaction necessary

I want to show you from the Word of God both the necessity and the blessedness of Christ's satisfaction of divine justice by his death on the cross. This is a doctrine of utmost importance. It is the glory of the gospel and the glory of the Christian religion. It is the satisfaction of divine justice by the death of Christ that distinguishes Christianity from all other religions. Take the cross out of Christianity, take away the satisfaction of Christ by his death upon the cross, and Christianity is of no more value and benefit to the souls of men than Judaism, Islam, or Hinduism. This is of paramount importance, because without satisfaction for sin, there could be no salvation from it.

The scriptures warn us of 'damnable heresies' brought in by false prophets. Among those damnable heresies, none is more common and none more destructive to the souls of men than the denial of Christ's satisfaction (Hebrews 10:26-29)[1].

Hebrews 2:9-10

Perhaps Hebrews 2:9-10 states the necessity of Christ's satisfaction for sin more clearly than any other single text.

'**We see Jesus**' – We see him with the eye of faith. We see him, because the Spirit of God has revealed him to us. We see that he is Jesus, our Saviour, the Christ of God. We see in him the fulness of the Godhead (Colossians 2:9), the fulness of grace (John 1:14; Colossians 1:19), and the fulness of redemption (Ephesians 1:7). We see him as Christ, our Redeemer, the Son of God, the Son of Man, the Lord our Righteousness. We see him as our all (1 Corinthians 1:31). Do you see him? If you do, flesh and blood has not revealed him to you, but our Father in heaven.

'**Who was made a little lower than the angels**' – He who made the angels was made a little lower than the angels. He was made of the seed of woman, made to be a man, 'made under the law, to redeem them that were under the law' (Galatians 4:4-5). This is the reason for the incarnation. This is why Christ was made a little lower than the angels ...

---

[1] The word 'unholy' in Hebrews 10:29, means 'common'. Those who make the blood of Christ a common thing, without efficacy, without merit, are without hope. There is no other sacrifice for sin.

'**For the suffering of death**' – The Son of God came into this world for the purpose of suffering death. He did not come to be an earthly monarch in Jerusalem. He did not come to establish a new religion. He did not come to be a reformer, or a mere example of morality and virtue. Christ, the Son of God, became a man so that he might die in the place of men and redeem them. He came here to die, because there was no other way for his people to be saved and live. We see this too, since he suffered and died in the place of his people, the Lord Jesus Christ is now ...

'**Crowned with glory and honour**' (Philippians 2:8-11) – Christ is exalted. That Man who died for us at Calvary is now crowned with glory, given all honour, as the Lord of all. The God-man, the Man-God, who died for us, now rules the world to save those people for whom he died (John 17:2). Now, look at the next line. Christ 'was made a little lower than the angels for the suffering of death...'

'**That he by the grace of God should taste death for every man**' – This statement, like all others, must be interpreted within its context and in the light of the entire Word of God. Is this a declaration that Christ died even for those for whom he refused to pray (John 17:9), for those who are not his sheep (John 10:11), for those who are vessels of wrath fitted to destruction (Romans 9:22), for those from whom he has hidden both his works and his grace (Matthew 11:20-25)? Of course not! Does this statement mean that Christ died for those who suffer the wrath of God in hell? No. That would be a declaration that there are some for whom Christ shed his blood in vain and would be a denial of the efficacy of his atonement. What, then, is the meaning of this statement? 'That he by the grace of God should taste death for every man'.

Christ died not merely as a good example, or merely for the good of men, but as the Surety, in the room and place of men. However, our translators, with no apparent reason except to make the sentence read more easily, added the word 'man'. In the Greek text there simply is no word in this verse that should be translated 'man'. The sentence literally should be translated, 'That he by the grace of God should taste death for every', or 'for all', or 'for every one'. The Lord Jesus Christ suffered and died upon the cursed tree for every one of the sons he would bring to glory (v. 10), for every one of the brethren he is not ashamed to own (v. 11), for every member of the church, in the midst of which he will sing praise (v. 12), for every one of the children God the Father had given him to save, for whose sake he assumed flesh and blood (v. 13), and for every one of Abraham's seed, God's elect, whom he took hold of to save (v. 16).

Why was the Son of God made so humble as to suffer and die for his people? What necessity was there for his humiliation and death in the room and stead of his people? Read verse 10 ...

'**For it became him**'– It was necessary, if God would save sinners and bring them to glory, that the Son of God must suffer in their room and stead all that the law and justice of God could demand. The scriptures plainly declare that there was a necessity for the death of Christ (Matthew 16:21; 26:29; John 3:14). It was necessitated by the decree of God (Acts 2:23); Christ's covenant engagements as our Surety (John 10:17-18); the prophecies of the Old Testament (Matthew 26:54); and the election of grace. God did not have to save anyone; but since he has chosen to save some, the only way he could save them was by the satisfaction of justice, through the sacrifice of his own dear Son.

When Paul says, 'it became him', that it was necessary for God to slay his Son to save his people, lest we begin to think that this implies some weakness in God, he immediately describes our God with these words – '**for whom are all things and by whom are all things**'. Here the Lord God is described as that One who is both the ultimate end and first cause of all things (Romans 11:36). All things are for him. He made all things for himself, for the glorifying of all the perfections of his nature (Proverbs 16:4; 2 Corinthians 5:18). And all things are by him. All things in nature, all things in providence, all things in redemption, and all things in grace are the work of our God.

'**In bringing many sons unto glory**' – This is an intimation of God's gracious designs toward his elect. Those whom Christ came to save are many. They were already the sons of God by eternal adoption and divine predestination long before Christ came to redeem them (Galatians 4:4-6). In the covenant of grace, our God declared, 'I will be their Father, and they shall be my sons and daughters'. We were chosen to be the children of God from eternity. We were given power and authority to become the sons of God and given the nature of God's sons in the new birth (John 1:12-13). We were openly and manifestly declared to be the sons of God when we believed by faith in Christ. Our faith in Christ does not make us God's sons. Adoption did that. Faith simply receives the adoption of sons and looks upon God through Christ as our Father (Galatians 4:6; Romans 8:15-16).

The sons of God are many, a great multitude which no man can number, ten thousand times ten thousand. They are the many chosen of God in electing love, the many for whom Christ gave his life a ransom, the many for whom his blood was shed for the remission of sins, the many made righteous by his obedience, the many for whom many mansions are prepared in the Father's house. Of these 'many sons', John Gill wrote …

> God has chosen them 'through sanctification of the Spirit and belief of the truth', to the obtaining of the glory of the Lord Jesus Christ! Christ died for them, and by means of his death, they receive the promise of eternal inheritance, and the inheritance itself. God calls them by his grace to eternal glory, and makes them 'meet to be partakers of the inheritance of the saints in light'.

The Person by whom God's elect are brought to glory is Christ, '**the Captain of their salvation**'. He is called 'the Captain' of our salvation, because he is the One in charge of it, the One responsible for it, the One whose arm alone has accomplished it.

As the Captain of our salvation, the Lord Jesus Christ was '**made perfect through sufferings**'. That is to say, the way, the means by which our great Saviour saved us and perfected, or completed his work as the Captain of our salvation, was by his perfect sufferings and death as our Substitute.

Apart from his sufferings for the satisfaction of justice there could have been no salvation. 'Though he were a Son, yet learned he obedience by the things which he suffered: And being made perfect, he became the Author of eternal salvation unto all them that obey him' (Hebrews 5:8-9).

It was necessary for Christ to suffer and die on the cross, under the wrath of God, to save his people. I repeat – he did not have to save us. But if he saved us, he could not save in any other way. Justice demanded it (Proverbs 16:6; 17:15; Romans 4:5; 1 Peter 3:18). This is what the Spirit of God teaches us in Hebrews 2:9-10: Since it was the design, purpose, and pleasure of the Almighty to bring some of the sons of men into eternal glory and happiness as the sons of God by Christ, it was necessary for Christ, the Son of God, to suffer all that the law and justice of God required for the punishment of sin, dying under the wrath of God as our Substitute.

I do not say that the satisfaction of Christ procures the love of God for us. It does not. The death of Christ is the fruit of God's love, not the cause of it. But I am saying that it is the death of Christ and the satisfaction of justice by his death that opens the way into the embraces of God's arms. We could never have been reconciled to God without the shedding of Christ's blood.

Again, John Gill has written:

> Let me observe to you something relating to experience, which you would do well to lay up in your minds. It may be of use to you hereafter, when you may be tempted to doubt of your interest in Christ's satisfaction. Have you any reason to believe that you have, at any time, had communion with God, in private

or in public, in your closet, or in the family, or in the house of God, under any ordinance, either the ministry of the Word, or prayer, or the Supper of the Lord? Then you may be assured Christ has made satisfaction for you; or you would never have enjoyed such communion.

Summary

Let me summarize the teaching of holy scripture with regard to the satisfaction of Christ by making six statements about it. These six facts are both plainly revealed throughout the scriptures and irrefutable.

1. All men and women by nature, since the fall of our father Adam, are sinners, alienated from God

'All have sinned and come short of the glory of God' (Romans 3:23). As sinners, we are alienated from the life of God and have become enemies unto God. The wages of our sin and enmity to God is death. Every transgression must receive its just recompense of reward (Hebrews 2:2). All sin must be punished, either in the sinner or in the sinner's Substitute. The law, being broken, accuses of sin, condemns the sinner, and demands death. Unless satisfaction is made, the sentence of the law must be executed. The sanction of the law is death. It can never be abrogated, changed, altered, or abated. God will never relax his justice. 'The soul that sinneth, it shall die!' (Ezekiel 18:2).

2. Yet, it is the will of God to save sinners

'He delighteth in mercy!' God has decreed the salvation of some. Christ came to save some. There are some people in this world that must be saved, because it is the will of God to save them; and God's will cannot be frustrated (John 10:16). Every sinner chosen in eternal, electing love must be saved (2 Thessalonians 2:13-14). Every predestined son must be saved (Romans 8:29-30). Every heir of the covenant must be saved (Ephesians 1:3-7). Every child of Adam whose name was written in the Lamb's Book of Life from the foundation of the world must be saved (Revelation 13:8). There is no possibility that even one of God's elect will perish!

3. However, it is impossible for a holy and just God to save any sinner apart from the satisfaction of justice (Hebrews 9:22)

God declares, 'I will by no means clear the guilty' (Exodus 34:7). Yes, God is omnipotent, almighty, and sovereign. He does what he will. I know of no one who declares that glorious truth more fully, more frequently, or more forcibly than I do. But God cannot do that which is contrary to his nature and character.

We do not rob God of his sovereignty when we repeat the declaration of scripture and say, 'God cannot lie'. He who is the Truth cannot lie. Neither do we rob God of his sovereignty when we assert this truth of holy scripture – God cannot forgive sin without the satisfaction of justice. The just, holy, and true God must punish sin.

4. The only way the justice of God's holy law and justice could ever be satisfied is by the substitutionary sacrifice of the Lord Jesus Christ (Job 34:23; Romans 3:24-26)

God could not die, and man could not satisfy; but the God-man both died and satisfied. Two facts demonstrate clearly that there was no other way for justice to be satisfied. Only the death of Christ upon the cross could do it.

The love of God the Father for his Son proves it. Would God almighty slay his darling Son if there were any other way to save his people consistent with his justice? Would the Father sacrifice the Son in vain? Perish the thought! Yet, if righteousness could have come to sinners in any other way, then the Holy Spirit tells us plainly, that 'Christ is dead in vain' (Galatians 2:21).

The prayer of Christ in Gethsemane proves the necessity of his satisfaction, too (Matthew 26:39). If the salvation of his people could be accomplished by any means other than his death upon the cross, would not God the Father have granted his tormented Son the desire of his soul?

> What can justice satisfy?
> Nothing but the blood of Jesus!
> What can God's law magnify?
> Nothing but the blood of Jesus!
> Oh, precious is the flow,
> That makes me white as snow!
> No other fount I know,
> Nothing but the blood of Jesus!

5. It is impossible for God, in his holiness, to punish any sinner for whose sins justice has been satisfied by the blood of Christ (Isaiah 53:11 Romans 7:14) – The law has no claim upon an executed felon. Toplady writes:

> Payment God cannot twice demand,
> First at my bleeding Surety's hand,
> And then again at mine!

6. Every sinner who trusts the Lord Jesus Christ has been chosen, redeemed, and called, and must be forever saved (Hebrews 11:1)

Faith in Christ is the result of grace, not the cause of it. This God given faith is the evidence of election, redemption, and calling. If salvation and eternal life is promised to all who believe on the Son of God, and that salvation and eternal life comes only to chosen, redeemed sinners, called by the Spirit, then I must conclude that if I trust Christ, God the Father chose me from eternity, the Lord Jesus Christ died for me at Calvary, and the Spirit of God has called me by his almighty grace.

What a horrible evil sin is: Nothing but the blood of Christ could make satisfaction for it. God almighty must and will punish sin. The death of Christ as the sinner's Substitute demonstrates the strictness of God's holy law. Yet, there is a way open for sinners to come to God. Christ is the Way. He has made satisfaction for sin. If you trust him, if you come to God by faith in him, he made satisfaction for your sin.

Let us ever admire and adore the perfections of our God (Psalm 85:10-11). Admire his love. Adore his mercy. Rejoice in his grace. Stand in awe of his wisdom, holiness, justice, and truth. All shine forth gloriously in the satisfaction of Christ. 'For it became him, for whom are all things, and by whom are all things, in bringing many sons to glory, to make the Captain of their salvation perfect through sufferings'. Divine wisdom found a ransom for our souls in Christ. Holiness approved of it. Justice is satisfied with it. Truth proclaims it.

'Whom God hath set forth to be a propitiation through faith in his blood, to declare his righteousness for the remission of sins that are past, through the forbearance of God'. (Romans 3:25)

Chapter 37

Three Aspects of Christ's Satisfaction

Gospel preachers speak frequently about the satisfaction of Christ, declaring that he has both made satisfaction for the sins of his people and that he shall forever be satisfied with the results of his finished work. Be sure you understand this. It is crucial to the gospel. Indeed, this matter of Christ making satisfaction and of Christ being satisfied is the gospel.

The Lord Jesus Christ satisfied the law and justice of God for his people when he suffered and died as our substitute upon the cursed tree. By obeying all the precepts of God's holy law as a man, he fulfilled it as our Representative and brought in everlasting righteousness for us. By dying under the curse of the law, bearing our sins, bearing its penalty to the full extremity of divine justice, dying as our Substitute under the wrath of God, our all-glorious Christ satisfied the wrath and justice of God for us.

Thus the Lamb of God put away the sins of God's elect by the sacrifice of himself. He has forever secured for his people complete, total immunity from all the evil consequences of their sins. He has secured the eternal salvation of God's elect by his satisfaction, making it impossible for God in justice to impute their sins to them.

Having satisfied the law and justice of God for us, we are assured that our great Redeemer shall see of the travail of his soul and shall be satisfied. He will see his people, every one of them saved; justified, sanctified, and glorified. Not one ransomed sinner shall perish under the wrath of God. This is the good news we declare in the gospel (Isaiah 40:1-2).

Briefly stated, that is the doctrine of Christ's Satisfaction. This matter of satisfaction is set before us in holy scripture as propitiation, atonement, and reconciliation.

Propitiation

The word 'propitiation' is used three times in the New Testament. In all three places we are told that Christ is our propitiation. The very same Greek word translated 'propitiation' in the New Testament is translated 'mercy seat' in the Greek version of Exodus 25:21 and in Hebrews 9:5.

The mercy seat, which covered the ark of the covenant and covered God's broken law, upon which the cherubim were fixed, upon which they constantly looked, was the place where the atonement blood of the paschal lamb was sprinkled. The mercy seat was the seat of divine majesty where God promised to meet his people in mercy. To the mercy seat men were bidden to look in hope of obtaining mercy from and communion with God through the blood of God's appointed sacrifice (typifying and pointing to the blood of Christ). Now we are bidden to come to the throne of grace that we may obtain mercy and find grace to help in time of need, because there Christ has sprinkled his blood.

The publican mentioned by our Lord in Luke's gospel had a glimpse of Christ as the one represented in the mercy seat. He cried,

'God be merciful (propitious) to me the sinner'. He sought mercy through the propitiatory sacrifice of the Lord Jesus Christ, the Messiah. Let us look at those places in scripture where this word propitiation is used in reference to our Lord Jesus Christ.

Romans 3:25

The first place where the word 'propitiation' is used this way is found in Romans 3:25. 'Whom God hath set forth to be a propitiation through faith in his blood, to declare his righteousness for the remission of sins that are past, through the forbearance of God'.

The Lord Jesus Christ was set forth by God the Father to be our propitiation. He is the one who has made propitiation for us, the one in whom propitiation is found, the one for whose sake God is propitious to sinners, and the one who is himself our Propitiation. Christ is our Mercy Seat. He alone is the place where God meets with sinners, receives us, and blesses us. He is the one by whom justice has been appeased. He is the one who is our Peace. He is the propitiatory Sacrifice for our sins. Just as God in the Old Testament types smelled the sweet savour of the typical, legal sacrifices, and was ceremonially content with them, so Christ's precious blood is a sweet smelling savour to him. John Gill said:

> His sacrifice was an offering of a sweet smelling savour to the Father. He was well pleased with it. It gave him content and satisfaction, because his justice was appeased by it, and the demands of his law were answered. Yea, it was magnified and made honourable.

How has God the Father set forth his dear Son as our Mediator to be the propitiation for our sins? Obviously, Paul does not suggest that the Son was compelled to be subservient to the Father. Not at all. This thing was agreed upon by both the Father and the Son. The Son was just as willing to be our Propitiation as the Father is willing to receive his propitiatory sacrifice. Yet, the Holy Spirit here tells us that it was God the Father who set forth his Son to be a propitiation. How has he done so?

Christ was set forth to be the propitiation for our sins in the eternal purposes and decrees of God. He is the Lamb of God who, verily, was foreordained before the foundation of the world to be slain as the ransom price and propitiatory sacrifice for his people. His sufferings and death as such were according to the determinate counsel and foreknowledge of God (1 Peter 1:19; Acts 2:23; 4:28).

God set forth his Son to be our Propitiation in all the promises, prophecies, and pictures of the Old Testament scriptures. He is the Seed of the woman promised to Adam and Eve in the Garden, who must come to crush the serpent's head. He is the paschal lamb, the brazen serpent, the morning and evening sacrifice, and the promised Substitute of whom the prophets wrote. In the fulness of time, the Son of God was set forth as our Propitiation in human flesh. He was actually made of a woman, made under the law, that he might redeem his people who were under the law.

Our Lord Jesus is still set forth to be the Propitiation for our sins, and shall be until time shall be no more in the gospel. In the Book of God, by the servants of God, and by the Spirit of God, as the gospel is preached Christ is set forth before men as the propitiation, the only and effectual propitiation, for sin.

1 John 2:2

Our Saviour is also called the propitiation for our sins in 1 John 2:1-2. 'My little children, these things write I unto you, that ye sin not. And if any man sin, we have an advocate with the Father, Jesus Christ the righteous: And he is the propitiation for our sins: and not for ours only, but also for the sins of the whole world'. Jesus Christ is the propitiatory sacrifice for the sins of God's elect Jews and Gentiles, throughout all the world, the sacrifice upon which God is merciful to us, being pacified towards us for all that we have done (Hebrews 8:12; Ezekiel 16:6).

1 John 4:10

We see the same thing in 1 John 4:9-10. 'In this was manifested the love of God toward us, because that God sent his only begotten Son into the world, that we might live through him. Herein is love, not that we loved God, but that he loved us, and sent his Son to be the propitiation for our sins'. Because of his great love for his people, God the Father sent his darling Son into the world to be the propitiation for our sins by offering up his soul and body as a sacrifice to divine justice to make atonement for us.

Atonement

As propitiation, or appeasement, is one aspect of Christ's satisfaction, a second aspect of it is atonement. The word 'atonement' is frequently used in the Old Testament in connection with the typical sacrifices of the law and the ceremonial (typical) expiation of sin (Leviticus 1:4; 4:20, 26, 31, 35; 5:6, 10, 13, 16, 18; 16:6, 10, 11, 16-18, 27, 30, 32-34; 17:11).

The basic meaning of the word 'atonement' is 'to cover'. As the ark Noah built for the saving of his house was covered with pitch, as the blood sprinkled on the mercy-seat covered God's broken law beneath it, as the blood sprinkled on the door posts and lintels covered every chosen family in Egypt, so the Lord Jesus Christ, by his sacrifice, the antitype of these, is a covering to his people, from the curses of the law we have broken, from the wrath of God we deserved, and from avenging justice of the holy Lord God to which our sins exposed us.

However, the word 'atonement' is only used one time in the New Testament. We find it only in Romans 5:11. 'And not only so, but we also joy in God through our Lord Jesus Christ, by whom we have now received the atonement'.

This atonement was made for us by Christ our Surety, Head, and Representative. The knowledge, blessing, and benefit of it, the application of it comes to us by the Spirit of God, who takes the blood, righteousness, and sacrifice of Christ and applies it to chosen, redeemed sinners, shows us our interest in the atonement, and causes us to receive the effect of it by trusting Christ. The effect of it is joy, peace, and comfort in the knowledge of redemption accomplished.

The word translated 'atonement' in the King James Version means and might be better translated 'reconciliation'. It is translated that way at times. The Hebrew word for 'atonement' is also translated, in some places, 'reconcile', or 'reconciliation' (Leviticus 6:30). The fact is, atonement and reconciliation for sin are essentially the same thing. Both imply a satisfaction made and accepted by God for sin. The word 'atonement' means 'at one with'. Believers are brought to be at one with God by the sin-atoning blood of Christ. As soon as we believe on the Son of God, we are at one with God, because God has reconciled us to himself by the death of Christ for us.

Reconciliation

The third aspect of Christ's satisfaction is reconciliation. 'And all things are of God, who hath reconciled us to himself by Jesus Christ, and hath given to us the ministry of reconciliation' (2 Corinthians 5:18). Ours is a ministry of reconciliation. We proclaim reconciliation accomplished and seek to persuade sinners, who are by nature haters of God, to be reconciled to him, bowing to and trusting his dear Son, the Lord Jesus Christ.

Reconciliation began with God himself, not with us. 'All things are of God', in nature, providence, and grace, 'Who hath reconciled us to himself by Jesus Christ'. Reconciliation began in the thoughts of his heart, which were thoughts of peace. It was brought up in the council chambers of eternity, and settled in the covenant of grace and peace before the world began. It was executed and accomplished by Christ, by his death, by the blood of his cross (Romans 5:10; Ephesians 2:16; Colossians 1:20-22).

The ransom price of Christ's precious blood was paid to God, against whom all sin is committed, whose law we have broken, and whose justice we have offended. The ransom price was paid to the Lawgiver, who is able to save and to destroy (Romans 5:10;

Ephesians 2:16). Christ's blood was shed to make reconciliation for sin, to make atonement for it (Daniel 9:24; Hebrews 2:17). Christ died to reconcile men and women to God, who are by nature sinners, 'children of wrath', and enemies in their minds to God (Romans 5:10; Ephesians 2:1-4; Colossians 1:21).

All who have been reconciled to God by the sin-atoning death of his Son shall, at God's appointed time, be reconciled to him in their hearts by the power and grace of his Holy Spirit (2 Corinthians 5:17-21). Reconciliation has been made for sinners by the death of Christ. The way is open for sinners to come near unto God and come with full assurance of faith. The way is Christ, his propitiation, and his atonement. God almighty sends his servants with the Word of reconciliation to persuade sinners to be reconciled to him. The motive by which God urges sinners to be reconciled to him is redemption accomplished and the blessed promise of all things new in Christ.

Propitiation is the appeasement of God's wrath by the blood of Christ. Atonement is union made between God and sinners meeting at the mercy seat ('the throne of grace' Hebrews 4:16), where Christ's blood covers our sins. Reconciliation is the reuniting of God and his elect in the person of his dear Son, both looking to the blood of atonement.

erefore if any man be in Christ, he is a new creature: old
js are passed way; behold, all things come new.
all things are God, who hath reconcile himself by
s Christ, and hath given to us the ministr nciliation;
vit, that God was in Christ, reconciling the wo to himself,
imputing their trespasses unto them; and committed
unto us the word of reconciliation. Now then we are ambassadors
for Christ, as though God did beseech you by us: we pray you
in Christ's stead, be ye reconciled to God. For he hath made
him to be sin for us, who knew no sin; that we might be made
the righteousness of God in him'.
(2 Corinthians 5:17-21)

Chapter 38

Reconciliation

A glorious promise

'Therefore if any man be in Christ, he is a new creature: old
things are passed away; behold, all things are become new' (v. 17).
Here is both a statement of fact regarding all true believers and a
glorious promise to all who shall trust the Lord Jesus Christ. All
who are in Christ by the experience of God's grace, in Christ by the
new birth, in Christ by faith, are new creatures in him.

This is a declaration of reconciliation accomplished. In the context
the Holy Spirit is not describing the believer's experience of
regeneration. Certainly, the Holy Spirit gives every called sinner a
new heart, a new will, and a new nature in regeneration. Christ is
formed in his elect by the regenerating, sanctifying grace and power
of God the Holy Spirit. But in 2 Corinthians 5 sinners are called to
Christ and persuaded to come to Christ by the gospel declaration of
that which the Lord Jesus Christ accomplished for sinners at Calvary.

2 Corinthians 5:17 declares that all who come to Christ, all who trust him, having been redeemed by him, are completely reconciled to God in him. If we trust Christ, we are new creatures in him. Our old record of sin has been thoroughly, completely purged away, forever eradicated from the books of law in the court of heaven, and all things have become new. We have a new record in heaven. It is a record of perfect righteousness (the righteousness of Christ imputed to us) and complete satisfaction, by the blood of Christ shed for us. Our sins cannot be found (Jeremiah 50:20) because Christ put them away.

A gospel proclamation

In the preaching of the gospel we do not offer reconciliation to sinners, or set before men terms and conditions of reconciliation. We proclaim reconciliation accomplished. 'And all things are of God, who hath reconciled us to himself by Jesus Christ, and hath given to us the ministry of reconciliation; To wit, that God was in Christ, reconciling the world unto himself, not imputing their trespasses unto them; and hath committed unto us the word of reconciliation' (vv. 18-19).

Reconciliation began in eternity, in the purpose of God. His thoughts toward his elect were thoughts of peace from eternity. Insofar as God's purpose is concerned, this matter was settled in eternity in the everlasting covenant of grace, and peace made between the three persons of the divine trinity before the world began (2 Samuel 23:5; Romans 8:28-31; Ephesians 1:3-6).

This reconciliation, which was purposed of God from eternity, was actually executed in time and accomplished by the Lord Jesus Christ at Calvary, who has reconciled us to God by his precious blood. In verse nineteen Paul explains what was going on at Calvary when God sacrificed his own dear Son in the place of chosen sinners. He says, 'God was in Christ, reconciling the world (the world of his elect) unto himself, not imputing their trespasses unto them'. The reconciliation accomplished by the shed blood of the Lamb of God was a reconciliation made for sin and for sinners, to make atonement for sin and to bring chosen sinners into an everlasting union of peace with God (Daniel 9:24; Romans 5:10; Ephesians 2:16; Colossians 1:20-22; Hebrews 2:17).

This reconciliation, purposed by God the Father and executed by God the Son, is effectually wrought and established in the hearts of God's elect when God the Holy Spirit speaks peace to their hearts by the gospel. When he gives life and faith to chosen, redeemed sinners, sprinkling their consciences with the sin-atoning blood of Christ, he graciously causes those who are by nature children of wrath, even as others, those who are by nature enmity against God, to be reconciled to him by the blood of Christ (Colossians 1:20-21). If you are in Christ, if you trust the Son of God, it is because there came a time when God sent a gospel preacher to you to proclaim to you the word of reconciliation in the power of his Spirit. Thereby he reconciled you to himself. Had he not done so, you would yet be among those who are haters of God.

A gracious persuasion

In verses 20-21, the apostle Paul tells us of how God conquered our hearts, subdued our spirits, brought us to our knees, and reconciled us to himself. 'Now then we are ambassadors for Christ, as though God did beseech you by us: we pray you in Christ's stead, be ye reconciled to God. For he hath made him to be sin for us, who knew no sin; that we might be made the righteousness of God in him'. It is by the revelation of Christ in a sinner's heart by the gospel that the Holy Spirit graciously and effectually persuades chosen, redeemed sinners to come to Christ. Once Christ is revealed in us in the day of his power, we are made willing recipients of his grace (Psalm 65:4; 110:3)

Enmity against God

Since the sin and fall of our father Adam, we are all by nature enemies of God (Romans 8:7; Ephesians 2:3; Colossians 1:21). 'The carnal mind is enmity against God'. This is just as true of God's elect in their natural state as it is of the reprobate. We are all by nature haters of God, and as such, 'children of wrath, even as others'. We are all 'alienated and enemies in our mind by wicked works', until God saves us by his grace.

First, the Spirit of God tells us that there is in every son and daughter of Adam a heart of enmity against God. (Romans 8:7). Every one of us is in his heart, not only the enemy of God, but enmity itself against God. What does that mean? It means that all men and women by nature hate God. Our natural hearts of flesh despise him. The very Being of God is obnoxious to fallen man. We all naturally wish that he did not exist. The nature, character, and perfections of God are odious to our proud flesh. We all naturally either deny or misrepresent the attributes of his holy Being, and frame an image of him in our minds as one altogether such as ourselves. The purposes and decrees of God, which men cannot bear, they insolently denounce. The providences of God we charge with inequality and unrighteousness, as though we were the judges of the Almighty!

The natural heart is no less insolent and hateful toward Christ. Everyone loves baby Jesus in the manger. But everyone despises Christ crucified. Man does not despise the fact that Christ died at Calvary; but all men do, by nature, despise the gospel message of Christ crucified, the message of the particular, effectual redemption of God's elect accomplished by Christ alone. Everyone loves the risen Jesus at Easter. But everyone despises the enthroned God-man, the sovereign Monarch of the universe. His dominion, his offices, and his ordinances, as presented in scripture, man abhors.

The same thing is true of God the Holy Spirit. We live in a day of such religious nonsense and foolishness that Pentecostalism has become accepted as the norm of religion. That fact itself ought to tell us that it is not of God. Everyone loves the spine tingling, tongue twisting, trance enhancing spirit of antichrist. But if you speak to religious people for just a few minutes about the sovereign Holy

Spirit, whose grace and power are always effectual, irresistible, and saving, you will discover that their sweet disposition of religion is just a covering for the acid hatred they harbour in their hearts against God. They do not know him. They will not receive him. And those things taught and revealed by him they consider foolishness.

This hatred of God is manifest openly in the hatred of all men for God's saints in this world. John Gill wrote:

> There is an old and implacable enmity between the seed of the woman and the seed of the serpent; the saints are hated by the world, because chosen and called out of the world. God's elect are themselves, until they are born of his Spirit, like Saul of Tarsus, hateful and hating one another.

The scriptures also tell us that there is an external enmity against God, which is manifest by the wicked works and sinful actions openly committed by sinners (Colossians 1:21). These outward acts of hostility against God are contrary to his nature and will, and are violations of his holy law. They are abominable in his sight and provoke his wrath. Men's sins stir up the wrath of the Almighty and cause it to be revealed from heaven against the children of disobedience. We all deserve God's wrath. Sins are breaches of his law. Sin separates man from God; and, unless God intervenes in grace, will forever separate man from God in hell. Our sins set us afar off from God, so that the natural man has no communion with, or access to the holy Lord God.

There is a just and righteous enmity on the part of God toward fallen man. The scriptures declare that there is legal enmity against fallen men. Fallen men are declared in scripture to be enemies of, traitors to, and rebels against the holy Lord God. Even God's elect were considered such when Christ died to make reconciliation for us. It is written, 'while we were sinners, Christ died for us, and when we were enemies, we were reconciled to God by the death of his Son' (Romans 5:8-10).

It is this law enmity that was slain by Christ, and removed by his death. There was never any enmity in the heart of God against his elect. He loves us with an eternal, everlasting love. But the law we broke, constantly broke from our youth up, had to be satisfied. Therefore, we could never approach or be accepted by God until the broken, violated law of God was satisfied.

Enemies reconciled

Reconciliation is a restoration of communion, fellowship, and peace between those who have been enemies. It supposes a former friendship. It implies a present alienation. In our case, it is such an alienation as could never be resolved by us.

The only way sinners could ever be reconciled to God is by the precious shed blood of his own dear Son, the Lord Jesus Christ. There is no other way possible for the holy Lord God to be both 'a just God and a Saviour'. Righteousness must be maintained. Justice must be satisfied. God could not save sinners in any way, except in a way that would magnify and honour his holy law. That is why Christ came here to die (Romans 4:24-26; 2 Corinthians 5:20-6:2; Galatians 2:21).

The means by which this reconciliation was made is the blood of Christ poured out unto death at Calvary as the sinners' sin-atoning Substitute. He alone is the Reconciler and Peace Maker. Sinners can never make peace with God, or reconcile themselves to him. No man can make satisfaction for his sins. It cannot be done by our works of righteousness, which are, themselves, impure, imperfect, and utterly sinful. Our imaginary works of righteousness are themselves just filthy rags before the Almighty. Repentance cannot atone for sin. Even faith in Christ does not contribute anything to the satisfaction of God's justice. Faith receives the atonement (Romans 5:11), but it does not make atonement or make atonement effectual.

There is nothing a sinner can do that will make reconciliation and peace for him. That which will make reconciliation and peace, no mere man can do. What is that? It is nothing less than fulfilling of the whole law, complete, perfect compliance (inward and outward, from the cradle to the grave) with all its demands, and the complete satisfaction of the law's infinite justice (Romans 8:3-4). Death is the sanction of the law and the wages of sin. That means that there can be no reconciliation made, but by death. The sacrifices of beasts could never put away sin (Hebrews 10:1-4). Though the whole world should suffer the wrath of God in hell forever, the death of mere mortals (and sinful mortals at that) could never atone for sin. There is no other way of peace, reconciliation, and atonement being made, but by the death of Christ, God's own dear Son. Only he, who is both God and man in one glorious person, could and did offer a sacrifice of such infinite merit and efficacy that the holy Lord God could, in strict justice, say, 'ENOUGH!'

'Being justified freely by his grace through the redemption that is in Christ Jesus'.
(Romans 3:24)

Chapter 39

Fourfold Justification

Perhaps the most important fact revealed in holy scripture is the one which men most presumptuously ignore, the fact that God is just. 'Justice and truth are the habitation of his throne'. It is not possible for us to understand the grace of God, the judgment of God, or the work of Christ until we have some understanding of the justice of God.

Because the Lord our God is just, he must always deal with men upon the grounds of strict justice. The justice of God is the rectitude and righteousness of his character, that which compels him to deal with all of his creatures in strict accordance with their deserts. Justice and holiness are as essential to the character of God as love and mercy. God can no more put aside his justice in his dealings with men than he can put aside love from his character. Because God is just, the only way he can save a guilty sinner, the only way he can bring a sinner into an eternal union of life with himself, is if he can make the sinner guiltless and sinless in the eyes of his own law and justice.

Justification

This act of God's matchless grace, by which he declares men to be guiltless and sinless, is what the apostle Paul calls 'justification'. Justification is a legal term. It means that God declares chosen, redeemed sinners guiltless, sinless, and perfectly righteous before his law. And when God declares that a person is guiltless and sinless, perfectly righteousness before him, that person really is, in the eyes of God, perfectly righteous. Our righteousness before God is not just a merciful supposition. It is a blessed reality in Christ. Every believer in the Lord Jesus Christ is truly justified, perfectly righteous in the sight of God.

But how is this justification accomplished? This is the great question of the ages. 'How can a man be justified with God? Or how can he be clean that is born of a woman?' (Job 25:4). How can God be just and yet justify the ungodly? Find the answer to that question and you have learned the gospel. If you have not found the answer to that question, you do not yet know the gospel.

Satisfaction

Because God is holy, just, and true, he demands an infinite satisfaction for sin. No man can ever be saved until he has suffered the just penalty of the law due unto his sins, so that his crimes and offences against the law of God no longer exist in the eyes of the law. God is as good as his word. He has declared, 'The soul that sinneth, it shall die'.

The Lord forbade Adam to eat of the tree of the knowledge of good and evil, saying, 'for in the day thou eatest thereof thou shalt surely die' (Genesis 2:17). No sooner did Adam eat of that tree than he and all his race died. When our father Adam (our divinely appointed federal head and representative) died, we all died spiritually. We began to die physically. We came under the curse of death eternally. Eternal death in hell is the sentence of man's sin against God, because mortal man can never make an infinite satisfaction for sin.

Righteousness

Not only does God require an infinite satisfaction for sin; he also requires of man perfect righteousness. No man will ever enter into heaven, in the eternal bliss of fellowship with God, no man will ever be accepted in God's presence, no man will ever be brought into union with the eternal God, until he is perfectly holy and righteous, even as God himself. The Holy Lord God says, 'Be ye holy, for I am holy'. He says, 'Be ye therefore perfect, even as your Father which is in heaven is perfect' (Matthew 5:48).

God requires total, absolute perfection. He will accept no one who is not perfect in holiness. Unless we render unto him a perfection of heart, perfection of thought, and perfection of life, with never so much as one deviation from absolute holiness, none of us shall ever see his face. If God ever accepted, delighted in, and was satisfied with anything less than absolute perfection, he would cease to be God.

Substitution

Is man therefore without hope? God requires an infinite satisfaction for sin. We cannot give it. God demands absolute perfection. We cannot perform it. Are we all hopelessly doomed? Must we all perish? Is there no hope for fallen man? Blessed be God, there is hope for sinners! He says, 'I have laid help upon one that is mighty'. The Lord God has appointed One in whom 'mercy and truth are met together; righteousness and peace have kissed each other'.

This is the good news of the gospel. God has set forth his own Son, the Lord Jesus Christ, as our Substitute and Representative. As our Substitute, Christ has done for us what we could not do for ourselves, putting away our sins, bringing in an everlasting righteousness, and accomplishing our justification. The Lord Jesus Christ has taken upon himself our nature. He is the God-man. The Son of God rendered unto God the perfection and righteousness, which God required of men. Our Lord Jesus Christ made an infinite satisfaction for sin, by pouring out his life's blood unto death at Calvary. All that he did, he did as the Representative and Substitute of God's elect; and all that he has done for us, we have done in him. Every true believer has both rendered perfect righteousness to God and made an infinite satisfaction for his sin in the Person of our all glorious Christ. Just as we sinned and died in the first substitute man (Adam – Romans 5:12), so we have obeyed God and become righteous by the second and last substitute Man (the Lord Jesus Christ – Romans 5:18-19).

As the result of Christ's finished work as our Representative and Substitute, it is a perfectly just thing for God to justify all who believe on him. In saving our souls and bringing us to heaven, the Lord God deals with us in exact accordance with justice. He gives us that which, in Christ, we deserve. The fact is, justice cannot allow one of those to perish for whom Christ lived and died and rose again. In this study, we will see that the scriptures declare that God's elect are justified in four ways. If we are justified, we are justified by the decree of God the Father in eternity, by the death of God the Son at Calvary, by the declaration of God the Holy Spirit in conversion, and by the display of good works before men.

The decree of God

First, our justification was accomplished by the decree of God the Father in eternity. In the mind and purpose of God all his elect were justified from eternity. Our justification was actually accomplished by God's sovereign purpose of grace in eternal predestination before the worlds were made. This is not a matter of speculation or hair-splitting theological precision, but a matter of unmistakable revelation. Read it for yourself in the Book of God, 'Moreover whom he did predestinate, them he also called: and whom he called, them he also justified: and whom he justified, them he also glorified' (Romans 8:30).

Our justification did not commence in time, but in eternity. Paul, speaking of God's eternal decree of predestination, here declares that all of God's elect were justified in his eternal purpose of grace. As John Gill put it, 'God's will to elect is the election of his people; so also his will to justify them, is the justification of them'. God's act of justification is entirely an act of his grace. It is God accounting and constituting us righteous, through the righteousness of his Son. From all eternity, God has looked upon his Son as the Substitute of his elect, and looking upon us in Christ, we are, and always have been, righteous in his sight.

In the mind and purpose of God, Christ is the Lamb slain from the foundation of the world (Revelation 13:8). Isaiah 53 is commonly read as a prophecy of our Saviour's death at Calvary; and it certainly is that. Yet, the passage speaks of that which was already done long before our Saviour's incarnation. God the Father set up his Son as our Surety, our Substitute, and our Redeemer, before the world began, as 'the Lamb slain from the foundation of the world', as that One in whom he delighted, and whose 'delights were with the sons of men' from eternity (Proverbs 8:30-31). As such, in his own mind, God the Father looked upon Christ his Son as having been slain for us from eternity. As Abraham sacrificed Isaac in the purpose and determination of his heart (Genesis 22:12), so our heavenly Father sacrificed his beloved Son and received his sacrifice for his people before the world began, making us 'accepted in the Beloved' (Ephesians 1:6). Because God our Father looked upon Christ as one already sacrificed for us before the world was, all the blessings of grace were given to us in him (Ephesians 1:3-7; 2 Timothy 1:9). Being accepted of God in Christ from eternity, we were granted grace, redemption, forgiveness, justification, and sanctification in Christ before the worlds were made. Thomas Goodwin wrote:

> We may say of all spiritual blessings in Christ what is said of Christ himself, that 'his goings forth are from everlasting'. In Christ we are blessed with all spiritual blessings (Ephesians 1:3). As we are blessed with all others, so with this also, that we were justified then in Christ.

Two facts compel us to look upon justification as an eternal act of God.

1. Had it not been for the fact that God looked upon his elect as being righteous and justified in Christ from eternity, he would have destroyed our race as soon as Adam sinned. God spared Adam and all the human race the full execution of the wrath threatened upon him, because there was in Adam's seed an elect race who must be saved. God spared Sodom until Lot was delivered from the city, so God spares this world for the sake of his elect who must be saved (2 Peter 3:9).

2. The Old Testament saints were justified by Christ, just as we are today, in exactly the same way and for the same reason. Their justification was just as full, complete, and perfect as ours (Hebrews 9:15, 22; Romans 3:25). All true believers were eternally justified in the purpose of God.

The death of Christ

Second, we are justified by the death of the Lord Jesus Christ, the Son of God, at Calvary (Romans 3:24-26). Though he is the Lamb slain from the foundation of the world, our Saviour was also slain in time for the redemption of our souls. Though God's elect were justified by his sovereign decree in eternal predestination, we were also justified by the precious shed blood of God's dear Son at Calvary.

The Bible does not teach that justification was merely provided, or made possible by the death of Christ. The Bible declares that justification was accomplished at Calvary. If it was merely provided or made possible for us, but is not accomplished until we believe, then our faith would be as much the cause of justification as the purpose of God and the sacrifice of Christ. But that is not the case. The Holy Spirit tells us plainly that when Christ died, those for whom he died were justified (Romans 3:24-26; 4:25).

C. H. Spurgeon understood this. He said, 'I must hold that, in the moment when Jesus Christ paid my debts, my debts were cancelled; in the hour when he worked out for me a perfect righteousness it was imputed to me; and therefore, I may, as a believer, say I was complete in Christ before I was born, accepted in Jesus, even as Levi was blessed in the loins of Abraham'.

When the scriptures declare that we are justified by the faith of Christ, or by faith in Christ, the meaning is not that our faith justifies us, but rather that Christ, the Object of our faith, justifies us. We are not justified by our act of faith in him, but by his faithful obedience to God for us as our Representative. Faith receives the blessedness of peace with God as the result of justification. It is written, Christ 'was delivered for (because of) our offences, and was raised again for (because of) our justification. Therefore being justified, we have peace with God through our Lord Jesus Christ' (Romans 4:25-5:1).

In his life of obedience to the law and will of God, the Lord Jesus Christ worked out a perfect righteousness for us. In him all God's elect have perfectly and fully obeyed God's holy law (Daniel 9:24; Jeremiah 23:6; 33:16; 1 Corinthians 1:30). In his death at Calvary, all for whom he died did themselves die, fully satisfying the demands of God's law and justice against us for sin (Galatians 3:13; 2:20; Romans 6:6-7; 8:1).

Since our Redeemer is both God and man in one Glorious Person, all that he has done is of infinite value for all who trust him. He has effectually accomplished the eternal justification of his people. He has obtained eternal redemption for us (Hebrews 9:12). He has put away the sins of his people (Colossians 2:13-15; Hebrews 9:26). He has perfected forever those who were set apart as the objects of his grace (Hebrews 10:14).

> Near, so very near to God,
> Nearer I cannot be,
> For in the Person of his Son,
> I am as near as He.

> In thy Surety thou art free,
>> His dear hands were pierced for thee:
> With His spotless garments on,
>> Holy as the Holy One.

This is complete, perfect justification. The law can require no more of us than perfect righteousness and infinite satisfaction (Ephesians 2:4-6). Toplady writes:

> Complete atonement Thou hast made,
>> And to the utmost farthing paid,
> Whate'er Thy people owed.
>> Nor can God's wrath on me take place,
> If sheltered in Thy righteousness,
>> And sprinkled with Thy blood.

> If Thou hast my discharge procured,
>> And freely in my room endured,
> The whole of wrath divine:
>> Payment God cannot twice demand,
> First at my bleeding Surety's hand,
>> And then again at mine.

We were eternally justified by the decree of God the Father before the world began. We were justified by the death of God the Son at Calvary. By virtue of, and upon the merits of, the life and death of Christ as our Substitute, God is both just and the Justifier of all who believe on his Son. Now, in perfect consistency with his justice, God forgives all the sins of all his people. 'He is faithful and just to forgive us our sins'. In Christ, God both punishes and saves the believing sinner.

The declaration of the Holy Spirit

Third, every true believer is justified by the declaration of God the Holy Spirit in conversion (Romans 4:25-5:1). When God the Holy Spirit regenerates the sinner, giving him life and faith in Christ, as that sinner looks to Christ alone as his Saviour and Redeemer, the blessed Spirit sprinkles the blood of Christ upon the conscience and speaks like a bailiff reading the verdict in court 'Justified!' Thus every believing sinner receives justification by faith in Christ.

Christ has justified us by his great sin-atoning sacrifice; and all who believe on him as Lord and Saviour receive the many benefits of his finished work. One of those many benefits which we receive by faith in him is justification.

Faith does not cause God to justify us. The obedience of Christ has done that. But faith, resting upon Christ alone as Saviour, obtains peace with God, even the peace of perfect, complete justification. Faith does not merit justification with God; but faith receives justification. Faith is not the basis upon which men are justified; but faith is the instrument by which justification is received.

Faith is essential; but it is not meritorious. Faith receives Christ; but it does not merit Christ. Faith receives the forgiveness of sin; but it does not merit forgiveness. Faith receives grace; but it does not merit grace. Faith receives justification; but it does not merit justification.

We were justified in the court of heaven by the decree of God the Father and by the death of God the Son. Then, in the experience of grace, we are justified in the court of conscience by the declaration of God the Holy Spirit.

The display of works

Fourth, all who know Christ, in the experience of grace, are justified by the display of good works before men (James 2:14-26). Yes, there is a sense in which we are justified by works, not before God, but before men. We justify our profession of faith in Christ by our works. Believers do not show their faith by creeds, confessions, and catechisms, but by their conduct. This is what the Holy Spirit teaches us in James 2:14-26.

James and Paul are not opposed to each other. In Romans Paul shows us the accomplishment of justification. James shows us the evidence of justification. If a person is a true believer in the Lord Jesus Christ, he will justify his faith and prove its reality by works of righteous obedience to God, even as Abraham did. Any faith that does not produce obedience to God is a false faith, a demonic delusion. It is not the faith of God's elect. Free grace is not opposed to good works. Free grace promotes good works (Titus 3:4-8, 14).

What are those works that justify our professed faith before men? What are those works that prove the reality of our profession? The Holy Spirit describes them in the book of James in a fourfold manner.

1. Good works are works of patient submission to the will of God (James 1:2-3).
2. Good works are works of genuine love toward the people of God (James 2:15-16). If we love each other, we bear one another's burdens, weep with those who weep and rejoice with those who rejoice. We provide for, care for, protect, and forgive those who are the objects of our love.
3. Good works are works of faithful obedience to the Word of God (James 2:21-23). Believers bow to the will of God in providence and obey the revealed will of God in scripture.
4. Good works are works of self-denial and sacrifice for the glory of God (James 2:23-25).

Every believer is eternally justified in the purpose of God by the decree of God the Father. All of God's elect were fully justified in time at Calvary by the death of God the Son. Every believer receives complete justification by faith in Christ, in the experience of grace, by the declaration of God the Holy Spirit in conversion. Every true believer is justified before men by the display of good works. Our justification is an eternal act of God, accomplished at Calvary, received by faith, and proved by works.

'Who shall lay any thing to the charge of God's elect?
It is God that justifieth'.
(Romans 8:33)

Chapter 40

'It is God that Justifieth'

Justification, as it is revealed and taught in the Word of God, is the imputation of Christ's righteousness to us, not the imparting of it, or the infusion of it. In the new birth, sanctification, the righteousness nature of Christ is imparted to the regenerate soul. In justification, it is imputed. That by which we are justified before God is not our experience of grace, and certainly not our own works of righteousness but the obedience and blood of Christ.

The word justify is never used in the Bible to represent any internal change in us. It is a strictly legal, forensic term. It is always used with reference to judicial matters (Deuteronomy 25:1; Proverbs 17:15; Isaiah 5:22; Matthew 12:37; Job 9:2-3; Psalm 143). We are justified freely by the grace of God through the redemption that is in Christ Jesus.

We who are by nature guilty sinners, justly condemned by God's holy law, being justified by the obedience and blood of Christ, are cleared of all charges, acquitted of all accusations, absolved of all guilt, freed from all condemnation, and declared to be worthy of eternal life in Christ. This is the confidence of faith of which the

Apostle Paul speaks in the eighth chapter of Romans. 'There is therefore now no condemnation to them which are in Christ Jesus, who walk not after the flesh, but after the Spirit ... Who shall lay any thing to the charge of God's elect? It is God that justifieth ... Who is he that condemneth? It is Christ that died, yea rather, that is risen again, who is even at the right hand of God, who also maketh intercession for us' (vv. 1, 33, 34).

This doctrine of free justification by the imputed righteousness of Christ is the very essence of the gospel (Romans 3:20-28; Galatians 2:16-17; Titus 3:5-7; Colossians 1:12). Every other doctrine of justification is plainly declared by the Spirit of God to be a false gospel (Galatians 1:6-7). This is the very foundation of true Christianity. Martin Luther called it 'The article of the church, by which it stands or falls'. It was the preaching of justification by grace alone which broke the shackles of papacy during the great Reformation. It is the preaching of justification by grace alone which will deliver chosen sinners from the bondage and tyranny of Arminian, free will, works religion today. This is the only ground of solid joy, peace, comfort, and hope there is for sinners before the holy Lord God. If my being just with God depends upon me, or must in some way be determined by me, then I have no hope. But, blessed be God, it is not man that justifieth. 'It is God that justifieth!' This great work of justification is the work of the triune God; Father, Son, and Holy Spirit.

God the Father

God the Father is set forth in holy scripture as the Justifier of his elect. He is specifically called such (Romans 8:33; 3:25-26; Isaiah 45:20). It is God the Father who, in scripture, is represented as having contrived the scheme and plan of justification from eternity. He found a ransom for us (Job 33:24). Our heavenly Father laid help upon One that is mighty to save (Psalm 89:19). He set up his Son as our Mediator, Surety, Representative, and Substitute before the world began (Proverbs 8:30-31). He accepted us in the Beloved as the Lamb slain from the foundation of the world (Ephesians 1:6). It was God the Father who, in the fulness of time, sent his Son into the world to execute his great scheme of grace (Romans 8:1-4; Galatians 4:4). God the Father accepts and is well pleased with the righteousness wrought by Christ as our Representative.

Once the Lord Jesus had wrought out righteousness for us, once he had magnified the law and made it honourable by both obeying all its precepts and principles and by satisfying all its justice and condemnation, it was our heavenly Father who approved of it and accepted it for us. Our heavenly Father has imputed, forever and irrevocably imputed, the righteousness of Christ to believing sinners (Romans 4:6-8; 1 Corinthians 1:30-31).

God the Son

Yet, (and this must be understood), God the Father could never have justified us without or apart from the perfect obedience and precious blood of his dear Son as our Substitute. Therefore God the Son is said to justify his people (Isaiah 53:10-12). The question was asked way back in the book of Job, 'How then can man be justified with God? or how can he be clean that is born of a woman?' (Job 25:4). To that question there is only one answer – Christ! 'For Christ is the end of the law for righteousness to every one that believeth' (Romans 10:4).

Jesus Christ, the Son of God, having fully obeyed and perfectly satisfied the law of God for us is 'the Lord our Righteousness', and we are made 'the righteousness of God in him'. This is the very language of the Bible (Jeremiah 23:6; 33:16; Romans 5:9; 19; 2 Corinthians 5:21).

The Lord Jesus Christ has the right and power to justify because he is God. Upon the authority of his own great name alone, he says, 'Thy sins be forgiven thee' (Matthew 9:2; John 8:11). As the God-man, our Mediator, 'He was delivered for our offences and raised again for our justification'. He arose from the grave as 'The Sun of Righteousness, with healing in his wings!'

As our legal, divinely appointed Head and Representative, our dear Saviour was made to be sin for us and punished to the full satisfaction of divine justice for our sins. Then, when he arose from the dead, declaring justification accomplished (Romans 4:25), he was himself justified from all sin (the sins of his people imputed to him) and we were and are justified in him (Isaiah 45:25; 50:8; 1 Timothy 3:16).

Our Lord Jesus is portrayed as the Angel before whom Joshua the High Priest stood in filthy garments being accused of Satan, the Angel of the covenant who clothed his chosen with the garments of salvation (Isaiah 61:10; Zechariah 3:1-4). That is exactly what the Son of God does for all his redeemed.

God the Holy Spirit

The work of our justification is also ascribed to God the Holy Spirit (1 Corinthians 6:11). It is the Holy Spirit who convinces chosen, redeemed sinners of their sin, of righteousness established and brought in by Christ, and of justice satisfied by the sacrifice of God's own Son at Calvary (John 16:8-11). It is God the Holy Spirit who works faith in us and causes us to look to Christ alone for justification (2 Corinthians 4:13; Colossians 2:12-13). It is the blessed Spirit of God who speaks peace to the believing sinner's heart, sprinkles the blood of Christ upon our consciences, and gives us peace with God, even the peace of perfect, full, complete, everlasting justification (Hebrews 9:14; 10:22).

Every justified sinner can and should make those same four, bold challenges of faith which the Apostle Paul raised in Romans the eighth chapter, with joy, confidence, and thanksgiving. 'Who shall lay any thing to the charge of God's elect? It is God that justifieth. Who is he that condemneth? It is Christ that died, yea rather, that is risen again, who is even at the right hand of God, who also maketh intercession for us. Who shall separate us from the love of Christ?' Blessed, forever blessed of God, is that sinner who can do so!

'I, even I, am he that blotteth out thy transgressions for mine own sake, and will not remember thy sins'. (Isaiah 43:25)

Chapter 41

The Blessed Forgiveness of Sin

I write from the perspective of one who has experienced the grace of God. God, in his infinite mercy and for reasons known only to himself has redeemed me, justified me, and saved me by his matchless grace through the blood and righteousness of his own dear Son, the Lord Jesus Christ. Though my sins are many, loathsome, and vile, the Lord God has blotted out all my sins, and forgiven me all my iniquities. He has put away my sins and purged my conscience of guilt by the blood of Christ.

This grace has come to me in spite of myself. I turned away from his gospel, and would have none of his reproofs. I cared not for the voice of his servant, nor for the instruction of his Word. The blessed Book of Life I would not read. My knees I refused to bend in prayer. My heart was set upon vanity. The actions of my life were so vile that I shall not share them with you, and my heart even more vile than my deeds. Yet, in the time of his love, by an act of almighty grace, the Lord God came to me and freely forgave me of all my sins. Now, I want all who read these lines to know the blessed forgiveness of sin in Christ.

The Lord our God, the one true and living God of heaven and earth, is a God who freely and abundantly forgives sin through the blood of his Son, the Lord Jesus Christ. This is what God himself says, 'I, even I, am he that blotteth out thy transgressions for mine own sake, and will not remember thy sins'.

Who?

Who are the people to whom God will be merciful, to whom the Lord God will grant forgiveness? In this passage our Lord clearly describes them. They are not good, righteous, and morally upright men and women. So long as a man thinks that he is good and righteous he will never obtain mercy from God. The characters to whom God says he will be merciful are sinners.

The grace and loving kindness of Jehovah is reserved for sinners. There is not a word of grace in holy scripture for self-righteous Pharisees. Our Saviour specifically said that he came not to call the righteous, but sinners to repentance. Until you see that your supposed righteousness is an abomination to God, you will never obtain the righteousness of God in Christ (Romans 10:1-4). Every promise of the gospel is made to sinners (Matthew 11:28-30; Isaiah 1:4-6, 18; 55:6-7). This is how God describes those people to whom he promises his mercy (Isaiah 43:22-24).

They were a prayerless people: 'Thou hast not called upon me'. Most likely they had said many prayers. They had repeated many forms of prayer. But no real prayer had ever come from their hearts to God. Their lips never breathed a living word to God. Yet, the Lord God says to these prayerless, graceless souls: 'I, even I, am he that blotteth out thy transgressions'.

These men and women despised God and his worship. The Lord looked past their words and gestures to their hearts, and said, 'Thou hast been weary of me, O Israel!' What a solemn charge! Yet, it is still true of multitudes! God has set before them the means of grace, and they are weary of his blessings. They are weary of reading his Word, gathering in his house, singing his praise, and hearing his gospel! Not only are these rich favours of heaven without attraction to them, they are wearisome things to them! Yet, even to such people, God says, 'I, even I, am he that blotteth out thy transgressions'. What grace! He who is our God is one 'who delighteth in mercy!'

Look at the character of these to whom God grants forgiveness again. There is no goodness in them. They are a thankless people: 'Thou hast not brought me the small cattle of thy burnt offerings'. They had their herds and flocks multiplied many times over. Yet, they offered no tribute of thanks to God, who had so bountifully blessed them. They did not even offer one of their small, sickly calves to him. Men and women who do not give thanks to God are worse than brute beasts. All we have, we owe to his bountiful hand. Dare a man rob God of his lawful and just tribute? These people did. They were a thankless people. Yet, the Lord God was gracious still. He said to them, 'I, even I, am he that blotteth out thy transgressions'.

Again, these people were an utterly useless people. 'Neither hast thou filled me with the fat of thy sacrifices … but thou hast made me to serve with thy sins'. It is well said that man was created in his chief end to glorify God. God made the sun, the moon, the stars, the beasts of the field, and the fish of the sea to honour his name. But there are many men and women who never give a thought, much less an effort, to the honour of God. Most people live for themselves, only and altogether for themselves. They are of no service to mankind. They are of no service to God. That is the state of our fallen race. Yet, the Lord says to such useless sinners, 'I, even I, am he that blotteth out thy transgressions'.

Once more, the Lord describes the character of these men and women to whom he would be gracious as a people who wearied him: 'Thou hast wearied me with thine iniquities'. They were religious people, very religious. But their religion was only a fig-

leaf by which they endeavoured to cover their sin and hide from
God. As they sat in the sanctuary of God, year after year, they
wearied him with their sins. Yet, the Lord says to these sinners, 'I,
even I, am he that blotteth out thy transgressions'.

Do you understand the doctrine of holy scripture? The grace and
mercy of God are for sinners. Christ died for sinners. The gospel is
sent to sinners. God saves sinners. God forgives sinners. He who is
the God of glory is the God who gives grace to needy sinners (Psalm
103:8-14).

What?

What is mercy's great deed? It is the blessed forgiveness of sin.
It is the glory of grace to forgive sin. It is the majesty of mercy to
forgive sin. It is the character of God to forgive iniquity and
transgression and sin (Exodus 34:5-7). This is an act of God alone.
He alone can forgive sin. His forgiveness is the only forgiveness we
need, desire and must have for the salvation of our souls and the
peace of our troubled consciences (Psalm 130:3-4).

What a surprising thing this is! The God against whom we have
sinned, whose name we have blasphemed, whose law we have
broken, the God whose grace we have despised is a God who forgives
sin. He says, 'I, even I am he that blotteth out thy transgressions'. It
is as constant as it is surprising. Certainly, it was done once, with
finality, when Christ died as our Substitute. But it is experienced
constantly as God speaks peace to the hearts of those who confess
their sins (1 John 1:9). This forgiveness of sin is the complete,
effectual, permanent forgiveness of all the sins of all who trust Christ.
God charged our sins upon his Son Jesus Christ, and they shall
never be charged upon us (Romans 4:8).

How?

The scriptures declare that God is holy, just, righteous, and true.
He has said, 'The soul that sinneth, it shall die'. Therefore I am
compelled to ask, how he can forgive sin? This much is certain:

God cannot forgive sin unless he can do so in a way that is honouring to his law and satisfying to his justice. In order for a holy God to forgive sin four things must be done: (1) The law of God must be honoured and perfectly obeyed. (2) The justice of God must be satisfied. (3) The sinner must be punished. (4) The sin must be removed.

There is only one way for a holy and just God to forgive sin. He can only forgive sin through the obedience and sacrifice of an all-sufficient Substitute. The Lord Jesus Christ, God's own dear Son, is that Substitute. In him, and only in him is there forgiveness with God (Romans 3:23-26; 1 John 1:7, 9). It is only in the crucified Christ that we can behold him, as he is, 'a just God and a Saviour' (Isaiah 45:20-22).

Why?

Why does the Lord God forgive sin? Hear his own words and rejoice: 'For mine own sake'. The greatest honour and glory of God is his mercy, his holy, righteous, and just mercy in forgiving sin (Psalm 106:8). He declares, 'I will establish my covenant with thee; and thou shalt know that I am the Lord: That thou mayest remember, and be confounded, and never open thy mouth any more because of thy shame, when I am pacified toward thee for all that thou hast done, saith the Lord GOD' (Ezekiel 16:62-63).

The promise

What is the promise God makes to sinners whose sins are forgiven by him? It is just this: 'I, even I, am he that blotteth out thy transgressions, and will not remember thy sins'. There are some things God cannot do. He cannot lie. God cannot break his covenant. He cannot forsake his people. He cannot be unjust. And the Holy, Lord God cannot remember the sins of his people. I do not mean that God is not aware of the fact that we have sinned. I mean that in so far as his law and justice are concerned, our sins do not exist; therefore, God cannot remember them. He will never remember our sins so as to treat us any the less graciously because of them. He will never remember our sins so as to bring them up and require payment for them while we live. God will not remember our sins when we stand before Him in judgment (Jeremiah 50:20). God will not remember our sins in the distribution of his heavenly crowns and gifts.

'If thou, Lord, shouldest mark iniquities, O Lord, who shall stand?
But there is forgiveness with thee, that thou mayest be feared'.
(Psalm 130:3-4)

Chapter 42

Questions About Forgiveness

Satan is a master deceiver. He is such a subtle, crafty deceiver
that he often uses the Word of God itself to confuse people. He is
particularly good at using scripture texts as stumbling blocks, which
he piles in the path of sinners seeking the Lord, or to trip and harass
God's pilgrims as they seek to follow Christ through this world. In
this study, I hope to clear away some of those stumbling blocks by
answering some questions about forgiveness. I cannot here answer
all the questions people have asked me about the forgiveness of
sins. It would be futile for me to attempt that. However, I have
carefully and prayerfully chosen seven questions which I want to
answer.

1. Are there varying degrees of sin, of guilt, and of punishment?
    Without question, the Word of God clearly teaches that there are
no varying degrees of innocence, righteousness, or holiness, and no
varying degrees of reward for the righteous in heaven. The teaching
of degrees of reward in heaven is totally contrary to the gospel of
God's free and sovereign grace in Christ. However, the scriptures
do teach us that there are varying degrees of sin, of guilt, and of
eternal punishment.

The papists teach that certain sins are venial (pardonable) in themselves, not deserving the wrath of God and eternal damnation, while other sins are mortal, deserving of God's wrath and eternal damnation. That distinction is purely a matter of papal invention, as are most of the doctrines of Rome. All sin deserves the everlasting wrath of God in hell. There are no exceptions. 'The wages of sin is death!' Spiritual, physical, and everlasting death, are the just reward of iniquity, transgression, and sin.

Yet, the Word of God tells us, in the plainest terms possible, that there are greater and lesser sins. Just as some breaches of the law were weightier than others, so the sins of men and women today are of a greater and lesser degree, depending upon the circumstances. Those who perish without the light of the gospel shall indeed perish forever under the wrath of God, but their punishment will be far less than that of those who go to hell pushing God out of their way. Read the scriptures for yourself, and you will see that this is clearly the teaching of the Inspired Volume (Romans 2:12; Matthew 11:20-24; Luke 12:47-48; John 19:10-11).

'God forgives iniquity, transgression, and sin', wrote John Gill, 'which include all sorts of sin; sins of the greatest magnitude, and of the deepest dye, are blotted out for Christ's sake. Such as are like crimson and scarlet become through him as white as wool, as white as snow. His blood cleanses from sin; every sin is forgiven, but the sin against the Holy Ghost (Matthew 12:31-32)'.

2. Will there be any forgiveness of sins in the world to come?

Some people reading Matthew 12:31-32 have erroneously concluded that our Lord there suggests that there is another day of grace yet to come in which sins shall be forgiven. Our Saviour there declares, 'All manner of sin and blasphemy shall be forgiven unto men: but the blasphemy against the Holy Ghost shall not be forgiven unto men. And whosoever speaketh a word against the Son of man, it shall be forgiven him: but whosoever speaketh against the Holy Ghost, it shall not be forgiven him, neither in this world, neither in the world to come'.

Our Lord here tells us that this sin of blasphemy against the Holy Spirit will never be forgiven. The text teaches no more and no less than that. Nowhere in holy scripture is there even the slightest hint of some state of purgatory or limbo between heaven and hell, or that there will be a second chance for grace, during some future tribulation period, or that there will be forgiveness at the day of judgment. Once this gospel age is over, the day of grace has ended. There is no hope beyond the grave for those who die without Christ. Those dying without forgiveness will spend eternity in hell with no hope of forgiveness (2 Corinthians 6:1-2).

3. Why is the sin of blasphemy against the Holy Ghost said to be unforgivable?

Matthew 12:31-32 does not suggest that any sin against the Holy Ghost, or every sin against the Holy Ghost is unpardonable. That cannot be the case, because every sin committed against God is committed against the Holy Ghost, as well as against the Father and the Son. He is God! The sin here spoken of is something more than a denial of his deity, and of his personality. It is more than a denial of the necessity of the operations of his grace on the souls of men in regeneration, conversion, and sanctification. It is also something more than vexing and grieving the Holy Spirit.

The Israelites certainly vexed and grieved him, as did Lot in Sodom, as did David in the matter of Uriah, as we all do both in our sinful thoughts and in our acts of sin. But these things are not unpardonable. The fact is a man may break all the ten commandments (We have all done so from our youth!), and not commit this sin against the Holy Ghost. This is a sin not against the law, but against the gospel. 'It lies in the denial of the great and fundamental truth of the gospel, salvation by Jesus Christ, in all its branches; peace and pardon by his blood, atonement by his sacrifice, and justification by his righteousness' (John Gill).

This blasphemy against the Holy Ghost is a sin committed after a person has received the knowledge of the truth, under the illuminations, convictions, and demonstrations of the Spirit of God;

and yet, through the instigation of Satan, and the wickedness of his own heart, knowingly, and wilfully, and maliciously denies this truth, and obstinately persists denying it. The person who commits this blasphemy never comes to repentance, and therefore he has no forgiveness, here nor hereafter.

'This is not', Gill continues, 'because the Holy Spirit is superior to the other divine Persons; for they are equal: nor through any deficiency in the grace of God, or blood of Christ; but through the nature of the sin, which is diametrically opposite to the way of salvation, pardon, atonement, and justification; for these being denied to be by Christ, there can be no pardon; for another Jesus will never be sent, another Saviour will never be given; there will be no more shedding of blood, no more sacrifice, nor another sacrifice for sin; nor another righteousness wrought out and brought in. Therefore, there remains nothing but a fearful looking for of judgment and indignation, to come on such persons'.

In Hebrews 10:26-29 the Holy Spirit himself shows us that this is the meaning of our Lord's words in Matthew 12:31-32. 'For if we sin wilfully after that we have received the knowledge of the truth, there remaineth no more sacrifice for sins, But a certain fearful looking for of judgment and fiery indignation, which shall devour the adversaries. He that despised Moses' law died without mercy under two or three witnesses: Of how much sorer punishment, suppose ye, shall he be thought worthy, who hath trodden under foot the Son of God, and hath counted the blood of the covenant, wherewith he was sanctified, an unholy thing, and hath done despite unto the Spirit of grace?'

4. What happens when a believer sins?

This question is very troublesome and perplexing to many. If I trust Christ now and am forgiven of all my past sins at this moment, what will happen when I sin again? Will the Lord turn against me again? Will I lose my salvation? Will I forfeit my interest in Christ and his salvation?

What does God say in his Word about this matter? When a believer sins, much happens, in his own heart and experience. He often loses the joyous knowledge of Christ's manifest presence. Our communion with him whom we most love is broken. Our heavenly Father chastens us sore. But our standing before God, our relationship with him, and our acceptance with him is not affected at all. Our acceptance with our God is a matter of grace, not merit. It is in Christ our Substitute, not in ourselves. It does not in any way depend upon us and cannot in any way be altered by us. Let wicked, self-righteous men do and say whatever they please in response to that, that is the teaching of this holy scripture (Romans 4:8; Psalm 32:1-2; 89:30-37; John 10:28; 2 Timothy 2:13; 1 John 2:1-2).

5. Should we pray for the forgiveness of sins?

Sometimes, when I am asked that question, I think to myself, 'How silly! What could it possibly hurt?' But I know that for some this is a serious question. Certainly, unbelievers ought to confess their sins and seek forgiveness by faith in Christ. However, we must never get the idea that praying for forgiveness and seeking it will be a substitute for believing on the Lord Jesus Christ. The unbeliever is not told to pray for forgiveness, but to believe on the Lord Jesus Christ (Acts 16:31).

Then the question arises, 'If our sins are already forgiven, is it right for us as believers to pray for forgiveness?' Rather than speculating about it, let's simply see what the Book of God says and the saints of God have done. Our Saviour taught his disciples (as believers) to pray for the forgiveness of their sins (Luke 11:2-4). Moses, God's faithful servant, prayed for forgiveness (Exodus 34:9). Not only did David seek forgiveness at the throne of grace (Psalm 25:11), he (writing by inspiration of God the Holy Spirit) declared plainly, 'For this shall every one that is godly pray unto thee in a time when thou mayest be found' (Psalm 32:5-6). Daniel's great prayer (Daniel 9) stands as an example of how believing, forgiven sinners ought always to seek God's face in Christ, confessing our sins and seeking forgiveness by his grace through blood atonement. Yes, believers must and should seek the forgiveness of sins (Hebrews 4:16).

6. Will the sins of God's elect be exposed in the day of judgment or in the world to come?

There are many who claim to believe in salvation by grace alone, through faith alone, in Christ alone, who yet hold people in bondage with the threat of some form of future punishment (the loss of rewards) and the promise of rewards for doing good. Such doctrine is contrary to scripture and to every doctrine of the gospel, and dishonours Christ in the most insulting manner. The scriptures tell us plainly that God's people will never suffer such humiliation and shame (Revelation 21:4). There is no such thing as partial righteousness or partial holiness. The basis of our acceptance with God in the day of judgment is the person and work of Christ our Substitute. The notion that Christ will expose the sins of his beloved bride on her wedding day is preposterous beyond imagination. The purpose of God in election, the purpose of Christ in redemption, and the purpose of the Holy Spirit in sanctification would all fall to the ground if we are found with even one spot of sin in that great and glorious day (Ephesians 1:3-6; 5:25-27; Jude 24-25).

7. How can I obtain the forgiveness of sin?

'If we confess our sins, he is faithful and just to forgive us our sins, and to cleanse us from all unrighteousness' (1 John 1:9). To confess our sins is much, much more than telling a man, or even the church of God about our evil deeds. It is much more than the acknowledgement that we have done some bad things. We confess our sins when we, like the publican, rip open our hearts before God, acknowledging the corruption and depravity of our hearts before him, looking to the blood of Christ for propitiation, and calling upon God for mercy through the merits of Christ's shed blood. The promise of holy scripture is this: To all who thus confess their sins, God is faithful to his Word, faithful to his covenant, and faithful to his own character, and just, through the blood sacrifice of his own dear Son, to forgive sin. That is grace! May God the Holy Spirit ever grant us grace to confess our sins, with the eye of faith cast upon the Lord Jesus Christ, and grant us the blessed knowledge of sins forgiven through the blood of Christ.

'Because the creature itself also shall be delivered from the bondage of corruption into the glorious liberty of the children of God'.
(Romans 8:21)

Chapter 43

'The Glorious Liberty of the Children of God'

This text speaks both of bondage and liberty, 'the bondage of corruption and the glorious liberty of the children of God'. 'The bondage of corruption' is that bondage into which sin has brought us. It is the bondage of nature, the bondage which makes us all miserable slaves and prisoners. This bondage of corruption is the forerunner of the everlasting torments of hell's bondage. Unless God intervenes, it will bring us into eternal misery at last.

All who live in the dungeon of sensuality and corruption, as the willing bond slaves of sin, dragged from place to place by the chains of envy, malice, anger, and wrath, shall spend eternity in the darkness and corruption of hell under the wrath of God, unless the Son of God makes them free.

'The bondage of corruption' holds multitudes in abject servitude to fashion, style, and social approval. It makes us all, by nature, slaves to our own corrupt passions; and that man who is a slave to his own passions is a slave to the worst possible despot. Physical slavery is the most immoral, debasing abuse of humanity imaginable. However, this 'bondage of corruption' is indescribably worse. This is the bondage, not of our bodies, but of our hearts, our minds, our souls! This satanic 'bondage of corruption' manifests itself in many ways. It is the bondage of sin, the bondage of the law, the bondage of social acceptance and approval, and the bondage of religious tradition, custom, and superstition.

The Lord Jesus Christ, the Son of God came into this world to deliver God's elect from 'the bondage of corruption into the glorious liberty of the children of God'. He came to set the captive free, to open the doors of the prison which held his people in captivity, to break the oppressive chains and shackles which held us captive to sin and Satan. Christ is the great Liberator of men's souls. He came to set his people free. Salvation is the deliverance of chosen, redeemed sinners by the grace and power of God 'into the glorious liberty of the children of God'.

The liberty of God's elect in Christ is, without question, a very controversial issue. But it is controversial only because of the prevailing errors of ascetic, legal religion, which have become so universally accepted that most people associate liberty with licentiousness and bondage with godliness. The fact is – all human religion is bondage, operates upon principles of bondage, and seeks to keep people in bondage.

We need plain, practical instructions about the matter of Christian liberty. Let us look into the Bible and see what God has to say to his people about their liberty in Christ. Every child of God needs to know that since Christ has made us free, it is our responsibility both to stand fast in the liberty of his grace, refusing to be brought again under the yoke of legal bondage, and to use the liberty he has given us for the glory of his name and the good of his people.

Our Liberator

Jesus Christ alone is the great Liberator of men. No one ever comes to enjoy true liberty before God, true liberty of heart and mind, true liberty in his soul, until he is set free by the merit of Christ's blood and the power of his grace. This liberty of grace is a blessed privilege of faith in Christ. Yet, there is a false liberty, which must be avoided.

Everything good, every work of God's grace is imitated by Satan. He is a master counterfeiter. Multitudes are deceived by him with a false liberty. Let all be warned. The word 'liberty' has been greatly abused by many. I have personally heard men use it to excuse and justify everything from Hollywood evangelism to homosexuality, from the ordination of women to the worship of idols. Do not be deceived. All is not liberty which men call liberty. May God graciously keep us from a false liberty that will bring us into eternal ruin.

Here are three common refuges, refuges of lies, into which people run in hope of finding liberty.

1. A religious profession – Multitudes are so naïve and gullible that they think a mere profession of religion is liberty from the curse of the law and the wrath of God. They think they are free because they profess that they are free.

2. Self-righteousness – Many grow weary of their evil ways and seek freedom by making an outward moral reformation. I fear that most of what passes for Christianity is nothing more than a reformation of life.

3. Antinomianism – Antinomianism is a vile, atrocious thing. It says, 'Since salvation is by grace, it does not matter how I live, or what I do'. God's servants today are frequently called antinomians, just as Paul was (Romans 3:8). We must not allow that slander to bother us. If lost religious men, clinging to their self-righteousness, accused our Master of being a glutton and a drunk, we should not expect to be treated any better.

It is impossible to preach salvation by grace alone and not be charged with the evil of antinomianism by slanderous legalists. However, we must constantly be on our guard against that form of licentiousness. Our glorious freedom from the law is not a licence to do evil.

May God the Holy Spirit keep us from a false liberty. It is far better to be in bondage and know it than to be in bondage and think your bondage is liberty. Yet, we must not fail to declare the fact that the Lord Jesus Christ truly does make sinners free (John 8:32-36; Romans 8:15; Galatians 4:6-7; 5:1).

True liberty, the liberty of grace, the liberty of life and peace in Christ is obtained only by the power and authority of God's eternal Son. Only the Son can make us free. Let me show you the significance of those words.

During the days of our Lord's earthly ministry there was a custom among the Greeks and Romans. When a man died, if he left slaves they became the property of his eldest son. If the son said, 'I proclaim these slaves, left to me by my father, free men', those slaves were forever free and could never be taken into slavery again. Under Greek and Roman law, that was the one, certain way by which a slave could obtain his liberty. If the son proclaimed freedom, the slave must go free.

Therefore, our Saviour said, 'If the Son therefore shall make you free, ye shall be free indeed'. Jesus Christ, the Son of God is the great Heir of promise. If he, the Son of God, makes you free, you shall be free indeed.

The Lord Jesus Christ purchased freedom for his people by his precious blood (Galatians 3:13). He comes to chosen, redeemed sinners in the preaching of the gospel and proclaims purchased, unconditional liberty to captives (Isaiah 61:1-3).

But the Lord Jesus Christ is more than a proclaimer of liberty. He accomplishes liberty, effectually bringing his elect into the glorious liberty of his grace by the power of his Spirit.

He breaks the power of cancelled sin;
He sets the prisoner free!
His blood can make the foulest clean;
His blood avails for me!

The instrument by which the Lord Jesus brings liberty to his people is the Word of God (John 8:32). The preaching of the gospel is like the blowing of the jubilee trumpet. The more clearly the truths of the gospel are preached and understood, the more fully liberty is enjoyed. Bondage comes from error. Liberty is the result of truth.

Liberty experienced

Faith in Christ brings God's elect into this 'glorious liberty of the children of God' (Galatians 4:1-7). The moment a sinner is born again by God the Holy Spirit and becomes (experimentally) a child of God by faith in Christ, he begins to enjoy true, lasting liberty before God. As we grow in the grace and knowledge of Christ, as we mature spiritually, we enjoy that liberty more fully; but the liberty is ours the moment we believe on the Lord Jesus Christ. It is both our privilege and our responsibility to walk in, enjoy, and protect this liberty, which the Lord Jesus purchased for us by his blood and gave to us by the power of his grace. Any return to bondage is giving up the liberty of grace (Galatians 5:1-4).

Let me describe that liberty which is ours in Christ Jesus. May God give us grace ever to promote it and walk in it for the honour of his name. In Christ we are free from sin, Satan, and the law. This is where the liberty of grace begins. When a person comes to Christ in faith, he is set free from that bondage in which all men by nature are held as prisoners and slaves.

The Lord Jesus Christ also frees his people from the bondage of sin (Romans 6:14-18). Believers are not free from the being of sin, the body of sin, or the acts of sin. All God's elect, so long as we are in this world, have to contend with sin. But in Christ we are no longer under the dominion of sin. The guilt of sin has been removed by the blood of Christ. The condemnation of sin has been removed by that same precious blood (Romans 8:1). The power of sin has been broken by the power of God's saving grace.

In salvation the Lord Jesus delivers his people from the power of Satan, too. By nature the devil holds a usurped dominion over all men, blinding them, binding them, deceiving them, and taking them captive at his will to do his bidding. In salvation the Spirit of God dethrones Satan. He enters the hearts of God's elect, binds the strong man, and takes his house. He turns men and women from the power of Satan to God. He translates us from the power of darkness into the kingdom of God's dear Son. Thus, the believer is no longer a slave to Satan to do his works and lusts. We are not yet freed from the temptations of the devil, or his roars; but we shall never be devoured by him!

The Lord Jesus Christ has also made us free from the law. This is a fact so plainly, constantly and forcefully stated in the New Testament that ignorance concerning it is utterly inexcusable (Romans 6:14,15; 7:4; 8:2; 10:4; Galatians 3:23-25). Christ is the end, the termination point, of the law for all believers. In Christ, because of his blood atonement, the believer is completely free from all the types and shadows of the ceremonial law, all the rigors of Old Testament dietary laws, all the statutes and curses of the law, and all the bondage, terror, and rule of the law as a way of life.

In Christ God's people have no covenant with the law, no curse from the law, no condemnation by the law, and absolutely no obligation to the law. Christ has satisfied all the law for us and we fulfil all the law by faith in him (Romans 3:31). The lives of God's people in this world are not ruled, governed, or motivated by rules and regulations, but by gratitude, love, and faith for the glory of God (1 John 3:23; 2 Corinthians 5:14).

Some may think, 'What can be wrong with teaching God's people to live by the ten commands as a rule of life?' Let me show you. It is a direct violation of the Word of God (Colossians 2:16-17). Legalism promotes pride and self-righteousness. Legalism always produces severity, judgmentalism, and a condemning spirit. Legalism denies the finished work of Christ and causes men to look not to him alone for everything, but to him and to themselves for assurance, sanctification, acceptance with God, worthiness before God, and peace with God. Many would have us believe, contrary to the scriptures, that having begun in the Spirit we must now make ourselves perfect by the works of the flesh (Galatians 3:1-3).

There can be absolutely no mixture of law and grace (Romans 11:6; Galatians 5:1-4). We must never wear a garment of linen and wool before God, or plow with the ox of grace and the ass of our own works in the same yoke. The liberty we have in Christ goes beyond mere doctrinal matters. According to New Testament teaching, it reaches to the common, everyday affairs of our lives.

Our liberty in Christ gives us total liberty from all the religious customs, traditions, and superstitions of men. Pharisees, both ancient and modern, impose heavy burdens upon the consciences of men and women, by which they make void the Word and commandments of God. We must never allow ourselves to become the servants of such things. We have no obligation to adhere to religious tradition. Indeed, we must not adhere to the oracles of men in spiritual matters (Matthew 15:1-6; Colossians 2:6-8, 16-18, 20-23).

Neither the Church of Christ, nor those men who are sent of God to preach the gospel, nor any other group of men have any right to add anything to the Word of God. We do not have the right to develop our own rules, dogmas, or doctrines. Neither local churches, nor religious denominations, nor councils, nor synods have authority to impose their opinions upon the consciences of God's saints. The Word of God alone is our rule of faith and practice.

In Christ, God's people are perfectly free to use every creature of God for their food, happiness, comfort, and satisfaction in this world. In the Old Testament things were divided into clean and unclean categories for the purposes of ceremonial purification. The Levitical law made the use of some things unlawful. But in this gospel age we are given liberty to use every creature of God. Nothing is common, or unclean of itself (Acts 10:14-15; Romans 14:14; 1 Timothy 4:3-4). We are perfectly free to use those things that are neither commanded nor forbidden of God, matters of indifference, as we see fit (Romans 14:2-3, 13-15, 20-23; 1 Corinthians 8:9-13). I will lay down no rules about those things. Let me simply offer a few biblical guidelines about the use of things which are matters of indifference.

1. Do not make any of these things a point of merit before God. Indifferent things become idolatrous if you make the use or non-use of them a means of obtaining favour with God, a means of religious devotion, or a means of obtaining peace of conscience.
2. Use all things in moderation. Eating is not wrong; but gluttony is. Drinking a glass of wine is not wrong; but drunkenness is. Entertainment is not wrong; but revelling is. Use all things wisely, abusing none.
3. Carefully avoid offending your brethren. To offend a brother is to cause him to go against his own conscience, doing something he thinks is wrong. This we must avoid at all costs to ourselves. My brother's conscience is more important than my own comfort, happiness, and satisfaction.
4. Make your use of all things subservient to the glory of God, the gospel of Christ, and the welfare of the church. In all things make love for Christ and his people the basis of your actions. Use all things wisely, for the glory of God, and abuse none.

John Gill gave this word of caution: 'Care should be taken, on the one hand, lest such things should be reckoned indifferent, which are not indifferent, and so any precept, or ordinance of God be neglected; and on the other hand, such as are indifferent, should not be imposed as necessary, which may lead to superstition and will-worship'.

Here is the essence of the glorious liberty that is ours as the children of God: In Christ we are free to worship and serve the Lord our God. No man can or will truly worship God except by faith in the Lord Jesus Christ. But all who are in Christ are free to do so (Ephesians 2:18). In Christ we are free to call upon God in prayer. In Christ we are free to enjoy all the ordinances of the gospel – Baptism – Church Fellowship – The Lord's Supper.

Those who are in Christ by faith have freely given themselves up as bond slaves to him. We hold ourselves, all that we are, and all that we possess in reserve for our Master, his cause, and his family.

> Ready to go, ready to stay,
> Ready my place to fill;
> Ready for service, lowly or great,
> Ready to do His will.

> All for Jesus, all for Jesus!
> All my being's ransomed powers:
> All my thoughts, and words, and doings,
> All my days and all my hours.
>
> Let my hands perform His bidding,
> Let my feet run in His ways;
> Let my eyes see Jesus only,
> Let my lips speak forth His praise.

Our great Saviour graciously grants his people deliverance from the fear of death (Hebrews 2:14-15). Through his incarnation, sufferings, and death he has delivered us, who, through fear of death, were all our lifetime subject to bondage. Death, formidable as it is, is no longer king of terrors to God's elect. We have no reason to fear the death of the body. Trusting Christ, believing that we are in him, and having a good hope that we shall ever be with him, we choose to depart this life and be with the Lord. We know that to die is gain. In the prospect of death and eternity, we can sing, 'O death, where is thy sting! O grave, where is thy victory!' We both live and die in hope of the resurrection. In Christ, we have no reason to fear the second, eternal death (Revelation 20:6). Being justified by his grace and redeemed by his blood, the second death has no power over God's elect.

> Bold shall I stand in that great day!
> For who aught to my charge shall lay?
> While through Thy blood absolved I am,
> From sin's tremendous curse and blame?

Liberty anticipated

Still, there is more. There is a glorious liberty yet to be revealed. It is this anticipated liberty, which is our blessed hope in Christ. This is the liberty that the sons of God shall have in the world to come. As soon as the believer dies, he shall be with Christ and with the spirits of just men made perfect. Then he shall be free from all sin. We will then be free from all the corruption and defilement of sin, free from the very being of sin, and free from all the evil consequences of sin.

I do not pretend to know all that awaits us in heaven. But this I do know. In heaven's glory we shall be free from every evil thing associated with our sin. Can you imagine what this liberty must be? We shall be free from all unbelief – Free from all doubts – Free from all fears – Free from all distresses – Free from all evil thoughts – Free from all temptations – Free from all strife – Free from all pride.

Then, when Jesus Christ comes again, these very bodies shall be raised to 'the glorious liberty of the children of God!' In the resurrection, these bodies shall no longer be sinful, but glorious. Our resurrection bodies shall not even bear the scars and pains of sin. Our bodies shall be free from every pain and disorder. Our very bodies shall be immortal! Body and soul shall be joined together in perfection. We shall be like Christ. We shall be with Christ. We shall never be in danger of the bondage of sin again! This is 'the glorious liberty of the children of God!'

'And such were some of you: but ye are washed, but ye are sanctified, but ye are justified in the name of the Lord Jesus, and by the Spirit of our God'.
(1 Corinthians 6:11)

Chapter 44

'Ye Are Sanctified'

In 1 Corinthians 6:11 the Holy Spirit shows us three great privileges that all of God's elect enjoy by his grace. These three things are true of every saved sinner. By nature we are all unrighteous, and therefore unfit to inherit and inhabit the kingdom of God; 'But ye are washed, but ye are sanctified, but ye are justified in the name of the Lord Jesus, and by the Spirit of our God'. These three things are essential elements of God's saving grace. Without them no one is or can be saved.

We must be washed, redeemed by the blood of Christ. This redemption, the atonement for our sins, was accomplished for all God's elect when Christ died at Calvary. 'Christ hath redeemed us from the curse of the law, being made a curse for us: for it is written, Cursed is every one that hangeth on a tree' (Galatians 3:13).

We must be sanctified by God the Holy Spirit. There is no salvation apart from sanctification. We must be made holy, or we cannot see God. This sanctification is accomplished for us and in us experimentally in regeneration, the new birth, when we are made new creatures in Christ and made to be partakers of the divine nature. 'According as his divine power hath given unto us all things that pertain unto life and godliness, through the knowledge of him that hath called us to glory and virtue: Whereby are given unto us exceeding great and precious promises: that by these ye might be partakers of the divine nature, having escaped the corruption that is in the world through lust' (2 Peter 1:3-4).

We must be justified before God by his grace. Our justification was accomplished by the Lord God, freely and graciously imputing the righteousness of Christ to us, declaring us to be righteous before him. As our sins were imputed to Christ, though he could never sin, so his righteousness has been imputed to every believer, though we could never do righteousness. We are 'justified freely by his grace through the redemption that is in Christ Jesus' (Romans 3:24). 'For he hath made him to be sin for us, who knew no sin; that we might be made the righteousness of God in him' (2 Corinthians 5:21).

All three of these privileges are works of grace. We do not wash ourselves, sanctify ourselves, or justify ourselves. God almighty, by distinct acts of grace, has washed us, sanctified us, and justified us. All three of these works of grace belong to all believers, without exception. The person who lacks any of these works of God's saving grace has not yet entered into the kingdom of God. He is lost, undone, and perishing in his sins. If you or I die without being washed, sanctified, and justified by the grace of God we will not be numbered with God's saints in the last day. You will notice that Paul did not hesitate to state that these believers at Corinth were all washed, justified, and sanctified. It is not possible for a person to be saved by the grace of God who is not washed, justified, and sanctified.

Remember Paul is writing to the church at Corinth, the only congregation which he calls carnal. These people were far from being what they ought to have been. In conduct and spirit, they were not exactly what you would call ideal Christians. Yet, Paul writes to them upon the basis of their professed faith in Christ and says, if you are in Christ, 'Ye are sanctified'.

What do you think of when you hear or read those words? The words 'saints', 'sanctify', 'sanctified', and 'sanctification', are used repeatedly throughout the scriptures, yet, few seem to understand what they mean as they are used by the inspired writers.

Errors

We are fairly comfortable in discussing redemption and justification, but not sanctification. With regard to this subject there is a great deal of confusion, and it needs to be cleared up. Errors regarding the doctrine of sanctification generally fall into one of three categories.

1. Pentecostalism teaches that sanctification is a second work of grace, whereby the believer is made totally free from sin and the old nature of sin is eradicated from his being. We know that such teaching is wrong for two reasons: – First, it is directly contrary to the Word of God. 'If we say that we have no sin, we deceive ourselves, and the truth is not in us' (1 John 1:8). – Second, it is contrary to every believer's experience. As honest men and women, we must confess our sinfulness. Though we are no longer under the dominion of sin, we have a continual struggle with sin. Sin is in us. It is mixed with everything we do. It mars everything we do. If a person says he is without sin, he is a liar. The truth is not in him.

2. The self-righteous legalist makes sanctification nothing more than an outward, legal morality. To him sanctification is accomplished by his separation from the world, his obedience to religious customs and traditions, and his abstinence from the use of things he considers evil. 'Touch not, taste not, handle not' is his creed.

3. Most of those who are regarded as orthodox, evangelical Christians teach that sanctification is the progressive increase of the believer in 'personal holiness'. We are told that the child of God attains higher degrees of holiness by his own works in sanctification,

until at last he is ripe for heaven, and that sanctification ultimately buds forth into glorification. Among these are both fundamentalists and some who regard themselves as reformed in doctrine.

One writer defined sanctification in these words: – 'Sanctification is progressive righteousness, which, of course, means that it is incomplete righteousness'. Another wrote, 'Sanctification is the personal holiness of the believer'. Usually this progressive, increasing righteousness is made to be the basis of the believer's assurance here and his heavenly reward hereafter.

The doctrine of scripture

Sanctification, as it is taught in the Word of God, is considerably different from the way it is commonly taught in theology books and from most pulpits. Let us properly appreciate the writings of men who have been used of God, from whom we may learn much. However, when they vary from the Word of God, we must vary from them. We must have no creed to defend, no confession to uphold, no denomination to answer to, and no catechism to teach, but this: 'Thus saith the Lord'.

Because sanctification is an essential element of salvation it is and must be, in its entirety, the work of God's free and sovereign grace in Christ. If salvation is by grace (And it is!), then all that is essential to salvation is by grace alone. Whatever sanctification is, it is the work of God alone. It is this fact, the fact that he is the One who sanctifies us that the Lord uses to encourage obedience in his people (Exodus 31:13; Leviticus 20:2).

The words used

What do the words 'sanctify' and 'sanctification' mean? These are Bible terms. We must turn to the Bible to find out what they mean. The word 'sanctify' is used in three distinct ways in the scriptures. The first meaning of the word 'sanctify' is 'to set apart', particularly, 'to set apart for God or for divine service'. Sanctification is taking something that is common and ordinary and setting it apart, separating it unto God's service alone. This is the first and primary meaning of the word as it is used in the Bible.

The seventh day was set apart for God (Genesis 2:3). This is the first time the word 'sanctify' is used in the Bible. 'And God blessed the seventh day, and sanctified it: because that in it he had rested from all his work which God created and made' (Genesis 2:3). The day was not altered at all. It was simply set apart, separated from the other days of the week for God's service alone. The basic meaning of the word 'sanctify', throughout the Bible, is 'to set apart'.

The firstborn of all the families of Israel were set apart for God (Exodus 13:2). The tabernacle, the altar, and the priesthood were sanctified unto the Lord, set apart for his use alone (Exodus 29:44). It is in this sense that our Lord Jesus Christ says he was sanctified (John 10:36). He was set apart from all other men to do the will of God, by God the Father. In this sense, our Saviour was sanctified by the Father and sanctified himself to do the work he was sent to do, to accomplish his Father's will in the redemption and salvation of his people (John 10:36; 17:19). When anything or anyone is sanctified, set apart to God and for God's service, that thing or that person is under God's special protection.

Second, as the word 'sanctify' is used in the Word of God, it means, 'to regard as holy', 'to treat as holy', and 'to declare that a person or thing is holy'. For example: God himself is frequently said to be sanctified by his people. We do not make God more holy. We do not separate God unto himself. We do regard him as holy, treat him as one who is holy, and declare that he is holy. That is what it is to sanctify the Lord God in your heart.

God commands us to regard him as holy. 'Sanctify the LORD of hosts himself; and let him be your fear, and let him be your dread' (Isaiah 8:13). Nadab and Abihu were consumed by the Lord, when they offered strange fire, because they did not reverence God's holiness. He said, 'I will be sanctified in them that come nigh me!' (Leviticus 10:3). Moses' sin in smiting the Rock the second time, for which he was not allowed to enter the land of promise, was just this – 'Ye believed me not, to sanctify me in the eyes of the children of Israel' (Numbers 20:12).

We have an even more familiar illustration of this in what is called 'The Lord's Prayer'. Our Saviour taught us to pray, 'Our Father, which art in heaven, Hallowed be thy name' (Matthew 6:9). The word 'hallowed' is simply another word for 'sanctified'. The meaning is, let your name be reverenced and adored through the whole earth. Let men regard your name as a holy and sacred thing.

The first meaning of the word 'sanctify' is to set apart for God. The second meaning is to regard, treat, and declare a person or thing as being holy. When a person is sanctified by God he is regarded by God as one who is holy, declared by God to be holy, and treated by God as one who is holy. All who are sanctified are under God's special care and protection. They are the apple of his eye. His beloved children. They are his anointed. God says to all creation, 'Touch not mine anointed!'

The third meaning of the word 'sanctify' is 'to actually purify something and make it holy'. This is more than a declaration. This is an actual change in the nature of things. The thing sanctified is not only set apart, and declared to be holy, it is actually made holy. When the Lord God was about to come down and give the law at Mount Sinai the children of Israel were required to make themselves ceremonially holy (Exodus 19:10-11). When Israel was about to cross the River Jordan God required them to first be purified (Joshua 3:5).

The words 'sanctify' and 'sanctification', as they are used in the scriptures, basically mean: (1) to set apart or separate for God, (2) to regard, treat, and declare something or someone as holy, and (3) to purify and make holy.

God's work

How are the people of God sanctified? Our sanctification, like our redemption and justification, is the work of God almighty in the trinity of his sacred Persons. We are sanctified by God the Father in election, by God the Son in redemption, and by God the Holy Spirit in regeneration. Sanctification is not something we do for ourselves. It is something God does for us and in us. The words 'sanctify', 'sanctified', 'sanctifieth', and 'sanctification' are used more than thirty times in the New Testament. We are said to be sanctified by the purpose of God, by the blood of Christ, by the Spirit of God, by faith in Christ, and by the Word of God. Never, not even once, are we said to sanctify ourselves. Sanctification is the work of God alone.

All believers were sanctified by God the Father in eternal election, set apart for him by God's decree, and separated unto him (Jude 1). This is the character of God's distinguishing grace. It sets some people apart from others and sanctifies them unto the Lord. We were secretly set apart for God in his secret, eternal decree of election before the world began. We were legally set apart from Adam's fallen race by the purchase of Christ at Calvary, when he ransomed us from the curse of the law. We were manifestly set apart and separated unto God by the effectual call of God the Holy Spirit in regeneration.

Every believer has been, in this sense, eternally sanctified, completely set apart by God and for God. The practical importance of this glorious doctrine is this: – That which has been set apart for God ought never be used for common purposes again. 'Ye are not your own. For ye are bought with a price: therefore glorify God in your body, and in your spirit, which are God's' (1 Corinthians 6:19-20).

We belong to the Lord our God. We are his special possession. Let us therefore consecrate ourselves to him and serve him in all things (Romans 12:1-2). We belong to God. Be assured, God almighty will always protect all who belong to him in all their appointed ways, even as he protected the ark of the covenant in the Old Testament (Psalm 91:3-13).

All of God's elect were perfectly sanctified by the blood of Christ when he died as our Substitute (Hebrews 10:10-14). Christ is our

Sanctification (1 Corinthians 1:30). We have been and are forever 'sanctified in Christ Jesus' (1 Corinthians 1:2). Believers are addressed throughout the Epistles as 'saints', that is as 'sanctified ones' in Christ. This is what I want you to see and rejoice in: – In the Lord Jesus Christ we who believe are regarded by God as perfectly holy, treated as if we were perfectly holy, and declared to be perfectly holy, because in Christ we are perfectly holy! We do not believe in imputed sanctification any more than we believe in imputed justification. We believe in imputed righteousness, by which we are both justified and sanctified. The righteousness of Christ has been imputed to us; and we are by his righteousness both justified from all things and declared to be holy, and sanctified, in the sight of God.

> With His spotless garments on,
> I am as holy as God's Son!

All believers are actually made holy by God the Holy Spirit in regeneration. Through the instrumentally of gospel preaching, the Spirit of God effectually applies the blood of Christ to the hearts of God's elect, purifying our hearts and implanting a new, holy nature within us. This is regeneration, the new birth. This is our sanctification by the Spirit (2 Thessalonians 2:13-14; 2 Peter 1:4; 1 John 3:9; 1 John 5:18).

Someone once wrote, 'We are a people with two natures, one that is holy and seeks after righteousness, and one that is corrupt and seeks after sin. However, these two natures are not equal in power. The divine nature rules and reigns; but the evil nature will not bow nor serve'.

While we live in this world we must continue to live with this old, sinful nature. We do have a new nature created in us, in the image of Christ, a nature that cannot sin. It is the old man that sins, not the new. It is written, 'Now if I do that I would not, it is no more I that do it, but sin that dwelleth in me' (Romans 7:20). In glorification the old man shall be totally eradicated from us, but not until then. That eradication of the old man is not a gradual, progressive thing. It is the radical, climactic change experienced by God's saints in death, and ultimately in resurrection glory.

Progressive sanctification?

Does the Word of God teach the doctrine of progressive sanctification? As it is commonly taught by men, the answer is, No. The Bible certainly does not teach progressive sanctification. Be sure you understand what I mean by that statement. The Bible does not teach that in sanctification our old nature becomes less sinful and more holy. 'Flesh is flesh'. It cannot be sanctified. The old man is not sent to the hospital for a cure. He is sent to the cross to be crucified. The Bible does not teach that by sanctification we who believe attain progressively increasing degrees of personal holiness and thereby improve our acceptance with God. Yet, the scriptures do clearly represent the work of sanctification in the believer as a present, continual work of grace (1 Thessalonians 1:3-7; 5:23-24).

The believer grows in his state of holiness, grows in grace, in knowledge, in love, in faith, in consecration, and in all other aspects of spiritual life; but he does not increase in holiness and righteousness. The child Christ Jesus was perfectly holy. Yet, he grew in that state of holiness. Even so, we are perfectly holy in Christ. We have a perfectly holy nature implanted in us (Luke 2:52; 2 Peter 3:18).

Sanctification cannot be properly spoken of as a progressive work. A person is either holy or he is unholy. There is nothing in between. You cannot be more or less holy. Yet, sanctification is a continual work. Being sanctified by God, born again by the Holy Spirit, every believer grows in the grace and knowledge of our Lord Jesus Christ.

Every living thing grows. We see more, feel more, do more, know more, repent more, believe more, and love more, as we grow in grace. In sanctification there is an ever-increasing faith, hope, and love in the hearts of God's elect. Wherever sanctification is found consecration of the heart, conformity to Christ in heart and life, commitment to Christ and his cause, love, devotion, confidence in, and submission to Christ, and confidence in Christ all increase. This growth in grace is the continual operation of God the Holy Spirit in sanctification. 'It is God which worketh in you both to will and to do of his good pleasure' (Philippians 2:13). This growth in grace is a work of grace accomplished by the Spirit of God through the use of those means of grace God has given (Psalm 119:9-16).

Tokens and evidences

Are there any tokens and evidences of sanctification in us? Am I one of those whom God has sanctified by his grace? Are you? If so, there are some things that will give clear evidence of our sanctification. A sanctified person is one who loves Christ and seeks his glory (1 John 3:14; 1 Corinthians 16:22). A sanctified person is one in whose heart and soul there is an unceasing warfare between flesh and spirit, between sin and righteousness (Galatians 5:17; Romans 7:14-22). A sanctified person is one who seeks after perfection (Philippians 3:7-10; Hebrews 12:14; 1 Peter 1:15-16). A sanctified person is one who is humbled before God, repenting, believing, and persevering (Philippians 3:13-14).

Do we know anything about sanctification by experience? If we are not sanctified, we are not saved. Let us ever weep over our sins. Confess them to God. But do not despair. Our acceptance with God is Christ alone! (1 John 1:9; 2:1-2). Would we grow in grace? Then let us 'keep our heart with all diligence; for out of it are the issues of life' (Proverbs 4:23). In all things, seek to imitate Christ. Follow his example, suffering with patience and serving one another. 'And the very God of peace sanctify you wholly; and I pray God your whole spirit and soul and body be preserved blameless unto the coming of our Lord Jesus Christ. Faithful is he that calleth you, who also will do it' (1 Thessalonians 5:23-24).

'Marvel not that I said unto thee, Ye must be born again'.
(John 3:7)

Chapter 45

'Ye Must Be Born Again'

These days, almost everyone talks about being born again; but virtually no one knows what the Word of God teaches about the new birth. For that reason the subject needs to be explained in simple, clear, unmistakable terms.

The religious world around us, in its apostate rejection of the truth of God, has made the new birth to be nothing more than making a decision, walking an aisle, and saying a prayer. Because of their abuse and error regarding the doctrine of the new birth, our tendency is to shy away from using the term 'born again', lest we be identified with those who deny the gospel of Christ. But, no matter how much men may pervert the language and the doctrine of Christ, our Lord's admonition to Nicodemus still stands. It is as necessary and urgent today as it was when he first made it two thousand years ago. This is my message to you right now, 'Ye must be born again!'

Perhaps some who read these words have never made any profession of faith in Christ. 'Ye must be born again!' Perhaps some who read these lines have been in the church for many, many years and are yet without Christ. You made a profession of faith a long time ago; but you are yet without life before God. May God the Holy Spirit cause you to hear this message and grant you his grace. 'Ye must be born again!'

Look at these five words, and ask God to give you wisdom and grace to understand what they mean. Here is a personal word – 'Ye'. This message is for you. Perhaps you are moral. Perhaps you are very religious. Perhaps you are even well instructed in doctrinal truth. So was Nicodemus. He was a highly respected religious leader, a Pharisee, and a ruler among the Jews. Nicodemus was a teacher who taught the teachers. He was a preacher, but more. Nicodemus was a preacher who taught preachers. He was a theologian. This was a man of highest rank in the Jewish church. But he was dead. He was without life before God. He was totally ignorant of all things spiritual. He was a lost man. If you are in his condition, if you are yet without life toward God, this is a word from God for you: 'You must be born again'.

Here is a pressing word – 'Must'. Time is short. 'What shall it profit a man if he gain the whole world and lose his own soul?' This is not a merely good recommendation. This is not simply wholesome advice. This is imperative. This is vital. This is a necessity. 'You must be born again!' Otherwise, you will perish in your sins. You will die under the wrath of God! Hell will be your portion forever!

Here is a passive word – 'Be'. The new birth is not something you do. It is something God does for you. A man has no more to do with his spiritual birth than he does with his natural birth. In this matter of regeneration man is passive. He has nothing to do with it (John 1:12-13). You cannot save yourself. You cannot give yourself life. You cannot be born again by something you do (Titus 3:4-6). No one has ever been born again by the exercise of his will, saying a prayer, doing good works, being baptized, making a decision for

Jesus, or even by faith in Christ. Faith in Christ is not the cause of
the new birth. Faith is the result of the new birth. We believe,
according to the working of God's mighty power, by the operation
of his grace (Ephesians 1:19; 2:8; Colossians 2:11-12). The new
birth is something done to you, for you, and in you by God's
sovereign, irresistible grace. It is not something you do. 'You must
BE born again!'[1]

Here is a powerful word – 'Born'. The new birth is a gift; but it
is not just any ordinary gift. This is the gift of life, eternal life.
When our Lord declares, 'Ye must be born again', he is saying you
must be the object and recipient of divine power. Just as God created
the world, God must create life in your soul. Just as God breathed
into Adam and made him a living soul, so God must breathe into
you the breath of life by his Spirit, or you will perish in your sins.
We are all spiritually dead, helplessly lost by nature. Man's only
hope is that God the Holy Spirit will give life. 'You must be born
again!'

Here is a profound word – 'Again'. The new birth is a mystery
of grace. It cannot be explained. It simply cannot be fully understood.
It is a work of God beyond our comprehension. Yet, this much is
certain, when our Lord says, 'Ye must be born again', his meaning
is twofold. The word 'again' has two meanings. First, it means,
'You must be born from above'. James tells us that 'every good and
perfect gift is from above, and cometh down from the Father of
lights, with whom is no variableness, neither shadow of turning'.
Then he tells us what he is teaching in the next verse. 'Of his own
will begat he us with the word of truth' (James 1:17-18).

Second, it means, 'You must be born a second time'. Our first
birth was of sinful parents, and we were born in their image. The
second birth is of God, and we are born in his image. The first birth

---

[1] I fully agree with what Martin Luther had to say in this regard. 'If any man
ascribes anything of salvation, even the very least thing, to the free will of man,
he knows nothing of grace, and he has not learned Jesus Christ rightly.'

was of corruptible seed. The second birth is of incorruptible seed. Our first birth is in sin. Our second birth is in righteousness. By our first birth we were polluted and unclean. By our second birth we become holy. Our first birth was fleshy and carnal. Our second birth is spiritual and makes us spiritual. By the first birth all men are foolish and ignorant. By our second birth we become wise unto salvation. By our first birth we were slaves to sin and the lusts of the flesh. By our second birth we are made free from the dominion of sin. By our first birth we are all children of wrath. By our second birth we are children of promise. Because we were all born wrong the first time, our Lord says, 'Ye must be born again'.

Our Lord said, 'Ye must be born again', because none shall ever enter into glory except those who are born again by the power and grace of God and made to live in and by the Lord Jesus Christ. In order for God to save a sinner two things must be done. God must do something for you and God must do something in you. Redemption is the work of God for sinners. Regeneration is the work of God in sinners. Both are the works of God. Man has nothing more to do with regeneration than he has to do with redemption. 'Salvation is of the Lord!'

> Not all the outward forms on earth,
> Nor rites that God has given,
> Nor will of man, nor blood, nor birth,
> Can raise a soul to heaven.
>
> The sovereign will of God alone
> Creates us heirs of grace;
> Born in the image of His Son,
> A new peculiar race.

Why must we be born again?
There are many answers that are given to that question in the Word of God. In the third chapter of John our Lord gave Nicodemus

three reasons why he must be born again. These three things make it imperative that you and I must be born again.

First, unless we are born again we cannot understand anything spiritual (v. 3). – 'Jesus answered and said unto him, Verily, verily, I say unto thee, Except a man be born again, he cannot see the kingdom of God'. The natural man is totally void of spiritual understanding. He may be a logical, reasonable, rational, and well educated person among men, but with regard to the things of God, he is as ignorant, foolish, and unreasonable as a madman. He has no capacity for spiritual knowledge (Romans 8:5; 1 Corinthians 2:14). The heart of stone is hard, cold, unbending, unaffected.

Until a person is born again, he cannot see the spiritual nature of God's law (Matthew 5:21, 27, 38, 43, 48), – the spiritual nature of sin (Matthew 15:17-19), – the glory of God in redemption (Romans 3:24-26), – the spiritual condition of his own heart (Jeremiah 17:9), – the spiritual nature of salvation (Ezekiel 36:25-27), or – the spiritual nature of obedience to God (1 Samuel 16:7; Romans 14:17). Human religion is carnal. It has to do with carnal things. In the kingdom of God all things are spiritual (John 4:23-24; Romans 14:17). Until a person is born of God, he simply cannot see spiritual things, he cannot see the spiritual nature of faith and worship (Philippians 3:3), – the true character of God (Exodus 33:18-34:7), and – the glory of God in Christ (2 Corinthians 4:6). The natural man cannot see the glory of God in Christ's suretiship, his incarnation, his obedience, his substitutionary atonement, or his ascension and exaltation as the God-man Mediator. The natural man just cannot see the gospel of the grace of God (2 Corinthians 5:18-21).

Second, unless you are born again by almighty grace you can never enter into the kingdom of God (v. 5). 'Jesus answered, Verily, verily, I say unto thee, Except a man be born of water and of the Spirit, he cannot enter into the kingdom of God'. You can reform your life without the new birth. You can be baptized without the new birth. You can join the church, be zealous in religion, teach a

Bible class, serve as a deacon or elder, you can even preach with great success without being born again. But unless you are born again, you will never enter the kingdom of God. Without the new birth, you will never be a part of the church and family of God. You will never have eternal life. You will never enter into the worship and fellowship of God's saints. You will never be admitted into the presence of God's glory in the bliss of heaven (Revelation 20:6; 21:27). Only new creatures will enter the New Jerusalem. Only holy men will walk into the Holy City. Only heaven born citizens will possess the bliss of heaven.

Third, 'Ye must be born again', because by nature we are fallen, sinful, depraved children of human flesh (v. 6). 'That which is born of the flesh is flesh; and that which is born of the Spirit is spirit'. All flesh is defiled. All flesh is corrupt. All flesh is sinful. All flesh is condemned. All flesh must die. Unless we are born of the Spirit, we will die in our sins, and our flesh[2] shall be justly damned.

What is the new birth?

No man can explain the mystery of the new birth. It is one of God's incomprehensible works. But there are several things in the Word of God which identify God's regenerating grace. To be born again is to be raised from the dead (Ephesians 2:1-5; Revelation 20:6). To be born again is to be made a partaker of the divine nature (2 Peter 1:4). In regeneration a new, Christ-like nature is created in our souls, so that men and women upon the earth are born in the image of God (Galatians 5:22). As John Gill expressed it, 'In regeneration there is that wrought in the soul which bears a resemblance to the divine nature, in spirituality, holiness, goodness, (and) kindness'. To be born again is to have Christ formed in us (Galatians 4:19). To have eternal life is to have the Lord Jesus Christ living in you (Galatians 2:20; Colossians 1:27). To be born again is

---

[2] The flesh is your natural, sinful self (Psalm 51:5; 58:3; Romans 5:12; Revelation 20:11-15).

to have a good seed implanted in you by grace (1 John 3:9-10). By nature we are all sprung from bad seed – Adam. But in regeneration we are sprung from good Seed – the Lord Jesus Christ.

To be born again is to be made new creatures in Christ (2 Corinthians 5:17). In the new birth, God the Holy Spirit gives chosen, redeemed sinners a new heart to know and love God. A new will to bow to the rule of Christ. A new mind to understand the things of God. A new, spiritual nature to know, enjoy, and live upon spiritual things. New eyes, eyes of faith, with which to see Christ. New ears with which to hear his voice. New hands, hands of faith, with which to lay hold of Christ and do his will. And, finally, new feet, with which to flee to Christ and walk with him in the newness of life. This is the great difference between the law and the gospel. The law demands everything, but gives nothing. The gospel demands nothing, but gives everything!

> 'Run, run, and work', the law demands,
> Yet gives me neither feet nor hands;
> But sweet, good news the gospel brings.
> It bids me fly, and gives me wings!
>
> With these my heavy soul may fly
> Away to Christ and reach the sky,
> Nor faint, nor falter in the race,
> But work with cheer and sing of grace!

How are men and women born again by the Spirit of God?

Anyone who understands the nature of man and the nature of the new birth realizes that divine, sovereign power and grace is required to give dead sinners life. Moral reason cannot give men life. Eloquence and logic cannot give men life. Emotional stirrings cannot give men life. A mere exercise of the will cannot give men life. 'Ye must be born again'. Only God himself can give dead sinners life (John 6:63).

Regeneration is the sovereign, irresistible work of God the Holy Spirit (v. 8). – 'The wind bloweth where it listeth, and thou hearest the sound thereof, but canst not tell whence it cometh, and whither it goeth: so is every one that is born of the Spirit'. At the time appointed by God, the Holy Spirit comes to the sinner, who was chosen by grace in eternal election and redeemed by Christ at Calvary, and creates life in that sinner by his sovereign, irresistible, effectual grace (Galatians 4:4-7).

The instrument by which the Holy Spirit causes men and women to be born again is the gospel of Christ (vv. 12-16). 'It pleased God by the foolishness of preaching to save them that believe'. 'Of his own will begat he us with the Word of Truth'. Sinners are 'born again, not of corruptible seed, but of incorruptible, by the Word of God which liveth and abideth forever … And this is the Word which by the gospel is preached unto you'.

In preaching the gospel God's servants call dead sinners to arise (Ephesians 5:14), knowing full well that they are preaching to dead sinners, knowing that they cannot hear and cannot obey the call. But knowing this, too: If God the Holy Spirit will be pleased to speak through them, though men are dead, the dead shall hear and live (John 5:25).

When is a sinner born again?

I have no interest in answering the foolish questions of men about the chronological sequence of events in a man's salvation. I am happy to leave that to theologians who have nothing better to do. However, I do want all who read these lines to know when a person may with confidence say, 'I am born again by the grace of God'. When you know Christ, you are born again (John 17:3). When you believe on Christ, you are born again (John 3:15, 36; see also Isaiah 45:22). When you have Christ, you are born again (1 John 5:10-13). – 'He that hath the Son hath life; and he that hath not the Son of God hath not life!' Get Christ and you get life. Miss Christ and you miss life.

'For many are called, but few are chosen'.
(Matthew 22:14)

Chapter 46

The Preaching of the Gospel

We rejoice in the blessed gospel doctrine of God's electing love. We rejoice to hear our Saviour say, 'Ye have not chosen me, but I have chosen you'. We say with the psalmist, 'Blessed is the man whom thou choosest'. But election alone never saved anyone. Election is not salvation. Election is unto salvation. It is not enough that we should be chosen to salvation. Before God almighty, in his holiness, justice and truth, could save chosen sinners, those who were chosen by him must also be redeemed. Election is the work of God the Father. Redemption is the work of God the Son.

How we rejoice in and give thanks to God for our redemption by Christ! Precious blood indeed is that blood which put away our sins! Every God taught sinner has learned to give thanks to God for that glorious gospel doctrine of limited atonement; particular, effectual redemption by Christ. Yet, even our redemption by Christ, though it guaranteed and infallibly secured the salvation of God's elect, is not salvation. Salvation involves the work of the Father and the Son; but it also involves the work of God the Holy Spirit in regeneration and effectual calling.

The effectual call of the Spirit is the Holy Spirit's work of effectual, irresistible grace, by which he draws all chosen, redeemed sinners to Christ, creating faith in them, granting them repentance, and converting them by almighty grace. This work of the Holy Spirit in effectual calling must be understood in two aspects: (1) The outward, external call of grace which comes to sinners by the preaching of the gospel; and (2) The internal call, which is the effectual operation of the Holy Spirit by which sinners are infallibly converted. In this chapter we will see what the Word of God teaches about the external call of the gospel.

It is this external call of the gospel which our Lord spoke of when he said, 'Many are called, but few are chosen'. The Son of God plainly declared that many, not all, but many, are called to repentance and faith in him by the preaching of the gospel, and that few of the many who are called are numbered among the chosen. The means by which this external call is given to sinners is the preaching of the gospel.

The utility of the gospel

God calls sinners to life and faith in Christ by the preaching of the gospel. Every time a true servant of God preaches the gospel of God's free and sovereign grace in Christ, electing love, redeeming blood, and saving grace, sinners are thereby called to Christ (2 Corinthians 5:20).

The preaching of the gospel is not an offer of Christ, of his grace, or of salvation by him. No preacher has the power to give grace and salvation. And no dead sinner has the power to receive God's grace and salvation in Christ. The preaching of the gospel is not an offer of Christ, or an invitation to sinners to receive Christ. The preaching of the gospel is a proclamation of the unsearchable riches of Christ, of his grace, of peace, pardon, righteousness, and life, and salvation by him (Isaiah 40:1-2).

This is God's appointed means of grace. God does not save sinners through the lies of false religion, but through the word of the truth of the gospel (Ephesians 1:13-14; 1 Corinthians 1:21; Romans 10:17; James 1:18; 1 Peter 1:23-25).

Universal message

The gospel call is universal in its scope. Our Master commands his servants to go into all the world and preach the gospel to all (Matthew 28:18-20). The gospel is a universal message of grace and salvation. We preach the gospel indiscriminately to all who will hear us, calling all to repentance and faith in Christ, just as our Lord commanded us. Yet, as we have observed already, even the outward preaching of the gospel is not absolutely universal. In the Old Testament, God sent his Word to Israel alone. During his earthly ministry, our Lord and his apostles went to the lost sheep of the house of Israel. In the Book of Acts, God's servants were frequently prevented from going to some places and sent to others. Even so, today our God sends the gospel to some and hides it from others. 'Many' are called, but not all.

Unconditional call

This call of sinners to repentance and faith in Christ is an unqualified, unconditional call. There are no conditions, qualifications, experiences, feelings, or anything else the sinner must meet, go through, or measure up to before he can trust Christ.

God almighty commands sinners, as sinners, to come to Christ (1 John 3:23). If God commands a person to do something, I presume it is all right for him to do it! God does not say, feel, do, get, experience, but 'believe!' The only terms of peace God sets before sinners is unconditional surrender to King Jesus. Gospel preachers stand before eternity bound sinners as God's ambassadors, sent with his terms of peace. They have no authority to change his terms, but simply proclaim them. Sinners must either surrender to the King, or be destroyed by the King.

Divine authority

This call of the gospel is given by divine authority. That man who is sent of God to preach the gospel is sent with a God given, divine authority, a divine authority which cannot be obtained by any means except the call and gift of God. It is an authority that cannot be obtained from any source other than God himself. He speaks as the very mouth-piece of the almighty (Matthew 10:40). When God speaks by a man, God strives with men (Genesis 6:3). When men resist the message delivered to them by a man who speaks in the power of God, they resist God the Holy Spirit (Acts 7:51-52).

This divine authority makes the preaching of the gospel a matter of urgent responsibility (Proverbs 1:23-31). Gospel preaching leaves sinners without excuse. If any will obey the gospel call, if any will trust the Lord Jesus Christ, he will save them. Indeed, if any hear his voice and obey the gospel, if any believe, he has saved them. Their faith is the evidence of his saving operations.

A sincere call

The call issued to sinners in the preaching of the gospel is a sincere call (Romans 10:1-4; Matthew 23:37). Arminians, free-willers, who despise the gospel of God's free grace, often attempt to repudiate the gospel of God's free and sovereign grace in Christ by saying, we are not sincere in preaching the gospel, or that belief in the doctrines of grace will dry up the zeal of God's people and make them anti-missionary. Nothing could be further from the truth. It was this gospel by which the apostles turned the world upside down. It is this gospel by which God's church still invades and prevails over the very gates of hell.

A gracious call

This gospel call is a most gracious call (Isaiah 1:18; 55:1-7). In infinite mercy and grace, God sends saved sinners to proclaim his free grace to perishing sinners, and uses the most gracious terms imaginable to persuade hell deserving men and women to come to Christ.

These are terms of grace: – 'Whosoever will, let him come!' – 'If any man thirst, let him come!' – 'Whosoever believeth on him shall not perish!' – 'Whosoever shall call upon the name of the

Lord shall be saved!' – 'He that believeth on the Son of God hath everlasting life!' – 'Come unto me, all ye that labour and are heavy laden, and I will give you rest!'

God's servants call needy sinners, reasoning with them, pleading with them in God's name, with God's authority, in Christ's stead, to trust Christ and be saved (Ezekiel 18:23, 32; 33:11). Were it not for the obstinate hardness of sinful hearts, all who hear the gospel would immediately see that only spiritual madness and utter insanity makes it necessary for preachers to plead with their souls.

In preaching the gospel we proclaim to guilty souls full pardon by the blood of Christ, perfect justification by the imputation of Christ's righteousness, complete cleansing from all sin, eternal life in Christ, immutable acceptance in the Beloved, infallible security in his grace, and peace, peace, blessed peace with God!

The power of God

Though it is, in itself, ineffectual for the saving of any, when accompanied by the power of God's Spirit, the preaching of the gospel is the power of God unto salvation (Isaiah 55:11; Romans 1:16-17). I have often been asked, 'If only the elect are going to be saved, why preach the gospel to all?'

Let me give you five answers to that question.

1. My Master has commanded us to preach the gospel to all (Matthew 10:27; 28:19; Mark 16:15; Acts 1:8).
2. God has chosen to save sinners through the foolishness of preaching.
3. We have no way of knowing who God's elect are until they believe the gospel (1 Thessalonians 1:4-5).
4. When we have faithfully preached the gospel to all men and women, we are pure from their blood (1 Corinthians 9:16; Ezekiel 33:7-9).
5. We preach the gospel to all, because God has promised by this means to save some.

We preach the gospel freely to all men, with earnestness, zeal, and unabated fervency, and with absolute confidence of success, because this is God's message, and because God will save his people by the gospel we preach.

'We are bound to give thanks alway to God for you, brethren beloved of the Lord, because God hath from the beginning chosen you to salvation through sanctification of the Spirit and belief of the truth: Whereunto he called you by our gospel, to the obtaining of the glory of our Lord Jesus Christ' (2 Thessalonians 2:13-14).

'Paul, a servant of Jesus Christ, called to be an apostle, separated unto the gospel of God, (Which he had promised afore by his prophets in the holy scriptures,) Concerning his Son Jesus Christ our Lord, which was made of the seed of David according to the flesh; And declared to be the Son of God with power, according to the spirit of holiness, by the resurrection from the dead: By whom we have received grace and apostleship, for obedience to the faith among all nations, for his name: Among whom are ye also the called of Jesus Christ'.
(Romans 1:1-6)

Chapter 47

What is it to Preach the Gospel?

Eternal election is the work of God the Father in salvation. The particular, effectual redemption of the elect is the work of God the Son in salvation. Effectual calling, or irresistible grace, is the work of God the Holy Spirit in salvation. Sinners cannot be saved without the Father's sovereign election, the Son's blood redemption, and the Spirit's effectual call. Every chosen sinner was redeemed at Calvary. Every chosen, redeemed sinner shall be called by the Spirit. Every chosen, redeemed, called sinner comes to Christ in faith and has eternal life.

There is no possibility that any sinner can be chosen by God the Father, redeemed by God the Son, and called by God the Holy Spirit, and yet perish in hell at last! To teach such nonsense is blasphemy! Such blasphemy exalts Satan above God, the free will of man above the omnipotence of God, and makes the triune God an utter failure in his purpose, work, and grace. It cannot be embraced or tolerated by anyone who knows God.

No one is saved apart from the effectual call of God the Holy Spirit. We rejoice to sing with the inspired psalmist, 'Blessed is the man whom thou choosest and causest to approach unto thee!' As none are saved without the effectual call of the Spirit, none are saved in this gospel age apart from the preaching of the gospel. Let no one deceive you in this matter. The issue is not whether or not God can save his people without the use of means. The issue is whether or not he will. We know that he will not, because he has revealed it plainly in his Word. Faith comes by hearing and hearing by the Word of God. It pleased God to save his elect by the foolishness of gospel preaching. All who are begotten of God are begotten of him by the gospel. All who are born again are born again by the incorruptible seed of God's Word, which is preached to them by the gospel.

These things are so plainly revealed in holy scripture that there is no excuse for error regarding them (Romans 10:17; 1 Corinthians 1:21; James 1:18; 1 Peter 1:23-25). Those who teach that God saves sinners apart from the preaching of the gospel fly in the face of holy scripture. It is therefore no surprise to see them favour emotionalism, experiences, dreams, custom, and religious tradition above the Word of God. The preaching of the gospel is God's chosen, ordained means of grace, by which he calls chosen, redeemed sinners to life and faith in Christ by the irresistible power and grace of his Holy Spirit.

If the preaching of the gospel is vital to the salvation of God's elect, as the New Testament universally declares that it is, then no questions can possibly be more important and pressing than the three I will answer in this study.

Who preaches the gospel?

We cannot do better, when we look for an example of a gospel preacher than the Apostle Paul. In Romans 1:1 we see how this inspired man describes himself and thus describes all who truly preach the gospel.

'Paul, a servant of Jesus Christ' – That man who truly preaches the gospel, that man who always preaches the gospel, that man who preaches the whole gospel, and that exclusively is a servant of the Lord Jesus Christ. Gospel preachers are the willing, voluntary bond-slaves of the Son of God. Notice how Paul describes himself. It is not, Rev. Paul, Dr Paul, Father Paul, or Pope Paul, but 'Paul, a servant of Jesus Christ'. This man counted it his highest honour to be a servant of Christ, not the servant, but a servant. He was just one servant among many; but he was a servant.

'Called to be an apostle (messenger)' – Gospel preachers are called and gifted of God to be his messengers, men sent with his message. A gospel preacher is a man with a message, a message from God, a message burning in his soul, which he must deliver. He is a man with a messianic call, a messianic purpose, and a messianic mandate.

If you ever run across a man with a mandate from God, or a man who even thinks he has a mandate from God, you will not have to wonder about it. You will know it. He will fit no mould, bow to no pressure, surrender no ground, make no compromise. Why should he? He has a mandate from God! That makes him utterly uncontrollable by anyone, except God who sent him. Moses and John the Baptist are two eminent examples of men with a mandate from God.

'Separated unto the gospel' – God's servants, true gospel preachers, are men who are separated unto the gospel. God's servants do not take this business of being God's servants lightly. They are men, like Jeremiah and Paul, separated unto the gospel. They are separated unto the gospel by God's decree, call, and gifts, by God's providence and grace, and by their own, ever increasing devotion and determination (Romans 1:9-17). That man who preaches the gospel of Christ is like Abraham's servant, who was sent to get a bride for his son Isaac. He will not be distracted from his work by either pleasure or pressure.

Who preaches the gospel? – Those men who are servants of Jesus Christ and called messengers of God almighty, men who are separated unto the gospel of God.

What is the gospel?

There are many other texts of scripture that could be used to show the answer to this question; but none are more emphatic and clear than the first six verses of the Book of Roman. In these six verses of scripture the Holy Spirit has given us five distinct, identifying characteristics of the gospel. Mark them carefully. Learn what they mean. Any gospel that fails to measure up to this standard is a false gospel and those who preach it are false prophets.

The gospel we believe and preach, the gospel of holy scripture, the only true gospel is here described as 'the gospel of God'. There are not many gospels, but one, and that one gospel is 'the gospel' which is 'of God'. It came from God. It reveals God. It is made known by God. It brings sinners to God. It glorifies and exalts God.

That gospel which is of God is that 'which he had promised afore by his prophets in the holy scriptures'. The gospel revealed in the New Testament is the gospel promised, portrayed, and typified in the Old Testament. As stated above, there is only one gospel, not two. God did not save sinners by works in the Old Testament. He saved them by grace, just like he does today. Noah was saved by grace, not by works. The scriptures do not say that God found grace in the eyes of Noah, but that Noah found grace in the eyes of the Lord. Enoch walked with God just like we do, by faith in Christ. Abraham was saved the same way we are. He believed God, he believed on the Lord Jesus Christ.

That gospel which is of God and according to the scriptures, promised in the prophets of the Old Testament, is 'concerning his Son, Jesus Christ our Lord'. The gospel is good news about a Person, the Lord Jesus Christ. It is not a set of doctrines, a proposition, or an offer. It is the blessed good news of the Person, work, and accomplishments of our Lord Jesus Christ.

Carefully study this description of Christ given by God the Holy Spirit. He is the Son of God, God the Son, the second Person of the Holy Trinity (1 John 5:7). He is Jesus, our Saviour, Deliverer, and Redeemer (Matthew 1:21). He is the Christ, Jehovah's Servant, his Elect, the Messiah, that One of whom it is written, 'He shall not fail!' He who is God our Saviour is our Lord, the Sovereign Monarch of the universe (John 17:2; Romans 14:9). He of whom the gospel speaks is God the eternal Son who was 'made of the seed of David, according to the flesh'. He was 'made of a woman, made under the law, to redeem them that were under the law'. Being made a man, he was made a man according to the direct, royal line of King David, to sit upon his throne forever. Then, after he had satisfied the law and justice of God for the sins of his people, which were imputed to him, by his death upon the cursed tree, our great Substitute was manifestly and indisputably 'declared to be the Son of God with power, according to the Spirit of holiness, by the resurrection from the dead'. It is this great God and Saviour revealed in the gospel by whom we have received grace, faith, and obedience.

This gospel, everything about this gospel, is 'for his name', for the glory, honour, praise, exaltation, and worship of his holy name. Here is a litmus test by which we must judge all religion, all doctrine, and all preaching. If it exalts the Lord Jesus Christ and the free grace of God in him, it is according to the gospel of God. If it exalts man, his will, his works, or his religious deeds, it is of the devil, the father of lies, the flatterer and deceiver of men's souls.

It is by this gospel, the glorious gospel of the all glorious Christ, that we who believe are 'the called of Jesus Christ'. 'We are bound to give thanks alway to God for you, brethren beloved of the Lord, because God hath from the beginning chosen you to salvation through sanctification of the Spirit and belief of the truth: Whereunto he called you by our gospel, to the obtaining of the glory of our Lord Jesus Christ' (2 Thessalonians 2:13-14).

What is it to preach the gospel?

I had the privilege of hearing Pastor Henry Mahan, when I was just a young man, raise and answer this question. I know of no better answer to this very important question than these five answers he gave to the congregation that night.

1. What is it to preach the gospel? It is to simply declare it. God never called a preacher to defend the gospel, apologize for the gospel, explain the gospel, or adorn the gospel. It is the preacher's job simply to declare the gospel (1 Corinthians 15:1-4).

2. To preach the gospel is to simply declare it, and to declare it as God's message. Our gospel is the gospel of God, not the gospel of the Reformers, the gospel of the Puritans, the gospel of the Calvinists, or even the gospel of the Baptists. The gospel we preach is God's message. If the message I preach is just my message, it may be heard or not without consequence. But if the message I preach to the souls of men is God's message, those who hear it must obey it, or suffer the consequences of ignoring and disobeying God.

3. To preach the gospel is to declare it as God's message for everyone. We do not have one message for the lost and another for the saved. We do not have one message for children and another for adults. We do not have one message for one group and another for another group[1].

Our message, the gospel of God, is a message for everyone. Our message is always the same. We preach the gospel for the salvation and sanctification of God's elect, for both evangelism and for edification, for conversion and for correction, for conviction and for comfort, to meet the needs of both dead sinners and of dying saints.

---

[1] The minute we start to specialize we compromise. If you try to make the gospel special for one group of people, you have to make it palatable to that group; and you cannot make the gospel palatable to sinners without compromising it.

4. If any man would preach the gospel of the grace of God, he must preach it as his own message (Romans 2:16; 16:25; 2 Timothy 2:8). Let me be clear. Gospel preaching is not talking to men about abstract religious, theological principles learned from a book. That man who preaches the gospel preaches the message of God which has been inscribed upon his heart by the finger of God with fire and burned into his soul as with a branding iron by the Word of God in the hands of God the Holy Spirit.

5. To preach the gospel is to declare it with a genuine desire that all who hear it may believe. Those who preach the gospel indifferently do not preach the gospel. They only go through the motions of preaching. God's servants do not preach with indifference, but with passion, as dying men to dying men. The gospel ought to be preached, as Luther said, 'as if I had just learned it today, as if you had never heard it before, as if you were sure never to hear it again, and as if I were certain that I would never preach it again'. Every gospel preacher can honestly say with Paul, 'My prayer and heart's desire to God for you is that you may be saved'. That is what it is to preach the gospel.

'Wherefore, holy brethren, partakers of the heavenly calling, consider the Apostle and High Priest of our profession, Christ Jesus'.
(Hebrews 3:1)

Chapter 48

'The Heavenly Calling'

In the opening words of Hebrews 3:1 the Holy Spirit tells us three things about all true believers, all who trust the Lord Jesus Christ: (1) All true believers are 'holy'. (2) All true believers are 'brethren'. (3) All true believers are 'partakers of the heavenly calling'.

There are some people in this world described by the Holy Spirit as 'the called' (Romans 1:6; 8:28). Those who are the called of Jesus Christ are God's elect, those sinners redeemed by the precious blood of Christ, who have been saved by his almighty, irresistible grace. All the rest of the elect shall be called, but those who are saved are 'the called', called from death to life, from unbelief to faith in Christ.

All who are privileged to hear the gospel preached are called externally, by the preaching of the gospel; but those who are saved, 'the called', have been called internally, effectually, and irresistibly by God the Holy Spirit. 'The called' are like the Thessalonian saints. Their election, redemption, and calling is made manifest by the fact that the Word of God has come to them, not in word only, but in the power of the Holy Ghost[1]. Salvation comes to chosen, redeemed sinners in the experience of grace by the almighty, irresistible, effectual call of God the Holy Spirit.

It is this call of which David sang, when he said, 'Blessed is the man whom thou choosest, and causest to approach unto thee'. This is the call the Apostle Paul was talking about when he said, 'God separated me from my mother's womb, called me by his grace, and revealed his Son in me'. Paul was talking about this internal, effectual call when he wrote to Timothy: – God 'hath saved us, and called us with an holy calling, not according to our works, but according to his own purpose and grace, which was given us in Christ Jesus before the world began, But is now made manifest by the appearing of our Saviour Jesus Christ, who hath abolished death, and hath brought life and immortality to light through the gospel: Whereunto I am appointed a preacher, and an apostle, and a teacher of the Gentiles' (2 Timothy 1:9-11).

Notice how the Apostle Paul describes this call of God. When he speaks of it, he seems to be so overwhelmed by it, in such awe of it that he cannot find words sufficient to describe it. He calls it …

- an holy calling (2 Timothy 1:9).
- the high calling of God (Philippians 3:14).
- the calling of God (Romans 11:29).
- your calling (1 Corinthians 1:26; Ephesians 4:4).
- the heavenly calling (Hebrews 3:1).

What is this call of God by which we are saved? What is this heavenly calling of which all who believe the gospel have been made partakers by the grace of God? It is described in many ways in doctrinal and theological works: – The Internal Call – The Effectual

---

[1] I remind you, there is no effectual call of grace apart from the preaching of the gospel. Yet, the preaching of the gospel will never produce life and faith in Christ without the effectual call of God the Holy Spirit.

Call – The Irresistible Call – The Call of Grace. All those terms are good and accurate. But how is this call described and explained in holy scripture? Here are seven texts, seven divinely inspired passages of scripture, in which our heavenly calling is described.

Called out of darkness – 1 Peter 2:9

'But ye are a chosen generation, a royal priesthood, an holy nation, a peculiar people; that ye should show forth the praises of him who hath called you out of darkness into his marvellous light'.

This internal, effectual, saving call of grace is a call out of gross darkness into God's marvellous light. As in the creation of the world, God commanded the light to shine out of darkness, so in the new creation of grace God the Holy Spirit shines in the hearts of chosen, redeemed sinners to give the light of the knowledge of the glory of God in the face of Jesus Christ (2 Corinthians 4:6)[2].

Before God saved us, we were like all other men, engulfed in the gross darkness of our own depraved hearts and spiritual ignorance. God's elect, in their state of nature, before they are converted, are just like all other men, totally ignorant of all things spiritual. We were all, by nature, ignorant of God, ignorant of ourselves, ignorant of Christ, ignorant of sin, ignorant of righteousness, ignorant of providence, ignorant of salvation, ignorant of the scriptures, and ignorant of the gospel. The natural man has absolutely no spiritual knowledge (John 3:5; 1 Corinthians 2:14).

Now, by the effectual call of the Holy Spirit, the eyes of our understanding have been opened, we are now made to see light and walk in light, as the children of light. God's people are children of light. They no longer grope about in darkness. They have the unction of the Spirit causing them to know all things. Believers have the

---

[2] 'When the apostle Paul was called by grace, a light surrounded him, as an emblem of that internal light which was sprung in him. After that, there fell from his eyes, as it had been scales, as a token of the removal of his former darkness and ignorance'. (John Gill)

mind of Christ, enabling them to understand all things (Proverbs 28:5; 1 John 2:20; 1 Corinthians 2:12-13, 15-16).

Believers understand the truth, believe the truth, and receive the love of the truth. Every regenerate man or woman rejoices in both the character of God and the ways of God. Believers all acknowledge their sin and sins, and the utter sinfulness of their righteousnesses. All who know God find in the effectual blood atonement of Christ the solitary basis for their hope and consolation before God. Saved sinners glory in the Lord, declaring with Jonah of old, 'Salvation is of the Lord!'

Being taught of God, regenerate, enlightened, saved sinners have the ability to distinguish between things that differ. They know the difference between grace and works. They know the difference between free grace and free will. We have been called out of darkness into God's marvellous light.

Called unto liberty – Galatians 5:13

'For, brethren, ye have been called unto liberty; only use not liberty for an occasion to the flesh, but by love serve one another'.

We were by nature children of wrath, even as others; but now, in Christ we are freed from all the curse and condemnation of God's holy law. We lived all the days of our lives as home born slaves, under the dominion of sin; but now, in Christ we have become the servants of righteousness. We spent all our days under the power and influence of Satan; but we are now Christ's free men. How we ought to thank God for the blessed liberation of grace! Satan, like a strong man armed, held me in a bondage worse than that of Egypt. Grace has set me free! 'The Lord brought us out of Egypt with a mighty hand' (Deuteronomy 6:20-23). 'Unto thee it was showed, that thou mightest know that the Lord he is God; there is none else beside him. Out of heaven he made thee to hear his voice, that he might instruct thee' (Deuteronomy 4:31-39). All who are born of God have been called unto liberty, even 'the glorious liberty of the sons of God'!

Called unto the fellowship of Christ – 1 Corinthians 1:9

'God is faithful, by whom ye were called unto the fellowship of his Son Jesus Christ our Lord'.

Not only have we been called out of bondage and into liberty, we have been called into the blessed liberty of intimate, sweet and lasting fellowship with the triune God in our all glorious Saviour, the Lord Jesus Christ!

God calls his people to abandon the world for Christ. Those who are called of God are called to forsake family and friends, like Abram, and follow Christ. We have been, and are continually called by our God, to 'love not the world, neither the things that are in the world'. The riches of this world, the recognition it lavishes upon men, and the religion it cherishes, we must purposefully despise (Deuteronomy 7:2-6, 25-26; 2 Corinthians 6:14-7:1; Revelation 18:4).

This is no great sacrifice. 'The heavenly calling' of which we are now partakers brings us into far better company than we ever knew before. We now have access to and communion with God the Father, God the Son, and God the Holy Spirit and blessed fellowship with his saints on earth, and even with his saints in heaven (Hebrews 12:22-23). God's house is open to us. The Lord's table is open to us. The very throne of God is open to us! What a privilege! We have been called into fellowship with the eternal God!

Called to peace – 1 Corinthians 7:15

'But if the unbelieving depart, let him depart. A brother or a sister is not under bondage in such cases: but God hath called us to peace'.

The call of God is a call to internal peace, peace of mind and peace of conscience; to which all men are utter strangers by nature. There is no peace to the wicked: but God has called us to peace. He has blessed us with it, with a peace that passes all understanding, with peace in the midst of the tribulations of the world, with a peace that the world can neither give nor take away. Our peace is a peace that arises from the blood and righteousness of Christ, and is part of that kingdom of God which is within us, into which we are brought by our heavenly calling.

We have also been called to peace amongst ourselves, and with all men. 'Let the peace of God rule in your hearts, to the which also ye are called in one body' (Colossians 3:15). We have been called unto peace.

Called unto holiness – 1 Thessalonians 4:7

'God hath not called us unto uncleanness, but unto holiness'.

The call of God is a holy calling. It is a call arising from a holy purpose – the purpose of God. It is a call based upon a holy principle – justice satisfied. A call that brings us into a holy position – justified and sanctified in Christ. It is a call which makes us a holy people, – 'an holy nation', – 'a peculiar people' ,– 'a royal priesthood'.

John Gill said, with regard to this call of God's elect;

> They are called out of a state of unholiness and sinfulness, into a state of holiness and righteousness; for being created anew in righteousness and true holiness, and created in Christ Jesus to good works, they are called to the exercise of them; to live holily, soberly, righteously, and godly, in this present evil world; 'God hath not called us unto uncleanness, but unto holiness', (1 Thessalonians 4:7) and 'hath called us to glory and virtue' (2 Peter 1:3), to glorious acts of virtue and goodness, becoming the nature of their call, and of him that has called them; 'As he which hath called you is holy' (1 Peter 1:15).

Called into grace – Galatians 1:6

'I marvel that ye are so soon removed from him that called you into the grace of Christ unto another gospel'.

We have been call by the grace of Christ. We have been called by the instrumentality of the gospel of the grace of Christ. We have been called into the blessed experience of the grace of Christ. We have been called to be partakers of and to enjoy all the blessings of the grace of Christ.

We have been called (1) out of darkness into light, (2) out of bondage into liberty, (3) out of the world into fellowship with God, (4) out of turmoil into peace, (5) out of uncleanness into holiness, (6) out from under the curse of God's law into the grace of our Lord Jesus Christ, and (7) out of the kingdoms of this world into God's kingdom and glory in Christ.

Called unto glory – 1 Thessalonians 2:12

'That ye would walk worthy of God, who hath called you unto his kingdom and glory'.

God has called us to a kingdom that is glory. He has called us into the possession of the kingdom of grace here, a kingdom that can never be taken away from us. He has called us to inherit a kingdom of glory hereafter. 'The Lord will give grace and glory'. This kingdom and glory to which he has called us is an everlasting kingdom.

Can you get hold of this? We have been called by the grace of God 'to the obtaining of the glory of the Lord Jesus Christ' (2 Thessalonians 2:14). 'When Christ, who is our life, shall appear, then shall ye also appear with him in glory'. All who are called are 'called in one hope of their calling' (Ephesians 4:4). All who are called have the same 'promise of eternal inheritance' (Hebrews 9:15). All who are called are called to and have been given the same glory for their eternal inheritance (John 17:22).

'Blessed be the God and Father of our Lord Jesus Christ, which according to his abundant mercy hath begotten us again unto a lively hope by the resurrection of Jesus Christ from the dead, To an inheritance incorruptible, and undefiled, and that fadeth not away, reserved in heaven for you' (1 Peter 1:3-4).

'And we know that all things work together for good to them that love God, to them who are the called according to his purpose'.
(Romans 8:28)

Chapter 49

'The Called'

There are several titles given to God's saints which appear to be specifically designed to display the fact that they are the objects and beneficiaries of God's peculiar, distinguishing, discriminating, sovereign grace and love in Christ. Believers are called 'the elect', 'the redeemed of the Lord', and 'the called'.

Those who are regenerated, those who are born of God, those who believe on and trust the Lord Jesus Christ are given this peculiar, distinct title, 'the called', to distinguish us from those who are not called. This is clearly the distinction made in Romans 8:28.

Obviously, (at least it is obvious to anyone whose brain has not been pickled by the vinegar of free will religion), the call spoken of here is not the outward, external, general call of the gospel, but the internal, effectual, irresistible call of God the Holy Spirit, by which we have been separated and distinguished from all other people. John Gill describes this effectual, irresistible call of grace, which comes to chosen, redeemed sinners by the sovereign power of God the Holy Spirit through the preaching of the gospel, as follows:

> Christ stands in the gospel-ministry, at the door of men's hearts, and knocks and calls. Having the key of the house of David, he opens the heart by the power of his grace, and lets himself in. In this way, and by this means, the Spirit and his graces are received. Men are called both to grace and glory by the gospel.

Called according to God's purpose

Those who are the called are called according to the sovereign will and purpose of God. Sinners are not called to life and faith in Christ because of their will, but because of God's will. We were not given life and faith in Christ because of what we did, or what we might do, but by what God did for us in eternity and in us in time. That which distinguishes God's elect from other people is the distinguishing grace and purpose of God. What could dead sinners ever do to attract God's attention and get him to call them?

Do you see how utterly absurd free will religion is? It is the religion of spiritual insanity. It was not our choice of God that caused him to call us, but his choice of us. 'We know that all things work together for good to them that love God, to them who are the called according to his purpose'. 'So then it is not of him that willeth, nor of him that runneth, but of God that sheweth mercy. For the scripture saith unto Pharaoh, Even for this same purpose have I raised thee up, that I might show my power in thee, and that my name might be declared throughout all the earth. Therefore hath he mercy on whom he will have mercy, and whom he will he hardeneth' (Romans 8:28; 9:16-18).

Salvation is not man's work. Salvation is not partially man's work and partially God's work. Salvation is not a co-operative effort between God and men. Salvation is God's work alone. 'Salvation is of the Lord!'

God almighty has, in his eternal purpose, determined the particular people whom he will call by his grace. He determined from eternity the time when he will call them; for as there is a time for every purpose, so there is a time for the calling of God's elect. It is called 'the time of love' (Ezekiel 16:8). Moreover, our great God determined from eternity the very place where his chosen ones shall be called. Also, he fixed from eternity the very means and circumstances of their calling, all according to his divine purpose.

Every aspect of our calling shows clearly that the whole thing is the result of the sovereign will and pleasure of God, who does all things after the counsel of his own will. Our wills had nothing to do with it. Our works contributed nothing to it. Josiah Conder wrote,

> 'Tis not that I did choose Thee,
> For, Lord, that could not be.
> This heart would still refuse Thee,
> Hadst Thou not chosen me.
> My heart owns none before Thee,
> For Thy rich grace I thirst,
> This knowing – If I love Thee
> Thou must have loved me first!

Called by irresistible grace

Those who are the called are called by the sovereign, irresistible grace of God. The great, impulsive, moving cause of the effectual call is the grace of God. The Apostle Paul describes the call of God as a call of grace; free, sovereign, undeserved, distinguishing grace. With him, every child of God gladly confesses, 'By the grace of God I am what I am', and that we now believe because 'God, who separated me from my mother's womb, called me by his grace' (1 Corinthians 15:10; Galatians 1:15).

God, as the God of all grace, calls his elect to grace and glory by Christ. The infinite, superabundance of his grace in Christ is displayed to chosen, redeemed sinners in this call. Indeed, the first open display of his grace, the first discovery of his love is made to God's elect in this call of grace. Then, seeing something of the infinite grace and love of God in Christ, by the revelation of the Holy Spirit, we were 'caused', compelled, and made willing to believe on the Son of God unto life everlasting (Psalm 65:4; 110:3) by the loving kindness of Christ, as the fruit and evidence of God's everlasting love for us. Therefore the time of calling is called a time of love (Jeremiah 31:3; Ezekiel 16:8; Zechariah 12:10).

The fact that this call is given to some and not to others demonstrates it is the effect of God's sovereign, distinguishing grace, and of his good will. It is grace alone that distinguishes the believer from the unbeliever; and every believer knows it (1 Corinthians 4:7). The fact that this call, as spoken of and illustrated in holy scripture always results in the one called having eternal life and faith in Christ, demonstrates the efficacy and irresistibility of it. 'Blessed is the man whom thou choosest and causest to approach unto thee'.

The called of Jesus Christ

Those who are the called are the called of Jesus Christ. This is what we are told in Romans 1:6 and 2 Timothy 1:9-10 – 'Among whom are ye also the called of Jesus Christ', – 'Who hath saved us, and called us with an holy calling, not according to our works, but according to his own purpose and grace, which was given us in Christ Jesus before the world began, But is now made manifest by the appearing of our Saviour Jesus Christ, who hath abolished death, and hath brought life and immortality to light through the gospel'.

Believers are described as 'the called of Jesus Christ', because the Holy Spirit calls those who were redeemed by Christ, to whom he is sent by Christ. This calling is ours only 'in Christ', in whom are hid all the treasures of God and by whom alone we receive all the blessings of his grace.

Let us never fail to observe the fact that the triune God has arranged everything in the whole scheme of salvation and grace to give all the glory to Christ, our Mediator and Saviour. Even the calling of grace was 'given us in him before the world began'. All grace is in Christ, comes to us from Christ, and gives all glory to Christ (Psalm 115:1).

Who are the called?

'The called' are called according to the purpose of God, by the grace of God, in the Son of God; but who are 'the called'? We are never left to guess about such things as this. These things are plainly revealed in the Word of God. Let's see what the Book of God says. I will not even comment on this, lest any who read these pages imagine I have twisted the scriptures to suit our doctrine. Let the Word of God stand alone. It needs no defence from me, or any other man. Read what the Book of God says and rejoice in it.

Those who are 'the called' are those who were chosen and predestinated unto salvation in Christ before the world began (Romans 8:28-31; 9:23-24). 'And we know that all things work together for good to them that love God, to them who are the called according to his purpose. For whom he did foreknow, he also did predestinate to be conformed to the image of his Son, that he might be the firstborn among many brethren. Moreover whom he did predestinate, them he also called: and whom he called, them he also justified: and whom he justified, them he also glorified. What shall we then say to these things? If God be for us, who can be against us?' God will 'make known the riches of his glory on the vessels of mercy, which he had afore prepared unto glory, Even us, whom he hath called, not of the Jews only, but also of the Gentiles'. The objects of election and effectual calling are the same. Those who were chosen in eternity are called in time; and those who are called in time were chosen in eternity.

Those who are 'the called' are those who are in Christ (Jude 1) – 'Jude, the servant of Jesus Christ, and brother of James, to them that are sanctified by God the Father, and preserved in Jesus Christ, and called'. We were from eternity in his hands as our Surety, in his loins as our Representative, in his care as our Shepherd, and in his heart as our Husband.

Those who are 'the called' are those who were redeemed and purchased by the precious blood of the Lord Jesus Christ at Calvary. Throughout the Word of God, election, redemption, and effectual calling are works of grace performed for the same people. We were chosen because God loved us, redeemed because God the Father chose us, and called by the Holy Spirit because the Father chose us, and the Son redeemed us. Is this, or is it not the teaching of holy scripture? Read Isaiah 43:1 and Zechariah 10:8, and see for yourself. 'But now thus saith the LORD that created thee, O Jacob, and he that formed thee, O Israel, Fear not: for I have redeemed thee, I have called thee by thy name; thou art mine', – 'I will hiss for them, and gather them; for I have redeemed them'.

Those who are 'the called' are those who appear the most unlikely to be called (Matthew 11:25; 1 Corinthians 1:26; James 2:5). Publicans and harlots go into the kingdom of God, being called of God, while scribes and pharisees sit around and debate about who is holiest, which church is the true church, where heaven is, when the Lord is going to come again, whether Adam had a navel, or where Cain got his wife! Sinners, real sinners, guilty, helpless, doomed, damned, ungodly, abominable, filthy sinners, are interested in just one thing – mercy! The people who need mercy, publicans and harlots, not good, religious people, are those who are 'the called'.

The testimony of holy scripture is crystal clear: – 'I thank thee, O Father, Lord of heaven and earth, because thou hast hid these things from the wise and prudent, and hast revealed them unto babes'. – 'Ye see your calling, brethren, how that not many wise men after the flesh, not many mighty, not many noble, are called'. – 'Hath not God chosen the poor of this world, rich in faith, and heirs of the kingdom which he hath promised to them that love him?'

Those who are 'the called' are those who ultimately are glorified with Christ (Romans 8:30) – 'Whom he did predestinate, them he also called: and whom he called, them he also justified: and whom

he justified, them he also glorified'. Those who are irresistibly called
are infallibly kept by the grace of God and shall be eternally glorified
with Christ. After all, he has called us to glory and honour!

Those who are 'the called' are all who trust the Lord Jesus Christ
(John 15:16; Colossians 2:12; Philippians 1:29). If any sinner calls
on Christ in faith, it is because he has been called by the effectual,
irresistible power and grace of God the Holy Spirit.

> Am I called? And can it be!
> Has my Saviour chosen me?
> Guilty wretched as I am,
> Has He named my worthless name?
> Vilest of the vile am I,
> Dare I raise my hopes so high?
>
> Am I called? I dare not stay,
> May not, must not disobey;
> Here I lay me at Thy feet,
> Clinging to the mercy-seat:
> Thine I am, and Thine alone;
> Lord with me Thy will be done.
>
> Am I called? What shall I bring,
> As an offering to my King?
> Poor, and blind, and naked I,
> Trembling at Thy footstool lie;
> Nought but sin I call my own,
> Nor for sin can sin atone.
>
> Am I called? An heir of God!
> Washed, redeemed by precious blood!
> Father, lead me in Thy hand,
> Guide me to that better land
> Where my soul shall be at rest,
> Pillowed on my Saviour's breast.

'But we are bound to give thanks alway to God for you, brethren beloved of the Lord, because God hath from the beginning chosen you to salvation through sanctification of the Spirit and belief of the truth: Whereunto he called you by our gospel, to the obtaining of the glory of our Lord Jesus Christ'.
(2 Thessalonians 2:13-14)

Chapter 50

The Character of the Call

In these two verses, God the Holy Spirit tells us that the only reason anyone believes the gospel, the only reason any fallen, depraved child of Adam worships our great and glorious, almighty, sovereign God, rather than a stump or a frog, the only reason any are not deceived with the rest of the world by the idolatrous, free will, works religion of antichrist is the fact that they have been chosen by God the Father, redeemed by God the Son, and called by God the Holy Spirit. Let us ever ascribe the whole of this great work to the triune God alone and praise him alone for it: – 'Not unto us, O Lord, not unto us, but unto thy name give glory, for thy mercy, and for thy truth's sake'.

Always pay close attention to the words of holy scripture. Too often we read the Word of God like we would read a newspaper, just scanning for the highlights. In the book of God the highlights are in the detail. Here the Apostle Paul, writing by divine inspiration, tells us five things that go right to the heart of the gospel.

The things here described are words of assurance given to every sinner who trusts Christ alone for redemption, righteousness, grace, and eternal life. If you have been granted faith in the Son of God, here are five things of which you ought to be assured by the Word of God. As surely as you trust Christ, these five things are true of you.

1. 'God hath from the beginning chosen you'. What blessed, good news that is! The holy Lord God chose you as the object of his special love and distinguishing grace in Christ before the worlds were made by his hand. Indeed, the reason why he made this world is that he chose you.

2. God chose 'you to salvation'. The Lord did not choose you to have a chance of salvation. He did not choose you to receive an offer of salvation. He did not choose you to hear about salvation. He chose you to save you. Election is unto salvation.

3. God chose 'you to salvation through sanctification of the Spirit'. The Lord God chose to save his elect in Christ, upon the ground of justice satisfied, by the irresistible grace and power of the Holy Spirit in regeneration. He saves, not only by imputing righteousness to you in justification, but also by imparting righteousness to you in regeneration. The Holy Spirit, in regeneration, sanctifies God's elect by giving them a new, holy nature, a nature created in the image of Christ in true holiness.

4. God chose 'you to salvation through sanctification of the Spirit and belief of the truth'. Faith in Christ, who is the Truth, is as essential to salvation as election, redemption, and regeneration. And this faith in Christ, who is the Truth, is inseparably connected with believing the truth of God revealed about Christ in the gospel. All who believe on the Son of God believed him 'after that we heard the Word of truth, the gospel of our salvation' (Ephesians 1:13).

5. God chose 'you to salvation through sanctification of the Spirit and belief of the truth, whereunto he called you by our gospel'. We need to understand the teaching of holy scripture in this regard. Chosen, redeemed sinners are brought into the blessed experience of God's grace in salvation only by the effectual call of God the Holy Spirit, which comes only through the preaching of the gospel.

The Word of God clearly teaches that the call by which we are saved has four distinct characteristics.

From God

First, the call by which we are saved is a call from God. It is 'God who hath called you unto his kingdom and glory', – 'God hath not called us unto uncleanness, but unto holiness'. It is the Lord God himself 'who hath saved us, and called us with an holy calling, not according to our works, but according to his own purpose and grace, which was given us in Christ Jesus before the world began, But is now made manifest by the appearing of our Saviour Jesus Christ, who hath abolished death, and hath brought life and immortality to light through the gospel' (1 Thessalonians 2:12; 4:7; 2 Timothy 1:9-10).

As in all other aspects of grace and salvation, all three Persons in the Holy Trinity are engaged in this call of grace. Sometimes the call is ascribed to God the Father. He has called us by his grace and revealed his Son in us. He has called us unto the fellowship of his Son. He called us by his Son, Jesus Christ (Galatians 1:15,16; 1 Corinthians 1:9; 1 Peter 5:10). Sometimes the call of grace is ascribed to God the Son, our Lord Jesus Christ. He is represented to us as Wisdom and as the eternal Logos (God the Word), who calls us to life and faith in himself (Proverbs 1:20-33; 8:1-4). God's saints are described as 'The called of Jesus Christ' (Romans 1:6).

However, this call of God is set before us in the scriptures primarily as that which is the office work of God the Holy Spirit, that blessed Comforter sent by the Father and the Son to reveal the things of Christ to the elect. 'There is one body and one Spirit, even as ye are called in one hope of your calling', called by the one Spirit, the Holy Spirit of God. It is God the Spirit who gives us life, who illuminates our hearts and minds, reveals Christ in us, and brings us into the liberty of the Sons of God. It is God the Spirit who brings chosen, redeemed sinners to Christ, creates faith in them, and speaks peace to their hearts through the blood of Christ, and teaches believing sinners to live in the blessed hope and expectation of eternal glory with Christ.

The effectual call is a divine work, arising from and accomplished by the will of God alone. It is not in any way or to any degree

dependent upon or determined by the works of man (2 Timothy
1:9), or the will of man (Romans 9:16). This is not a mere fine point
of theological orthodoxy. It is vital. If you make the call of God to
be dependent upon or determined by the works of man you contradict
scripture which states, 'It is the Spirit that quickeneth. The flesh
profiteth nothing' (John 6:63). As this effectual call is God's work
and God's work alone, it is always irresistible. I hope you have
learned to love the term 'irresistible grace'. Grace that can be resisted
is not grace at all. A call that can be resisted will never save anyone.
It is only irresistible grace that makes doomed, damned, dead sinners
willing in the day of God's power (Psalm 110:3).

The call of the Spirit is an irresistible call, because when God
works none can hinder. When God calls, sinners who are dead in
trespasses and sins rise out of their graves and live at his omnipotent,
all commanding voice, just as Lazarus came forth out of his grave
at the call of Christ. That call cannot be resisted. It carries with it
life-giving, resurrecting power. This irresistible call of the Holy
Spirit is issued to God's elect with the same power that was exerted
in raising Christ himself from the dead. If we believe on the Son of
God, we believe because the omnipotent God of grace has given us
life by 'the exceeding greatness of his power to us-ward who believe,
according to the working of his mighty power, which he wrought in
Christ, when he raised him from the dead' (Ephesians 1:18-20).

By the gospel

Second, the call of God by which we are saved is a call by the
gospel. Paul told the Thessalonian believers that God had called
them to salvation by the gospel, which he preached to them (2
Thessalonians 2:13-14). He told the Ephesians that they came to
believe on the Lord Jesus after that they heard the word of truth, the
gospel of their salvation accomplished in Christ (Ephesians 1:13).

This is a matter of immense importance. 'It pleased God by the
foolishness of preaching to save them that believe'. God does not
by-pass the means that he has ordained for the salvation of his elect.
To suggest that he may is utterly ludicrous. If it is God's pleasure to

save his elect by the preaching of the gospel, the only reason he would ever do otherwise would be if he were caught in a bind and could not do things the way he pleases! We never need to be concerned that the Almighty might get caught in a bind.

God saves his elect, gives them life and faith in Christ, by the sovereign power of his Spirit, only through the instrumentality of the preaching of the gospel. Let men say what they will in opposition to that statement, offering example after example of others who have been 'saved' without the use of means. That leaves us with two choices. We can either build our doctrine on the shifting sand of human reason and experience, or we can build our doctrine on the plain statements of holy scripture. We must build our doctrine on the plain statements of holy scripture, no matter how much they may contradict and nullify our thoughts and experiences.

The scriptures do address this issue plainly and forcibly, setting before us this fact: God saves his people by the gospel. He does not save sinners without the gospel, apart from the gospel, or by believing a false gospel. 'I am not ashamed of the gospel of Christ: for it is the power of God unto salvation to every one that believeth'; – 'So then faith cometh by hearing, and hearing by the word of God'; – 'For after that in the wisdom of God the world by wisdom knew not God, it pleased God by the foolishness of preaching to save them that believe ... Unto them which are called, both Jews and Greeks, Christ the power of God, and the wisdom of God. Because the foolishness of God is wiser than men; and the weakness of God is stronger than men'; – 'Every good gift and every perfect gift is from above, and cometh down from the Father of lights, with whom is no variableness, neither shadow of turning'. Chosen, redeemed sinners are 'born again, not of corruptible seed, but of incorruptible, by the word of God, which liveth and abideth for ever. For all flesh is as grass, and all the glory of man as the flower of grass. The grass withereth, and the flower thereof falleth away: But the word of the Lord endureth forever. And this is the word which by the gospel is preached unto you' (Romans 1:16; 10:17; 1 Corinthians 1:21-25; James 1:17; 1 Peter 1:23-25).

This fact places upon the shoulders of every believer, every local church, and every gospel preacher a tremendous burden of responsibility (Ezekiel 33:7-9; 1 Corinthians 9:16). Our God has left us in this world to preach the gospel to the generation in which we live for the salvation (the ingathering) of his people, the building of his kingdom, and the honour of his name, promising that our labour shall never be in vain (1 Corinthians 15:58). His Word will not return void (Isaiah 55:11).

It is the great privilege and responsibility of every preacher to seize every opportunity God puts before him to preach the gospel. God has not sent his servants out to defend creeds and reform society. He has sent his servants to preach the gospel. It is not enough merely to preach, or merely to preach the doctrinal facts and moral lessons of holy scripture. The Word of God has not been preached until the gospel has been preached.

As it is the responsibility of gospel preachers to preach the gospel, it is the responsibility of every believer and every local church to use everything God puts in their hands and seize every opportunity he gives us for the furtherance of the gospel. If we faithfully meet these responsibilities and sinners refuse to believe the gospel, their blood is forever upon their heads; we have delivered our souls and are free of their blood. If we refuse to meet these responsibilities, their blood shall forever be upon our heads.

Of grace

Third, the call by which sinners are saved is a call of grace. The Apostle Paul ascribed his salvation experience on the Damascus road to the fact that God 'called him by his grace' (Galatians 1:15). This call of God is a matter of pure, free, undeserved grace.

God, as the God of all grace, calls sinners to grace and glory by Christ. The super-abundance of God's grace is displayed in this call. As we have seen, the first open display of grace and discovery of love to a sinner is made when he is called. It is then that God brings salvation, life, and immortality to light by the gospel (2 Timothy 1: 9-10). It is by this call that we were drawn with loving kindness, as a fruit and evidence of God's everlasting love for us. Therefore, the time of our calling is called the time of love (Jeremiah 31:3; Ezekiel 16:8). When we think of the call of God as the work of his grace, let us ever remember three things.

1. The call of God's grace is the fruit of his everlasting love for us (Jeremiah 31:3).
2. The call of God is issued to chosen sinners according to his sovereign will and good pleasure (Mark 3:13; Romans 9:16).
3. The call of God is without repentance (Romans 11:29).

Like all God's operations of grace, the call by which we are saved is unchangeable, irreversible, and irrevocable. Those who are called of God to life and faith in Christ shall be preserved safe to the kingdom and glory of God and shall most certainly enjoy it in all its fulness. It is written 'faithful is he that has calleth you, who also will do it' (1 Thessalonians 5:24).

Here is the happiness and joy of this doctrine. Those who are called of God are assured by his Word of their election; for 'whom he did predestinate, them he also called'. Election and calling always go together. The one is the fruit, effect, and evidence of the other (2 Peter 1:10). Election is revealed and known by the call of the Spirit through the ministry of the Word (1 Thessalonians 1:4-5).

Being called of God, we are also comfortably assured of our justification in and by Christ. 'Whom he called, them he also justified'. If the Lord has called me, then I am justified. Therefore, I have every reason to conclude that I am safe from all charges, from all condemnation, and from wrath to come.

Moreover, if the Lord has called me, if he has granted me faith in Christ, I must, believing his Word, conclude that I shall at last enter into and possess eternal glory with Christ. Are we not assured that all who are called of God are justified, and that those who are justified by God, 'them he also glorifies'? John Gill rightly tells us, 'Between calling grace and eternal happiness, there is a sure and an inseparable connection'.

Unto glory

Fourth, the call of God, by which we are saved, is a call unto glory. It is a call unto a state of happiness and bliss in another world. God 'hath called you unto his kingdom and glory' (1 Thessalonians 2:12). He has called us to possess a kingdom of grace here, which cannot be removed, and to inherit the kingdom of glory hereafter, which is an everlasting one. The Lord God, the God of all grace, has called us 'to the obtaining of the glory of the Lord Jesus Christ' (2 Thessalonians 2:14; John 17:22; Colossians 3:4), and to eternal glory by Christ Jesus (1 Peter 5:10). Imagine that! We have been called by God to 'lay hold on eternal life' (1 Timothy 6:12) and to obtain an eternal inheritance.

What does this mean? It means that we shall most assuredly enjoy eternal, heavenly glory; having a meetness for it through the grace of God and the blood and righteousness of his dear Son. Indeed, by Christ's blood and righteousness, we have a right to it (1 Peter 1:3-4; Hebrews 9:15)

All who are born of God are 'called in one hope of our calling' (Ephesians 4:4) to partake of the same inheritance with the saints in life, and to enjoy the same blessed hope laid up for them in heaven, for which hope of righteousness we wait by faith, through the Holy Spirit, trusting Christ alone as our all-sufficient Saviour. That inheritance of the saints for which we wait is the very glory of our Saviour (John 17:5, 22). The very glory given to Christ as a man, as our God-man Mediator, shall be ours! Can you grasp that? You and I who are called of God are 'heirs of God and joint-heirs with Jesus Christ!' It is for this reason that David sang, 'Blessed is the man whom thou choosest, and causest to approach unto thee, that he may dwell in thy courts: we shall be satisfied with the goodness of thy house, even of thy holy temple' (Psalm 65:4).

'Thy people shall be willing in the day of thy power, in the beauties of holiness from the womb of the morning: thou hast the dew of thy youth'.
(Psalm 110:3)

Chapter 51

Conversion

Conversion is the turning of God's elect to Christ by the power of his grace. It is a willing turn of rebels to Christ as their King, surrendering to his dominion. Yet, it is a turning that is caused by God's free grace. We turn to him because he has turned us by his grace. This is exactly what we read in Jeremiah 31:18-20, where the Lord tells us of Ephraim bemoaning himself.

> I have surely heard Ephraim bemoaning himself thus; Thou hast chastised me, and I was chastised, as a bullock unaccustomed to the yoke: turn thou me, and I shall be turned; for thou art the LORD my God. Surely after that I was turned, I repented; and after that I was instructed, I smote upon my thigh: I was ashamed, yea, even confounded, because I did bear the reproach of my youth. Is Ephraim my dear son? is he a pleasant child? for since I spake against him, I do earnestly remember him still: therefore my bowels are troubled for him; I will surely have mercy upon him, saith the LORD.

In Psalm 80 a prayer is offered before the throne of grace which sinners everywhere would be wise to take up as the cry of their hearts before God: – 'Turn us again, O God, and cause thy face to shine; and we shall be saved'. – 'Turn us again, O God of hosts, and cause thy face to shine; and we shall be saved'. – 'Turn us again, O LORD God of hosts, cause thy face to shine; and we shall be saved' (vv. 3, 7, 19).

Yet, unlike regeneration and effectual calling, conversion is not something in which we are passive. Conversion is both God almighty turning us, and us willingly turning, under the influence of his grace, to him. Stephen Charnock expressed the difference between regeneration and conversion in these words, 'Regeneration is the motion of God towards and upon the heart of a sinner. Conversion is the motion of a sinner towards God'.

Conversion is the willing response of the newborn soul to the effectual call of God's grace. As John Gill put it, 'Conversion lies in a man's turning to the Lord actively, under the influence of divine grace, being thoroughly convinced that there is salvation in no other but in Christ'.

Repentance, faith, and conversion always go hand in hand. They are inseparable gifts of God's grace (Acts 11:18-21). Here is the Holy Spirit's description of what happened when Peter preached the gospel to Cornelius and his household, and when the disciples went everywhere preaching the gospel among the Jews and the Gentiles.

When they heard these things, they held their peace, and glorified God, saying, Then hath God also to the Gentiles granted repentance unto life. Now they which were scattered abroad upon the persecution that arose about Stephen travelled as far as Phenice, and Cyprus, and Antioch, preaching the word to none but unto the Jews only. And some of them were men of Cyprus and Cyrene, which, when they were come to Antioch, spake unto the Grecians, preaching the Lord Jesus. And the hand of the Lord was

with them: and a great number believed, and turned unto
the Lord (Acts 11:18-21).

Notice once more that great emphasis is placed upon the
instrumentality of gospel preaching in the gracious operations of
God. As in regeneration and in effectual calling, so also in conversion,
the Lord God is pleased to save his elect through the instrumentality
of gospel preaching (James 5:19-20). James tells us, by divine
inspiration, that God uses human instrumentality to accomplish his
purpose of grace toward chosen sinners. Those standing by his tomb
could not raise Lazarus from the dead; but they could take the stone
away from the mouth of the tomb. What they could do, they were
responsible to do and graciously allowed to do (John 11:39).

God is pleased, in his infinite, inscrutable wisdom, to work the
conversion of his elect by the instrumentality of converted sinners.
'Instrumentality is the plan of the universe' (C. H. Spurgeon). In
the new creation it is God's invariable rule that he converts sinners
by the instrumentality of converted sinners. Specifically, sinners
are converted by the instrumentality of other sinners who, in one
way or another, preach the gospel to them. There are several things
that need to be stated and clearly understood in this regard.

1. The use of human instruments is in no way a necessity with God.
It is his pleasure.
2. The employment of human instruments in the work of saving his
people is honouring to God, both as an act of amazing, condescending
grace and as an act of infinite wisdom and sovereignty.
3. If God almighty is pleased to use you, or me, or any other human
being for the conversion of his elect, it will be the conferring of the
highest possible honour upon us.

Psalm 110
      The LORD said unto my Lord, Sit thou at my right hand,
until I make thine enemies thy footstool. The LORD shall
send the rod of thy strength out of Zion: rule thou in the

midst of thine enemies. Thy people shall be willing in the day of thy power, in the beauties of holiness from the womb of the morning: thou hast the dew of thy youth (Psalm 110:1-3).

This is a coronation psalm. It describes the coronation of the Lord Jesus Christ as our King. Having accomplished our redemption by the sacrifice of himself, having finished the work which his Father gave him to do as our Mediator, having fulfilled all the Father's will as our Surety, 'The LORD said unto my Lord, Sit thou at my right hand, until I make thine enemies thy footstool'.

Once our Lord Jesus was crowned as the omnipotent Prince and King of the universe, the sceptre of righteousness was put in his hands, he was given power, dominion, and authority over all flesh for the saving of his people, with this blessed promise – 'The LORD shall send the rod of thy strength out of Zion: rule thou in the midst of thine enemies'.

But where are his people? A king without subjects is no king at all. The title of 'King' is a mockery if there are no people, no subjects to the king. Where, then, shall the Christ of God find subjects who shall at last fill up the fulness of him that filleth all in all?

Sometimes we fear that God is saving no one; that our labour is in vain. We preach the gospel to hard-hearted, obstinate sinners, to proud, dead, self-righteous religionists, to a valley full of dead, dry bones. Frequently, we almost despair, wondering, 'Where shall we find subjects for this great King, our God and Saviour and King? Where shall we find men and women willing to bow to the Son of God?' Then, when we read this third verse, our fears are silenced and laid to rest. 'Thy people shall be willing in the day of thy power, in the beauties of holiness from the womb of the morning: thou hast the dew of thy youth'. Our all glorious Christ, our great King shall never lack for a people to serve him, because all his people are made willing in the day of his power to be his subjects forever. Here are five promises made by God the Father to God the Son, when he crowned him King over all things.

A promised people

You will notice that this promise from the Father to the Son has reference to a specific people. It concerns 'thy people' and no one else. God's concern is for his people. Everything he does is for his people. When he has done everything, fulfilled all his purpose, all his will, and all his desire, every one of those here spoken of as 'thy people' shall be with the Son of God in glory. Who are these who are called 'thy people'? They are God's chosen people (2 Thessalonians 2:13-14), his covenant people (Jeremiah 31:31-34), his redeemed people (Isaiah 43:1), his preserved people (Jude 1), his called people (Romans 8:28), his loved people (Jeremiah 31:3).

A promised persuasion

Look at the next three words of this promise: – 'Thy people shall be willing'. The text does not read, might be, or should be, or could be, but 'shall be willing!' 'Knowing therefore the terror of the Lord we persuade men', or try to persuade them; but here is a matter of certainty, absolute certainty.

The Arminian, Adam Clarke, wrote, 'This verse has been woefully perverted. It has been supposed to point out the irresistible operation of the grace of God on the souls of the elect, thereby making them willing to receive Christ as their Saviour'.

That is precisely what the verse teaches. The only person who cannot see it is either totally blind, wilfully ignorant, or incapable of understanding the simplest forms of English grammar. No sinner, our Saviour said, can or will come to him until he is made willing by God's omnipotent grace. All who are thus made willing do come to him in true conversion. Grace makes chosen, redeemed, called sinners willing to confess their sin, trust Christ as their Substitute, bow to Christ as their Lord, cast off their filthy rags and receive Christ as Jehovah-tsidkenu (The Lord Our Righteousness), hang everything on the blood, righteousness, intercession, and power of Christ, our Divine Mediator, and do his will as his servants. Grace makes sinners willing to give themselves and theirs to him, as their reasonable service, parting with all, and follow Christ.

A promised power

'Thy people shall be willing in the day of thy power'. Here the Lord God promises his darling Son a specific day when his power shall be manifest, revealed, made known, and experienced by each of his people to the saving of their souls.

Notice that the promise says nothing about the day of the sinner's power, or the preacher's power. It speaks of the day of Christ's power. The day of his power is any day the Lord God enables his servant to preach the gospel effectually to the hearts of chosen sinners in the power of his Spirit, any day when the Holy Spirit comes to chosen sinners in the omnipotent power of his saving grace. Calvin translates this verse, 'at the time of the assembling of their army'. In other words, whenever there is an army needed there will be an army assembled for the cause of Christ and his glory.

A promised purity

Look at this text and rejoice in the promised purity. The Lord swore to his darling Son, 'Thy people shall be willing in the day of thy power, in the beauties of holiness'. The Lord God will save his people, but only on the grounds of perfect holiness by the satisfaction of Christ and his imputed righteousness. His people, all of them, shall be brought to him in the beauties of holiness, in justification, in sanctification, and ultimately in glorification (Jude 24-25).

A promised praise

Read the rest of the text: '... in the beauties of holiness from the womb of the morning: thou hast the dew of thy youth'. Those who are converted by the grace of God are born from the womb of the morning, mysteriously born of God in the morning of his grace, according to the purpose of God in eternal election. Those who are converted by the grace of God are the dew of Christ's youth. They are compared to the dew of the morning because, like morning dewdrops, they are a great multitude, which no man can number. These chosen, redeemed converted sinners are the dew of Christ's perpetual youth, who shall bring praise to him for all eternity.

'My sheep hear my voice, and I know them, and they follow me: And I give unto them eternal life; and they shall never perish, neither shall any man pluck them out of my hand. My Father, which gave them me, is greater than all; and no man is able to pluck them out of my Father's hand. I and my Father are one'. (John 10:27-30)

Chapter 52

'They Shall Never Perish'

Sheep are weak, helpless, defenceless creatures. They have no strength to withstand their enemies. If they are lost, they cannot find their way home again. If sick, they cannot fight off their disease. If threatened, they cannot run fast enough to escape danger. If attacked, they cannot defend themselves.

The only security sheep have is in their shepherd. If their shepherd is wise, good, and strong, they are secure. If the sheep survive, if they live and flourish, the honour belongs to the shepherd. If the sheep perish, the blame belongs to the shepherd. It is the shepherd's responsibility to keep the sheep. Knowing these things, those who are the Lord's sheep rejoice to hear him say, 'My sheep hear my voice, and I know them, and they follow me: And I give unto them eternal life; and they shall never perish, neither shall any man pluck them out of my hand. My Father, which gave them me, is greater than all; and no man is able to pluck them out of my Father's hand. I and my Father are one'.

The doctrine of our Lord in this text is very plain and obvious: We who believe are Christ's sheep; weak, helpless, defenceless creatures. The Lord Jesus Christ, the Son of God, is our Shepherd, wise, good, and strong. Because Christ is our Shepherd, we are secure in him. This is what the Son of God, our dear Shepherd, says concerning all his sheep: 'They shall never perish!' With those words, the Son of God declares the absolute, infallible, unwavering security of God's elect in Christ.

I realize that some pervert the doctrine of holy scripture concerning the eternal security and preservation of God's elect in Christ. Some twist it into a lie to the eternal ruin of their souls. They attempt to justify their ungodliness by claiming to believe in God's sovereignty to the exclusion of all responsibility. They try to soothe their consciences with the delusion that they really are saved, though they live in utter, abhorrent ungodliness. Others cry, 'Such teaching as that promotes lawlessness and antinomianism'. Because they must be ruled by law, they presume that everyone must. Because they are forced servants and mercenary soldiers, they presume that there is no such thing as voluntary obedience to the Son of God.

I regret such perversions; but I will not hold back the truth of God for fear that some godless wretch will pervert it or be offended by it. Our Lord never hesitated to proclaim the truth, even when he knew the people to whom he was preaching would twist his words, pervert his doctrine, or be offended by the gospel he preached. When our Master preached the fulfilment of the law his enemies said, 'He is an enemy of the law'. When he preached election they took up stones to kill him. When the Son of God preached the free forgiveness of sin they said, 'He is the friend of publicans and sinners, a promoter of licentiousness'. When the Lord Jesus Christ preached moral freedom, freedom of conscience, his enemies said, 'He is a glutton and a wine bibber'.

Following the example of Christ, I want all who read these lines to know and rejoice in the absolute security and preservation of God's elect in Christ. Some of you may be confused by this doctrine. Some may twist and pervert my doctrine to the ruin of their own souls. But, for those who believe God, the doctrine set forth in this chapter will be full of comfort, assurance and joy for their souls.

Perseverance

Without question, the Word of God teaches the perseverance of the saints. Those who are born of God must and shall persevere. They will continue in the faith of Christ. God's elect both believe and keep on believing. The true believer begins in faith, lives in faith, and dies in faith. True faith never quits (Matthew 10:20; John 8:31; 1 Corinthians 15:1; Colossians 1:23; Hebrews 3:6, 14). The Word of God is very clear in this matter: Only those who continue in the faith shall enter into glory. This is the doctrine of the final perseverance of the saints.

Preservation

However, the Bible also teaches the preservation of God's elect in Christ. Those who are truly born of God will most certainly persevere in faith, because we are preserved in Christ by almighty grace. Not one of God's elect shall ever perish. The Word of God teaches the preservation of the saints just as plainly, just as fully, just as forcibly as it teaches the perseverance of the saints. Perseverance is the believer continuing in faith. Preservation is God keeping his people in faith. Perseverance is the believer holding Christ by the hand of faith. Preservation is Christ holding the believer by the hand of grace.

> Jesus is our God and Saviour,
> Guide, and Counsellor, and Friend:
> He will never, never leave us,
> Nor will let us quite leave Him.

Having Christ as our Shepherd, all of God's sheep are absolutely secure in his hands. It is not possible for any true believer to perish, because we are preserved by the grace of God in Christ.

A divine distinction

Here is a divine distinction: – 'My sheep hear my voice, and I know them, and they follow me'. Let men denounce it as they may, the God of the Bible does distinguish between men. He chooses some and passes by others. He redeems some and leaves others under the curse. He calls some and rejects others. He saves some and does not save others. Grace is God's prerogative. He has mercy on whom he will have mercy (Romans 9:16; Hebrews 2:16).

Our Lord clearly teaches his sovereignty in salvation in this chapter. He said to the unbelieving Jews who refused to believe his word, 'Ye are not of my sheep'. He told them that the reason for their unbelief was the fact that they were not his sheep (v. 26). The gift of faith and all other grace is reserved for God's elect.

Catch these words and let them sink into your heart. God our Saviour says of you and I who believe, these people are 'my sheep'. In everlasting love, by sovereign grace, the Son of God has distinguished us from all other people, and made us to be his own sheep, his own peculiar possession.

All who believe are Christ's sheep by a distinct election. We became his sheep by his own eternal choice. In the covenant of grace God branded his sheep and set a hedge about them, securing their eternal salvation (v. 16). The Lord Jesus says, 'I know them'. His knowledge is the peculiar knowledge of his elective, omniscient love. Blessed word of grace this is. Christ knows his sheep! He knows who they are, where they are, what they are, all that they have done and all that they have been, what he will make of them, when he will be gracious to them, and how to bring them home.

We are his sheep by a distinct purchase, too. 'I am the good shepherd: the good shepherd giveth his life for the sheep ... As the Father knoweth me, even so know I the Father: and I lay down my life for the sheep' (vv. 11, 15). The Lord Jesus Christ laid down his life for his sheep, in the place of his sheep, in our room and stead. He offered himself as a voluntary sacrifice for sin. He died as a vicarious Substitute, suffering the penalty of the law for his sheep. He accomplished redemption for us as a victorious Saviour.

God's elect are made to be his by a distinct call: – 'He calleth his own sheep by name, and leadeth them out', – 'My sheep hear my voice, and they follow me'. This is that special irresistible call that Christ issues to his sheep alone. It is always effectual. It always accomplishes salvation. It always brings the sheep to the Shepherd. The good Shepherd calls his own sheep, and no one else (v. 3). He calls his sheep by name. When he calls them, he effectually leads them out. Out of darkness into light! Out of bondage into liberty! Out of death into life! And they follow him. 'These are they that follow the Lamb whithersoever he goeth'. Do you hear the Shepherd's voice?

The Lord assures us of something else, regarding his sheep. His sheep will not follow a stranger. They know truth from error (v. 5; 1 John 2:20, 27). Those who are his sheep are taught of God; and, being taught of God, they have the mind of Christ and are enabled by his Spirit to discern truth from error in all matters spiritual.

A divine gift
Here is a divine gift: – 'I give unto them eternal life'. This is one reason why we must believe in the eternal security of God's elect. Eternal life is the gift of God. It is not God's offer to men, but God's operation in men. Eternal life comes to chosen, redeemed sinners as a matter of free grace. Man does not have eternal life by nature. Eternal life does not evolve from man's sinful heart by some mysterious process of 'spiritual evolution'. It is given to men graciously. It is performed in the heart by the power of God's sovereign grace. The very word 'give' forbids the idea that eternal life comes to men as a matter of debt or reward. 'The gift of God is eternal life'. There was nothing in our hearts or conduct, which caused God to bestow eternal life upon us (Jeremiah 31:3; Romans 8:30; Ephesians 2:1-4). There is nothing in the believer's heart or conduct, which can cause God to take away his gift of eternal life (Isaiah 54:10; Psalm 89:30-36).

R. L. Dabney wrote, 'God was not induced to bestow his renewing grace in the first instance by anything which he saw meritorious and attractive in repenting sinners; and therefore the subsequent absence of everything good in them would be no new motive to God for withdrawing his grace'. Think about that.

It is contrary to the nature and character of God to take away his gifts so freely bestowed (Romans 11:29). This gift of eternal life is a gift freely bestowed. It is in no way dependent upon the contingencies of this present, mortal existence. If we acknowledge that eternal life is entirely the gift of God, in no way earned by or dependent upon the goodness of man, it must be concluded that those to whom eternal life is given are eternally secure in Christ (Ecclesiastes 3:14).

Any child who has not been blinded by religious error must recognize that eternal life must of necessity be eternal. I realize that 'eternal life' refers more to the quality of the believer's life union with Christ than it does to the duration of his life. But it certainly implies a life of eternal duration. When our Lord says, 'eternal' he means eternal. How can life be eternal if it comes to an end? If I have received from God the gift of eternal life, it is not possible for me, by any act of mine, or upon any grounds, to lose it and perish. 'The gift of God is eternal life'. That which is born of God, the new nature created in us by the power of God cannot sin and cannot die (1 John 3:5-9).

The believer's life must be eternal because it is a life in union with Christ. We who believe are so really and truly joined to Christ that we cannot possibly perish, unless he also perishes. We are truly one with Christ. He says, 'Because I live, ye shall live also'. This union between Christ and his people is an immutable, indissoluble union. We are married to Christ (Hosea 2:19-20; Ephesians 5:30). We are members of Christ's body, the church (Ephesians 1:23). Can you imagine Christ with a maimed body? Perish the thought! Yet, his body would not be complete if so much as one member were lost.

The believer's life in Christ must be a life of eternal duration, because we are preserved in life by the power and grace of God the Holy Spirit (Ephesians 1:14; 4:30). The Holy Spirit was sent into the world both to call and to preserve God's elect. He is the Giver of life and the Preserver of life. The Spirit of God is the seal of the new covenant (Ephesians 1:13-14; 4:30). A seal is a mark of ownership. It is that which keeps something legally secure. A seal suggests permanent freshness. A seal means everything is okay!

A divine promise
Here is a divine promise: – 'I give unto them eternal life; and they shall never perish'. Our Lord Jesus here makes a blanket, unconditional promise. It takes into consideration all times, all circumstances, all contingencies, all events, and all possibilities. Our Lord says, concerning all his sheep, I give unto them eternal life', and because they are my sheep and I give eternal life to them, 'they shall never perish'.

What if they are babes in Christ and their faith is weak? 'They shall never perish'. What if they are young men in Christ and their passions are strong? 'They shall never perish'. What if they are old men and their vision grows dim? 'They shall never perish'. What if they are tempted? 'They shall never perish'. What if they are tried? 'They shall never perish'. What if all hell breaks loose against them? 'They shall never perish'. What if they sin? 'They shall never perish'. What if they sin again? 'They shall never perish'. What if they fall? 'They shall never perish'. What if they fall seven times a day? 'They shall never perish'. What if they fall seventy times in a day? 'They shall never perish!'

This promise takes in all the flock. 'They shall never perish'. Not one of Christ's sheep shall ever perish; no, not even one! This is not a distinctive privilege reserved for a favoured few. It is a common mercy to all the chosen flock. If you are a believer, if you trust the Lord Jesus Christ, if you have received eternal life, you shall never perish! Christ himself has promised it. No, you cannot even sin away the grace of God bestowed upon you in Christ. Noah's fall did not alter God's grace. Abraham's weakness did not make God's grace less strong. Lot's wickedness did not make him less righteous before God. David's crime did not cause him to perish. Peter's denial of the Lord did not cause his Lord to deny him. 'Salvation is of the Lord!' Christ's sheep shall never perish.

This doctrine of the believer's security in Christ is in every way consistent with all revealed truth. It is most surely believed among the people of God. Deny this promise and with it you deny every promise of God. If one word from God cannot be believed, no word from God can be believed. Here are seven reasons why the sheep of Christ shall never perish.

1. The promise of God must be fulfilled – 'They shall never perish' (2 Timothy 2:19; 1 John 3:19).
2. The purpose of God cannot be frustrated (John 6:37-40). God's covenant cannot be disannulled. God's purpose in election cannot be overturned. The suretyship engagements of Christ cannot be defeated (Hebrews 2:13).
3. The redemptive work of Christ cannot be nullified (Isaiah 53:10-11).

The book of God declares an actual, literal, accomplished, substitutionary redemption. Since Christ died for his sheep, in their room and in their place, they cannot and shall not die. He paid all our debts. We have no debt to pay. He bore all our punishment. There is no punishment left for us to bear. Christ satisfied the offended justice of God for us. There is nothing left for us to bear, and nothing for us to satisfy. Justice pleads as strongly as mercy for the eternal salvation of those people for whom Christ died at Calvary (Romans 5:10; 8:31-34). If even one of those for whom Christ died were to perish, then his purpose in dying for them would be frustrated (Ephesians 5:25-27; Galatians 1:4-5; Titus 2:14). If even one of those for whom Christ died were to perish, then he could never see of the travail of his soul and be satisfied.

4. The believer's justification in Christ is an irreversible act of grace. The trial is over. The court of heaven has pronounced an irreversible verdict upon us – 'Justified!' God will not impute sin to a believing

soul (Romans 4:8). God has put away our sins forever by the sacrifice of his Son. Our acceptance before God is in Christ. Our justification is free, full, and forever!

5. The work of God's grace can never be defeated (Philippians 1:6). That which God has begun he will carry on to perfection. God is willing to complete his work in us. God is wise enough to complete his work in us. God is strong enough to complete his work in us. Without the least presumption, every true believer may gladly sing,

> The work which God's goodness began,
> The arm of His strength will complete;
> His promise is yea and amen,
> And never was forfeited yet:
> Things future, nor things that are now,
> Not all things below nor above,
> Can make Him His purpose forego,
> Or sever my soul from His love.
>
> My name from the palms of His hands,
> Eternity will not erase:
> Impressed on His heart it remains
> In marks of indelible grace:
> Yes, I to the end shall endure,
> As sure as the Earnest is given,
> More happy, but not more secure,
> The glorified spirits in heaven.

6. The intercessory work of Christ must prevail (John 17:9-11, 15, 20; 1 John 2:1-2).

> Our cause can never, never fail,
> For Jesus pleads and must prevail!

7. The seal of the Holy Spirit cannot be broken (Ephesians 1:13-14).

A divine security

Here is a divine security: – 'Neither shall any man pluck them out of my hand'. We are preserved in the heart of his love. We are preserved in the hands of his power. 'All thy saints are in thy hands'. We are in the hands of Christ our God and Saviour. We are always in his hands. What a blessed place to be! This is the place of our security. These are the hands that were pierced to redeem us. These are the hands of omnipotent power. These are the hands that hold the reins of universal dominion. These are the hands that hold us in life. These are the hands of God himself: – 'My Father, which gave them me, is greater than all; and no man is able to pluck them out of my Father's hand. I and my Father are one' (John 10:29-30).

Man's response

This blessed doctrine of the believer's security in Christ always draws a strong response from men. The self-righteous religionist says, 'That is a dangerous doctrine. Such a doctrine will lead men into sin'. The presumptuous professor of religion will say, 'Let us sin that grace may abound'. The true believer will say, 'Such marvellous grace compels me to give my heart to Christ in undivided love, praise, and devotion'. Read again Romans 11:33 - 12:2. Grace produces gratitude; and gratitude produces devotion.

Perhaps you are asking, 'How can I know that this word of grace is for me?' This word of grace is for every self-confessed sinner who trusts Christ alone as Lord and Saviour. If I trust him, it is for me. If you trust him, it is for you. Do you hear the Shepherd's voice? Do you follow Christ? If so you have eternal life; and you shall 'never perish'.

'For by grace are ye saved through faith; and that not of yourselves: it is the gift of God: Not of works, lest any man should boast'.
(Ephesians 2:8-9)

Chapter 53

Salvation As God Describes It

With all the babble, confusion, and religious nonsense there is in this world, – in this age when the house of God seems to lie in a heap of ruins, – in this day of obvious divine judgment, – in this day in which we and our fathers have been kindling the wrath of God for generations, burning incense to other gods, it would be wise for us to go through all the ruins of God's house, like Hilkiah, the high priest during the days of Josiah, and search for the book of God. Like that faithful man pick it up, dust it off, and read it. Then, after reading it, like that godly young king, we would be wise to inquire of the Lord concerning the words of this book.

I think it would be both wise and profitable for us to lay aside our church creeds, catechisms, and confessions of faith, all of them! Lay aside our theology books, religious papers, religious traditions, customs, and even the opinions of great men of the past. How I wish we could do that! How I wish I could get men and women to simply hear what God says in his Word about his salvation! Try to forget, for just a little while, what Calvinism says about salvation, what Arminianism says about salvation, and what Catholicism says about salvation, and try to find out what God says salvation is. Can you do that? Can you lay aside everything you have ever thought, heard, and learned about salvation from all other sources, and look into the Word of God to see what God has to say about this thing called salvation?

At the very outset I want you to see that everywhere salvation is spoken of in holy scripture, everywhere it is illustrated, everywhere it is explained, it is presented to us just as it is right here in Ephesians 2:8-9: – 'For by grace are ye saved through faith; and that not of yourselves: it is the gift of God: Not of works, lest any man should boast'. Here God the Holy Spirit tells us four things about God's salvation. These four things are always characteristic of God's saving operations. Wherever salvation is found, wherever salvation is experienced, these four things are both obvious and gladly acknowledged.

1. Salvation is by grace alone.
2. Salvation is through faith alone.
3. Salvation is in Christ alone.
4. This salvation by grace alone, through faith alone, in Christ alone is accomplished entirely without works of any kind on the part of the one who is saved.

Be sure you understand this. We are saved without works! Our relationship with God certainly determines what we do; but what we do, either good or bad, has absolutely nothing to do with our relationship with God. This is the doctrine of holy scripture. Salvation is the work of God alone, a gracious work of God wrought for and in chosen sinners, without their aid or assistance, through the mediatorial work of the Lord Jesus Christ and the gracious, irresistible operations of the Holy Spirit.

In this study, we will look at seven passages of holy scripture to see how God himself describes salvation. Here are seven Bible descriptions of salvation. It is not my present purpose to expound these various texts of scripture in their context. I simply use them to demonstrate how God himself has described his great work of salvation in his Word. Salvation, as God describes it, is called ...

'Thy salvation'

The very first time the word 'salvation' is used in the Word of God, it was used by Jacob in his prophetic words to his sons regarding the twelve tribes of Israel in Genesis 49:18. The old patriarch said, 'I have waited for thy salvation, O Lord'. Whatever the Bible teaches about salvation, it is talking about something that is the particular property and prerogative of God alone. 'Salvation is of the Lord!' and 'salvation is the Lord's' (Exodus 12:13; 2 Chronicles 20:15, 17; Isaiah 40:10-11; 41:13-14).

Salvation is God's work alone, God's possession alone, and God's prerogative alone. He gives it to whom he will. This is the clear testimony of scripture despite all that men may say to the contrary. A popular religious leader said recently, 'Since salvation is essentially the work of God alone, everything must depend upon man's willingness to allow God to save him'. That is not the language of the Bible (John 1:11-12; Romans 9:16). Whenever we think of salvation, we ought to remember these two words: – 'Thy Salvation'. Salvation is the Lord's. It belongs to him, comes from him, and goes back to him. God planned it. God purchased it. God performs it. God preserves it. God perfects it. God shall have the praise for it.

'Eternal salvation'

'And being made perfect, he became the author of eternal salvation unto all them that obey him' (Hebrews 5:9). Our Lord Jesus Christ is the author of an 'eternal salvation'. Though it was purchased at Calvary by Immanuel's precious blood, though it is wrought in the hearts of chosen sinners, by God the Holy Spirit at the appointed time of love in regeneration, salvation is an eternal work of God. It was devised and secured, predestinated and purposed, and, in the mind of God, it was performed, finished, and perfect in the covenant of grace before the world began. Read your Bible and you will see that this is so.

It really does not matter what Calvinism, Arminianism, or all the creeds and confessions in the world say about the matter. The only thing that really matters is this: What does the Book of God say? The Book of God declares that God's salvation is an 'eternal salvation'. Christ is the Lamb of God slain from the foundation of the world (Revelation 13:8). All who believe on Christ in time were loved of God, chosen, adopted and predestined to salvation before God made the worlds (Ephesians 1:4-6). We were redeemed, justified, called and glorified in Christ from eternity (Romans 8:28-30). We were accepted in the Beloved before we were ruined in Adam (Ephesians 1:6). We were blessed of God with all spiritual blessings of salvation and grace in Christ before the worlds were made (Ephesians 1:3; 2 Timothy 1:9-10). Our salvation in time is neither more nor less than the outworking of our 'eternal salvation' in Christ.

'The common salvation'

'Jude, the servant of Jesus Christ, and brother of James, to them that are sanctified by God the Father, and preserved in Jesus Christ, and called: Mercy unto you, and peace and love, be multiplied. Beloved, when I gave all diligence to write unto you of the common salvation, it was needful for me to write unto you, and exhort you that ye should earnestly contend for the faith which was once delivered unto the saints' (Jude 1-3).

Certainly, Jude does not mean for us to think of God's salvation as something that is ordinary and cheap. Not on your life! But he does mean for us to understand that salvation is the same wherever it is found. It is the same in the experience of all who are saved. Every true child of God has experienced and possesses the same common salvation. All are saved by grace alone, through faith alone, in Christ alone.

We do not all experience grace the same way. Paul's experience was not the same as Lydia's. Both experienced the same grace, but not the same way. The experience of grace is not always the same. Our needs are the same. The grace is the same. The results are the same. But the experience of grace varies greatly[1]. Still, all who are saved possess and enjoy 'the common salvation'. All who are born of God have a common Saviour, a common family, a common hope, a common blessedness, and a common inheritance.

'Your own salvation'

'Wherefore, my beloved, as ye have always obeyed, not as in my presence only, but now much more in my absence, work out your own salvation with fear and trembling' (Philippians 2:12). What a blessed description this is of God's salvation. If you are saved, the salvation you have is 'your own salvation'. God devised it for you. Christ purchased it for you. The Holy Spirit brought it to you and wrought it in you. It is yours forever! If you trust the Lord Jesus Christ, all that is included in that word 'salvation' is your personal property and possession forever. It belongs to you by the gift of the grace of God.

Here is an admonition: – 'Work out your own salvation with fear and trembling'. That does not mean, 'Work that you might be saved'. It means, 'Work outwardly what God has worked inwardly' (Philippians 2:1-5; Matthew 5:16; Titus 3:8, 14). Here is an assurance: – 'For it is God which worketh in you both to will (to desire) and to do of his good pleasure'. Read 1 Thessalonians 5:23-24. If you are saved, the salvation God has wrought in you is 'your salvation'.

'So great salvation'

'How shall we escape, if we neglect so great salvation; which at the first began to be spoken by the Lord, and was confirmed unto us by them that heard him?' (Hebrews 2:3). God's salvation is called, 'so great salvation' because it comes from the great God. It is

---

[1] This fact is beautifully and clearly illustrated in the healing of the blind men mentioned in Mark's gospel (Mark 8:22-25 and 10:51-52). Both received the same blessing, by the same grace, from the same hands; but their experience of it was different.

salvation for great sinners. It comes to us through the merits of the great Saviour. It flows from the great reservoir of God's great mercy, love, and grace. It secures for us a great inheritance in heaven. So great is God's salvation that no words can adequately describe it.

'Everlasting salvation'

'But Israel shall be saved in the Lord with an everlasting salvation: ye shall not be ashamed nor confounded world without end' (Isaiah 45:17). Salvation is eternal both ways. It is from everlasting and to everlasting. If salvation is God's work, it is an everlasting work (Ecclesiastes 3:14). Sinners saved by grace shall never perish. We are saved beyond the reach of condemnation, or even danger. God's love is an everlasting love (Jeremiah 31:3). God's election is everlasting election (Malachi 3:6). God's grace is everlasting grace (Romans 11:29). Christ's redemption is an everlasting redemption (Hebrews 9:12). The Spirit's seal is an everlasting seal (Ephesians 1:14).

'Salvation to our God'

God's salvation shall return to him in everlasting praise. We are repeatedly told, throughout the Old and New Testaments, that God's reason for saving sinners is for the praise, honour, and glory of his own great name. So it shall be. The salvation of God's elect shall bring forth everlasting praise to him.

This is what we are told in Revelation 7:9-12. 'After this I beheld, and, lo, a great multitude, which no man could number, of all nations, and kindreds, and people, and tongues, stood before the throne, and before the Lamb, clothed with white robes, and palms in their hands; And cried with a loud voice, saying, Salvation to our God which sitteth upon the throne, and unto the Lamb. And all the angels stood round about the throne, and about the elders and the four beasts, and fell before the throne on their faces, and worshipped God, Saying, Amen: Blessing, and glory, and wisdom, and thanksgiving, and honour, and power, and might, be unto our God for ever and ever. Amen'.

'That we should be to the praise of his glory, who first trusted in Christ. In whom ye also trusted, after that ye heard the word of truth, the gospel of your salvation: in whom also after that ye believed, ye were sealed with that holy Spirit of promise, Which is the earnest of our inheritance until the redemption of the purchased possession, unto the praise of his glory'.
(Ephesians 1:12-14)

Chapter 54

'Your Salvation'

That great, glorious, eternal, everlasting, common salvation which God has wrought in us is distinctly ours. If you are saved, if you are a believer, if you are a child of God, God's salvation wrought in you is 'your salvation!' There are five things clearly taught in these three verses about your salvation and mine.

Divine praise
Child of God, that salvation, which God has given you and wrought in you by his omnipotent grace, is a salvation designed for divine praise. – 'That we should be to the praise of his glory'. That salvation revealed in holy scripture always honours the Lord God. It is a salvation becoming the character of God. If a person's salvation does not honour God alone, his salvation is but a delusion.

The great, ultimate purpose of God in all things is the glory of his own great name. That is why he has saved us (Psalm 106:8). This is the end of predestination, election, adoption, redemption, and calling: – 'That we should be to the praise of his glory'. God has saved us that his glory might be revealed in us (1 Corinthians 4:6), that his glory might be revealed and displayed in us (Ephesians 2:7), – that we should ascribe all praise, honour, and glory to him alone for all our salvation (Psalm 115:1), – that we should give thanks to God alone for all the benefits and blessings of grace (Ephesians 1:3-6), – that we should so order our lives by the gospel that we glorify the triune God in all things (1 Corinthians 10:31), – that we should do all things with a view to the glory of God (1 Corinthians 6:19-20).

Divine trust

The salvation of God's elect is a salvation based upon a divine trust: – 'That we should be to the praise of his glory, who first trusted in Christ'. The Holy Spirit here informs us that God the Father trusted his Son as our Mediator and covenant Surety long before we came to trust him (John 6:37-39). He trusted his elect sons into the hands of his Son to save them. He trusted his chosen sheep into the hands of his Son as the good Shepherd to bring them all safely into his heavenly fold.

A divine gift

All who are born of God obtain and enjoy salvation by a divine gift: – 'In whom ye also trusted, after that ye heard the word of truth, the gospel of your salvation'. The Object of all true saving faith is a 'whom', not a what! – 'In whom ye also trusted'. How is it that we came to trust in the Lord Jesus Christ?

We heard the word of truth. The gospel of the grace of God is called the word of truth, more correctly, the word of the truth, for many reasons. It came from the God of truth. It speaks of Christ who is the truth. It is revealed by the Holy Spirit, the Spirit of truth, who leads us into all truth. It is this word of the truth by which the Spirit of God sets sinners free. This is that incorruptible seed by which all heaven-born children are born of God. This is that word which by the gospel was preached unto us, by which we were granted life and faith in Christ by the Spirit of God (1 Peter 1:23-25; Romans 10:17).

The word of the truth, which we heard, not by word only but by the power of God the Holy Spirit, is called 'the gospel of your salvation'. Here we are told that the Holy Spirit, when he regenerates and calls sinners from death to life and gives them faith in Christ, does so by declaring to them, declaring in their hearts what Christ has done for them. We came to know the Lord when God the Holy Spirit brought the light of the gospel into our souls, when God, who commanded the light to shine out of darkness, shined in our hearts and granted us the light of the knowledge of the glory of God in the face of Christ (2 Timothy 1:9-10; 2 Corinthians 4:6).

A divine seal

Our salvation in Christ is a salvation secured by a divine seal. – 'In whom also, after that ye believed, ye were sealed with that Holy Spirit of promise'. Do not be confused by those who would use this text to teach some sort of mystical second work of grace. The sealing work of the Spirit is mentioned after the experience of faith, because our salvation is attested to and revealed only after we believe. This is not a privilege reserved for a few special, very saintly saints. Rather, this blessing of grace is here declared to be the possession of all who believe. Actually, we have a threefold seal from God.

1. The seal of the Father's foreknowledge (2 Timothy 2:19).
2. The seal of the Son's love (Song of Solomon 8:6; 4:12; Revelation 7:3).
3. The seal of the Spirit's work of grace (Ephesians 4:30).

A divine pledge

The salvation here described, that salvation which belongs to all who are the objects of God's everlasting love; chosen, redeemed, and called in Christ, all who are born of God, is a salvation assured by a divine pledge: – 'Which is the earnest of our inheritance until the redemption of the purchased possession, unto the praise of his glory'. The seal of the Spirit is that which gives us the assurance of salvation. The Spirit of God is the earnest, quite literally the down payment or earnest money, of our inheritance, assuring us of it until the resurrection, here called the redemption of the purchased possession. All who have been redeemed by the ransom price of Christ's sin-atoning blood are, at God's appointed time of love, redeemed by the saving power of God's outstretched arm in effectual, irresistible regenerating grace, and shall in the last day be redeemed (delivered) from all the evil consequences of sin in resurrection glory, being perfectly conformed to Christ. With this great salvation, we have this great promise: – 'Ye shall not be ashamed nor confounded world without end'.

'We know that all things work together for good to them that love God, to them who are the called according to his purpose'. (Romans 8:28)

Chapter 55

Divine Providence – That Which Quietens Our Fears

The gospel of God's free and sovereign grace in Christ is specifically designed to minister comfort to God's elect in this world of sin and sorrow. In fact, the Lord God directly commands his servants, in preaching the gospel, to comfort his people (Isaiah 40:1-2). That is my aim as I endeavour to instruct you in the blessed doctrines of the gospel, as I try to set before you the glorious character and gracious operations of God our Saviour.

With that in mind, allow me to show you three of my favourite texts of scripture. I certainly do not mean to imply that these three texts are of any greater importance and authority than other portions of God's Word. That is not the case. We know that 'all scripture is given by inspiration of God, and is profitable for doctrine, for reproof, for correction, for instruction in righteousness' (2 Timothy 3:16).

Still, there are some passages of holy scripture that God the Holy Spirit graciously uses to minister to our own heart's needs and become our favourites. Here are three of my favourites. They set forth the three most precious, delightful, soul-cheering truths of the gospel by which my faith is continually strengthened, my soul is continually encouraged, and my heart is continually comforted in this world so constantly filled with trials, temptations, and troubles. My three favourite texts are Psalm 115:3, 2 Corinthians 5:21, and Romans 8:28. Look at them with me.

Psalm 115:3

'Our God is in the heavens: he hath done whatsoever he hath pleased' (Psalm 115:3). Here the psalmist David plainly declares the great supremacy and glorious sovereignty of our God. Our God is supreme over all the gods of the world. He who truly is God, is God who rules over all things, at all times, in all places, absolutely. He is the absolute, unrivalled Sovereign of the universe, who always does his will in heaven, earth, and hell. 'He has his way in the armies of heaven and among the inhabitants of the earth; and none can stay his hand, or say unto him – What doest thou?' The God I worship, trust, and love is in total control of the universe!

2 Corinthians 5:21

'He hath made him to be sin for us, who knew no sin; that we might be made the righteousness of God in him' (2 Corinthians 5:21). With those words, the Apostle Paul sets before us the effectual, substitutionary sacrifice and atonement of our Lord Jesus Christ. The Son of God was made to be sin for his people. He died under the wrath of God for God's elect, for every sinner who trusts him. Thus he accomplished our redemption and obtained our eternal salvation. As he was made to be sin for his people by divine imputation (having our sins imputed unto him!), even so, by that same divine imputation, all for whom he died are made to be the very righteousness of God in him (having his righteousness imputed unto us!).

Romans 8:28

'We know that all things work together for good to them that love God, to them who are the called according to his purpose' (Romans 8:28). Here the inspired Apostle declares the holy, wise, good, adorable providence of our God. Nothing is more comforting to a believer's heart, nothing so effectually quietens our fears as the assurance of our heavenly Father's good providence. Any study of divine providence ought to reprove our hearts because of our horrible, inexcusable unbelief, while, at the same time, encouraging us truly to trust our great, gracious, glorious God. I will share with you five statements I heard Pastor Henry Mahan make in a message I was privileged to hear many years ago. I found them to be like barbed arrows piercing my heart. I trust they will be the same to you. These are five heart-piercing, convicting, humbling facts.

1. We have entirely too many fears for a people to whom the Lord God has said, 'Fear thou not; for I am with thee: be not dismayed; for I am thy God: I will strengthen thee; yea, I will help thee; yea, I will uphold thee with the right hand of my righteousness' (Isaiah 41:10).

Why cannot we believe God? Has he not proved his great faithfulness to us? David heard God's promise and believed him. His faith in God gave quietness to his heart. God's promises quietened his fears. Did they not? He spoke in quiet, confident faith when he said, 'Yea, though I walk through the valley of the shadow of death, I will fear no evil: for thou art with me; thy rod and thy staff they comfort me' (Psalm 23:4). 'I will both lay me down in peace, and sleep: for thou, Lord, only makest me dwell in safety' (Psalm 4:8). 'When my father and my mother forsake me, then the Lord will take me up' (Psalm 27:10).

2. We have far too much anxiety and worry about earthly, material things for a people to whom the Son of God has said, 'And why take ye thought for raiment? Consider the lilies of the field, how they grow; they toil not, neither do they spin: And yet I say unto

you, That even Solomon in all his glory was not arrayed like one of these. Wherefore, if God so clothe the grass of the field, which to day is, and to morrow is cast into the oven, shall he not much more clothe you, O ye of little faith?' (Matthew 6:28-30).

It is written in the scriptures, 'My God shall supply all your need according to his riches in glory by Christ Jesus' (Philippians 4:19). Why should I worry, fret, and pace the floor by day and by night, when God my Saviour has promised that my Father will for his sake provide me with everything I need in this world? Why should I concern myself about that which God, who cannot lie, has promised?

'Therefore take no thought, saying, What shall we eat? or, What shall we drink? or, Wherewithal shall we be clothed? (For after all these things do the Gentiles seek:) for your heavenly Father knoweth that ye have need of all these things. But seek ye first the kingdom of God, and his righteousness; and all these things shall be added unto you. Take therefore no thought for the morrow: for the morrow shall take thought for the things of itself. Sufficient unto the day is the evil thereof' (Matthew 6:34).

3. We have far too many doubts concerning God's mercy, love, and grace for a people to whom the Lord Jesus Christ has said, 'All that the Father giveth me shall come to me; and him that cometh to me I will in no wise cast out' (John 6:37).

The Lord of Glory declared, 'I give unto them eternal life; and they shall never perish, neither shall any man pluck them out of my hand' (John 10:28). Many of us have trouble here. I acknowledge that I do. My shameful, sinful, baseless doubts are inexcusable. I will not attempt to justify them or excuse them. Upon what grounds dare we call into question the mercy, love, and grace of God? We have absolutely no reason to entertain any doubt concerning him! Shall the God of heaven fail to perform his promise? Perish the thought!

The scripture says, 'He that believeth on the Son of God hath everlasting life'. I believe the Son of God. I have life. That is not a presumptuous statement. Indeed, it would be the utter height of arrogant presumption to say otherwise. How dare a man call into question the promise of God, ever? Paul was a sinner, just like us, saved by grace, just like us. He did not question God's promise, neither should we (2 Timothy 1:12; 4:6-8; Romans 8:31-39).

What shall we then say to these things? If God be for us, who can be against us? He that spared not his own Son, but delivered him up for us all, how shall he not with him also freely give us all things? Who shall lay any thing to the charge of God's elect? It is God that justifieth. Who is he that condemneth? It is Christ that died, yea rather, that is risen again, who is even at the right hand of God, who also maketh intercession for us. Who shall separate us from the love of Christ? ... I am persuaded, that neither death, nor life, nor angels, nor principalities, nor powers, nor things present, nor things to come, Nor height, nor depth, nor any other creature, shall be able to separate us from the love of God, which is in Christ Jesus our Lord.

I will not doubt God's love because of something I have thought, or said, or done. His love is unconditional and free. I will not question his grace because of my sin. His grace superabounds where sin is found. I will not be suspicious of his mercy, because I do not deserve his mercy. His mercy is for the undeserving. I will not doubt his faithfulness because of my unfaithfulness. His faithfulness stands forever (2 Timothy 2:13, 19).

4. We spend entirely too much time grumbling and complaining about our trials and troubles for a people to whom the Lord Jesus has said, 'These things I have spoken unto you, that in me ye might have peace. In the world ye shall have tribulation: but be of good cheer; I have overcome the world' (John 16:33).

We should not be surprised when troubles come our way. We ought to be surprised when they do not come. As long as we live in this world, we are going to have trials, troubles, temptations, and sorrows.

> God in Israel sows the seeds
> Of affliction, pain and toil.
> These spring up and choke the weeds
> That would else o'er spread the soil.

Every ounce of gold that has ever been perfected and made valuable has been refined by fire. If God puts the gold of his grace in us, he will also make us pass through the fire. He declares, 'Behold, I have refined thee, but not with silver; I have chosen thee in the furnace of affliction' (Isaiah 48:10). 'Beloved, think it not strange concerning the fiery trial which is to try you, as though some strange thing happened unto you' (1 Peter 4:12).

Trouble is not a strange thing. For the believer, the absence of trouble is a strange thing. Yet, when we meet with some great difficulty, some heavy trial, some heart-breaking sorrow, though we may not say it, our first shameful, wicked thought is usually, 'Why me?' Our first thought really ought to be: – 'Why not me?'

> Shall I be carried to the skies,
> On flowery beds of ease,
> While others fought to win the prize,
> And sailed through bloody seas?

Our trials are nothing compared to what others have had to endure before us. Our sorrows are nothing compared to the sorrows our Master endured to have us. Our griefs are nothing compared to the glory that shall be revealed in us!

5. We have entirely too much attachment to this world and to this present life, for a people who are looking for a city whose Builder and Maker is God. 'For we know that if our earthly house of this tabernacle were dissolved, we have a building of God, an house not made with hands, eternal in the heavens'.

We know that 'to be absent from the body is to be present with the Lord'. We have a desire to depart and be with Christ, which is far better. Believers are a people who long to be with Christ. Yet, it is so difficult for us to be torn loose from this present existence called life. I cannot explain that. I just know it is so.

I also know that the only way for us to be delivered from these carnal principles, the only way we will ever be delivered from the cares of this world, the only way we will ever be saved from our fears, concerns, doubts, grumblings, and attachments to this world is to find something better. Our religious works will be dropped like a hot potato, if we ever see and get hold of Christ's finished work. Our boasted good deeds will be of no value, if we are allowed and made to see what Christ has done for sinners by his obedience and death as our Substitute. Our righteousnesses will appear to us as they really are, as filthy rags, if ever we behold the righteousness of God in Christ. Our goodliness will wither and die like mown grass in a furnace, if we ever see the goodness and glory of God in Christ (Isaiah 6:1-6). If ever we see Christ, there will be no more argument about our goodness, debate about our worth, and fuss about our will.

Even so, our fears, our doubts, our grumblings, our complaints against our little trials, our complaints against our God's providence and purpose will disappear in proportion to the faith we have in his promises (Isaiah 43:1-5; 46:4).

'But now thus saith the LORD that created thee, O Jacob, and he that formed thee, O Israel, Fear not: for I have redeemed thee, I have called thee by thy name; thou art mine. When thou passest through the waters, I will be with thee; and through the rivers, they shall not overflow thee: when thou walkest through the fire, thou shalt not be burned; neither shall the flame kindle upon thee. For I am the LORD thy God, the Holy One of Israel, thy Saviour: I gave Egypt for thy ransom, Ethiopia and Seba for thee. Since thou wast precious in my sight, thou hast been honourable, and I have loved thee: therefore will I give men for thee, and people for thy life. Fear not: for I am with thee: I will bring thy seed from the east, and gather thee from the west ... And even to your old age I am he; and even to hoar hairs will I carry you: I have made, and I will bear; even I will carry, and will deliver you'.

The more we believe his 'I will', the less we will fear. The less we believe his 'I will', the more we will fear. May God the Holy Spirit cause us to believe that which he has revealed in Romans 8:28, teach us to understand it, give us grace to walk in the light of it, and daily apply it to our hearts effectually to quieten our fears. 'We know that all things work together for good to them that love God, to them who are the called according to his purpose'.

'And we know that all things work together for good to them that love God, to them who are the called according to his purpose'.
(Romans 8:28)

Chapter 56

The Providence of God

God moves in a mysterious way,
His wonders to perform.
He plants His footsteps in the sea,
And rides upon the storm.

William Cowper

Divine providence is the daily, constant, sovereign rule of our God over all things for the accomplishment of his eternal purpose of grace in predestination. Predestination is the sovereign, eternal, immutable, unalterable purpose of God almighty, by which he ordained and ordered, according to his own will and good pleasure, all things that come to pass in time. Divine providence is the accomplishment of God's sovereign will and purpose. Providence is God bringing to pass in time (sovereignly, absolutely, and perfectly) what he purposed in eternity. Predestination is God's purpose. Providence is God's execution of his purpose.

Be sure you understand the doctrine of holy scripture with regard to the providence of God. Nothing in the universe happens by luck, chance, fortune, or accident, or by blind fate. Everything that comes to pass in time was purposed by our God in eternity, and is brought to pass by his wise, adorable, good providence. Nothing comes to pass in time that God did not purpose in eternity, in sovereign predestination. Nothing comes to pass in time except that which God sovereignly brings to pass in his providence. All that God predestinated in eternity and brings to pass in his providence is for the good of his elect and the glory of his name. This is clearly and incontrovertibly the teaching of holy scripture (Psalm 76:10; Proverbs 16:4, 9, 33; 21:1; Daniel 4:34, 35, 37; Isaiah 46:9-11; Romans 11:33-36).

This delightful, soul-cheering doctrine is taught and exemplified throughout the Word of God; but it is nowhere stated more clearly and explained more fully than in Romans 8:28: – 'We know that all things work together for good to them that love God, to them who are the called according to his purpose'. May God the Holy Spirit, who inspired these words, effectually inscribe them upon our hearts for the glory of Christ, enabling us in all things to believe, worship and give thanks unto our God.

A delightful persuasion

First, the Holy Spirit speaks of a delightful persuasion, a persuasion which the apostle Paul assumed (assumed because he was inspired of God to make the assumption) that all true believers have in common. He says, 'We know ...'

The word 'know' in this sentence refers to a knowledge beyond speculation, theory, doctrine, or even sound judgment. It is the knowledge of a confident, assured persuasion based upon fact and experience. Paul says, 'We (all believers) know'. How do we know? What is the basis of this knowledge? Is this a pipe dream; or a matter of established fact?

This is a matter of established fact. We know these things by the revelation of our God in holy scripture (Psalm 84:11; 91:1-16;

Proverbs 12:21; Hosea 2:18). We know these things and walk in the comfort of God's providence because of the inner witness and anointing of the Holy Spirit, who teaches us all things, by whom we have the mind of Christ (1 John 2:20; 1 Corinthians 2:16). We know the wisdom and goodness of God's adorable providence, because we have experienced it. Evangelist Rolfe Barnard used to say, 'We only believe what we experience'. He was exactly right. Are you persuaded, really persuaded of what Paul teaches us here? If you are, you have a persuasion that will keep your soul in peace. Indeed, this is the only persuasion that will keep your soul in peace: – 'When sorrows like sea billows roll'.

A divine providence

Second, the Holy Spirit here reveals a divine providence by which all things are ordered, ruled, and disposed of in time: – 'We know that all things work together for good ... ' Providence is God's government of the universe. This is a subject of deepest importance. If we have a proper view of God's providence, we will see the hand of God and the heart of God in everything, in all the experiences of our lives. Let us never talk like the unbelieving Philistines who said, 'It was a chance that happened to us' (1 Samuel 6:9). Believers do not talk like that. Believing souls ascribe their sorrows, the judgments of God, and even the cursing of their enemies to the hand of their heavenly Father's wise and good providence (Job 1:21; 1 Samuel 3:18; 2 Samuel 16:11-12).

God is not idle. He is the one person who is always on the job. He never needs to rest, recuperate, or regroup! God almighty, our God and heavenly Father, is always at work, governing the world. Ignorant, unbelieving rebels often think, 'God is not doing a very good job of running this world'. I have often heard fools say, 'If God is running everything, then this or that would not happen'. I have frequently heard preachers and religious leaders speak of sickness, poverty and war, sin, crime and cruelty, famine, earthquakes and death, as things over which God has no control. Nonsense!

Basic Bible Doctrine

Could not the almighty easily put an end to these things? Of course he could, and soon shall; but God almighty will not be dictated to by his creatures. Who are we that we dare set ourselves up as instructors to the all-wise God? He 'worketh all things after the counsel of his own will'. I do not pretend that any child of God discerns the depth of God's providence, or understands how all the works of providence are meshed together. Faith does not demand an accounting from God. Faith bows to him.

We recognize that God's providence is mysterious (Romans 11:33-36). His judgments are a great deep. His ways are past finding out. But these things are certain: – God always has his way, – his ways are not our ways, – His way is always right and best.

God's providence is as minute as it is mysterious (Matthew 10:30). Our God has ordained the number of hairs on the heads of all. Not even a worthless sparrow falls to the ground without his decree. God's providence is all-inclusive. God rules everything, great and small, everywhere, and at all times. Our God is in control of all inanimate matter. He who created all things rules all things. At his word the Red Sea parts and a path of dry ground is made in the Jordan River for his people. 'The Lord hath his way in the whirlwind and in the storm, and the clouds are the dust of his feet'. When his servants were cast into the burning and fiery furnace, he made the fire as cool and comfortable as the evening breeze for his own.

Our great God is in total control of all irrational creatures. At his bidding frogs, flies, and locusts filled Egypt; and at his bidding they left. He prepared a whale to swallow his servant Jonah and directed the whale to the right place to spit him out. At his command the rooster crowed for the sake of his fallen saint, Peter. It is written, 'The Lord hath prepared his throne in the heavens; his kingdom ruleth over all!'

Our God and heavenly Father controls (absolutely and totally) all rational creatures too. He controls all men and women everywhere, good and bad, in the good they do and in the evil they perform. All angels, all demons, and Satan himself are under the total control of our God (Psalm 76:10; Isaiah 14:24-27). Nothing in God's universe breathes or wiggles contrary to his decree (Isaiah 46:9-13). Satan is not a rival to our God, but his vassal!

We have no trouble believing that God controls good things and good people; but those are not the things that bother us. It is the bad stuff that disturbs us. I want to know who is in control of wickedness and evil. That is the One I will worship. Many have a lot of trouble with this. They do not understand that God truly is God, as fully in control of hell as he is in heaven, as totally in control of wickedness as of righteousness (Proverbs 16:4, 33; 21:1; Acts 2:23; 4:27-28).

What about sin? What about the fall? 'God allows sin because he is able to overrule it for his own glory. God is not the author of sin; but he is the controller and director of sin. God is not the causative force, but the directing agent in the sins of men. Men are rebellious; but they have not pushed God off his throne. They are not out from under his control' (C. D. Cole).

God's providence is mysterious and minute; and God's providence is good! 'All things work together for good to them that love God, to them who are the called according to his purpose'. No event in history is isolated from any other event. We may not be able to see how; but all things are connected to all other things: – 'All things work together'. What does Paul mean when he says that? He does not necessarily mean for us to understand that all things work together for the immediate, temporal good of God's elect, though I am convinced that is true. Paul's doctrine in Romans 8 is this: – All things work together for their spiritual, eternal good, both individually and collectively.

That which is truly good for us very often appears to be the exact opposite. It appeared to be a very bad thing for Paul to be on his way to Damascus; but nothing could have been better. He was doing that which was utterly horrible; but God was doing that which was perfectly good. That woman with an issue of blood for twelve, long years was brought by that which appeared to be very bad to touch the Lord Jesus by faith. Seated with Christ in Glory, she praises him for both the grief that brought her to him and the grace she found in him.

This is what I am saying: It is good for me to know Christ and be found in him. If God has to hurt me, or hurt my child to get my attention and then turn my eyes and my heart to Christ, that is good! It is good for me. It is good for me to fellowship with God and walk humbly before him, however he arranges it. It is good for me to be a blessing to others, however God is pleased to bring it to pass. It is good for me to be weaned from this world, however the Lord is pleased to wean me. It is good for me to be a better pastor and preacher, regardless of the cost. It is good for me to continue in the faith, no matter what else may be lost. It is good for me to finish my course with joy, no matter what sadness is experienced in the course. It will be good for me to die in the faith, though I must die to self day by day. It will be good for me to rise in glory and be like Christ, no matter what my heavenly Father has arranged to bring it to pass.

Whatever God sees fit to use to accomplish these things for us and in us is good! At your leisure, read Psalm 107 again. There we are given a detailed view of God's providence. 'All things work together for good'. As a wise, skilled pharmacist mixes medicine, our heavenly Father wisely mixes exactly the right measure of bitter things and sweet to do us good.

Too much joy would intoxicate us. Too much misery would drive us to despair. Too much sorrow would crush us. Too much suffering would break our spirits. Too much pleasure would ruin us. Too much defeat would discourage us. Too much success would puff us up. Too much failure would keep us from doing anything. Too much criticism would harden us. Too much praise would exalt us. Our great God knows exactly what we need. His providence is wisely designed and sovereignly sent for our good! Let him therefore send and do what he will. By his grace, if we are his, we will face it, bow to it, accept it, and give thanks for it.

> I welcome all His sovereign will,
> For all His will is love.
> And when I know not what He does,
> I'll wait for light above.

God's providence is always executed in the wisest manner possible. We are often unable to see and understand the reasons and causes for specific events in our lives, in the lives of others, or in the history of the world. Our lack of understanding does not prevent us from believing God. We bow to his will, which is evident in his works of providence, and say, 'O the depth of the riches both of the wisdom and knowledge of God! How unsearchable are his judgments, and his ways past finding out!'

All God's works of providence are executed in perfect holiness and righteousness. Even the way he uses the evil works of men and devils is totally free of sin on his part. Though he has predestined and permits deeds of wickedness, sin cannot be imputed to the Almighty. Let men think and say what they will, these two things are plainly revealed in holy scripture: (1) 'All things are of God' (2 Corinthians 5:18). (2) 'The Lord is righteous in all his ways, and holy in all his works' (Psalm 145:17).

God's providence demands and deserves our unceasing praise.

We should give to him the glory of all; observe with wonder and gratitude, the various steps of it (his providence) respecting ourselves and others; and put our trust in him for things temporal and spiritual; and at all times cast our care upon him, who cares for us; seeing it is, and always will be, well with the righteous, in time and to all eternity. (John Gill)

A designated people

'We know that all things work together for good'. If we stop there and read no further, we would be forced to say, 'That is not so'. The simple fact of the matter is that all things do not work together for good to everyone. There are many against whom all things work for evil. The text makes sense, and is true only when the entire sentence is read, 'We know that all things work together for good to them that love God, to them who are the called according to his purpose'.

God's providence, in all its details, is designed and accomplished for his elect, those who love him and are the called according to his purpose. Whenever we think about God's providence, we must never forget that divine providence is for a designated people. Everything that is, has been, or shall hereafter be is brought to pass by the hand of our God for the good of his people. Who are these people? Can they be identified with certainty? Indeed they can. You cannot identify God's people in this world by their clothes, their church, their creed, their confession, their conversation, or even their conduct. But they can be identified.

God's elect are identified by their faith (Philippians 3:3). 'For we are the circumcision, which worship God in the spirit, and rejoice in Christ Jesus, and have no confidence in the flesh'. God's people are identified by their love. They are a people who love God. In many respects believers and unbelievers are very much alike, especially if the unbeliever is religious and moral. But here is a marked distinction. True believers, and they alone, love God (Romans 8:7). We love God in his revealed character (1 Corinthians 16:22). We love him because he is who he is, and does as he does. We love our God in all his relations to us. We love him as our Father, our King, our Portion, and our Inheritance. Without question, all who love God recognize and confess that our love for him is caused by his love for us (1 John 4:19); but we do love him. With Peter, we declare, 'Lord, thou knowest all things; thou knowest that I love thee'.

Believers are also identified by their calling: – 'Them who are the called'. Let the Arminian, the free-willer, try as he may to get around the eighth chapter of Romans, here it stands to declare forever the glorious gospel doctrine of God's free, sovereign, effectual, irresistible grace in Christ. Those who believe are 'them who are the called'. If language means anything, this text asserts that there are some people in this world who are called and others who are not called. Our faith in Christ and love for God is the result of this call (Ephesians 2:1-4).

A declared purpose

Fourth, here is a declared purpose, according to which God almighty rules, governs, and disposes of all things: – 'We know that all things work together for good to them that love God, to them who are the called according to his purpose'. We are not left to figure out what that purpose is. It is plainly stated in verses 29-31: – 'All things work together for good to them that love God, to them who are the called according to his purpose. For whom he did foreknow, he also did predestinate to be conformed to the image of his Son, that he might be the firstborn among many brethren. Moreover whom he did predestinate, them he also called: and whom he called, them he also justified: and whom he justified, them he also glorified. What shall we then say to these things? If God be for us, who can be against us?'

This grace by which we believe, by which we love God, by which we are called, this great providence which works all things together for our good is according to God's eternal purpose to save us. The evidence of our calling is our faith in and love for God as he has revealed himself to us in Christ. The evidence of our election and redemption is our calling. The cause of our election, redemption, and calling is God's sovereign, eternal purpose of grace toward us in Christ (2 Timothy 1:9-10).

He who is God indeed is the God of providence, the God who rules all things, and rules all things well. How we ought to trust him! Ever remember, our heavenly Father is God all-wise, good, and omnipotent. He is too wise to err, too good to do wrong, and too strong to fail.

'Christ is the end of the law for righteousness to everyone that believeth'.
(Romans 10:4)

Chapter 57

'Christ is the End of the Law'

'Christ is the end of the law'. It is entirely correct to do with that statement exactly what the whole religious world says we must not do with it. Take it and run with it just as far as possible. There is no sense in which Christ is not the end of the law. He is the fulfilment of the law, the conclusion of the law, the finality of the law, the object of the law, the reason why the law was given, and the termination of the law.

'Christ is the end of the law for righteousness'. There is no righteousness of any kind, justifying righteousness or sanctifying righteousness, to be had by our personal obedience to the law. It is written, 'If righteousness come by the law, then Christ is dead in vain!'

Christ is not the end of the law for everyone. The Son of God did not fulfil the law's demands for everyone. He is the end of the law for God's elect, for all who trust him. 'Christ is the end of the law for righteousness to everyone that believeth'.

Holy, just and good

When the apostle Paul declares, 'Christ is the end of the law', he is not telling us that the law is evil. It is not (1 Timothy 1:8-9). It is an evil thing to misuse the law; but the law is not evil. Writing by divine inspiration, the apostle tells us those apostate religious leaders who try to mix law and grace, who try to put believers under the yoke of bondage, desiring to be teachers of the law, do not know what they are talking about, 'understanding neither what they say, nor whereof they affirm'. The law was never intended, in any sense, for those who are righteousness before God. The law was given for the unrighteous. The law is not evil. It is holy, just, and good. It would be well if all men lived in conformity to the law's commands, both in outward practice and in inward principle. Indeed, it is ordained of God and used by all civil governments to protect society from those who would otherwise disregard all respect for the rights, property, and lives of others.

Delight in the law

When the scriptures affirm, as the New Testament constantly does, that Christ is the end of the law and that believers are entirely free from the law, the Spirit of God certainly is not suggesting that believers are free to break, or disregard God's holy law. Not only is the believer not free to break the law, he has no desire to do so. To those who believe, God's commandments are not grievous (1 John 5:1-3). Every child of God in this world truly delights in the law of God after the inward man (Romans 7:22). If we could, we would love God with all out hearts. If we could, we would love our neighbour as ourselves. But we do not have the ability to do so.

Bible doctrine

I am fully aware that the creeds, confessions, and religious dogma of almost every Protestant or Baptist denomination, as well as those written by papists, stringently affirm that there is a sense in which believers are yet under the law. (That fact alone ought to be enough to convince us that it is contrary to holy scripture!) But the Word of

God declares exactly the opposite, and states the believer's freedom from the law with such frequency and clarity that error in this regard is utterly inexcusable. In Christ every believer is entirely free from the law, because Christ is the end of the law for righteousness to everyone that believeth'. 'We are not under law, but under grace' (Romans 6:14-15). We have been crucified with Christ, and we are 'become dead to the law by the body of Christ' (Romans 7:4). There is no sense in which it may be said that the believer is under the law (Romans 8:1-4; Galatians 2:19-21; 3:1-3, 13, 18-19, 21-26; 4:9-11, 21, 30; 5:1-5; Colossians 2:8-23).

> I defy anyone to find a solitary text of scripture in the New Testament that uses the law to motivate, inspire, regulate, or even guide the believer. Believers are motivated by love, inspired by gratitude, regulated by grace, and guided by the Holy Spirit. The whole Word of God, the complete revelation of his will is our law. Our lives are governed by love, not by fear. We walk by faith, not by legislation. We walk in the Spirit, not in the flesh (Romans 8:9-14; Galatians 3:3).(Scott Richardson)

Our law, our rule of life, is not one section of scripture[1], but the whole revealed will of God in holy scripture. We take the Word of God in its entirety as our only rule of faith and practice. However, we rejoice in the fact that we are no longer ruled, motivated or governed by the law. We do not live before God upon legal principles. Therefore we sing with joy,

> Free from the law, oh, happy condition!
> Christ has redeemed us from every transgression.

---

[1] Frequently, the word 'law' is used in the Old Testament, particularly in the Psalms, to refer to the whole Word of God, the whole revelation of God and his will in holy scripture. Sometimes the Word 'law' is used to refer to the ceremonial, dietary and sometimes to the civil law given to [continued over]

In Christ, the children of God, those who live in the Spirit, those who walk by faith, are entirely free from the law. We have no covenant with the law. We live under a covenant of grace. We have no commitment to the law. Our commitment is to Christ, who obeyed the law for us. We do nothing by constraint of the law. 'The love of Christ constraineth us'. We fear no curse from the law. 'Christ hath redeemed us from the curse of the law, being made a curse for us. For it is written, Cursed is everyone that hangeth on a tree'.

False accusations

Because the doctrine of the believer's freedom from the law is so clearly and universally taught in the scriptures that it cannot, upon any grounds, be refuted, those who refuse to bow to the Word of God have only one other course of action by which to persuade men against it: Slander. They attempt to justify themselves and their doctrine by making the doctrine of holy scripture and those who teach it appear vile. Men often accuse us of being antinomians. They accuse us of promoting licentiousness. They censure us and warn others to avoid contact with us, as though our liberty in Christ were some kind of spiritual leprosy. But we will not again be entangled with the yoke of bondage. We will not attempt to reach the throne of God by climbing Mount Sinai. We will simply trust the grace of God streaming to us from the wounds of our crucified Saviour, finding all our righteousness and all our redemption in that One who died for our sins at Mount Calvary.

---

the nation of Israel. The word 'law' is often used to refer specifically to the ten commandments as recorded in Exodus 20. These ten commandments are commonly referred to as 'the moral law' by preachers and theologians. However, you will search the Word of God in vain to find a separation between the ten commandments and the other laws given by the hand of Moses to the children of Israel. When the scriptures declare that believers in Christ are free from the law and that Christ is the end of the law the declaration is that we are free from all the Mosaic law (civil, dietary, economic, and moral) by which the nation of Israel was governed in the Old Testament.

Be warned

Let all who seek God's favour by their obedience to the law be warned: – 'Christ is become of no effect unto you, whosoever of you are justified by the law; ye are fallen from grace'. Show me a man who trusts his own righteousness, his own obedience, his own devotion, his own feelings, or anything else of his own as a basis of acceptance with God to any degree or for anything, and I will show you a man who is entirely lost, a man to whom the blood of Christ, the righteousness of Christ, and the grace of Christ are worthless.

'Christ is the end of the law'

The law of God is that which we ought to dread above all things, for the sting of death is sin and the strength of sin is the law. The law condemns us and demands our execution. In solemn terms, it appoints for us a place among the damned. 'For it is written, Cursed is everyone that continueth not in all things which are written in the book of the law to do them' (Galatians 3:10).

Yet, man has a strange infatuation with the law. Like the gnat that is drawn to the candle that will destroy it, man by nature is drawn to the law for righteousness, when all the law can give is destruction. The law can do nothing else but reveal sin and pronounce condemnation on the sinner (Romans 3:19-20).

Still, we cannot get men to flee from the law. They are so enamoured with their own self-righteousness and their own self-worth that they will cling to the law with a death grip, though there is nothing to cling to. They prefer Sinai to Calvary, though Sinai offers them nothing but death. Listen to the Word of God. If the opinions of men, or your own opinions contradict the Word of God, 'Let God be true and every man a liar'.

– The law was never given to save sinners; and it can never serve that purpose (Galatians 2:16).

– The law was never given to motivate the people of God to holiness and service; and it cannot serve that purpose. The one thing that God requires is a willing heart (2 Corinthians 8:12; 1 Corinthians 6:19-20; Romans 12:1-2).

– The law was never given as a rule of life, or standard of conduct for the believer; and it cannot serve that purpose (Romans 3:28, 31; 1 John 3:23).
– The law was not given to produce sanctification in the believer; or even to be a measure of sanctification, and it cannot serve such purposes (Galatians 3:1-3). Christ is our sanctification!

The law was given to point men to Christ for salvation. The law was given to show man his guilt, sin, and need of a Substitute. This is the law's only purpose; and it serves that purpose well (Romans 3:19-22). The thunders of Sinai drive us away and point us with its lightning bolts to Calvary and to Christ who is the end of the law.

'For Christ is the end of the law for righteousness to every one that believeth'.
(Romans 10:4)

Chapter 58

How and to Whom is Christ the End of the Law?

Knowing something of the just severity and strict demands of God's holy law, – knowing that the law demands, 'The soul that sinneth it shall die', – knowing that the law demands, 'It must be perfect to be accepted', – knowing the utter terror of the law, – when, knowing all these things, I read this great and glorious statement, 'Christ is the end of the law', I immediately want to know, – how and to whom? Don't you?

How?

How is Christ the end of the law? What does Paul mean when he says that Christ is the end of the law? There are four obvious and clear answers to that question.

1. Paul means for us to understand that the Lord Jesus Christ is the end of the law's purpose

He is the purpose and object of the law. The law was given to lead us to Christ. The law was our schoolmaster to bring us to Christ. Once it has served that purpose, it has no other function

(Galatians 3:24-25). The law is the sheriff's deputy who shuts men up in prison for their sin, concluding them all under condemnation, so that they may look to the free grace of God in Christ for deliverance. This is the purpose of the law. It empties, that grace may fill. It wounds, that grace may heal. The law was given to lead sinners to faith in Christ, by showing them the impossibility of salvation in any other way. As Spurgeon once put it: 'The law is God's black dog, by which he fetches his sheep to the Shepherd.'

How does the law perform its work? How does the law bring men to Christ? The law exposes our sin (Romans 7:7-9). The law shows us what the result of our sin must be: separation from God and death: – 'The soul that sinneth, it shall die' (Ezekiel 18:20). The only way any man can obtain mercy from God is to approach him with a bloody sacrifice, the blood sacrifice of God's own darling Son.

The law reveals our utter helplessness (Psalm 24:3-4). Anyone who thinks he can keep the law and thereby win God's favour simply does not know what the law requires. 'Tell me, ye that desire to be under the law, do ye not hear the law?' (Galatians 4:21). The law demands both perfection and satisfaction. If a sinner ever sees what God requires in his law, he will beg for a Mediator (Exodus 20:1-19).

The law shows us our great need of Christ as our Substitute. Our only hope before God is that God himself will send One who is able and willing to satisfy his holy law for us. We must have a Substitute, one who is able to make us righteous, one who is able to redeem (Romans 3:24-26). Give me Christ. I want nothing to do with God's naked law! The law strips. Christ covers. The law condemns. Christ pardons. The law kills. Christ gives life. Not only is Christ the purpose and object of the law, the One to whom the law points ...

2. He is also the fulfilment of the law (Isaiah 42:21)

He has magnified the law and made it honourable. Our Lord said, 'I came not to destroy the law, but to fulfil the law'. The law demands complete obedience, without one spot or speck, failure or flaw. The law demands holiness, righteousness, perfection. The terms of the law cannot be lowered, not even in order to save God's elect.

God's holy law demands complete satisfaction. It will settle for nothing less than the death of every transgressor. Yet, in Christ all God's elect possess everything the law demands. His life is ours, for we lived in him representatively. His obedience is ours, for we obeyed God in him representatively. His death is ours, for when he died we died in him representatively (Romans 5:19). In Christ we are free from the law's curse (Romans 8:1; Galatians 3:13). In Christ we fulfil the law. We fulfil it by faith in him (Romans 3:31).

3. Christ is the termination of the law

Yes, you read that right. Christ is the end of the law in the sense that he is the termination of the law. Dead is just about as terminated as you can get; and Paul tells us that if we are truly married to Christ we are dead to the law (Romans 7:1-4).

Christ has terminated the law as a covenant of life: – 'We are not under the law, but under grace'. Christ has terminated the law's curse and penalty (Romans 8:1-4; Galatians 3:13). In Christ, every believer has a just, righteous claim of merit upon all the blessedness of everlasting glory (Psalm 32:1-2). In him we are worthy of our heavenly inheritance (Colossians 1:12). Do you see the sweet mystery of salvation by the substitutionary work of Christ? The law has no claim upon those for whom Christ died. The curse spent itself on our Redeemer. We are dead to the law. We are righteous, justified, guiltless, innocent in Christ.

Christ is the fulfilment and termination of all the law's prophecies, types, and ceremonies. He has, in every sense of the word, made an 'end' of the law.

4. 'Christ is the end of the law for righteousness'

Let this be clearly understood. No man can obtain righteousness of any kind, to any degree, of any merit before God by the works of the law (Galatians 2:21). God requires perfect righteousness and absolute 'holiness without which no man shall see the Lord' (Matthew 5:20; Hebrews 12:14). We have no righteousness of our own, and we have no ability to produce righteousness (Isaiah 64:6).

The Lord Jesus Christ established that righteousness for his people, meeting all the law's demands as our Representative (Philippians 3:8-10). The righteousness of the law is found only in Christ (1 Corinthians 1:30-31). He is the Lord our Righteousness. We have no righteousness, neither for justification nor for sanctification, except Christ who is made of God unto us wisdom, righteousness, sanctification, and redemption.

To Whom?

To whom is Christ the end of the law? 'Christ is the end of the law for righteousness to everyone that believeth'. Do you see the stress of the text? It is just this: – 'To everyone that believeth'. The one issue of vital importance is this: – 'Dost thou believe on the Son of God?' If you believe, Christ is the end of the law to you. If you do not believe, you are yet under the curse of God's holy law.

If we would be saved we must submit to the righteousness of God. We must trust Christ alone for righteousness. Our sin cannot be put away, except by his blood atonement. We cannot be made holy before God, except by Christ. If we refuse to submit to the righteousness of God in Christ, we must forever perish in hell. This great, all-glorious, gracious Saviour bids weary, helpless sinners come to and find rest for their souls, the rest of perfect atonement and perfect righteousness, by which we have perfect, perpetual acceptance with the holy Lord God (Matthew 11:28-30).

We must never attempt to serve God upon a legal principle (Colossians 2:16-23). God will not accept legal obedience. We must never allow anyone to bring us back into bondage, no not for a moment. We must never trust our own righteousness. If anyone endeavours to do anything to gain God's favour, to improve his standing in God's favour, keep God's favour, or merit anything from God, he has missed Christ altogether, missed the gospel entirely, and knows nothing of the grace of God in Christ, who is 'the end of the law' (Galatians 5:2, 4). Self-righteousness sticks to human flesh like leaches. Shake it off. Flee from it. Cling to Christ alone for all your hope before God. He is 'The Lord our Righteousness'.

'Wherefore then serveth the law? It was added because of transgressions, till the seed should come to whom the promise was made; and it was ordained by angels in the hand of a mediator'. (Galatians 3:19-29)

Chapter 59

'Wherefore then Serveth the Law?'

False teachers crept into the Church at Galatia and convinced many that they must seek to live by the law, that the believer's justification and sanctification were not accomplished by grace alone. They taught, we must be saved by grace, by faith in Christ; but we must also keep the law if we would be saved. Paul boldly and dogmatically asserted that there can be no mixture of law and grace.

In Romans 11:6 he says, if you add your works to the grace of God, for justification, for sanctification, or for righteousness of any kind before God, then you deny the grace of God altogether and are lost, totally ignorant of the grace of God, without Christ, and without hope before the Holy Lord God.

In Galatians 2:21, after dashing in pieces the notion of mixing law and grace, he makes this bold, dogmatic assertion: – 'I do not frustrate the grace of God: for if righteousness come by the law (justifying righteousness or sanctifying righteousness), then Christ is dead in vain!'

Paul could not have used stronger language to state his case. He declares that those who teach that righteousness may be obtained before God by personal obedience to the law both frustrate the grace of God and assert that Christ died for nothing!

In Galatians 3:19-29 Paul, being inspired by the Holy Spirit, anticipated the carping of the legalists who would denounce his doctrine. He knew they would come along and say, 'If the law has nothing to do with the believer, if it has nothing to do with our justification and nothing to do with our sanctification, if it is not to be used as a rule of life, why was it given? What is its use?' That is the question he answers in these eleven verses. 'Wherefore then serveth the law?' These eleven verses of divine inspiration tell us the purpose of God's law.

It was added because of transgressions, till the seed should come to whom the promise was made; and it was ordained by angels in the hand of a mediator. Now a mediator is not a mediator of one, but God is one. Is the law then against the promises of God? God forbid: for if there had been a law given which could have given life, verily righteousness should have been by the law. But the scripture hath concluded all under sin, that the promise by faith of Jesus Christ might be given to them that believe. But before faith came, we were kept under the law, shut up unto the faith which should afterwards be revealed. Wherefore the law was our schoolmaster to bring us unto Christ, that we might be justified by faith. But after that faith is come, we are no longer under a schoolmaster. For ye are all the children of God by faith in Christ Jesus. For as many of you as have been baptized into Christ have put on Christ. There is neither Jew nor Greek, there is neither bond nor free, there is neither male nor female: for ye are all one in Christ Jesus. And if ye be Christ's, then are ye Abraham's seed, and heirs according to the promise. (Galatians 3:19-29)

Verse 19 'Wherefore then serveth the law? It was added because of transgressions, till the seed should come to whom the promise was made; and it was ordained by angels in the hand of a mediator'.

'The law was added because of transgressions'. The law of God, (The ten commandments and the legal precepts of worship, civil government, and daily life given in the Old Testament) was never intended to be a means of righteousness, a means of grace, or a means of salvation. It was not given as a code of moral ethics. It was not given as the believer's rule of life. It was not given as a motive for Christian service. It was not given as a measure of sanctification. It was not given to be the grounds of our assurance. It was not given as a basis for reward in heaven.

The purpose of God's holy law is to identify and expose man's sin, shutting him up to Christ alone for acceptance with God (Romans 3:19; 5:20). Before any man is converted, he must be convinced of his sin and guilt. We preach the holy law of God to convince men of their sin. Before any man is given the newness of life in Christ, he must be slain by the law. The law is God's deep cutting plow, by which he breaks up the fallow ground of a man's heart and conscience, and prepares the soil for the gospel. This plowing is a difficult, but necessary, process.

The law was given until, 'The Seed should come to whom the promise was made'. The Seed spoken of here is Christ. The promise spoken of is the promise God the Father made to God the Son before the world began. That promise was the promised gift of grace, salvation, and eternal life by the Holy Spirit to his elect. It was a promise made on condition of Christ's obedience and death, upon condition of righteousness established by him for us as our Substitute (Galatians 3:13-14).

I am not guessing about this. The context declares it. The Mosaic law, given at Mount Sinai, was given to Israel in the hands of a mediator, who was but a man. But the promise was given to Christ our Mediator from God our Father; and these two are one God! That is the meaning of Paul's next words.

Verse 20 'Now a mediator is not a mediator of one, but God is one'.

God the Father promised eternal life to his elect before the world began. But he made the promise to Christ as our Covenant Surety (Titus 1:1-3). We who believe have obtained this promise of eternal life in Christ, because he purchased it and effectually obtained it for the seed of Abraham, Abraham's true, spiritual seed (Galatians 3:13-14; Hebrews 9:12; 2:16).

Verse 21 'Is the law then against the promises of God? God forbid: for if there had been a law given which could have given life, verily righteousness should have been by the law'.

What a plain statement this is! It is utterly irrefutable. The law, which was given by Moses, cannot be contrary to the promise of eternal life to God's elect before the world began. It is absurd, monstrously absurd, to imagine that God would have sacrificed his darling Son for nothing! If righteousness could be obtained by us doing something, God would never have sacrificed his Son at Calvary to bring in righteousness for us! To suggest such a thing is to declare that 'Christ is dead in vain' (Galatians 2:21).

Verses 22-23 'But the scripture hath concluded all under sin, that the promise by faith of Jesus Christ might be given to them that believe. But before faith came, we were kept under the law, shut up unto the faith which should afterwards be revealed'.

The law was not given to make us righteous, but to shut us up to Christ. The law of God, in holy scripture, concludes all under sin. We are by birth, nature, choice, and practice under sin, under its dominion, corruption, penalty and curse (Romans 3:19-23).

The scripture declares that we are under sin specifically for this reason: – 'That the promise (the same promise he has been discussing throughout the chapter, the promise of grace, salvation, and eternal life) by faith of Jesus Christ might be given to them that believe'.

Read those lines carefully and understand the gospel. Grace, salvation, and eternal life come to chosen sinners upon the ground of and because of the faith, faithfulness, or faithful obedience of Jesus Christ as our Substitute. It was Christ alone who brought in everlasting righteousness for us. It was Christ alone who redeemed us. It was Christ alone who put away our sins. It was Christ alone who made atonement for us by satisfying the justice of God with his own blood. It was Christ alone who, with his own blood, obtained eternal life for us! Our faith in him has no part in the accomplishment of these things!

What does faith do? Nothing! Faith receives! Believing God, every sinner who believes, has been given grace, salvation, and eternal life by God the Holy Spirit, because God the Father promised it and God the Son purchased it! 'Salvation is of the Lord!'

Before faith came, that is before we came to trust Christ, before God gave us faith in his Son, 'we were kept under the law'. As we are told in Ephesians 2, we were by nature children of wrath, just like everyone else. Though we were justified from eternity by God's decree and justified at Calvary by Christ's blood atonement, we knew nothing about it. We lived under the curse and condemnation of God's law. Our first convictions, our first thoughts toward God, filled us with terror. The law condemned us, condemned us justly. When the law came, sin revived, and I died! That is what Paul said (Romans 7:9); and that is what every believer experiences. We were thus, by the terror of the law on our consciences damning us, shut up to Christ. Look at it in verse 23: – 'Shut up unto the faith which should afterward be revealed'.

Verse 24 'Wherefore the law was our schoolmaster to bring us unto Christ, that we might be justified by faith'.

The law's purpose, function, and use is to bring sinners to Christ. Once it has served that purpose it has no other function. That is exactly what we are told in verse 25.

Verse 25 'But after that faith is come, we are no longer under a schoolmaster'.

What does that mean? It means exactly what you think it means. It means spiritually what Martin Luther King proclaimed with the passage of the Civil Rights Bill. 'Free at last! Free at last! Thank God Almighty, I'm free at last!' Salvation comes to sinners (I mean salvation in its entirety, in the totality of all that is included in that word 'salvation') by faith in Christ, not by the works of the law. Is that, or is it not, the doctrine of holy scripture? Read the next verse.

Verse 26 'For ye are all the children of God by faith in Christ Jesus'.

Paul wrote to these Galatians in exactly the same way as any pastor would address a congregation of professed believers. He took them at their word. Because they professed faith in Christ, he charitably assumed that their profession was genuine. Therefore he says, 'Ye are the children of God by faith in Christ'.

The Apostle is not suggesting that our adoption into the family of God is the result of our believing. It is just the other way around. Our faith in Christ is the result of our adoption. We were adopted, by God before the world began, in divine predestination (Ephesians 1:5). It was our adoption which sent the Holy Spirit to us in effectual, regenerating grace. Our adoption in election was the cause of Christ's atonement and the Spirit's call (Galatians 4:3-7; 1 John 3:1).

Verse 27 'For as many of you as have been baptized into Christ have put on Christ'.

Paul does not imply here that there were some in the church who were baptized and some who were not, or that there were some Christians who submitted to the gospel ordinance of immersion in the name of Christ and some who did not. His language here simply implied that there might have been some among them (as there might be in any assembly), who though baptized in water, yet did not know Christ. John Gill explained the text correctly, saying, 'Those who are truly and rightly baptized, who are proper subjects of it, and to whom it is administered in a proper manner, are baptized into Christ'.

Paul is not suggesting that by baptism we are brought into union with Christ, but into communion with him. When baptism is an act of faith in and obedience to Christ, believers are baptized in the name of Christ, by the authority of Christ, according to the doctrine of Christ, in obedience to the command of Christ, into the body of Christ, and in hope of the resurrection with Christ.

All who have truly been baptized into Christ have put on Christ, both before we were baptized and when we were baptized. Before we were baptized we put him on as the Lord our righteousness. We put him on as our robe of righteousness. When we were baptized we put on Christ by public profession, declaring him to be our Lord and King, declaring ourselves to be his voluntary servants forever, resolving to walk with him in the newness of life.

Verse 28 'There is neither Jew nor Greek, there is neither bond nor free, there is neither male nor female: for ye are all one in Christ Jesus'.

All who are in Christ are one in him. In Christ, all social, economic, racial barriers are dissolved. The only place in the world where race, gender, and social status make no difference is in Christ, in the Church of Christ (Colossians 3:10-11). Grace alone can make sinful men and women truly one. God's elect really are one in Christ.

Verse 29 'And if ye be Christ's, then are ye Abraham's seed, and heirs according to the promise'.

'And if ye be Christ's' – nothing else really matters. If you belong to Christ, by the Father's election, the Son's redemption, the Spirit's call to faith in him; if you believe on the Son of God, all is well. If not, you are going to hell! 'And if ye be Christ's, then are ye Abraham's seed'. If you believe on the Lord Jesus Christ, you are the object of God's love, the recipient of his grace, and 'heirs according to the promise!' If you believe on the Lord Jesus Christ, you are God's forever and he is yours! You are heirs of God and joint heirs with Jesus Christ, according to the promise of eternal life which God, who cannot lie, made to his Son before the world began!

'Now we know that what things soever the law saith, it saith to them who are under the law: that every mouth may be stopped, and all the world may become guilty before God'.
(Romans 3:19)

Chapter 60

The Purpose of God's Holy Law

The person who knows the proper place of the law and the glory of God's free grace, the person who can rest in Christ alone for all that the law requires and all that justice demands, knows the gospel. But that person who mixes law and grace, in any measure whatsoever, as a matter of acceptance before God, has not yet learned the gospel aright.

No two things in the world are more completely opposed to one another, more mutually exclusive, than law and grace. They are as opposite as light and darkness. They can no more agree than fire and ice. Like oil and water, law and grace simply will not mix. The scriptures are explicitly clear in asserting this fact (Romans 11:5-6).

'Even so then at this present time also there is a remnant according to the election of grace. And if by grace, then is it no more of works: otherwise grace is no more grace. But if it be of works, then is it no more grace: otherwise work is no more work'.

Yet, there is an amazingly well established opinion in the distorted minds of men that law and grace will mix! Though law and grace are diametrically opposed to one another, the depraved human mind is so void of spiritual understanding, and so thoroughly turned away from God, that the most difficult thing in this world for man to do is to discriminate between law and grace. Man insists on mixing that which God has positively put asunder. Because of his foolish ignorance, man wants to find some legal standing before God. This is the thing that Paul opposes throughout all of his epistles. He expends every effort to destroy every remnant of legalism among God's people.

Free from the law

In Christ, all who believe are free, totally free from the law. That fact cannot be stated too emphatically. There is absolutely no sense in which believers are under the law.

The word law is used 160 times in the New Testament epistles. Not once, not even once, in those 160 references is there a single hint that the believer is in some way, to some degree, for some reason, motivated by, ruled by, under the dominion of, or obligated to the law. Let's look at just a few of the plain, obvious statements of holy scripture dealing with this, the most persistent of all heresies.

Romans 6:14-15 – 'For sin shall not have dominion over you: for ye are not under the law, but under grace. What then? Shall we sin, because we are not under the law, but under grace? God forbid'.

Romans 7:4 – 'Wherefore, my brethren, ye also are become dead to the law by the body of Christ; that ye should be married to another, even to him who is raised from the dead, that we should bring forth fruit unto God'.

Romans 8:3-4 – 'For what the law could not do, in that it was weak through the flesh, God sending his own Son in the likeness of sinful flesh, and for sin, condemned sin in the flesh: That the righteousness of the law might be fulfilled in us, who walk not after the flesh, but after the Spirit'.

Romans 10:4 – 'For Christ is the end of the law for righteousness to every one that believeth'.

Galatians 3:24-25 – 'Wherefore the law was our schoolmaster to bring us unto Christ, that we might be justified by faith. But after that faith is come, we are no longer under a schoolmaster'.

1 Timothy 1:8-10 – 'But we know that the law is good, if a man use it lawfully; Knowing this, that the law is not made for a righteous man, but for the lawless and disobedient, for the ungodly and for sinners, for unholy and profane, for murderers of fathers and murderers of mothers, for manslayers, For whoremongers, for them that defile themselves with mankind, for menstealers, for liars, for perjured persons, and if there be any other thing that is contrary to sound doctrine'.

Was Paul opposed to the law? Did he think the law was an evil thing? Certainly not! In Romans 7, he shows us his own and every true believer's attitude towards God's holy law. 'The law is holy, and the commandment holy, and just, and good ... We know that the law is spiritual ... I delight in the law of God after the inward man'.

The true believer recognizes the purpose of the law; and he highly reveres the law. It is his desire to live in perfect compliance with everything revealed in the law. Recognizing the law's perfection, he refuses to seek acceptance with God on the basis of legal obedience. It is our reverence for the law that keeps us from trying to live by the law. It is the perfect holiness and strict, unbending demands of God's law and justice, which drive us to Christ. This is not licentious doctrine, but holy doctrine.

C. H. Spurgeon once illustrated this fact by telling his congregation of the experience of one Dr Chalmers, who said, 'I preached morality until there was scarcely a moral person left in the parish. I preached righteousness and goodness until I could hardly find a decent, honest man anywhere around me'. Then God saved the man. He began preaching Christ crucified and salvation by the free grace of God in him, and things changed.

That is exactly what Paul told Titus would happen whenever the gospel is faithfully preached.

'But after that the kindness and love of God our Saviour toward man appeared, Not by works of righteousness which we have done, but according to his mercy he saved us, by the washing of regeneration, and renewing of the Holy Ghost; Which he shed on us abundantly through Jesus Christ our Saviour; That being justified by his grace, we should be made heirs according to the hope of eternal life. This is a faithful saying, and these things I will that thou affirm constantly, that they which have believed in God might be careful to maintain good works. These things are good and profitable unto men' (Titus 3:4-8).

We do not teach Sabbath keeping because God forbids it; but we keep the Sabbath rest by faith in Christ: – Christ is our Sabbath. We do not teach circumcision because our Lord forbids it; but we are the circumcised. God the Holy Spirit has circumcised our hearts by the saving operations of his grace in the new birth. We do not teach tithing because God plainly forbids us taking anything from anyone by constraint of law. 'God loveth a cheerful giver!' But all believers give. We give ourselves to Christ. Giving themselves to Christ, God's elect cheerfully give of their means to support the cause of Christ.

Three great difficulties

Seeking the conversion of sinners, endeavouring to persuade men to believe on the Lord Jesus Christ, we are faced with three great difficulties.

The first real difficulty in conversion is to get a person lost, really lost. The hardest thing in the world to find is a sinner who is really lost. I know that all who are without Christ are lost in the sense that all are under the wrath of God; but few know it. There are very few men and women walking the streets of any city anywhere in this world who know they are lost, so thoroughly and completely lost that no religious rite or ceremony, no system of works, no law, no code of morality can do them any good. Joseph Hart expressed it in one of his hymns:

> What comfort can a Saviour bring,
> To those who never felt their woe?
> A sinner is a sacred thing;
> The Holy Ghost hath made him so.

There are many who will admit that they are weak, and need a little help. There are some who will even admit that they are sinful, and in need of some atonement. But there are few people in this world who will acknowledge that they are totally and eternally lost, in need of salvation by pure grace alone. Only the Holy Spirit can produce a lost sinner. The first thing that must be done is to get a man lost. Only real sinners seek real grace. Only God the Holy Spirit can convince a sinner that he is a sinner, lost, undone, and under the curse of God's holy law without Christ.

The second real difficulty in conversion is teaching lost sinners the gospel of the free grace of God in Christ. There are few people in this world who have ever heard the gospel, and fewer still who ever really learn it. The gospel of God's free, sovereign, saving grace in Christ proclaims salvation to lost sinners without anything in return from them, – requiring nothing from them. Salvation is the free gift of God, from beginning to end. Even repentance, faith, and good works are gifts of his grace.

It is very difficult for proud sinners to learn the gospel, because it is opposed to our pride. It is opposed to our wisdom. It is opposed to our religious prejudices. It is opposed to our traditions. The gospel contradicts everything the natural man thinks about spiritual things (1 Corinthians 2:9-16). God's way is always exactly the opposite of man's way.

The third great difficulty in conversion is bringing lost sinners to rest in Christ alone, trusting him alone for everything they need for acceptance with the holy Lord God (1 Corinthians 1:30-31). We must rest entirely upon Christ. We must never go beyond that. We are to live all the days of our lives trusting that same grace and love that first took us in. We are chosen, redeemed, called, justified, sanctified, and kept by grace alone. 'As ye have therefore received Christ Jesus the Lord, so walk ye in him' (Colossians 2:6).

> Here I raise mine Ebenezer;
> Hither by Thy help I'm come:
> And I hope by Thy good pleasure
> Safely to arrive at home.

We place no hope whatsoever in our obedience to the law of God. We have neither salvation, nor sanctification, nor reward by our obedience to the law. We trust nothing but Christ alone; and we trust him for all things. Everything God requires from and gives to sinners is in Christ (Ephesians 1:3-14).

One purpose

The law of God has but one proper use spiritually. I grant, the law restrains unrighteous men from behaving as they would were there no penal consequences for their offences (1 Timothy 1:8-10). But spiritually the law has only one proper, lawful use. It was given for only one purpose. It was not given as a code of moral ethics. It was not given as the believer's rule of life. It was not given as a motive for Christian service. It was not given as a measure of sanctification. It was not given to be the grounds of our assurance. It was not given as a basis for reward in heaven. The only purpose of God's holy law is to identify, expose, and condemn man's sin, shutting him up to Christ alone for acceptance with God.

Romans 3:19 – 'Now we know that what things soever the law saith, it saith to them who are under the law: that every mouth may be stopped, and all the world may become guilty before God'.

Romans 5:20 – 'Moreover the law entered, that the offence might abound. But where sin abounded, grace did much more abound'.

Before any sinner is converted, he must be convinced of his sin and guilt. That is the only lawful use of the law. Before any man is given the newness of life in Christ, he must be slain by the law. Remember, the law is God's deep cutting plow, by which he breaks up the fallow ground of a sinner's heart and conscience, and prepares the soil of his heart for the gospel. This plowing is a difficult, but necessary process. Yes, there must be more than legal conviction; but legal conviction is an essential part of gospel conviction (John 16:8-11).

Our only hope

The sinner's only hope before God is free grace, free grace that flows to chosen sinners upon the ground of righteousness fulfilled and justice satisfied. This is Paul's doctrine. This is the doctrine of holy scripture. This is the doctrine of the gospel.

Romans 3:19-31 – 'Now we know that what things soever the law saith, it saith to them who are under the law: that every mouth may be stopped, and all the world may become guilty before God. Therefore by the deeds of the law there shall no flesh be justified in his sight: for by the law is the knowledge of sin. But now the righteousness of God without the law is manifested, being witnessed by the law and the prophets; Even the righteousness of God which is by faith of Jesus Christ unto all and upon all them that believe: for there is no difference: For all have sinned, and come short of the glory of God; Being justified freely by his grace through the redemption that is in Christ Jesus: Whom God hath set forth to be a propitiation through faith in his blood, to declare his righteousness for the remission of sins that are past, through the forbearance of God; To declare, I say, at this time his righteousness: that he might be just, and the justifier of him which believeth in Jesus. Where is boasting then? It is excluded. By what law? of works? Nay: but by the law of faith. Therefore we conclude that a man is justified by faith without the deeds of the law. Is he the God of the Jews only? is he not also of the Gentiles? Yes, of the Gentiles also: Seeing it is one

God, which shall justify the circumcision by faith, and uncircumcision through faith. Do we then make void the law through faith? God forbid: yea, we establish the law'.

God the Holy Spirit inspired the Apostle to say exactly the same thing to the saints at Galatia. He means for us to get the message.

Galatians 2:19-21 – 'For I through the law am dead to the law, that I might live unto God. I am crucified with Christ: nevertheless I live; yet not I, but Christ liveth in me: and the life which I now live in the flesh I live by the faith of the Son of God, who loved me, and gave himself for me. I do not frustrate the grace of God: for if righteousness come by the law, then Christ is dead in vain'.

> The law demands a weighty debt;
> And not a cent will it abate.
> The gospel points to Jesus' blood,
> And says, 'He made the payment good!'
>
> The law provokes man oft to ill,
> And hardened hearts makes harder still.
> The gospel shows Immanuel's heart
> And melts this hardened sinner's heart!
>
> 'Run, run, and work', the law commands,
> But gives me neither feet nor hands.
> Much sweeter news the gospel brings.
> It tells me Christ did everything!

'For I was alive without the law once: but when the commandment came, sin revived, and I died'.
(Romans 7:9)

Chapter 61

'When the Commandment Came'

In this text the Apostle Paul, writing by divine inspiration, tells us of three things he experienced, three things by which he was brought to faith in Christ. These three things are experienced, to a greater or lesser degree, by all of God's elect. Here are three things that happen to every truly converted soul.

1. 'I was alive without the law once'

When Paul says that he was alive without the law, he does not mean that he had never heard or read the law before, or that he did not know it. Of all men in his day, Saul of Tarsus was probably more fully acquainted with and knowledgeable of the law of God (in the killing letter of it) than any other. He knew and understood the letter of the law very well.

When the Apostle says, 'I was alive without the law once', his meaning is this: There was a time when the law of God had never come home to my heart and conscience, I never knew the spirituality of the law. I never knew what the law demanded.

Saul of Tarsus was a lost religious man. He was zealous, devoted, and strict. He kept the law, in its letter, all the days of his life. Yet, he was as lost as the most debased barbarian who ever lived in the darkest corners of heathendom. Like all in that state and condition, he was totally convinced that everything was well with his soul.

Though he was dead in sin, he was full of religious life. He had great joy; but it was a false joy. He enjoyed great peace; but it was a false peace. He walked with great confidence; but it was a false confidence. Saul of Tarsus was a man of steadfast hope; but it was a false hope. He had great faith; but it was a false faith. He lived with complete assurance that all was well with his soul; but it was a false assurance. His religion was altogether a satanic delusion. He was deluded by a false security.

Saul's proud, self-righteous security made him very zealous in his religion. He looked down upon others with disgust and scorn. He held those whom he looked upon as sinners in utter contempt. He became a ferocious persecutor. As soon as a person thinks he is better than others, he becomes the judge of others; and the next step is to carry out his sentence upon others.

There are many things which support men and give them security in self-righteous religion. Saul of Tarsus lacked none of those things which give men a false security. First and foremost, that proud Pharisee was ignorant of the law's spiritual character (Romans 7:7). 'Like the rest of the Pharisees', wrote John Gill, 'he thought the law only regarded the outward actions, and did not reach to the spirits or souls of men, the inward thoughts and affections of the mind'.

Self-righteousness stems from a failure to understand the spiritual character of the law of God. Uncleanness of mind in God's eyes is as obnoxious as uncleanness of life. An unclean thought is adultery. Anger is murder. Covetousness is theft. Love of self is idolatry.

Saul had the respectability and esteem of high office in the church. He was a Pharisee of the Pharisees. He came behind no one in matters of religious devotion. Read the third chapter of Philippians. Saul of Tarsus was a remarkable, highly respected figure in the religious world.

This man rested in a false evidence of God's love and favour. He thought external reformation was an indication of God's favour (John 8:39-41). The fact is, evidence based assurance is false assurance. The believer's assurance of salvation is Christ. It is the assurance of faith (Hebrews 11:1). Saul strengthened his carnal security by comparing himself to those who were, in his opinion, more profane and wicked than he was. He was one of those men, utterly repugnant to God, who thought he was 'holier'[1] than others (Isaiah 65:1-5). Saul the Pharisee had that love of self which causes a man to overlook his own faults and exaggerate the faults of others (Matthew 7:3-5).

Moreover, he was deceived with a wrong idea of God's justice. He did not realize that the law of God demands perfection and that the justice of God requires an infinite atonement for every deviation from his holy law.

Through all of these things, the god of this world had blinded his mind, lest the light of the glorious gospel of Christ should shine unto him. Like some of you, Saul of Tarsus was a man lost in religion. His religion kept him from Christ. He said, 'I was alive without the law once'. Saul of Tarsus had such a high opinion of his own personal holiness that he actually presumed that he was good enough to meet whatever demands the holy Lord God required! He was alive without the law. He felt perfectly comfortable with himself. He was, in his considered opinion of himself, good enough for God!

2. 'When the commandment came, sin revived'

Before the commandment came, piercing his heart and soul, sin was a dead thing to him. He had mortified the flesh. He had sanctified himself, at least outwardly. He did not believe that there was really any great sin in him. In his own estimation, and in the eyes of others, Saul was a truly holy man.

---

[1] The only time in the entire Word of God where the word 'holy' is used in a relative sense when applied to man is found in Isaiah 65:5, where those who vainly imagine that they make themselves 'holier' than others by what they do or do not do are exposed for what they really are: – 'a smoke in God's nose!'

What does Paul mean by this statement? – 'When the commandment came, sin revived?' He means for us to understand that the law exposed his sin. The law came crushing into his soul, exposing his inward lusts. He particularly uses the expression of the law, 'Thou shalt not covet' (Romans 7:7), as the thing which stirred up his lusts, the enmity of his heart against God. The law aggravated his sin. Thus, 'sin revived'.

For the first time in his life, Saul felt himself to be a guilty sinner. This conviction of sin is not an easy thing to experience; but it is necessary. Without it, no man will ever be saved. A person's sin must be exposed to himself, or he will never come to Christ.

3. 'And I died'

At last, Saul was slain by the law. His mouth was stopped. He stood guilty before God. What was it in this man that died? It was that which ought never to have lived. It was the great 'I'. 'Sin revived, and *I* died'. The law killed it. 'I' was so secure. 'I' was so proud. 'I' was so holy. 'I' was so zealous. But now '*I* died'. Any man whose heart has been exposed to the light of God's holy law sees himself as a vile, obnoxious, rotting corpse of human flesh.

What does the Apostle mean by this statement – 'I died'? He means for us to understand that he was made to see, for the first time in his life, that he was justly condemned to die. All his hopes from his past life of self-righteousness died. All his hopes regarding the future died.

He had broken the law of God, and all his efforts to keep it in the future could never atone for his sin. All his tears of repentance, all his sorrowful cries, all of his sincere confessions, all his best deeds, could not mend God's broken law. Toplady writes:

> Could my tears forever flow,
> Could my zeal no languor know,
> All for sin could not atone;
> Thou must save and Thou alone.

The thunderous bolts of Sinai dashed all his hopes to the ground. The iron cold sword of the law had wounded and slain his spirit. Then, but not until then, did this broken man cry, 'Lord, what wilt thou have me do?'

Have you ever been slain by God's holy law? I hope you have. Perhaps, even as you have read these lines, God the Holy Spirit has slain you by the law. Has he made you to know yourself a sinner, a real sinner, utterly lost and undone before God? If so, read on. There is good news for sinners. Christ died for sinners. God, for Christ's sake, saves sinners. May God graciously compel you to fall down before the throne of the sovereign Christ, suing for mercy, crying like the needy publican of old: – 'God, be merciful to me, the sinner', – 'Lord, if you will, you can make me whole'.

In Galatians 3, this same man declares, 'I through the law am dead to the law', because he had been crucified with Christ (Galatians 3:19-21). Once his carnal hopes were slain, once he was made alive by grace, once Christ was revealed in him, he saw and rejoiced to see that he was 'dead to the law'. The same is true of every believer.

How can we be dead to the law? Once the law has exacted all its demands, once all its justice has been executed and the criminal is dead, he is dead to the law. The law cannot require anything more from the executed felon. That is exactly what happened at Calvary. All the sins of God's elect were imputed to the Lord Jesus Christ. When he was made to be sin for us, the fire of God's holy wrath fell on him, and fell on his people in him. When he died, all his people died. Thus, when the fire of God's law and justice consumed our Substitute and he consumed it, we became 'dead to the law – through the law!'

'Do we then make void the law through faith? God forbid: yea, we establish the law' (Romans 3:31). By faith in Christ, we who believe fulfil the law of God. That is the only way any sinner can fulfil the law. Being freed from the law in Christ, being dead to the law and married to Christ, we must never allow anyone to bring us back under the yoke of the law (Galatians 5:1-4).

'Come unto me, all ye that labour and are heavy laden, and I will give you rest. Take my yoke upon you, and learn of me; for I am meek and lowly in heart: and ye shall find rest unto your souls. For my yoke is easy, and my burden is light.' (Matthew 11:28-30)

Chapter 62

Blessed Sabbath Rest

The text that heads this page is a call to rest. Here the Son of God, the Lord of glory, the God-man Mediator, our all-glorious Christ, bids weary, heavy laden sinners to come to him and find rest for their souls. Call it a command, if you like. When the King of the universe bids you do something, his bidding is a command. Call it an invitation, if you wish. I have no problem with that either. When the all holy, infinite God condescends to speak to hell-bent, hell-bound sinners, when he bids those sinners come to him and live, that is the sweetest, gentlest, most tender, gracious, and merciful invitation in the world! Whether we hear these words as a command, or hear them as an invitation, it matters not. The only thing that matters is that we hear them.

Here is Christ's word to lost, ruined, guilty sinners: – 'Come unto me, all ye that labour and are heavy laden, and I will give you rest. There is no salvation to be had, but by coming to Christ. There can never be any true, peaceful, satisfying rest for our souls, except we come to Christ, trusting him alone as our Lord and Saviour, trusting his blood as our only atonement and his obedience as our only righteousness. Only Christ can give weary sinners rest.

Here is the Master's word to us all, both to the unbeliever and the believer: – 'Take my yoke upon you, and learn of me; for I am meek and lowly in heart: and you shall find rest unto your souls'. In all circumstances of life we find rest unto our souls only as we voluntarily submit to the rule and dominion of the Son of God as our Lord and King. The only way to find rest is to willingly slip our necks under his yoke. When we do and only when we do, we will find that his yoke really is easy and his burden really is light. I bid you now, whatever your circumstances, take the Master's yoke upon you, and find rest unto your soul. Take upon you the yoke of his grace, bowing to him as your Lord (Luke 14:25-33). Take upon you the yoke of his doctrine, his gospel, bowing to him as your Prophet (Jeremiah 6:16). Take upon you his yoke of providence, trusting him as your God and Saviour (Psalm 31:1, 5, 7, 15). Only in this way do we find rest for our souls.

'Come unto me, all ye that labour and are heavy laden, and I will give you rest. Take my yoke upon you, and learn of me; for I am meek and lowly in heart: and ye shall find rest unto your souls. For my yoke is easy, and my burden is light'. The call of the gospel is a call to rest, the blessed rest of faith in Christ. It is this rest that the Old Testament sabbath day pointed to and typified. All things relating to sabbath law in the Old Testament pointed to the necessity and blessedness of that rest of faith which believers enjoy in Christ. In this study we will see from the Word of God what was required for the keeping of the sabbath in the Old Testament law, what the purpose of that law was, and why we do not and must not keep the Old Testament sabbath today.

Non-essential

Sabbath observance is not essential in the worship of God. The first observance of a sabbath day mentioned in holy scripture is in Genesis 2:2-3, where we are told, 'God ended his work which he had made; and he rested on the seventh day from all work which he had made. And God blessed the seventh day and sanctified it; because that in it he had rested from all his work which God created and made'.

Though it is not mentioned by name, here we see the first observance of a sabbath rest. The Lord God himself rested on the seventh day from all his work. That is what it is to keep the sabbath. It is to rest from all your work. Though he kept the sabbath, there was no other mention of it for 2,000 years. Adam never kept a sabbath day, either before or after the fall. Yet, he worshipped God and walked with him. Abel never observed a sabbath day; but he worshipped God. Enoch walked with God; but he never observed a sabbath day. Noah found grace in the eyes of the Lord; but we never read of him observing the sabbath. Abraham was the friend of God; but he did not keep a ceremonial sabbath day of any kind.

Throughout the days of the patriarchs, (Abraham, Isaac, and Jacob), though God was believed, worshipped, loved and honoured by his people, not one of his people kept a sabbath day. Even Joseph, that great, eminent type of Christ, never once observed a sabbath day.

Were these men antinomians? Were they evil, licentious, wicked men? To even suggest such nonsense is offensive. These were men, all of them, who walked with God. They were holy, righteous, believing men. They did not keep a sabbath day, because God did not require them to do so. Yet, they worshipped God! My point is just this: Sabbath observance is in no way essential to the worship of God.

Sabbath established

The ordinance of sabbath observance was established by God in the wilderness at the same time that manna was given from heaven (Exodus 16:22-30). The manna portrayed God's provision of life in Christ, the Bread of Life. The sabbath portrayed God's provision of rest in Christ. It is specifically called, 'the rest of the holy sabbath unto the Lord'. 'So the people rested on the seventh day'.

The children of Israel were commanded not to do any work on the sabbath. They were not even allowed to pick up manna on the seventh day of the week! In Exodus 20:8-11, God's law strictly prohibited everyone from doing any work on Saturday, and even prohibited him from having anyone under his authority do any work.

Those who would impose upon us the carnal ordinance of sabbath keeping, those who would bring us back under the yoke of bondage to the law, compelling us to keep the sabbath day, compel us to do what they themselves cannot do. I know that many teach sabbath keeping as a rule of life. They would impose upon God's saints strict rules and regulations for sabbath day observance. But all their teaching and preaching in that regard is sheer hypocrisy. Not one of them observes the sabbath day. Their teaching regarding the sabbath are just 'a fair show in the flesh' (Galatians 6:12-13), no more. Their pretended reverence for the law of God, when closely examined, reveals a total disregard for God's law. They sift through the commandments, pick out what they like, and simply ignore the rest. Let me show you what I mean.

Here are four things required in God's law for the observance of the sabbath day. If the sabbath day is observed, it must be observed in such a way as to include all four of these things.

1. The sabbath day must be observed on Saturday, the seventh day of the week (Exodus 20:10). Sunday is not the sabbath day. It never has been. Sunday is once called 'the Lord's Day', but only once, and then with no instructions of any kind about the matter. It was the day of Christ's resurrection. But nowhere in the Bible are we commanded, or even permitted, to observe the sabbath on Sunday.
2. No work can be done on the sabbath, none (Exodus 20:10). Works of necessity and works of mercy were permitted on the sabbath; but no one was allowed to do any work of any kind for himself, or to benefit himself. If you want to keep the sabbath day, in accordance with God's holy law, then you must not, under penalty of death, light a fire for cooking (Exodus 35:3), gather wood for burning

(Numbers 15:32-36), carry any burden (Jeremiah 17:21-22), travel (Exodus 16:29), or do any business (Amos 8:5). Anything which might be construed as a matter of personal profit or pleasure was expressly forbidden on the sabbath day (Isaiah 58:13; 56:2; Ezekiel 20:12, 21). The essence of sabbath worship was absolute, unreserved, unconditional, all-encompassing self-denial. It was an utter renunciation of self and an utter dedication of one's self to the Lord God.

3. In addition to these things, any genuine observance of the sabbath day necessitates a return to the ceremonial law of the Old Testament. The sabbath day cannot be observed without the offering of a double sin-offering, a double meal offering, and a double drink-offering; and those offerings must be made in the temple at Jerusalem (Numbers 28:9-10).

4. There is one more point, which cannot be ignored. Those who insist upon keeping the sabbath must also demand the execution of all sabbath breakers (Exodus 31:15). The very same law that required the observance of the sabbath also required the death of those who broke the sabbath. If a man wants to keep the sabbath, he must also be willing to stone to death anyone who breaks the sabbath, even his own son or daughter.

Do you know anyone who observes the sabbath day this way? I do not. Not even the most orthodox Jew, the most strict Adventist, or the most heretical Russellite in the world observes such a sabbath. Those who pretend to observe a Sunday sabbath do not even come close to the requirements of God's Word regarding sabbath observance.

It is obvious that no one observes the sabbath day in a literal sense, and no one has for 2,000 years! Jews do not observe it. Catholics do not observe it. Protestants do not. Reformed people do not observe it. Those who pretend to observe it only make a mockery of the sabbath by their hypocrisy. Their sabbath keeping is nothing but a fleshy show!

Why not keep a sabbath day?

Why do we not observe a sabbath day? Why do we refuse to observe a literal sabbath day? What can be wrong with setting aside the first day of the week and requiring God's saints to keep it as a sabbath day unto the Lord? Should we not at least allow the observance of a sabbath day by those who want to do it?

We do not and must not observe any literal sabbath day for precisely the same reasons we do not and must not observe the Jewish Passover or any other legal ceremonies of the Old Testament. The sabbath day which God required the Jews to keep was, like all the other carnal ordinances of the law, only a temporary, typical ritual of the law, which represented, portrayed, and typified the Lord Jesus Christ and our redemption by him.

When the Lord God established the sabbath, when he instituted that ordinance of worship, he gave two reasons, and only two reasons, for its observance.

1. The sabbath day was to be observed by Israel as a symbol of God's rest (Exodus 20:8-10). It represented the completion of God's work, the finality of creation, and God's total satisfaction with it. Though God's creation has been marred by sin, though the slime of the serpent's trail has polluted it, the Book of God speaks of a time called the time of restitution. The sabbath day portrayed that day when all things shall be restored to God; and that restitution began when Christ died and rose again (Acts 3:21; Colossians 1:20).
2. The observance of the sabbath was designed by God to be a constant reminder to Israel of their redemption out of Egypt. As such, it was a picture of our redemption by Christ (Deuteronomy 5:15). Like all other aspects of the Mosaic law, the sabbath was a picture prophecy of our perfect redemption by Christ. As the Jews rested from all their works on the seventh day of the week (eating the manna, the bread of life, which God gave them without any works of their own being done), believers find perfect rest in the Lord Jesus Christ.

We do not and cannot observe a legal, literal sabbath day, because Christ is our sabbath, and we rest in him! In the New Testament epistles (Romans - Revelation), the sabbath is only mentioned in two places. It is mentioned in the four gospels and in the book of Acts many times in connection with the Jews and Jewish worship. But in those Epistles that prescribe all ordinances of divine worship in this gospel age, it is mentioned in just two places (Colossians 2:16-17; Hebrews 4:3-9).

Colossians 2:16-17 – 'Let no man therefore judge you in meat, or in drink, or in respect of an holyday, or of the new moon, or of the sabbath days: Which are a shadow of things to come; but the body is of Christ'.

As we have seen the Apostle Paul, writing by divine inspiration, forbids the observance of a legal sabbath day on the basis of the fact that in Christ every believer is completely, totally, entirely, and forever freed from the law (Romans 7:4; 10:4).

Hebrews 4:3-9 – 'For we which have believed do enter into rest, as he said, As I have sworn in my wrath, if they shall enter into my rest: although the works were finished from the foundation of the world. For he spake in a certain place of the seventh day on this wise, And God did rest the seventh day from all his works ... There remaineth therefore a rest to the people of God'.

The word 'rest' in these verses is the word normally translated 'sabbath'. Here we are told that all who believe on the Lord Jesus Christ keep the sabbath spiritually, truly keep the sabbath by faith in him. How do we keep the sabbath by faith? Just like our God kept the first sabbath. We come to Christ, believing on the son of God, ceasing from our works and resting in him. This is our Saviour's word of grace to poor, needy, troubled, heavy-laden sinners: – 'Come unto me, all ye that labour and are heavy laden, and I will give you rest. Take my yoke upon you, and learn of me; for I am meek and lowly in heart: and ye shall find rest unto your souls. For my yoke is easy, and my burden is light'.

'There remaineth therefore a rest to the people of God. For he that is entered into his rest, he also hath ceased from his own works, as God did from his. Let us labour therefore to enter into that rest, lest any man fall after the same example of unbelief'. (Hebrews 4:9-11)

Chapter 63

The Sabbath that Remains

Sabbath keeping is not a matter of indifference. It is not one of those areas about which the scriptures give no specific instructions. In fact, the instructions given in the Word of God about sabbath keeping are very specific and clear.

Like circumcision, the passover, and all other aspects of legal, ceremonial worship during the Old Testament, the legal sabbath day was established by our God to be a sign, picture, and type of grace and salvation in Christ. This is not a matter of speculation and guesswork. This is exactly what God says about the matter in Exodus 31:13: – 'Verily my sabbaths ye shall keep: for it is a sign between me and you throughout your generations; that ye may know that I am the Lord that doth sanctify you'.

Forbidden ordinances

Because sabbath keeping was a legal type of our salvation in Christ during the age of carnal ordinances, like the passover and circumcision, once Christ came and fulfilled the type, the carnal ordinance ceased. In the New Testament, we are strictly and directly forbidden to keep any of those carnal ordinances. In fact, we are plainly told that those who attempt to worship God on the grounds of legal ordinances are yet under the curse of the law. They have not yet learned the gospel.

Circumcision is forbidden as an ordinance of divine worship (Galatians 5:2, 4). Those who have their babies sprinkled to bring them into the church and kingdom of God, to seal them into the covenant of grace, attempting to retain the carnal ordinance of circumcision, by their act of sprinkling that child deny the gospel of salvation by grace alone. They deny the necessity of heart circumcision by the Spirit of God[1].

Passover observance is forbidden since Christ our Passover has been sacrificed for us (1 Corinthians 5:7).

Those who continue to offer up sacrifices to God, either for atonement, or penance, or to gain a higher degree of divine favour, or to prevent his anger, by their sacrifices deny that Christ's death at Calvary was an effectual satisfaction for the sins of his people. If something must be added by me to his blood and his righteousness, then his blood and his righteousness are totally useless.

In exactly the same way, those who attempt to sanctify themselves by keeping a carnal sabbath deny that Christ is enough to give us perfect acceptance with the thrice holy God. As Paul puts it in Colossians 2:23, they make an outward show of spirituality and wisdom; but it is all will-worship. Such pretences of humility are nothing but the satisfying of the flesh. Not only that, the whole matter of sabbath keeping is strictly forbidden by the Holy Spirit in

---

[1] I do not suggest that all who practice infant sprinkling, calling it the New Testament equivalent of circumcision, know that their practice implies such a denial of the gospel; but the implication cannot be denied. It is as clear a denial of the gospel as the papists' mass.

Colossians 2:16-17. Since the Lord Jesus Christ has, by his death
at Calvary, blotted out the handwriting of the ordinances that was
against us, since he nailed God's broken law to the cross and put
away our sins, he alone is our sabbath. We rest in him. All carnal
sabbath keeping, any form of it, is strictly forbidden on the basis of
the fact that in Christ all true believers are totally free from the law
(Romans 7:4; 10:4).

The sabbath that remains

Yet, the New Testament does speak of a sabbath keeping that
remains for the people of God (Hebrews 4:9-11). The children of
Israel perished in the wilderness because of unbelief. They could
not enter into God's typical rest in the land of Canaan; they could
not enter into that typical picture of God's salvation because of
unbelief (Hebrews 4:1-6).

Though that unbelieving generation perished in unbelief, the
purpose of God was not and could not be hindered. There is an elect
multitude who must and shall enter into his rest (Hebrews 4:6).
However, that typical rest given by Joshua in the land of Canaan
was not the rest purposed and purchased for God's elect. It was
only typical of that blessed rest of faith that is ours in Christ (Hebrews
4:7-8).

It is this remaining sabbath rest that is discussed in Hebrews
4:9-11[2]. The scriptures declare, and declare very plainly, that the
Old Testament sabbath day finds its fulfilment and complete
accomplishment in Christ. All true believers, all who trust Christ
keep the sabbath by faith in him.

---

[2] The word 'rest', which is used over and over and over in Hebrews 3
and 4, means to repose back, to lay down, to be at peace, to cease from
work, to be at home. But, the word translated 'rest' in verse nine is an
entirely different word. The word here translated rest means 'sabbatism',
or 'a keeping of a sabbath'.

Christ's rest

First, the Holy Spirit here declares that the Lord Jesus Christ has entered into his rest, and his rest is glorious, because he has finished his work (Isaiah 11:10; 2 Corinthians 5:17-21; Romans 8:34; Hebrews 10:11-14), and his rest is glorious, just as Isaiah 11:10 declared it would be. Our Saviour's rest in heaven is his glory. In fact, as indicated by the marginal translation of the last sentence of Isaiah 11:10, his rest is his glory. As God the Father rested on the seventh day, because his work of creation was finished; so God the Son rested in the seventh day of time and entered into his rest forever, because he has finished his work of making all things new for his people (Romans 8:34; Hebrews 10:11-14).

Read Matthew 28:1. This is a very remarkable verse of scripture. I wish all who read these lines could read this text in its original language: – 'In the end of the sabbath, as it began to dawn toward the first day of the week, came Mary Magdalene and the other Mary to see the sepulchre'.

The verse quite literally reads, 'In the end of the sabbath, as it began to dawn toward the sabbath'. I take the verse to mean this. When the Lord Jesus Christ died at Calvary and rose again, the old sabbath of the law ended and the new sabbath of grace began. I cannot conceive any other interpretation of Matthew's words.

Behold our exalted Saviour! Do you see him seated yonder upon his throne in heaven? There he sits in the undisturbed, undisturbable serenity of his absolute sovereignty! His rest is his glory (John 17:2; Philippians 2:9-11; Isaiah 45:20-25). He has finished his work (John 17:4; 19:30). He has brought in everlasting righteousness by his obedience and obtained eternal redemption by his blood. Because Christ has finished his work, the salvation of his people is certain (Hebrews 9:12). The works were finished before the foundation of the world in God's purpose. They were finished in time when the God-man took his seat in heaven as our forerunner (Hebrews 6:20). There is no more work to be done. Christ did it all. Since he has finished his work, he sits down in his glory. There he is resting; and his rest is his glory!

The sinner's rest

Second, the Holy Spirit declares that every sinner who believes on the Lord Jesus Christ keeps the sabbath by faith by entering into his rest (Hebrews 4:3, 9-10): – 'For we which have believed do enter into rest ... There remaineth therefore a rest to the people of God. For he that is entered into his rest, he also hath ceased from his own works, as God did from his'. We keep the sabbath of faith, a spiritual sabbath, not a carnal one. We rest in Christ, trusting his finished work, by faith entering into his rest.

The believer's life is a perpetual keeping of the sabbath. None of us keeps it perfectly. Our best faith in this world is still unbelief. But we do keep this blessed sabbath rest sincerely, ever looking to Christ, ever coming to Christ, ever resting in Christ (Matthew 11:28-30).

Our all glorious Christ gives rest to every sinner who comes to him in faith. He says, 'Come unto me, all ye that labour and are heavy laden, and I will give you rest'. Horatius Bonar wrote:

> I heard the voice of Jesus say,
> 'Come unto Me and rest;
> Lay down, thou weary one, lay down
> Thy head upon My breast!'
> I came to Jesus as I was,
> Weary, and worn, and sad;
> I found in Him a resting-place,
> And He has made me glad!

The Lord Jesus Christ has given and continually gives us rest. He gives us the rest of complete pardon (Isaiah 45:22; Ephesians 1:6), perfect reconciliation (2 Corinthians 5:17; Colossians 1:20-21), absolute security (John 10:27-30; Philippians 1:6; 1 Thessalonians 5:24), and of his special providence (Romans 8:28).

As the ceremonial sabbath of the law portrayed a strict, universal consecration to God, so this blessed sabbath of faith involves the perpetual consecration of ourselves to our God and Saviour, the

Lord Jesus Christ (Matthew 11:29-30). We keep the sabbath of faith when we wilfully, deliberately take the yoke of Christ. If we would keep the sabbath, it involves much, much more than living in religious austerity one day a week. To keep the sabbath is to bow to Christ's dominion. To keep the sabbath is to learn of him what to believe, how to live, what to do, how to honour God. To keep the sabbath is to bow to his will.

How can a troubled, weary, heavy-laden, tempest tossed sinner obtain this blessed sabbath rest? I can tell you, both from experience and from the Word of God, there is only one way we can enter into his rest. We have to quit working! We have to trust Christ alone for everything!

Labour to enter in

Third, we must labour to enter into that great, eternal rest of glory with Christ in heaven. 'Let us labour therefore to enter into that rest, lest any man fall after the same example of unbelief' (Hebrews 4:11). There is a great, eternal sabbath to be obtained. 'There remaineth therefore a rest (a sabbath) to the people of God' (Hebrews 4:9) – an eternal remembrance of redemption, an eternal, perfect consecration to Christ, an eternal rest!

Some have already entered into that rest. 'For he that is entered into his rest, he also hath ceased from his own works, as God did from his' (Hebrews 4:10). I have already shown you that this refers to Christ as our covenant Surety and Mediator; but it also refers to all God's elect. There are many who cannot enter in because of unbelief. They simply cannot give up their own works as grounds of righteousness before God.

Those who have entered into their heavenly rest have ceased from their own works. Their days of labour and toil are forever ended. They now serve God night and day, perfectly and without end; but there is no toil or labour involved in their service. Those who have entered into the blessed rest of faith in Christ have also ceased from their own works. They have quit trying to win, keep, or improve standing in God's favour by their own righteousness.

Believers simply trust Christ alone for righteousness (1 Corinthians 1:30; Philippians 3:7-10). Then, there are some who 'must enter therein'. There is an elect multitude of redeemed sinners who yet must enter into this blessed rest.

'Let us therefore labour (strive) to enter into that rest, lest any man fall after the same example of unbelief!' I cannot think of a better way to expound those words than by taking the words of the apostle Paul in Philippians 3:7-14 for an inspired commentary on them.

> But what things were gain to me, those I counted loss for Christ. Yea doubtless, and I count all things but loss for the excellency of the knowledge of Christ Jesus my Lord: for whom I have suffered the loss of all things, and do count them but dung, that I may win Christ, And be found in him, not having mine own righteousness, which is of the law, but that which is through the faith of Christ, the righteousness which is of God by faith: That I may know him, and the power of his resurrection, and the fellowship of his sufferings, being made conformable unto his death; If by any means I might attain unto the resurrection of the dead. Not as though I had already attained, either were already perfect: but I follow after, if that I may apprehend that for which also I am apprehended of Christ Jesus. Brethren, I count not myself to have apprehended: but this one thing I do, forgetting those things which are behind, and reaching forth unto those things which are before, I press toward the mark for the prize of the high calling of God in Christ Jesus.

The penalty for not keeping the sabbath is still death. 'He that believeth on the Son hath everlasting life: and he that believeth not the Son shall not see life; but the wrath of God abideth on him' (John 3:36). If we would be saved we must keep and satisfy the whole of God's law. There is only one way we can do that. We keep the law by faith in Christ, only by faith in Christ. 'Do we then make void the law through faith? God forbid: yea, we establish the law' (Romans 3:31). Believing on the Lord Jesus Christ we offer the holy Lord God everything his holy law demands – perfect righteousness and perfect satisfaction. Come to Christ and rest forever! This is the sabbath that remains.

'If thou turn away thy foot from the sabbath, from doing thy pleasure on my holy day; and call the sabbath a delight, the holy of the LORD, honourable; and shalt honour him, not doing thine own ways, nor finding thine own pleasure, nor speaking thine own words: Then shalt thou delight thyself in the LORD; and I will cause thee to ride upon the high places of the earth, and feed thee with the heritage of Jacob thy father: for the mouth of the LORD hath spoken it'.
(Isaiah 58:13-14)

Chapter 64

When Can We 'Call the Sabbath a Delight'?

Isaiah 58 is a difficult chapter for many to understand; but there is no need for the difficulty. Without question, this chapter was particularly addressed to the Jews during the time of their Babylonian captivity. In it God gave his people some much needed instruction about worship. But, if we limit the text and its interpretation to the Jews, it is meaningless to anyone today. So, that certainly is not the full scope of the chapter. It was written for us (Romans 15:4).

In these fourteen verses the Lord God gives us crystal clear instructions about worship today. Indeed, the promises made in verses 8-14 cannot be fully applicable to anyone other than the saints of God in this gospel age who 'worship God in the Spirit, rejoice in Christ Jesus, and have no confidence in the flesh' (Philippians 3:3).

Empty ceremonies

Verses 1-4 show us the sin and folly of empty religious rituals and ceremonies without faith in Christ, the abomination of a mere form of godliness without the power of it.

> Cry aloud, spare not, lift up thy voice like a trumpet, and show my people their transgression, and the house of Jacob their sins. Yet they seek me daily, and delight to know my ways, as a nation that did righteousness, and forsook not the ordinance of their God: they ask of me the ordinances of justice; they take delight in approaching to God. Wherefore have we fasted, say they, and thou seest not? wherefore have we afflicted our soul, and thou takest no knowledge? Behold, in the day of your fast ye find pleasure, and exact all your labours. Behold, ye fast for strife and debate, and to smite with the fist of wickedness: ye shall not fast as ye do this day, to make your voice to be heard on high.

Here, the Lord God charges lost religionists with exercising religious ceremonies and rituals for the mere gratification of the flesh! Multitudes there are to whom the charge is applicable. Let us not be numbered among them.

That person whose religious exercises, no matter how devout they appear to be, result in them sitting in judgment over others, debating and striving with the fist of wickedness, endeavouring to gain favour with God, that person performs their religious duties only for the gratification of their own lusts.

True worship

Verses 5-7 show us that the essence of worship is heart and spirit, mercy and grace, kindness and love. These are the marks of true and pure religion, the evidences of genuine humility and faith.

Is it such a fast that I have chosen? a day for a man to afflict his soul? is it to bow down his head as a bulrush, and to spread sackcloth and ashes under him? wilt thou call this a fast, and an acceptable day to the LORD? Is not this the fast that I have chosen? to loose the bands of wickedness, to undo the heavy burdens, and to let the oppressed go free, and that ye break every yoke? Is it not to deal thy bread to the hungry, and that thou bring the poor that are cast out to thy house? when thou seest the naked, that thou cover him; and that thou hide not thyself from thine own flesh?

True religion is merciful, gracious, and kind (James 1:26-27). True worshippers, even in the legal dispensation, worshipped God in the Spirit and in truth, seeking to honour him and endeavouring to serve the needs of others by doing them good. Grace experienced makes people gracious; not harsh and demanding, but kind and forgiving. True faith always 'worketh by love'.

Faith's blessedness

Verses 8-12 of Isaiah 58 display the blessedness of faith in Christ and obedience to the gospel.

Then shall thy light break forth as the morning, and thine health shall spring forth speedily: and thy righteousness shall go before thee; the glory of the LORD shall be thy rereward. Then shalt thou call, and the LORD shall answer; thou shalt cry, and he shall say, Here I am. If thou take away from the midst of thee the yoke, the putting forth of the finger, and speaking vanity; And if thou draw out thy soul to the hungry, and satisfy the afflicted soul; then shall thy light rise in obscurity, and thy darkness be as the noon day: And the LORD shall guide thee continually, and satisfy thy soul in

drought, and make fat thy bones: and thou shalt be like
a watered garden, and like a spring of water, whose
waters fail not. And they that shall be of thee shall build
the old waste places: thou shalt raise up the foundations
of many generations; and thou shalt be called, The
repairer of the breach, The restorer of paths to dwell in.

The light and life of free, sure, and everlasting grace (v. 8), the
blessed satisfaction and contentment of faith toward God (v. 9;
Philippians 4:12; 1 John 5:14), and the delightful privilege of
usefulness as instruments of mercy and grace in the hands of God
(vv. 10-12) are things belonging to God's saints in every age in this
world. It is promised to Abraham and his children, 'Thou shalt be a
blessing!' (Genesis 12:2). Those who are blessed of God are made a
blessing to others.

Delightful sabbath
In verses 13 and 14 the prophet of God, with the inspired vision
of prophecy, looks beyond the carnal, Jewish sabbath and sees in it
a picture of Christ, who is the true sabbath, and the blessed rest of
faith in him[1].

If thou turn away thy foot from the sabbath, from
doing thy pleasure on my holy day; and call the sabbath
a delight, the holy of the LORD, honourable; and shalt
honour him, not doing thine own ways, nor finding
thine own pleasure, nor speaking thine own words:
Then shalt thou delight thyself in the LORD; and I
will cause thee to ride upon the high places of the
earth, and feed thee with the heritage of Jacob thy
father: for the mouth of the LORD hath spoken it.

---

[1] This becomes obvious when we observe that Isaiah's exhortation: – 'Call the
sabbath a delight, the holy of the Lord', literally reads, 'Call the sabbath a
delight the Holy One of the Lord'.

When can we, when do we, 'Call the sabbath a delight'? We can and do call the sabbath a delight only when we are brought to the blessed rest of faith in Christ, who is our sabbath, when we keep the sabbath of faith, ceasing from our own works and resting in Christ alone for our entire acceptance with God.

When a person turns from his way, from his sin, from the pleasure of his depraved heart, and from this world to the Lord Jesus Christ, finding rest in him, he finds that Christ, in whom he rests, is a delight, a luxury, and that faith in him is an honour. Indeed, all who trust Christ delight themselves in him, triumph over all their foes in him, and shall at last obtain the full heritage of the heavenly Canaan, called here 'the heritage of Jacob'. 'For the mouth of the Lord hath spoken it'.

The legal sabbath

We need to understand that the sabbath which God required the Jews to keep was only a temporary, typical ordinance, which represented Christ and our redemption by him. When the Lord God instituted sabbath keeping to the Jews in the legal dispensation, he gave two reasons for it.

First, the sabbath was to be kept as a symbol of God's rest (Exodus 20:8-11). It represented the completion of God's creation and the satisfaction of God in his work. Though God's work of creation has been marred by the sin and fall of our race, the sabbath day portrayed a blessed day of glorious rest called 'the times of restitution of all things' (Acts 3:21; Colossians 1:20; Ephesians 1:10), when all things shall be restored to God.

Second, the sabbath day was a constant reminder of Israel's redemption out of Egypt. It was a picture of our redemption by Christ (Deuteronomy 5:15). In other words, the sabbath day, like all other aspects of the Mosaic law, was a picture prophecy of our perfect redemption by Christ. As the Jews rested on the seventh day of the week from all their works, so believers find perfect rest and peace in the Lord Jesus Christ.

Christ our sabbath

We can and will call the sabbath a delight only when we understand that Christ is our sabbath. We do not observe a literal, legal sabbath day, because Christ is our sabbath, and we rest in him. I know many who pretend to keep a literal sabbath day. Many try their best to delight in legal sabbath work. But I do not know a sabbatarian in the world who really delights in his attempts at sabbath keeping, not a single one. Every sabbatarian I know finds the yoke of their legal observance oppressive and galling. It is a spiritual flagellation they feel they must perform in order to be holy.

Sabbath keeping, like animal sacrifices, was a part of the Old Testament law. It has nothing to do with New Testament worship. I know that the sabbath day is frequently mentioned in the four gospels and the Book of Acts, during that transitional period in which the church of God passed from the Old Testament era into the New. However, it is always mentioned in connection with the Jews and Jewish worship in the temple, or in their synagogues. It is mentioned only two times in all the Epistles (Romans – Revelation).

In Colossians 2:16-17 we read, 'Let no man therefore judge you in meat, or in drink, or in respect of an holyday, or of the new moon, or of the sabbath days: Which are a shadow of things to come; but the body is of Christ'. Here the apostle Paul forbids the observance of legal sabbath days in any form. He does so on the basis of the fact that in Christ God's elect are entirely free from the law (Romans 7:4; 10:4).

In Hebrews 4:3-4, 9-11 the sabbath that remains in this gospel age is called 'rest'. Here the Apostle shows us that all who believe on the Lord Jesus Christ keep the sabbath in a spiritual way. That is to say, they and they only truly keep the sabbath by faith in him, by resting in him.

Finished work

We can an will call the sabbath a delight when we realize that our all glorious Saviour, the Lord Jesus Christ, our Mediator, has entered into his rest, and his rest is glorious, because he has finished his work (Hebrews 4:10; Isaiah 11:10). Our Saviour's rest in heaven is glorious and it is his glory: – 'His rest shall be glory!' As God rested on the seventh day, because his work of creation was finished, so the God-man our Mediator has entered into his rest in heaven, because he has made all things new for his people, having finished his work of redemption (Romans 8:34; 2 Corinthians 5:17-21; Hebrews 10:10-14).

Behold our exalted Saviour! Do you see him seated upon his throne in heaven? There he sits in undisturbed and undisturbable sovereign serenity! His rest is his glory (John 17:2; Philippians 2:9-11). That exalted God-man, as our divinely appointed Representative, has fulfilled all the legal sabbath requirements for us, even as he did all the other requirements of the law. Now, in heaven, he is keeping an everlasting sabbath rest (Isaiah 53:10-12). And his rest, which is his glory, tells us that he has finished his work (John 17:4; 19:30), the salvation of his people is certain (Hebrews 9:12), and all his enemies shall soon be made his footstool (Hebrews 10:13). There is no more work to be done. Christ did it all! When all the work was done for us, our blessed Saviour entered into his rest. Now, all who find rest in him call that sabbath a delight!

Sabbath rest

All who believe on the Lord Jesus Christ keep the sabbath by faith (Hebrews 4:3), because we have entered into his rest; and we call this blessed sabbath rest of faith in Christ a delight, the delight of our souls. We do not yet keep the sabbath perfectly, because we do not yet trust our Saviour as we should. We do not yet trust him perfectly. But we do keep the sabbath truly and sincerely by faith. Our sabbath observance is not a carnal, literal thing. We do not keep a sabbath day. God forbids that (Colossians 2:16-17). We keep the sabbath spiritually by faith.

Remember, the sabbath day was ordained by God in the ceremonial worship of the Jews in the Old Testament as a symbol of God's rest after creation and as a reminder of the Jews redemption out of Egypt. The essence of sabbath observation was self-denial and consecration to God. Anything personally profitable or pleasurable was expressly forbidden (Isaiah 56:2; 58:13; Ezekiel 20:12, 21). Sabbath observance was, in its essence, an unconditional, all-encompassing, self-denial. It was a renunciation of self and a dedication of one's self to God. That is exactly the way we observe the sabbath spiritually by faith in Christ, not one day in seven, but all the days of our lives. The believer's life is a perpetual keeping of the sabbath!

The Lord Jesus Christ gives rest to every sinner who comes to him in faith. He says, 'Come unto me, all ye that labour and are heavy laden, and I will give you rest' (Matthew 11:28). Are you labouring and heavy-laden under the load of sin and guilt? Do you long for rest? In your inmost soul do you struggle hard with sin, longing to find peace with God? Will you hear what the Lord Jesus says? 'Come' – That is: believe, trust, rely upon me. 'Come unto me!' – Not to the preacher. Not to my church. Not even to my doctrine. But 'Come unto me, and I will give you rest!' When a sinner comes to Christ, he ceases working for God's favour, because he rests his soul upon the finished work of his Substitute (1 Corinthians 1:30-31).

Yet, this sabbath of faith involves more than a ceasing from our works and the remembrance of our redemption by Christ. It also involves, in its very essence, the consecration of our lives to our dear Saviour (Matthew 11:29-30). We keep the sabbath of faith and find rest unto our souls as we wilfully, deliberately, wholeheartedly surrender to Christ as our Lord. If we would keep the sabbath, truly keep the sabbath, it will take considerably more than going to church on Sunday and reserving one day a week for religious exercises! We keep the sabbath by putting ourselves under the yoke of Christ's dominion, submitting to his will in all things, learning of him what to believe, how to live, and how to honour God. As we do, we find that his yoke is easy and his burden is light. When we submit to Christ's dominion, when we bow to his will, we find rest for our souls and 'call the sabbath a delight!'

'Take heed therefore unto yourselves, and to all the flock, over the which the Holy Ghost hath made you overseers, to feed the church of God, which he hath purchased with his own blood'.
(Acts 20:28)

Chapter 65

The Church of God

Believers cannot exist in this world in spiritual health without the strength, ministry, support, and help of a local church family. It is, therefore, of utmost importance that every child of God know the purpose and value of the church of God in this world and commit himself to it.

The text, which heads this page, is taken from the book of Acts. One great purpose of that book, which is really a brief history of the early church, is to show us how God works in this world through his church. It is the inspired record of the progress of the church during its first thirty years of existence in this world. The most prominent figure in the church during those first thirty years was the Apostle Paul. It is this man, Paul, who is speaking in chapter 20. He is giving a solemn charge to the elders at Ephesus regarding their responsibilities as the servants of God. He says, 'Take heed therefore unto yourselves, and to all the flock, over the which the Holy Ghost hath made you overseers, to feed the church of God, which he hath purchased with his own blood'.

What is the church of God?

It cannot be denied that the word 'church' is used in at least three ways in the New Testament. First, it is used to describe all true believers of all ages, both those of the Old Testament and those of the New, both those on the earth and those in heaven. Considered in this sense, the church is universal, made up of all true believers. It is the mystical, spiritual body of Christ and the Bride of Christ. It is that spiritual body of which Jesus Christ is the Head (Ephesians 1:22; 5:25-27).

Second, the word 'church' is used to describe local, visible assemblies of professed believers in a given place. In every local church there are both believers and unbelievers, wheat and tares, sheep and goats, true possessors of faith and false professors of faith. Every local church has in its membership both the true and the false. Still, every local assembly of men and women who profess faith in Christ and the gospel of his grace is set forth as a local church, and is called 'the church of God' (Romans 16:1-5).

Third, the word 'church' is used to describe all true gospel churches at any given time in the world. Obviously, I do not mean to suggest that the church of God is made up of all churches and denominations. However, it does include all true New Testament churches at any given time in the world. We are one in Christ, one in purpose, one in heart, and one in desire. All true gospel churches are one in this world (1 Corinthians 10:32; 12:28).

In Acts 20:28 Paul is addressing the elders of a particular local assembly at Ephesus, or perhaps elders from several local assemblies in the Ephesus area. In either case, the words 'the church of God' in this text have reference to the local church. Here Paul tells us three things about the church of God, which are true of every local, gospel church.

1. The church belongs to God. Grace Baptist Church of Danville is 'the church of God' at Danville, Kentucky. I am not talking about the building in which we meet, but about the people who meet here. We are 'the church of God'. This church does not belong to the

Baptist denomination, or to me, or even to the church members. It belongs to God exclusively. We are God's people and God's property. God chose us to be his people in sovereign election before the world began (2 Thessalonians 2:13). God redeemed us to himself by the precious blood of his dear Son, the Lord Jesus Christ (Titus 2:14). God called us to himself by the irresistible power and grace of his Spirit, creating spiritual life within us and giving us faith in Christ (Colossians 1:12-14).

These things are true of all true believers. Though there may be unbelievers among us, we all profess to be believers, so these things are true of us collectively as a local church. This is the church of God. Let all beware. He that harms God's church touches the apple of God's eye (1 Corinthians 3:16-17)[1].

2. The church of God is a flock of sheep. It is called 'the flock of God', because it is made up of Christ's sheep. 'A church of Christ is compared to a flock of sheep, being in Gospel order, folded together and feeding in the same pasture, attending the Word and ordinances, under the care of shepherds appointed by Christ the chief Shepherd' (John Gill). Before we were converted, we were sheep going astray from our God and Saviour (Isaiah 53:6). After conversion, God's people are compared to sheep, because they are meek, inoffensive, patient, and totally dependent upon Christ, who is our Shepherd.

God's church is well compared to a flock of sheep, because sheep are far from perfect. They are a good bit less than what we might consider ideal creatures. Sheep are silly, ignorant, helpless, defenceless, straying, dirty, needy animals that cannot even bear their young alone. Therefore, they need and must have shepherds, pastors, to care for them. It is the pastor's responsibility to feed the sheep with knowledge and understanding, protect the sheep with his very life, lead the sheep by going before them, comfort the sheep with the gospel, help the sheep in trouble, and sometimes to gently carry the sheep in loving arms. However, contrary to the opinions

[1] What I have said here, relating to the local assembly of which I am a member is, of course, true with regard to all local churches, all true gospel churches.

of many, it is never his responsibility to discipline and chasten the sheep. The Chief Shepherd alone has the ability to do that.

3. The church of God was purchased by the blood of Christ, who is God. Paul describes the church as being 'the church of God, which he hath purchased with his own blood'. The purchaser of the church is God himself. The price of the purchase was 'his own blood'. The purchase was made by the legal payment of our debt, the satisfaction of justice, to ransom our souls from the hands of divine justice and the penalty of the law. It was a particular purchase. Christ purchased his church. All God's elect, the chosen members of this church, were purchased by Christ. It was a complete purchase. Christ purchased all his people at once out from under the curse and penalty of the law (Galatians 3:13). It was an effectual purchase. When he is finished with all things, all for whom the Son of God died shall stand before the holy Lord God in perfect holiness (Ephesians 5:25-27).

What is the purpose of the church?

Why did our Lord establish his church in this world? Why did the apostles gather believers into local churches in every city? What is the purpose of our existence as a local church? In 1 Timothy 3:15-16, the apostle Paul tells us that the church is 'the pillar and ground of the truth'.

We are not the source of truth; but we are the pillar and ground of the truth. We are not the devisors of truth, but the dispensers of truth. It is our responsibility to preserve the truth, promote the truth, and proclaim the truth of God in the generation in which we live. Truth is the legacy we have received from the preceding generation; and truth is the legacy we must leave to the generation to come. That particular body of truth, which we are responsible to maintain, is the gospel of Christ. Our creed is 'Christ and him crucified'. The truth we maintain and declare is the great 'mystery of godliness', redemption by Christ, the incarnate God. Let us never lose sight of our divinely ordained purpose in this world.

How is the Church to be governed?

At first, the church was under the direct government of Christ himself. Then, it was governed by the apostles of our Lord. They, by the direction of God the Holy Spirit (Acts 6), appointed deacons to relieve them of the mundane duties of watching over matters of money, property, and the care of widows. As the apostles died out, the pastors they had appointed in different places had the responsibility of being overseers of the churches. Sometimes the pastor is called 'elder', and sometimes 'bishop' in the New Testament. But wherever you read the words 'elder', 'bishop', and 'pastor' in the New Testament, the men mentioned are the same, they are pastors, under-shepherds to Christ, overseers of the church, spiritual rulers in the house of God.

The church of God is not a political body, or a business corporation, or a social club or organization to be ruled by the democratic vote of the people or the whims of men. The commonly accepted practice of congregational rule among Baptist churches is totally without foundation in the Word of God. The church of God is a kingdom, under the rule of Christ. It is governed by Christ's appointed pastors, through the Word of God, as they are taught and led by the Spirit of God (Hebrews 13:7, 17).

It is the pastor's responsibility to rule in the house of God (1 Timothy 3:1-7). He does not rule by bullish force, or intimidation, or legislative power; but he does rule. He is to rule in the house of God in precisely the same way a husband is to rule in his own house. The pastor rules the house of God by the Word of God. He rules by his own example of faith and faithfulness. As God's overseer, he rules the church in love, love for Christ, love for the truth, and love for the people of God. The pastor must rule the house of God as he is led by the Holy Spirit, for the glory of God.

I know that giving one man such power over so many can be a very dangerous thing, if that man is not himself ruled by the Spirit of Christ. Many have suffered greatly by the abuse of pastoral authority. However, the answer to the problem of abuse is not to restrict the pastoral office, but rather to seek the direction of the

Holy Spirit in choosing a pastor, carefully following the guidelines of holy scripture, and praying for God's mercy and grace to abide upon, preserve, and keep the pastor in the way of truth, faith, and righteousness.

When a local church is ruled by the voice of the people, there is no limit to the evil that may be done. In the Word of God, I find four places, only four, where the course of action for God's people was decided and determined by the congregation (Exodus 32:1-6; Numbers 16:1-4; 1 Chronicles 13:1-14; Acts 12:15-26). The results are a commentary on the subject of congregational rule. In Exodus 32:1-6, the children of Israel are seen dancing naked around the golden calves. In Numbers 16:1-4, they tried to kill God's prophet, Moses. In 1 Chronicles 13:1-14, the Lord made a breach upon the people, because they defiled the ark of God. In Acts 1:15-26, the church chose an apostle God had not ordained. The axiom of democracy is 'the people are always right'. But in spiritual matters the majority is almost always wrong. The majority almost never rules according to the mind of God.

It is the responsibility of God's church to follow and obey that man who rules over it as pastor by the will of God. Again I emphasize the importance of local churches exercising great care in calling a pastor. They should get to know all they possibly can about him. Make certain that he measures up to the requirements laid down in holy scripture. If he does not measure up, no matter how well he can preach, no matter how likeable he appears to be, he must not be called as pastor. Once a man has been called as pastor, the church has placed herself under his rule. If he is God's man, it will be a blessed relationship. If he is not, it will be disaster.

It is every believer's responsibility to yield a voluntary subjection and obedience to your pastor as God's messenger to your soul. It is an obedience based upon love and trust. If you are not happy with your pastor, if you have reason to question his ability to faithfully watch over your soul, you can do one of two things: (1) You can ask God to remove him, and wait for him to do it. Or, (2) you can quietly remove yourself from his rule. In either case, you had better be very sure of what you are doing. You must never dare to assume that it is your responsibility to remove your pastor. That is God's work.

How do people unite with and join the church?

A person is united with the church universal when he is united with Christ by faith. A local church must be joined by some public act. Many think church membership is insignificant; and there are some who place too much importance upon it, making church membership a basis of hope before God. Still, in the New Testament, believers did publicly unite with one another in local churches (Acts 9:26-27; Romans 16:1-2).

A local church is an assembly, or congregation, of believing men and women, united to Christ and one another in love. A local church is a society of saved sinners, knit together by the Spirit of God. According to the pattern laid down in Acts 2, four things are necessary for membership in the church of God.

1. You must hear Christ preached (vv. 14-40).
2. You must believe the gospel (v. 41).
3. You must confess Christ in baptism (v. 41).
4. You must be compelled by Christ, by the direction of his Spirit to unite with his people. You must make a public identification with and commitment to the people of God (vv. 41-47).

Every local church, if it is truly the church of God, is an habitation of God through the Spirit (Ephesians 2:20-22; 1 Corinthians 3:16). The church is more than a mere unit of men. It is a union of hearts. It is more than a bare uniformity of doctrine, though that is important. It is a union of spiritual life in Christ (Ephesians 4:1-7). We are 'one body', united to Christ our Head. We are made to live by and in 'one Spirit'. We all have 'one hope'. Our hope is Christ our Substitute. We all submit to 'one Lord', our crucified and exalted Redeemer. We all live by 'one faith', the faith of Christ who loved us and gave himself for us. The object of our faith is One – Christ.

The doctrine of our faith is one – the gospel. The goal of our faith is one – the glory of God. We have all been buried with Christ by 'one baptism' into his death. We all worship 'one God', who is the Father of us all.

Those are the things that characterize the church of God. If those things describe any local church, it is 'the church of God'. If they do not, it is just another religious club, with a name that it lives, but is dead!

What does church membership involve?

It is one thing to have your name on a church role, but it is something else to be a member of the church of God. Church membership is an alliance of hearts to one another in Christ. It is a voluntary commitment of love, a loving commitment to Christ and to one another for Christ's sake. To unite with the church of God is to make a public commitment to the worship of Christ, the gospel of Christ, and the church of Christ.

Church membership involves commitment to the worship of our Lord Jesus Christ. Local church families come together to read his Word, sing his praise, observe his ordinances, call upon his name, and be instructed in his gospel (Acts 2:42).

It involves commitment to the gospel of Christ. All true churches are united in the defence of the gospel and the furtherance of the gospel. For this reason, we assemble to hear the Word, give to publish the Word, and go forth to proclaim the Word. Together believers as a local assembly support one man to give himself to the ministry of the Word, so that he may feed their souls with knowledge and understanding (Jeremiah 3:15). Together they help supply the needs of pastors, missionaries, and evangelists around the world, so that they may publish the gospel without distraction by carnal cares. Together they publish the gospel around the world that others might know the gospel and worship our God.

Church membership involves commitment to the church of Christ. Believers are committed to one another for Christ's sake. In a local church the members of the family are devoted, their very hearts are devoted to one another (Philippians 2:1-4). God's people love each other, pray for each other, encourage each other, and forgive each other. That is the way families live.

Why should I join the church of God?

Perhaps you have been debating the matter of church membership in your mind. You may be looking for biblical reasons to join the church of God. I could give you numerous reasons from the scriptures why you should unite with a local New Testament church; but I will give you just one. If you are a believer, if you trust Christ, if you are born again by the grace of God, here is one reason why you should unite with the church of God, you need us! You need the regular ministry of the gospel. You need the fellowship of God's family. You need the help, strength, and encouragement of your brethren (Hebrews 10:24-25).

The church of God is neither more nor less than an assembly of men and women whose hearts are united together in the faith of the gospel, the fellowship of the Spirit, and the love of Christ. Every true local church has all that any church should have.

A Priesthood: The priesthood of every believer in Christ.

An Altar: Christ Himself.

A Sacrifice: The blood of Jesus Christ.

A Law: The law of Christ our Head, the law of faith and love.

A Creed: The Word of God, the Revelation of Jesus Christ.

A Message: Jesus Christ and him crucified.

A Programme (with activities for every age-group): Prayer, praise, and preaching.

A Goal for which we strive earnestly: The Glory of God.

As Moses said to Jethro, his father-in-law, so I say to saved sinners everywhere: – 'Come, thou, with us and we will do thee good'.

'Then they that gladly received his word were baptized: and the same day there were added unto them about three thousand souls ... And they continued steadfastly in the apostles' doctrine and fellowship, and in breaking of bread, and in prayers ... And fear came upon every soul: and many wonders and signs were done by the apostles. And all that believed were together, and had all things common; ... And sold their possessions and goods, and parted them to all men, as every man had need ... And they, continuing daily with one accord in the temple, and breaking bread from house to house, did eat their meat with gladness and singleness of heart ... Praising God, and having favour with all the people. And the Lord added to the church daily such as should be saved'.
(Acts 2:41-47)

Chapter 66

Three Gospel Ordinances

In Acts 2 Peter preached the gospel to a great multitude on the day of Pentecost. He simply told them the wondrous story of redemption and grace by Christ, and proclaimed the glorious exaltation of Christ as Lord and King of the universe. He preached with the power of God the Holy Spirit upon him; and three thousand people were converted by the grace of God, baptized, and united with the church in one day!

Three things characterized this early church, three things which were tokens of God's blessings upon his people at Jerusalem, baptism, church membership, and the Lord's supper. These are things which should be of great interest and concern to every believer. They are matters about which every local church needs to be informed and well established. In this study we will examine what the Word of God has to say about our responsibilities as believers regarding these ordinances of the gospel.

We recognize the fact that the church of God is made up of all true believers in every age. God's elect are his church. Some are in heaven, and some are on the earth. Yet, we are all one body in Christ (Matthew 16:18; Ephesians 1:22-23; 3:15-16; 5:25-27; Hebrews 12:22-24). We also recognize that the New Testament places great emphasis upon the importance of the local church (Matthew 18:20; 28:18-20; 1 Timothy 3:15).

The great commission was given to and is carried out by local churches. Local churches support, maintain, and send out pastors, missionaries, and evangelists to preach the gospel. Local churches administer the ordinances of Christ. The local church is a family, a brotherhood, a body of believers united together in Christ (1 Corinthians 12:25-27). Every local church should be a miniature of the church universal, a habitation of God through the Spirit (Ephesians 2:20-22; 4:1-7).

Our relationship to the church of Christ is a matter of obedience to Christ himself. The importance of a believer's relationship and faithfulness to the local church cannot be overemphasized. It is a great privilege and blessing to be a part of a true gospel church. With this great privilege, we assume a great responsibility. Our relationship with the church of Christ, in great measure, reveals our relationship to Christ.

Obviously, I cannot begin to explain all that the Bible teaches about baptism, church membership, and the Lord's supper in a single chapter. That is not my intention. I want to simply give you a brief definition of these three things and encourage you to honour our Lord by faithful obedience to him in these three areas.

Baptism

Baptism is the believer's confession of faith in Christ (Romans 6:1-11). If we want to know what the Bible teaches about a specific doctrine, we must go to that place in the Bible where that doctrine is taught and explained. Romans 6 explains the meaning of believer's baptism.

What shall we say then? Shall we continue in sin, that grace may abound? ... God forbid. How shall we, that are dead to sin, live any longer therein? ... Know ye not, that so many of us as were baptized into Jesus Christ were baptized into his death? ... Therefore we are buried with him by baptism into death: that like as Christ was raised up from the dead by the glory of the Father, even so we also should walk in newness of life ... For if we have been planted together in the likeness of his death, we shall be also in the likeness of his resurrection: ... Knowing this, that our old man is crucified with him, that the body of sin might be destroyed, that henceforth we should not serve sin ... For he that is dead is freed from sin. ... Now if we be dead with Christ, we believe that we shall also live with him: ... Knowing that Christ being raised from the dead dieth no more; death hath no more dominion over him ... For in that he died, he died unto sin once: but in that he liveth, he liveth unto God ... Likewise reckon ye also yourselves to be dead indeed unto sin, but alive unto God through Jesus Christ our Lord. (Romans 6:1-11)

What is baptism? Baptism is a symbolic picture of the gospel (Acts 22:16; 1 Peter 3:21). It is the means by which believers publicly confess faith in and consecration to the Lord Jesus Christ, showing symbolically how God has saved us through the death, burial, and resurrection of Christ as our Substitute. By this means, we publicly identify ourselves with Christ, his gospel, and his people.

Baptism is a publicly avowed commitment to the glory of Christ. All believers are to be baptized, and only believers. Nowhere in holy scripture is there even a hint of unbelieving children being baptized. The solitary requirement for any to be baptized is faith in Christ; but that faith is the condition that must be met before any can be baptized (Acts 2:38-41; 8:37).

How is baptism to be performed? The answer to that question is so obvious in scripture that the question itself is ridiculous. Baptism cannot be performed except by immersion. Not only is it true that none were baptized in the New Testament by any other means, the very word 'baptize' means 'to immerse'. Immersion is not a mode of baptism. Immersion is baptism. Without immersion, there is no baptism (Matthew 3:13-17; Acts 8:38; Colossians 2:12).

Why should all true believers be baptized? Again, the scriptures are clear. Our Lord commands it (Mark 16:15-16). Baptism is not an option, but a requirement. All who believe on the Son of God are required by him to be baptized. It is the answer of a good conscience to God (1 Peter 3:21).

Can a person be saved without baptism? Certainly! All who are saved are saved without baptism. Salvation is the work of God's free and sovereign grace alone. Our works of obedience have absolutely nothing to do with God's gift of grace and salvation. Yet, it must be understood that obedience to Christ is the fruit of God's grace. Anyone who wilfully refuses to obey the ordinances of God is not saved. God's people are not rebels. They obey God's commands; and to us his commands are not grievous.

Should believers ever be rebaptized? No! If a person has been baptized since believing the gospel, there is no reason for him to ever be baptized again. However, if a person was immersed before God granted him faith in Christ, in some profession of false religion, then he needs to be baptized and confess Christ. Baptism in the New Testament is the believer's public confession of faith in and allegiance to the Lord Jesus Christ.

Church membership

Church membership is the believer's fellowship and communion with Christ in his body, the church. Many think little of church membership. Many who profess to be believers are not identified with or committed to any local church. Whatever their reason is, they are wrong. In the New Testament, men and women who followed

Christ, by one means or another, applied for and obtained
membership in local churches. They publicly identified themselves
with and committed themselves to the church of God (Acts 9:26;
Romans 16:1).

Church membership is for believers only. A local church is a
body of believers, voluntarily united together in the name of Christ
for the glory of Christ, the furtherance of the gospel, the salvation
of God's elect, and mutual edification. In many ways church
membership is similar to baptism. Though I was baptized before I
moved to Danville, when I joined Grace Baptist Church, I publicly
identified myself with this congregation and its doctrine. I publicly
committed myself to this church. I said, 'Thy people shall be my
people and thy God shall be my God'.

The fellowship of believers in a local church is vital to their
spiritual welfare. The believer's spiritual growth in the grace and
knowledge of our Lord Jesus Christ is in many ways dependent
upon his relationship to and fellowship with the body of Christ.
Believers need the fellowship of other believers. We need the
encouragement of our brethren. We need the strength of our brethren.
We need one another. The first signs of apostasy are usually seen in
the neglecting of the assembly of God's saints (Hebrews 10:24-29).
Membership in a local, gospel church basically involves these three
things:

1. Commitment

Church membership is an avowed commitment to the body of
Christ (Philippians 2:1-4). The church of Christ is my family. I am
committed to my family. I prefer my family to myself. I seek the
welfare of my family above my own welfare. I seek the happiness
of my family above my own happiness. I seek the comfort of my
family above my own comfort.

God's people are a family; and the members of God's family are
committed to one another. Commitment is dependability, faithfulness,
and loyalty. It always requires a measure of self-denial and self-
sacrifice. It always requires some effort. I pray for my family, support

my family, serve my family, speak well of my family, promote my family, and enjoy the company of my family. My family can count on me. That is what commitment involves. Church membership involves commitment to the family of God.

2. Communion

Church membership also gives us the privilege of communion and fellowship with the body of Christ. 'Behold, how good and how pleasant it is for brethren to dwell together in unity' (Psalm 133:1). We love the fellowship of God's people, because in the fellowship of God's people we find fellowship with Christ (Matthew 18:20). Our Saviour still walks in the midst of the seven golden candlesticks and makes himself known in his churches.

Blessed are those people who are members of a gospel church that enjoys sweet unity and fellowship in the gospel. Let all who are so blessed of God pray that he will ever enable them to zealously guard and promote that unity of the Spirit and bond of peace which he has given them (Ephesians 4:1-6). This unity is not a mystical, or even an emotional thing. The unity of Spirit, the bond of peace that makes a gospel church strong, is a unity of doctrine. All God's people hold the same doctrine. It is the doctrine of Christ. This unity of the Spirit is an agreement of hearts. All who are born of God love the same thing and seek the same thing. We love God our Saviour, seek his glory, his will, and the interests of his kingdom. This unity of the Spirit, the bond of peace that makes local churches strong, involves a willing submission to one another for Christ's sake (Ephesians 5:18-25). Like any earthly family that is strong and united, the family of God is made up of frail, sinful men and women who have many faults; but, loving one another, they cover one another's faults, forgive one another's wrongs, prefer one another's happiness and welfare, and gladly yield to one another's desires.

A true, gospel church is a fellowship of real, sincere love (Ephesians 4:32-5:1). Church membership is more than having your name on the same church register. It is commitment to the body of Christ and communion with Christ in his body. It involves ...

3. Care.

Membership in a local church involves care for the body of Christ (1 Corinthians 12:24-27). The people of God care for and take care of one another. They care for one another in their own local assembly and care for believers everywhere. Without denominational organization, the force of ecclesiastical hierarchy, or pressure from any group outside itself, gospel churches give to the aid of and seek to assist, support, and promote faithful pastors, missionaries, and other churches around the world.

The Lord's supper

The Lord's supper is the believer's remembrance of Christ. One of the most blessed privileges we have in this world is coming together at the Lord's table to celebrate our redemption by eating the bread and drinking the wine set before us at the Lord's table.

This is not an ordinance shrouded in mystery. It is a very simple, but very precious, picture of our redemption by Christ. Every child of God needs to understand what the Lord's supper is, so that he may receive it, enjoy it, and profit by it to the fullest possible degree (1 Corinthians 11:23-30).

Why was the Lord's supper given? It is a symbolic remembrance of Christ and what he has done for us. Like baptism, the Lord's supper sets the gospel before us in picture. The unleavened bread represents his body, the wine represents his blood sacrificed for us. Eating the bread and drinking the wine is a picture of faith feeding upon Christ and his sacrifice. The Lord's supper is a vivid, pictorial proclamation of the gospel.

What are the elements to be used in the Lord's supper? I know that this is a matter of great controversy with some; but the controversy ceases once the meaning of the ordinance is understood. The Lord's supper can be observed only by eating unleavened bread and drinking wine. Why?

1. When Melchizedek, who was a type of Christ, met Abraham, he brought forth bread and wine as the symbols of God's blessing through a sacrifice (Genesis 14:18-20).

2. In the original institution and in all the New Testament churches, the Lord's supper was observed by the use of unleavened bread and wine.

3. Only these elements, unleavened bread and wine, can properly portray our Saviour and his work of redemption.

The unleavened bread represents the spotless, sinless, holy body of our Lord Jesus Christ. The breaking of the bread represents the crushing of our Saviour's body in death to accomplish our redemption. The wine represents the pure, holy, sinless blood of Immanuel, by which our sins were washed away and the covenant of grace was ratified. The two, bread and wine, body and blood separated implies the certain death of our Redeemer.

Who should observe the Lord's supper? When we come together for the observance of this blessed ordinance, we come to the Lord's table. The Lord's table is open to all the Lord's children (Acts 20:1-7). Not only is the Lord's table open to all his children, all his children are commanded by him to receive it. Like baptism, this is not an optional thing. The Son of God does not tell us we ought to do this. He says, 'this do'. The ordinances of divine worship are not optional.

When should the Lord's table be observed? The scriptures lay down no fixed time. Therefore, we must not insist upon any. Yet, three things are obvious:

1. In the New Testament it was observed on the Lord's day.

2. Because it is called the Lord's supper, and because it was originally so, I think it should be observed in the evening.

3. It is to be observed often. Throughout the book of Acts it was observed every week.

What makes us worthy to observe this holy ordinance? Multitudes have been taught to fear receiving the Lord's supper because of personal unworthiness. I would be very fearful if I thought for a moment that I had any personal worthiness to partake of God's ordinance. Our worthiness before God is not in us, but in Christ.

That which makes us worthy of baptism and church membership makes us worthy to receive the Lord's supper; and that is faith in

Christ. Nothing else! Christ is our worthiness. Those who are united to Christ are worthy to receive the bread and wine, for they, and they alone, discern the Lord's body. They know their need of a Substitute and understand how that Christ accomplished redemption by the sacrifice of himself. Those who do not believe are not worthy, because they do not discern the Lord's body. They do not discern the need of our Lord's incarnation. They do not discern the righteousness established by Christ's obedience. They do not discern the satisfaction of justice by the sacrifice of Christ's body upon the cursed tree.

The basis of our faith is the Word of God alone. We must add nothing to it and take nothing from it. We must obey every precept of the Word. We must follow every precedent of the Word. We must reverence every ordinance of Christ given in the Word. It is our responsibility to obey Christ and keep his ordinances, exactly as he gave them. We need never fear doing what our Lord commands us to do.

– Baptism is the believer's confession of faith in Christ.
– Church membership is fellowship and communion with Christ in his body.
– The Lord's supper is the believer's blessed remembrance of Christ.

'For the LORD God is a sun and shield: the LORD will give grace and glory: no good thing will he withhold from them that walk uprightly'.
(Psalm 84:11)

Chapter 67

Grace and Glory

What is heaven? Do God's saints go to heaven immediately when they leave this world? What is the condition, or state, of the saints' existence in heaven? Who shall enter into heaven's glory? Upon what grounds do the saints enter into heaven?

These are the questions I hope to answer in this study. I realize at the outset that I can do no more than scratch the surface of this great subject. The glory that awaits God's saints in heaven and the vastness of our inheritance with Christ is light years beyond the scope of our puny brains. I have no hope of exhausting this subject. I have purposefully avoided all matters of vain curiosity and speculation. It is my purpose to set forth some of those things which are plainly taught in the Word of God about the glorious state of God's saints in heaven.

Psalm 84 is described in the title as 'A Marching Song'. In the eleventh verse God's pilgrims are inspired in their march through this world with these words of promise: 'The Lord will give grace and glory'. The Psalmist takes our minds away from ourselves and calls our attention to 'The Lord', Jehovah, our great God and

Saviour. We must not look to ourselves in any measure for either grace here or glory hereafter. Be sure you understand this. We must not look to ourselves in any measure for either grace here or glory hereafter. The source of grace and glory is the Lord. The security of grace and glory is the Lord. Christ alone is the Rock of our salvation. To him alone we must look for grace and glory.

Gifts

'The Lord will give grace and glory'. The word 'give' declares that neither grace nor glory can be earned, merited, or purchased by man in any way. This text, like all the Word of God, puts us upon the footing of grace. God cannot be obliged by man to bestow his grace; and he cannot be obliged by man to bestow glory. Both grace and glory are free gifts of God; and where he gives one he is sure to give the other.

Inseparable gifts

Grace and glory are inseparable gifts. They are really the same thing. Grace is glory in the seed. Glory is grace in full bloom. Glory begins in grace; and grace is completed in glory. Someone said, 'Grace is glory begun, and glory is grace consummated. Grace is glory in the bud, and glory is grace in the fruit. Grace is the lowest degree of glory, and glory is the highest degree of grace'. These are two great and marvellous gifts, which God bestows upon the fallen sons and daughters of Adam in Christ. The first thing he gives is grace. The last thing he gives is glory. These two gifts comprehend all others.

Grace

'The Lord will give grace'. How we love that word 'grace'. Grace is God's riches at Christ's expense. In the life, experience, and hope of the believer everything is of grace, from the beginning to the end. Every believer gladly confesses, 'By the grace of God I am what I am'.

Oh, to grace how great a debtor,
Daily I'm constrained to be!
Let that grace, LORD, like a fetter,
Bind my wandering heart to Thee.

Read this promise in the boldest letters imaginable and rejoice.
'The Lord will give grace!' The promise comes from God the Lord.
The Lord God almighty, the great Jehovah, the triune God will most
certainly, by his own irresistible power, according to his own
sovereign will, give grace, freely and irreversibly.

To whom?

To whom will the Lord give grace? We know that he will give
grace. It is asserted plainly. Someone is going to get grace from
God; but who? The Lord God will give grace to his own elect
(Romans 9:15-16). Grace belongs to God. It is his sovereign
prerogative to give it to whom he will. There are some among the
fallen sons of men whom God has chosen to be the recipients of his
grace (John 15:16; Matthew 11:25-27). Not one of those chosen in
electing love, before the foundation of the world, to be a vessel of
mercy shall fail to receive that grace before passing out of this world.

The Lord will give grace to every sinner redeemed by Christ's
precious blood. Every sinner redeemed and purchased by Christ
shall be his and shall obtain grace. Christ did not die for nothing!
All whom he redeemed by blood shall have the grace of forgiveness
(Ephesians 1:7; Colossians 1:14). All whom he purchased shall have
the grace of reconciliation (Colossians 1:20). All for whom Christ
was made a curse shall have the grace of free justification (Romans
8:34; Galatians 3:13). All for whom Christ was made to be sin shall
have the grace of righteousness (2 Corinthians 5:21). All for whom
he died shall have the grace of eternal life (John 10:8, 27).

The redemption Christ accomplished in his death is an effectual
redemption, which infallibly secures grace for all his redeemed ones.
Not one of those whom Christ has redeemed from among men shall

perish. Not one of his blood bought sheep shall be lost. Not one member of his body shall be ruined. Not one part of his bride, the church, shall be destroyed. Those whom Christ has redeemed shall most assuredly obtain grace (Ephesians 5:25-27; John 10:16). God's sovereign election and Christ's effectual redemption inspire us to preach the gospel fervently to every creature, because we know that 'the LORD will give grace' to his chosen, blood bought people (Isaiah 53:9-11).

The Lord will give grace to every believing sinner. We do not know who God's elect are, or whom Christ has redeemed, except as they believe the gospel. Yet we are assured by God that every believer is both elect and redeemed, because God promises grace to all who believe (Mark 16:16; John 1:12-13; 3:14, 15, 36; Romans 10:9-13). Indeed, if you and I believe on the Son of God, the Lord has given us grace already. That faith by which we believe is itself the gift and operation of God's grace (Ephesians 2:8; Colossians 2:12).

The long and short of the gospel is this: If you believe on the Lord Jesus Christ, if you trust his precious blood alone for your salvation and eternal acceptance with God, he will give you grace. I know that a sinner cannot believe unless he has grace. I also know that you cannot have grace unless you believe. To every believing sinner it is promised, 'The LORD will give grace'.

What grace?

What is this grace, which God promises to give? The psalmist does not say, 'The Lord will give some grace', 'graces', or 'a grace'. The text reads, 'The Lord will give grace'. The implication is that wherever the Lord gives any grace, he gives all grace. 'The Lord will give' regenerating grace (Ephesians 2:1-5), justifying grace (Romans 5:1-11), sanctifying grace (Hebrews 10:10-14), preserving grace (Philippians 1:6), instructing grace (John 16:13), directing grace (Proverbs 3:5-6), comforting grace (John 16:7; Lamentations 3:21-26), reviving grace (Isaiah 57:15), and sufficient grace (2 Corinthians 12:9).

> He giveth more grace when the burdens grow greater,
> He sendeth more strength when the labours increase;
> To added affliction He addeth His mercy,
> To multiplied trials, His multiplied peace.

How?

How does the Lord give us his grace? God gives his grace to sinners mediatorially, through Christ our Mediator, through the use of the means he has ordained. Without question, God's saving grace comes to chosen sinners before they seek it (Isaiah 65:1). Yet, those who are sought of God are caused by grace to seek him; and he promises that all who earnestly seek him shall find him (Jeremiah 29:13-14).

Believers are people who seek the Lord and seek his grace in Christ continually. He gives grace to those who seek it by prayer, through his Word, and in the keeping of his ordinances. These are the means by which God's grace is constantly bestowed upon his saints in this world. God gives us his grace seasonably. As our days demand, his grace is given. The Lord our God gives us his grace readily. He is always ready to be gracious. The Lord our God gives us his grace constantly.

> At home, or abroad, on the land and the sea,
> As thy days shall demand shall thy strength ever be!

Read this promise as broadly as you will. It is to you, child of God, in every condition and circumstance of life, 'The LORD will give grace'. He will give you grace to serve Him (2 Corinthians 12:9). He will give you grace to suffer for him (Philippians 4:13). He will give you grace to endure temptations (1 Corinthians 10:13). He will give you grace to die in him (2 Timothy 4:6-8).

Who?

Who is it that will give grace? 'The Lord will give grace!' Grace is the gift of God alone. You will not get grace from yourself, from the church, from some imaginary priest, at some imaginary altar, or from the law of God. If we would get grace, we must get it from God alone. The only way God gives grace is through Christ (John 1:16-17). Look to Christ! Trust Christ! Believe Christ! Cling to Christ! As we do, 'The Lord, will give grace!'

Glory

'The Lord will give glory'. The psalmist says, 'The Lord will give grace and glory'. That little connecting word, 'and', is more precious than gold. It is an indestructible rivet, forever uniting grace and glory. There are many who seem determined to take the rivet out; but they cannot. The text does not say, 'The Lord will give grace and perdition', or 'grace and purgatory', but 'The Lord will give grace and glory'. The text does not promise glory without grace. You can no more have glory without grace than you can have grace without glory. The two are riveted together. What God has joined together let no man put asunder.

If we have grace, we shall have glory, too. God will not give one without the other. Grace is the bud. Glory is the flower. Grace is the fountain. Glory is the river. Grace is the first fruit. Glory is the full harvest. If we have grace, we shall never perish. We shall have glory. But those who do not have grace here shall never have glory hereafter. It is not possible for any to be glorified who have not first been justified. You cannot reign with Christ in glory if Christ does not reign in you by grace. Grace and glory are inseparable gifts of God. 'The Lord will give grace and glory'.

What is the glory that he shall give? I am fully aware that no puny, earthly brain can comprehend it (1 Corinthians 2:9). But God has revealed something of the glory that awaits us, that our hearts may be drawn to it (1 Corinthians 2:10).

The glory of heaven

The glory we are to receive is the glory of heaven. Whatever heaven is, God will give. It is a place of indescribable beauty. It is a state of indescribable bliss. Whatever may be meant, by the figurative language that describes it[1], all of heaven shall be ours forever. The Lord will give the perfection of glory without measure to all to whom he has given grace without measure. You and I who trust Christ shall sit down with Abraham, Isaac, and Jacob at the throne of Christ the Lamb in the kingdom of God.

The glory of eternity

The glory God will give is the glory of eternity. Eternity! Who can define it? No one on earth can fathom the meaning of the word 'eternity'. We always confound eternity with time. We speak of the 'endless ages of eternity'. But there are no ages in eternity in the sense that we measure time. Eternity will never pause, decline, or approach its conclusion. We will never grow weary of eternity. We will never grow weary in eternity. Eternity is unchanging bliss.

The glory of Christ

Moreover, the glory God will give his saints is the glory of Christ, our Mediator, Surety, and Covenant Head (Romans 8:17; John 17:5, 22). Whatever that glory is which Christ has as our Mediator, as the reward of his perfect obedience to God, we shall have when we see him as he is in heaven. My heart pants to know, by actual experience, the meaning of what I have just written. Oh, to know the glory that awaits us! Now we look through a glass darkly. We long to see him face to face, to have the clouds of darkness swept away, that we might know and enter into his glory! In the serene atmosphere of heaven, we shall not only see the King in his beauty, but also possess his glory!

The glory of victory

This glory will be the glory of total victory. We are more than conquerors through Christ our Lord (Romans 8:32-39). By the grace

---

[1] The streets of pure gold, the gates of pearl, the walls of jasper, the crowns, the palms, the harps, the songs, the river of the water of life, the trees bearing fruit, the tree of life, all that these things describe heaven is.

of God and the blood of the Lamb, we shall yet be victorious over the world, the flesh, and the devil (Romans 16:20). Death shall do us no harm, sin shall bring us no more grief, Satan shall tempt us no more, when the Lord gives us glory.

The glory of a perfect nature

The glory the Lord will give us is the glory of a perfect nature (Ephesians 5:25-27; Jude 24-25). This was and is the purpose and goal of God in predestination, election, redemption, and regeneration. God's work will not fail to accomplish his purpose. In heaven we shall have a perfect nature, spotless, sinless, incorruptible; – bodies without weakness, sickness, decay, or death; – souls incapable of temptation, sin, care, or trouble; – hearts free of unbelief, sorrow, and pain; – and wills in complete harmony with God's will. Imagine that! In glory we will possess perfect natures! Holiness, perfect holiness shall be ours!

The glory of perfect rest

The glory promised in our text is the glory of perfect rest (Hebrews 4:9-11). Heaven's glory shall be a perpetual sabbath, an endless day of perfect peace, perfect happiness, perfect security. Spurgeon once said,

> It shall not be possible for a man to have a wish ungratified, nor a desire unfulfilled. Every power shall find ample employment without weariness. And every passion shall have full indulgence, without so much as a fear of sin.

This is rest! This is glory! We shall want what our Saviour wants, do what our Saviour wills, love what our Saviour loves, and live for our Saviour's glory perfectly.

This glory is a gift of God's rich, free, abundant grace in Christ. 'The LORD will give grace and glory'. There is not a soul in heaven that came there by his own merit. There is not a crown in heaven earned by the works of men. There is not a note of self-righteousness to mar the song of the redeemed. Glory is the gift of God.

When?

When will the Lord give us this glory? Some will receive glory very soon. For some it will, perhaps, be a while yet. But of this we can be absolutely sure: – 'The Lord will give glory' as soon as our work here is done, no sooner and no later. And 'the Lord will give glory' at the hour he has purposed from eternity, no sooner and no later. Let us ever comfort one another with these words: – 'The Lord will give grace and glory'. Our trials and troubles here are not worthy to be compared with the glory that awaits us (Romans 8:18).

'So I returned, and considered all the oppressions that are done under the sun: and behold the tears of such as were oppressed, and they had no comforter; and on the side of their oppressors there was power; but they had no comforter. Wherefore I praised the dead which are already dead more than the living which are yet alive'.
(Ecclesiastes 4:1-2)

Chapter 68

Where Have They Gone?
What Are They Doing There?

The wise man, Solomon, after considering 'all the oppressions that are done under the sun', the tears of the oppressed in this world, the power of those who oppress, and the fact that there is no comfort for God's saints in this world of woe, said, 'I praised the dead which are already dead more than the living which are yet alive'. In the book of Revelation, we read a similar statement: – 'Blessed are the dead which die in the Lord' (14:13).

Yet, when you and I go to the funeral home and graveside to bid our loved ones good-bye, we are filled with sorrow and weeping. Why is that so? If the one God has taken is an unbeliever, the grief and sorrow is understandable. Those who die without Christ die under the wrath of God! If our sorrow is the sorrow of parting friends, that, too, is understandable. None of us like to part with cherished friends and loved ones. But if the sorrow is the sorrow of those who have no hope, uncontrollable anguish, or even anger at God for having taken someone we love, that is neither understandable nor excusable. Such sorrow reveals both ignorance and unbelief: ignorance of the blessed state of God's saints in heaven, and unbelief regarding the Word of God, the promises of the gospel, and the finished work of Christ. God's saints in heaven, our departed friends are alive and well. Though their bodies have died and have been laid in the earth, they are now more alive and more full of happiness than ever before.

Immediate glory

First, I want you to see from the Word of God that the soul of a redeemed sinner, immediately after death, enters into heaven, into a state of everlasting happiness. It is not my intention to answer the foolish questions of infidels and heretics. Neither will I allow myself to be sidetracked by the foolish speculations of ignorant men and women about life after death. My purpose in this chapter is threefold:

1. Comfort and instruct God's saints,
2. Persuade sinners to seek Christ, and
3. Honour God in the process.

Therefore, everything I have to say about the wonder of immortality will be written with utter simplicity, appealing to no authority but the Word of God.

You and I are men and women with immortal, undying souls. Though these bodies must die and rot in the earth like the brute beasts, our souls will exist forever. As soon as you die your soul will enter into a state of endless happiness or misery. Man does not die like a dog. When your dog dies, that is all. It ceases to be. But when you die, that is not all. Your soul lives on, not in a state of sleep, insensitivity, and inactivity, but in the fulness of life and consciousness. Therefore, our Lord urges this question: – 'What will it profit a man if he should gain the whole world and lose his own soul?'

The souls of believers, redeemed sinners, men and women who have been made righteous before God by the righteousness of Christ imputed to them, the souls of God's saints return to God at death. Our departed brothers and sisters, as soon as they closed their eyes in death, opened them again in glory. There they shall remain until the second coming of Christ. When Christ comes again in his glory, he will bring them all with him, raise their bodies from the dust, and reunite their bodies and souls in resurrection glory. Believers yet living when Christ comes back then shall be changed, glorified, and caught up into glory to be forever with the Lord (1 Thessalonians 4:13-18).

I will not now say anything about the horrible state of the wicked and unbelieving after death. They shall immediately, as soon as they close their eyes in death, wake up in the torments of hell. O sinner, how I wish you could realize the fearfulness of your condition. The wrath of God is upon you. If you die without Christ, you must be forever damned! To die without Christ is to die without hope! But for the believer, things are different. The believer, as soon as he dies, is alive forever. At once his soul goes home to God in heaven (2 Corinthians 5:1-9).

The Word of God, when speaking of the believer's death, always represents it as an immediate entrance into heavenly blessedness and glory. There is no delay. Actually, for the believer, death is not death at all, but the beginning of life. Our Lord said, 'Whosoever liveth and believeth in me shall never die' (John 11:26). God's elect never die! The death of the body is the liberty of the soul. As soon as our souls are freed from this body of sin and death, we shall enter heaven.

When the righteous perish from the earth they live in uprightness forever (Isaiah 57:1-2). The righteous are those men and women who are born of God, made righteous by grace: in justification by imputed righteousness and in regeneration by imparted righteousness. When the righteous die, they are taken away from evil. They enter into a world of peace. Their bodies are in the grave, but their souls rest in the arms of Christ (Hebrews 4:9-11). They walk in their uprightness. God reckons the righteousness of Christ imputed to us to be our righteousness. And he makes it ours. In heaven, our departed brethren walk in their uprightness, in spotless purity and holiness, in shining robes of bliss and glory.

As soon as a believer dies, he is carried by God's angels into heaven, Abraham's bosom, the place of endless comfort (Luke 16:22-25). 'Abraham's bosom' was a Jewish expression referring to the place of heavenly happiness prepared for God's saints between death and the resurrection.

Every believing sinner, as soon as he dies, is taken to be with Christ in Paradise (Luke 23:43). Paradise is heaven, the garden of God (Revelation 2:7). It is the third heaven into which Paul was raptured for a brief visit (2 Corinthians 12:2-4), during his pilgrimage here. Paradise is the place of the divine majesty, the place of happiness, pleasure, and endless delight. It was to Paradise that Christ went as soon as he died, to obtain eternal redemption for us (Hebrews 9:12). It is a place of assured blessedness, promised to sinners who seek the mercy of God in Christ. Our Lord Jesus said, to the dying thief, 'Today (immediately) shalt thou (assuredly) be with me (in endless company) in paradise'.

Death for the believer is gain, infinite, immeasurable, gain (Philippians 1:21, 23). Paul believed that, as soon as he departed from this world, he would immediately be with Christ in blessed communion. Believing the Word and promise of God, he looked upon death as a desirable thing.

What is the state of the saint's life between death and the resurrection? I will not say more than the Bible says; but this much I know: The souls of God's saints are not floating around in the sky. They have gone to a specific place, where Christ is. They are assembled as a glorified church (Hebrews 12:22-23). Their souls exist in a recognizable form (Luke 16:23; Matthew 17:3).

Do God's saints in heaven have a body between death and the resurrection? A physical body? No – a spiritual body, a heavenly form, a house for their souls? Most definitely (2 Corinthians 5:1). Every believer, as soon as he leaves this body enters into heavenly glory with Christ. It is this assurance of heavenly glory and bliss that makes death a desirable thing for the believer.

Welcome relief

For the believer the death of his body and the freeing of his soul is a welcome relief (Philippians 1:21-23; Revelation 14:13). While living in this world, we seek to be content with God's good providence. We want to glorify him by living before him in faith, resigning all things to his will. We would not change our lot in life, even if we could. Our heavenly Father knows and always does what is best.

I am not weary of life. I cannot imagine a man in this world having a happier, more tranquil, blessed life than I have. I am blessed of God with a loving, devoted wife and family. I have the blessed privilege of being a part of a gospel church in the sweet fellowship of Christ. I am honoured to be a preacher of the gospel. But life in this world, at best, is a burden to the heaven born soul. In this tabernacle we groan (2 Corinthians 5:1-4). We groan for life! Our hearts cry, 'O wretched man that I am! Who shall deliver me from this body of death!' In this body we struggle with sin. In heaven we shall be free from sin! In this body we are tempted and often fall. In heaven we shall never be tempted and shall never fall. In this body we weep much. In heaven we shall weep no more. In this body we long to be like Christ. In heaven we shall be like Christ. In this body we long for Christ's presence. In heaven we shall forever be with Christ!

I have many friends in heaven whom I dearly love. I miss them. I do not sorrow for them; but, oh, how I envy them! When an eagle is happy in an iron cage, when a sheep is happy in a pack of wolves, when a fish is happy on dry land, then, and not until then, will my soul be happy in this body of flesh! Death for this man will be a welcome relief (Psalm 17:15).

A real place

I have shown you from the scriptures that God's saints, as soon as they die, enter into heaven, and that death for the believer is a welcome relief. I have already shown you that our departed friends have gone to heaven. They have not gone to purgatory. They are not asleep. Our friends who have left us are in heaven. Where is heaven? That is a question I cannot answer. God has not told us. Heaven is a place somewhere outside this world, somewhere outside time. But it is a place, a real place. Heaven is the place where Christ is. Heaven is the place to which he has promised to bring us (John 14:1-3). Heaven is the place where our departed friends are right now (Hebrews 12:22-23). Read 2 Corinthians 5:1-8. In eight verses Paul tells us four things about our death and entrance into heaven.

1. Death is the dissolving of this earthly body. This body is of the earth. This body is only suitable for the earth. This body must return to the earth. The dissolution of this body is no cause for sorrow. It will be like taking off a shoe that hurts my foot, a welcome relief! It will be like laying aside a tool that is no longer needed. It will be like tearing down a tent to move into a house.
2. In heaven, we shall have another house for our souls. 'In my Father's house are many mansions', houses, dwelling places. Our heavenly house shall be a house not made with hands, a house prepared by Christ, a house suitable to our glorious life.
3. As soon as this earthly tabernacle is dissolved, we shall enter that house Christ has prepared for our souls in heaven. There will be no lapse of time, no delay between the dissolving of this body and our entrance into our house in glory.
4. This is not a matter of conjecture, but of certainty. Paul says, 'We know'. We know by the revelation of God in holy scripture, by the earnest of the Spirit (v. 5), and by faith in Christ (v. 7).

What happens to the believer after death? Do you ask me, 'Where have our departed friends gone?' They have gone to heaven. They have gone home. They have gone to be with Christ!

Heavenly employment

What are God's saints doing in heaven? The scriptures speak sparingly with regard to the saints' employment in heaven; but these five things are plainly revealed in the book of God.

1. God's saints in heaven are celebrating and adoring the perfections of God in Christ (Revelation 5:11-12; 7:11-12). Yonder, in Glory Land, redeemed sinners, heavenly saints, ever celebrate and praise the triune God for his glorious holiness, omnipotent power, infinite wisdom, covenant goodness, saving grace, invariable faithfulness, and everlasting love!

2. God's saints in heaven are delightfully employed in beholding the glory of God in the face of Christ (John 17:24). Oh, my soul, what will it be to behold the glory of our Redeemer? We shall forever behold him as he is, with a constantly increasing knowledge of him. Heaven is the Garden of God where the Rose of Sharon is in full blossom; and the fragrance of it perfumes the whole place. Heaven is to behold Christ forever, never taking our eyes off him, and never wanting to.

3. God's saints in heaven are employed in the constant exercise of every spiritual grace. Faith ceases because it is no more needed. Hope is no more because the saints in heaven have their hope fulfilled. But love never ends. There all God's children truly love one another perfectly.

4. God's saints in heaven are employed in the unending service of Christ (Revelation 7:14-15). They are engaged in prayer (Revelation 6:10). They sing the songs of grace to the praise of God, ever celebrating God's electing, redeeming, regenerating, justifying, sanctifying, preserving grace in Christ.

5. God's saints in heaven are engaged in constant, uninterrupted fellowship, communion, and conversation with one another and with the holy angels. We cannot here even begin to imagine what the conversations of saints and angels must be around the throne of God; but this much is sure, they speak constantly about Christ and the rich, free grace of God in him.

Make certain that you are in Christ. Take comfort with regard to those who have gone to heaven. Be assured that our weary, troublesome lives will end soon; and they will end well (2 Corinthians 4:17-5:1). A God given and God sustained faith in Christ is not only sufficient to enable the most feeble believer to overcome the corruptions of the flesh, the allurements of the world, and the temptations of the devil, but also to give him an easy, triumphant passage through death into glory (Exodus 15:16-18). In a sense, faith's last work shall be its greatest. When we are leaving this world, our bodies may convulse with pain, physical unconsciousness may set in, and we may have many spiritual struggles. Yet, once our souls are freed from this body of flesh, we shall be blest with such a sight and sense of our blessed Redeemer as we never had and never could have in this mortal state (Acts 7:55).

> So I returned, and considered all the oppressions that are done under the sun: and behold the tears of such as were oppressed, and they had no comforter; and on the side of their oppressors there was power; but they had no comforter. Wherefore I praised the dead which are already dead more than the living which are yet alive (Ecclesiastes 4:2).

'For the Son of Man is as a man taking a far journey, who left his house, and gave authority to his servants, and to every man his work, and commanded the porter to watch. Watch ye therefore: for ye know not when the master of the house cometh, at even, or at midnight, or at cockcrowing, or in the morning: lest coming suddenly he find you sleeping. And what I say unto you, I say unto all, Watch'.
(Mark 13:34-37)

Chapter 69

The Second Coming of Christ

In the holy scriptures we are assured that our Lord Jesus Christ is coming again. Soon, that One who died as our Substitute at Calvary, arose from the dead, and ascended up into heaven, the exalted God-man, our Lord and King, shall appear on this earth again, in the brightness of his glory, taking vengeance upon all his enemies and bringing the salvation of his elect to its consummate glory. We are also assured that no one knows, or can know, when Christ shall appear. Our Lord has graciously hidden that from us. No man knows, or can know, the exact hour, or day, or even the exact millennium! Those who pretend otherwise are deluded. It is positively evil for us to pry into such matters (Matthew 24:36; Mark 13:32; 1 Thessalonians 5:1; Acts 1:7). However, the scriptures do teach us many things about our Lord's second coming. Those things that are revealed we should seek to know.

The house of God

Our Lord Jesus here compares his church and kingdom to a man's house. The church on earth is the house of God (1 Timothy 3:14-16). Every true gospel church is the peculiar, distinct house of God. There is something almost mystical about the assembled body of Christ. As we gather in his name to worship our God, each local assembly in which the Lord God is truly worshipped becomes the dwelling place and temple of the triune God!

In 1 Timothy 3 Paul speaks of the local church as 'the house of God ... the pillar and ground of the truth'. In Ephesians 2:22, we read that the local Church, every true gospel Church, is 'an habitation of God through the Spirit'. 1 Corinthians 3:16, declares, with regard to the assembled saints in any given place, 'Know ye not that ye are the temple of God, and that the Spirit of God dwelleth in you?' Our Lord Jesus Christ promises in Matthew 18:20, 'Where two or three are gathered together in my name, there am I in the midst of them'. In this parable (Mark 13:34) our Saviour speaks of the church on earth as his own house, his distinct dwelling: – 'For the Son of man is as a man taking a far journey, who left his house'.

The church is called his house because he is the Foundation stone upon which it is built. Just as every stone of a building rests on the foundation, so every believer rests on Christ alone. Christ is the Rock upon which we are built, the sure Foundation of our souls. He is 'The Stone of Israel' (Genesis 49:24; Isaiah 28:16; Acts 4:11-12; Romans 9:33; Ephesians 2:20; 1 Peter 2:6-8). Were it not for the foundation, the whole house would fall into ruins. The floods of judgment and winds of adversity would sweep it away. Were it not for Christ, we would all be swept away by God's anger. But that cannot be! We are rooted, and grounded, and built upon him.

Our Lord rightfully calls the church his house because he alone is the Builder of it. The church is not built by men, not even by faithful men, much less by the entertainment, gimmicks, tricks, and tomfoolery of modern religion. Christ alone builds his Church (Matthew 16:18). Every stone in the building has been placed there by the hands of Christ. Christ himself has taken every stone from the quarry. Look unto the rock whence ye were hewn, and the hole of the pit whence ye were digged. We were all embedded in the world, in sin, in ungodliness and death, and just as firmly so as a rock in the quarry. Only the hands of our omnipotent Saviour could dig us out of the pit.

Our Lord Jesus Christ carries every stone dug from the pit of fallen humanity, and lays it on the Foundation. Once the stone has been quarried, it cannot lift itself; it needs to be carried, and built upon the foundation. We cannot build ourselves on the Son of God. We must be built on him. The hewn stone is carried on the shoulder of the great Master Builder and laid in its ordained place, exactly according to the eternal blueprint of grace. Every stone in this building, which is his house, has been hewn, carried, and put in place by the Son of God. This house is very properly called his house, since he builds every stone of it.

The church is his house because he owns it. Not only does he build it with his hands; he bought it with his own precious blood (Acts 20:28). He purchased his church legally, satisfying all the demands of divine justice for his people. The Son of God purchased his church particularly, having loved it with an everlasting love (Ephesians 5:25). Our Lord's purchase of his church effectually guarantees the everlasting glory of it (Ephesians 5:26-27).

The church of God is called his house because this is where he dwells with his family. Wherever a man's family is, that is his home. Wherever a man's mother and sister and brother dwell, that is his home. This, then, must be Christ's home, for he stretched forth his hand toward his disciples, and said: 'Behold my mother and my brethren; for whosoever shall do the will of my Father which is in heaven, the same is my brother, and sister, and mother'.

A long journey

Our Lord Jesus Christ is like 'a man who taking a far journey' (Mark 13:34). Though the church on earth is his house, and though he dwells with us spiritually, our Saviour is not here physically. He is risen, ascended, exalted and glorified in heaven.

He has gone to take possession of heaven in our name, as our Representative (Hebrews 6:20). When a man goes abroad to purchase a piece of property for himself and his family, he goes on a far journey ahead of his family, in order to take possession of the property. That is what Christ has done for us. He lived and died in order to purchase eternal redemption for his people. He has gone into heaven to take possession of it for us (Hebrews 9:12).

Do you trust Christ as your Surety? Do you believe the Son of God? If you do, then heaven is yours already. You already hold the title deed in your hands. You possess it now and shall possess it forever! Perhaps, you are thinking, 'How can I be a possessor of heaven when I have never been there?' Christ your Surety has taken possession of it in your name.

Look at your Surety, my brother, my sister, in the glory land that is very far off. He calls it ours! 'These things have I spoken unto you, that your joy may be full'. Heaven is our inheritance right now. We possess it now in Christ by eternal predestination (Ephesians 1:11), by legal purchase (Hebrews 9:12), by proxy (Hebrews 6:20), and by divine pledge (Ephesians 1:11-14; 4:30).

Our Lord Jesus has gone into heaven to make intercession for us, to ever plead our cause at the throne. He has gone to intercede for his lost sheep and for his needy family in this world. He has gone to procure all blessings of grace for us. He has gone far above all heavens, there to appear in the presence of God for us, and to ask the very things we need, and to send down all the treasures of heaven upon us. The Lord Jesus has gone to glory to intercede for his sinning saints (1 John 2:1-2).

Our Saviour has gone to prepare a place for us. His word to us is: – 'Let not your heart be troubled: ye believe in God, believe also in me. In my Father's house are many mansions: if it were not so, I would have told you. I go to prepare a place for you. And if I go and prepare a place for you, I will come again, and receive you unto

myself; that where I am, there ye may be also' (John 14:1-3). The
Lord Jesus is preparing a place for us. There we soon shall be.
There we shall be with him, with him in the place he has prepared
for us forever!

His servants

Our Lord Jesus Christ has left us here upon the earth to be his
servants, to serve the interests of his house, his kingdom, and his
glory in this world (v. 34). All God's people are his servants. Each
one has been set in this world, in the place where God has put him,
to serve him in a specific way: – 'For the Son of man is as a man
taking a far journey, who left his house, and gave authority to his
servants, and to every man his work, and commanded the porter to
watch'.

Pastors, elders, and missionaries (gospel preachers whatever the
field of their calling), are servants, and have their work assigned
them. God's preachers are porters who throw open the door of the
house to poor, needy sinners, bidding them 'Come in'. They are
also stewards of the gospel (2 Corinthians 4:1-7), the treasure of
the house, who must rightly divide the Word of truth. Faithful gospel
preachers are men who feed the church of God with knowledge and
understanding (Jeremiah 3:15). Those men who are set over the
house of God are set upon the walls of Zion as watchmen, too
(Ezekiel 33:1-11).

Some people think that preachers alone are God's servants. That
is not so. Christianity is not a spectator sport! Look at our text: –
'He gave to every man his work'. All believers are Christ's servants.
We all have our work to do. I have my work assigned to me; and
you have your work assigned to you. Let us do it faithfully. When
our Saviour found us, he said, 'Go, work in my vineyard'. Find out
what the Lord would have you to do in his vineyard, and do it with
all your might.

Learn to keep to your own work. Each of us has his own peculiar
work assigned to him. We must not leave it. 'Let every man abide in

the same calling wherein he was called'. It is not for me to choose what I will do for Christ. It is mine to do what he has given me the opportunity and ability to do. If you are the Lord Jesus Christ's, you have your work to do for him where you are. Even in poverty, sickness, and in time of great trial, you are Christ's servant and have your work to do for him there as much as the most influential servant of Christ in the world. The smallest twinkling star is as much a servant of God as the mid-day sun. Live for Christ and serve him where you are. That is the place of your service.

The Master comes

Our blessed Master is coming back again, we know not when. The Lord Jesus does not say, 'The Master shall come'. He declares, 'The Master cometh'. 'Behold, he cometh!' Our Master is coming now. 'Watch ye therefore: for ye know not when the master of the house cometh, at even, or at midnight, or at the cockcrowing, or in the morning: lest, coming suddenly, he find you sleeping' (vv. 35, 36).

Yes, our Redeemer is coming again. The whole Bible bears witness to this fact. The Master of the house has been away on his journey for a long time; but he will return. When our Lord left his disciples and ascended up into heaven, a cloud received him out of their sight. As they gazed upon their ascending Lord, looking steadfastly into heaven, the angels said: – 'Ye men of Galilee, why stand ye gazing up into heaven? This same Jesus which is taken up from you into heaven, shall so come in like manner as ye have seen him go into heaven'. He went up in a cloud. He shall come in the clouds.

When Christ comes again, he will appear with unannounced suddenness. The whole Bible bears witness to this as well. Our Master's return shall be 'as a snare shall it come on all them that dwell on the face of the whole earth', – 'The day of the Lord so cometh as a thief in the night', – 'Ye know not when the master of the house cometh'.

His coming will be sudden, sudden to the world, and sudden to the children of God. 'In such an hour as ye think not, the Son of Man cometh'. 'Ye know not when the master of the house cometh, at even, or at midnight, or at cockcrowing, or in the morning'. But at the appointed hour, he shall come again!

Watch

'And what I say unto you I say unto all, Watch' (v. 37). The gospel preacher must watch. Each one must watch over his own soul. Yet, he must watch over the souls of those committed by divine providence to his care. Each believer must watch over his own soul, too. Do not read that word lightly. 'Watch!' Watch against sin. Watch against slothfulness and indifference. Watch against unbelief. Watch against worldliness and the love of the world! Watch for Christ! Do not look for signs, but for the Saviour. As you go about your business of serving him, do so upon the tiptoe of faith in blessed expectation of his appearing: – 'Looking for that blessed hope, and the glorious appearing of the great God and our Saviour Jesus Christ!'

Should any read these lines who are yet without Christ, let the Master's word ring in your heart. 'Watch!' Oh, Christless souls, how dreadful your case is! Death may take you suddenly to eternity! How sudden it often is. You may have no time for repentance, not even the space of a breath to pray! The coming of Christ in judgment shall be more sudden still. You know neither the day nor the hour. You are without God! Without Christ! Without atonement! Without righteousness! Without peace! Without hope! Oh, what will you do in the day of the Lord's fierce anger?

'But I would not have you to be ignorant, brethren, concerning them which are asleep, that ye sorrow not, even as others which have no hope. For if we believe that Jesus died and rose again, even so them also which sleep in Jesus will God bring with him. For this we say unto you by the word of the Lord, that we which are alive and remain unto the coming of the Lord shall not prevent them which are asleep. For the Lord himself shall descend from heaven with a shout, with the voice of the archangel, and with the trump of God: and the dead in Christ shall rise first: Then we which are alive and remain shall be caught up together with them in the clouds, to meet the Lord in the air: and so shall we ever be with the Lord. Wherefore comfort one another with these words'.
(1 Thessalonians 4:13-18)

Chapter 70

When Jesus Comes

Get hold of this blessed fact and ever walk in the awareness and anticipation of it: – Our Lord Jesus Christ is coming again. Just as he came in humiliation to redeem his people, he shall come a second time in power and great glory to resurrect his people from the grave and to reign upon the earth. The promise was given when our Lord ascended up to heaven in glory: – 'This same Jesus, which is taken from you into heaven, shall so come in like manner as ye have seen him go into heaven'. We are 'looking for', anticipating, 'that blessed hope, and the glorious appearing of the great God and our Saviour Jesus Christ'.

There is much about our Lord's second coming that we cannot know until he appears. We must not attempt to pry into that which God has not revealed. Yet, there is much that is revealed in holy scripture about the glorious advent of our King. I want to show you, from the Word of God, what is going to happen when the Lord

Jesus comes again. Here are five facts plainly revealed in the Word
of God about Christ's return.

1. Our Lord could appear at any moment (Revelation 1:7). There is
nothing necessary to prepare for the second coming of the Lord
Jesus Christ. The time is at hand. 'Lift up your heads, your
redemption draweth nigh'. Indeed, the sense of scripture is that our
glorious Redeemer is presently coming; he is on his way now. We
should live, moment by moment, in anticipation of his glorious
appearance.
2. Our Lord is coming in power and great glory (2 Thessalonians
1:7-10). The Bible nowhere speaks of our Lord coming in secret to
rapture the church and then coming again in judgment seven years
later. The second advent of Christ will be a climactic thing. Suddenly,
he shall appear in glory.
3. Our Lord will come in a real body (Revelation 1:7). I will not
attempt to say what the glory of his body will be; but two things are
sure: Christ will come in a physical body, the same body in which
he hung upon the cross. His body will be so glorious, so bright, so
dazzling, that every living creature shall see him, and the earth shall
melt before him.
4. When Christ comes a mighty resurrection shall take place (John
5:28-29). There shall be a resurrection of the just, those who have
been justified freely by the grace of God through the redemption
that is in Christ Jesus. God's elect shall be raised to immortality,
life, and eternal glory. The body of flesh shall be gathered from the
dust, and in those bodies we shall see the Lord, our Redeemer (Job
19:25-27).

There shall also be a resurrection of the unjust, those who are
without righteousness before God. The ungodly, the unbelieving,
shall also be raised, their bodies shall become immortal and united
to their souls, so that they may endure everlasting damnation in
hell.
5. At the second coming of Christ, this world shall be destroyed and
he will create new heavens and a new earth (2 Peter 3:10-14; Romans

8:18-23). God's saints will not spend eternity floating around like ghosts in the air. In these very bodies, we shall live forever upon the new earth. Heaven shall be brought to the earth. Righteousness shall reign here. The paradise of God, the Heavenly City, shall be with men.

The Apostle Paul was inspired of God the Holy Spirit to encourage and comfort his brethren there and believing men and women in all succeeding ages with some plain, simple, easy to understand words of instruction and assurance about Christ's glorious second advent. 1 Thessalonians 4:13-18 is taken entirely up with that blessed hope set before us in the New Testament.

Thessalonica was a large and prosperous city of commerce. Paul came to this city after leaving Philippi, and stayed for about three weeks, preaching every sabbath day. His ministry there was greatly blessed of God. Some Jews, a large number of Gentiles, and many women were converted. This group of new converts was the beginning of a gospel church in Thessalonica. These are the people to whom Paul addressed this his first inspired letter.

The unbelieving Jews of the city were so upset by Paul's success that they raised an angry mob and assaulted the house of Jason where Paul was staying. Paul and Silas escaped by night and went to Berea, and from there they came to Athens. But, being concerned about the welfare of this young church, Paul sent Timothy back to Thessalonica to confirm, establish, and comfort God's saints. He wrote this letter and sent it to the church there, hoping to encourage them in their afflictions and sufferings, and exhort them to stand fast in the faith of Christ and the ordinances of the gospel.

Here are five words of comfort given to believing sinners upon the earth by God the Holy Spirit about the second coming of our Saviour. Our divine Comforter here gives us a word of comfort about our departed friends (vv. 13-15), our Lord's return (v. 16), the living saints (v. 17), our glorious reunion (v. 17), and our final position (v. 17).

Our departed friends

First, we are given a word of comfort about our departed friends (vv. 13-16): – 'But I would not have you to be ignorant, brethren, concerning them which are asleep, that ye sorrow not, even as others which have no hope. For if we believe that Jesus died and rose again, even so them also which sleep in Jesus will God bring with him. For this we say unto you by the word of the Lord, that we which are alive and remain unto the coming of the Lord shall not prevent (go before, *or* precede) them which are asleep ... The dead in Christ shall rise first'.

We have all been to the funeral home. We have taken many to the cemetery. We all have many friends and loved ones who died in the faith. Here Paul admonishes us not to be in sorrow for those who are taken from us, as though we had no hope.

Without question, there is sorrow when a loved one is taken from us. Believers are not unfeeling stoics. Yet, if the one taken from us is a believer, if he has died in Christ, there is no reason for us to be in despair, or to sorrow and mourn as those who have no hope. Do not be ignorant about those who are taken from us.

When the believer dies, he simply falls asleep in the arms of Christ (John 11:11-13; Acts 7:54-60). What could be more comforting than that? It is truly a blessed thing, a thing to be desired, to fall to sleep in the arms of Christ. It is the believer entering into his long awaited sabbath, his rest, with the Lord. The body falls to sleep, and the soul awakes (Revelation 14:13).

Be sure you understand our Lord's teaching about this. It is only the body that sleeps in the grave. The soul never sleeps. At death the soul enters into a state of activity, such as cannot be known in this world. There is no such thing as soul sleep. Immediately upon the death of the body, the soul enters into a temporary state, an intermediate body, in which it lives between death and the resurrection (2 Corinthians 5:1-10; Luke 16:19-31). The children of God go immediately into the bliss of heaven (Luke 23:43; Philippians 1:21-23; Revelation 7:15-17). The unbelieving go immediately into hell (Luke 16:22-23).

None of God's elect die until it pleases the Lord to bring them home. They have left us because the Saviour has taken them to himself! Our departed friends are with the Lord. They are beholding his glory, feeding upon the Tree of Life, and drinking from the Fountain that flows from the throne of God. Why should we weep for them?

When our Lord comes again, their bodies shall be raised from the graves. Those who have died in the faith will lose nothing by having fallen to sleep in Christ. They shall be raised first. We who are alive when Christ comes will have to wait for a moment (really just a split second!), until the dead in Christ arise. It will be glorious waiting, but we will have to wait (vv. 15-16).

May God graciously teach us to live confidently in the hope of the resurrection. The resurrection of Christ secured the resurrection of his people. Christ is called the first fruits of the resurrection, the firstborn from the dead. If he is the first, there must be at least a second. The resurrection of the body is that for which we hope (1 Corinthians 15:17-23; 52-54).

Though this hope of the resurrection was not so bright in the Old Testament church as it is today, it was clearly revealed even to the saints of that age (Psalm 16:9-11; 17:15; 73:24). The wise man said, 'The wicked is driven away in his wickedness: but the righteous hath hope in his death' (Proverbs 14:32). This is what I am saying, Christ arose as our Surety, and as surely as he arose, all who are in him must also rise from the dead (Colossians 3:1-4).

Our Lord's return

Second, Paul gives us a word of comfort about the second coming of our Lord Jesus Christ (v. 16). – 'For the Lord himself shall descend from heaven with a shout, with the voice of the archangel, and with the trump of God: and the dead in Christ shall rise first'.

This is the blessed hope we anticipate. The Lord himself shall descend from heaven. He came once and was despised and rejected of men. He came once in humiliation and sorrow to suffer and die. But he is coming again in power and great glory to reign. In this earth, in the place where the battle was fought and the victory won, King Jesus must reign gloriously.

Our great King shall return with a shout of triumph and victory. The voice of the archangel will go forth and the trump of God shall sound. The trumpet-blast will announce the coming of the great King. It will sound the glorious year of jubilee for God's elect. (Then we shall be free!) The trumpet-blast will announce the mighty conquest of our King. Death will be swallowed up in victory. Satan will be thrown into the lake of fire. Every rebel will be crushed with the rod of his strength and consumed with the brightness of his glory.

Our Lord's coming will be public, visible, and audible. The reverberating sound will go through the universe. Every eye shall see him. All of God's elect shall be gathered unto him from the four corners of the earth. The wicked shall wail because of him, and the saints shall rejoice (2 Thessalonians 1:7-10).

Lift heart and head with hope and joy in anticipation of this great day. Our Lord, Our Redeemer, is coming again! He is coming for his bride. He is coming himself. He is coming ~~soon~~ NOW! Christ the one who stood as my Surety in the covenant! The one who lived for me in perfect righteousness! The one who died for me at Calvary! The one who intercedes for me in heaven! The Lord Jesus Christ is coming for me!

The living saints

Here is a word of comfort regarding the living saints (v. 17): – 'Then we which are alive and remain shall be caught up together with them in the clouds, to meet the Lord in the air: and so shall we ever be with the Lord'.

'We shall not all sleep, but we shall all be changed' (1 Corinthians 15:51). There will be a remnant of God's elect living upon the earth. At the last day, in a moment, in the twinkling of an eye, we shall all be caught up and changed. A glorious transfiguration shall take place. Like Elijah, we shall be swept up into glory in a full array. It could happen today. Blessed thought! Blessed hope!

Our glorious reunion

Fourth, here is a word of comfort concerning our glorious reunion (v. 17): – 'We shall be ... caught up together with them in the clouds to meet the Lord in the air'.

The air is spoken of in scripture as the sphere of Satan's power. He is called 'the prince of the power of the air'. The transfiguration and reunion of Christ's redeemed ones will take place right in the heart of Satan's territory! The Lamb that was slain, and all the hosts of his elect shall be victorious and Satan shall be shamed, mocked, and defeated. Yes, the fiend of hell must be loosed for a little season; but his days are numbered. Soon, King Jesus will throw the old serpent into the lake of fire. And, at that moment, a glorious reunion shall take place. All the saints of God shall be united. This appears to be the order of things:

1. Christ will descend.
2. The dead shall be raised.
3. The living shall be snatched up to meet the Lord.
4. The world shall be destroyed and recreated.
5. We shall come to the earth with Christ.

The word here translated, 'meet' is only used four times in the New Testament (Matthew 25:1, 6; Acts 28:15). It always implies a friendly encounter. One of the old writers explained the use of this word like this: – 'When a king enters the city the loyal go forth to meet him; the criminals, in confinement, await their judge'. It is in this way that the Kingdom of God shall come to the earth (Revelation 21:1-5).

In that blessed hour, Christ shall see of the travail of his soul and shall be satisfied. All who were given to him in the everlasting covenant, redeemed by him at Calvary, called by his Spirit, and all for whom he has made intercession these two thousand years shall be with him. They shall see his face. There shall be one fold and one Shepherd. And they shall be one (John 10:16).

Our final position

Then, Paul gives us this word of comfort regarding our final
position (v. 17): – 'So shall we ever be with the Lord' (Revelation
22:3-5). We have been redeemed by him. We shall be made like him
(1 John 3:2). Then we shall be forever with him. Our Lord Jesus
Christ has gone to prepare a place for us, and when his intercessory
work is done and all his elect are saved, he shall come again and
receive us unto himself that where he is, there we may be also.
Then, his great prayer shall be answered (John 17:24). Earth's
greatest blessing is to find him. Heaven's greatest honour is to be
with him. This is promised to all who trust him.

'Wherefore comfort one another with these words' (v. 18). The
Master has given us his word: – 'Let not your heart be troubled: ye
believe in God, believe also in me. In my Father's house are many
mansions: if it were not so, I would have told you. I go to prepare a
place for you. And if I go and prepare a place for you, I will come
again, and receive you unto myself; that where I am, there ye may
be also' (John 14:1-3). Our departed friends are safe. Our risen
Lord is coming again. We shall soon be changed. Soon the whole
family of God shall be united. We shall forever be with the Lord.

'And God shall wipe away all tears from their eyes; and there shall be no more death, neither sorrow, nor crying, neither shall there be any more pain: for the former things are passed away'. (Revelation 21:4)

Chapter 71

Will there be Degrees of Reward in Heaven?

Will there be degrees of reward in heaven? This is a question around which there has been much controversy throughout the history of the church. Many men whose doctrine has been thoroughly biblical in other areas have been in grave error concerning rewards. I know that I will not settle the controversy surrounding this question in this brief study. That is not my purpose. It is my responsibility to teach those things which become sound doctrine and build up God's elect in the faith of Christ, so that you will not be 'tossed to and fro, and carried about with every wind of doctrine, by the slight of men, and cunning craftiness!'

The issue by which this question must be settled is very clear. Is God's salvation, in its entirety, the work of his free grace in Christ, or is it not? If, as the scriptures everywhere assert, our salvation is altogether the work of God's free grace, if our works have nothing to do with it, and heavenly glory is but the consummation of that salvation, then there can be no degrees of reward in heaven.[1]

---

[1] Salvation involves all that is required to bring a sinner from the ruins of the fall into the glory of heaven.

Without question, salvation is by grace alone, through faith alone, in Christ alone. No part of salvation can be, in any measure, attributed to the will, worth, or works of man (2 Timothy 1:9; Ephesians 2:8-9; Romans 11:6). If it is possible to separate heavenly rewards from salvation, then one might imagine that there shall be degrees of reward in heaven; but if heaven and the glorious inheritance of the saints in heaven is only the consummation of salvation, then the doctrine that there shall be degrees of reward in heaven is but another subtle way of teaching salvation by works! It is impossible to separate heavenly glory from salvation.

The doctrine

What is the doctrine of those who teach degrees of reward in heaven? I realize that some who teach that there are degrees of reward in heaven may have slightly different opinions than others; but basically their doctrine is the same. I do not wish to put words into the mouths of others. So, I will give you the doctrine in the words of one of its leading proponents.

Rewards are offered by God to a believer on the basis of faithful service rendered after salvation. It is clear from scripture that God offers to the lost salvation and for the faithful service of the saved, rewards. Often in theological thinking salvation and rewards are confused. However, these two terms must be carefully distinguished. Salvation is a free gift (John 4:10; Romans 6:23; Ephesians 2:8-9), while rewards are earned by works (Matthew 10:42; Luke 19:17; 1 Corinthians 9:24-25; 2 Timothy 4:7-8). Rewards will be dispensed at the Judgment Seat of Christ (2 Corinthians 5:10; Romans 14:10). The doctrine of rewards is inseparably connected with God's grace. A soul being saved on the basis of divine grace, there is no room for the building up of merit on the part of the believer. Yet, God recognizes an obligation on his part to reward his saved ones for their service to Him. Nothing can be done to merit salvation, but what the believer has achieved for God's glory God recognizes in His great faithfulness with rewards at the Judgment Seat of Christ'. (Merrill F. Unger)

Here are five things involved in the teaching that there will be degrees of reward in heaven, as stated by Mr Unger.

1. Salvation is limited to the initial experience of conversion. – In the Word of God no such separation exists. The scriptures never separate one part of salvation from another (Matthew 10:22; Romans 8:28-30; 13:11; 2 Corinthians 2:10; 2 Timothy 1:9; 1 Peter 2:4).
2. It is possible for a person to be saved and not be a faithful servant of Christ. – Nothing can be more contrary to the words of our Lord (see Luke 14:25-33). There is no such thing as a believer who does not live in submission to Christ as his Lord. Believers do not always act faithfully; but they are all faithful. To be a believer is to be a saint (sanctified) and to be numbered among 'the faithful in Christ Jesus' (Ephesians 1:1).
3. Men and women, by their service to God, put God under obligation to reward them. – What an atrocious statement! Is it possible for a sinful man or woman to do anything to merit God's favour, to earn God's blessing? Can a mere man oblige the Almighty? We are debtors to God. He is not, and cannot be made to be, a debtor to us![2]
4. There will be two judgment days, one for believers and another for unbelievers. – The Word of God never hints at the idea that Christ will come again twice, once in secret and then in open, or that there will be two distinct resurrection days, or that there will be

---

[2] Let the reader ask himself: 'What have I ever done, or even thought, that is worthy of God's acceptance?' If, as every child of God humbly acknowledges, sin is mixed with all we are and do (1 John 1:8-10) and our very righteousnesses are filthy rags in the sight of the infinitely holy Lord God (Isaiah 64:6), we certainly cannot 'oblige' the Almighty on account of our deeds!

two separate days of judgment. Such fabrications are but the inventions of men, in an attempt to make the Word of God fit into their theological systems.

5. Believers will yet have to suffer for their sins! – The doctrine of degrees of reward in heaven unashamedly declares that those for whom Christ has suffered all the wrath of God, whose sins he put away, will yet suffer in heaven for their sins after God saved them, that they will suffer the shame of loss in the presence of those who earned a greater measure of glory, those who by their great goodness obliged God to give them a greater inheritance! The Lord God says otherwise. He declares that he will never charge his people with sin (Romans 4:8; 8:32-34). The doctrine of degrees of reward in heaven is nothing less than a Protestant version of purgatory. Heavenly glory is not everlasting sorrow, but everlasting bliss.

Implications

Such doctrine has unavoidable implications. If the doctrine of degrees of reward in heaven is accepted then it must be acknowledged that heaven's glory is not the reward of grace, but the payment of a debt. It must be acknowledged that heaven is not a place of unmingled joy as the scriptures assert (Revelation 7:15-17; 21:1-5; 22:2-5), but a place of mingled joy and grief. If the doctrine of degrees of reward is accepted, it must also be accepted, contrary to the plainest statements of divine Revelation, that God does withhold some good things from them that walk uprightly, and some evil shall fall upon the just (Psalm 84:11; Proverbs 12:21). Again, if the doctrine of degrees of reward in heaven were accepted, then we would be forced to conclude, in direct opposition to the universal teaching of holy scripture that the blood of Christ and the righteousness of Christ will not alone be sufficient for our acceptance with God, that some part of God's favour, some of the blessings of God, must be earned by us, that salvation is partly a matter of works and not altogether the gift of God's free grace in Christ. These implications are inescapable, and utterly blasphemous. Yet, they must be accepted, if we accept the doctrine of degrees of reward in heaven.

Why has this issue been stated so dogmatically? Why have I dealt with this so pointedly? It could have been passed over with little or no notice. Few, if any, would have realized its omission. Here are five reasons for my decision to write as I have on this matter.

1. The doctrine of degrees of reward in heaven is totally without foundation in the Word of God. Not one passage referred to in support of this doctrine even hints that some saints will have more and some have less in heaven. Not one of the crowns mentioned in the Bible are said to be given only to certain believers. All the saints before the throne have the same golden crowns, crowns which they gladly cast before the feet of the Lamb (Revelation 4:10).

2. It is totally contrary to the plain statements of holy scripture. Here are eight passages of scripture, given without comment, which utterly nullify the absurd doctrine of degrees of reward in heaven.

> – Matthew 20:1-16 'For the kingdom of heaven is like unto a man that is an householder, which went out early in the morning to hire labourers into his vineyard. And when he had agreed with the labourers for a penny a day, he sent them into his vineyard. And he went out about the third hour, and saw others standing idle in the marketplace, And said unto them; Go ye also into the vineyard, and whatsoever is right I will give you. And they went their way. Again he went out about the sixth and ninth hour, and did likewise. And about the eleventh hour he went out, and found others standing idle, and saith unto them, Why stand ye here all the day idle? They say unto him, Because no man hath hired us. He saith unto them, Go ye also into the vineyard; and whatsoever is right, that shall ye receive. So when even was come, the lord of the vineyard saith unto his steward, Call the labourers, and give them their hire, beginning from the last unto the first. And when they came that were hired about the eleventh hour, they received every man a penny. But

when the first came, they supposed that they should have received more; and they likewise received every man a penny. And when they had received it, they murmured against the goodman of the house, Saying, These last have wrought but one hour, and thou hast made them equal unto us, which have borne the burden and heat of the day. But he answered one of them, and said, Friend, I do thee no wrong: didst not thou agree with me for a penny? Take that thine is, and go thy way: I will give unto this last, even as unto thee. Is it not lawful for me to do what I will with mine own? Is thine eye evil, because I am good? So the last shall be first, and the first last: for many be called, but few chosen'.

– Romans 8:17 'And if children, then heirs; heirs of God, and joint-heirs with Christ; if so be that we suffer with him, that we may be also glorified together'.

– Romans 8:29 'For whom he did foreknow, he also did predestinate to be conformed to the image of his Son, that he might be the firstborn among many brethren'.

– Ephesians 1:3 'Blessed be the God and Father of our Lord Jesus Christ, who hath blessed us with all spiritual blessings in heavenly places in Christ':

– Ephesians 5:25-27 'Husbands, love your wives, even as Christ also loved the church, and gave himself for it; That he might sanctify and cleanse it with the washing of water by the word, That he might present it to himself a glorious church, not having spot, or wrinkle, or any such thing; but that it should be holy and without blemish'.

– 1 John 3:1-2 'Behold, what manner of love the Father hath bestowed upon us, that we should be called the sons of God: therefore the world knoweth us not, because it knew him not. Beloved, now are we the sons of God, and it doth not yet appear what we shall be: but we know that, when he shall appear, we shall be like him; for we shall see him as he is'.

– Jude 24 'Now unto him that is able to keep you from falling, and to present you faultless before the presence of his glory with exceeding joy'.

Can there be degrees of holiness, degrees of perfection, degrees of faultlessness, degrees of glorification? Nonsense!

1. The doctrine of degrees of reward, of heavenly rewards earned by personal obedience, makes service to Christ a legal, mercenary thing

Such doctrine promotes pride. If one person could obtain a bigger crown, a higher rank, or a greater nearness to God by his works than another, he would have every reason to polish his halo, strut around heaven, and have those poor, crownless people, living in the back street slums of the New Jerusalem, bow and scrape before him.

Not only does the doctrine promote pride, it threatens punishment. It attempts to put God's people upon a legal footing before God, threatening the loss of reward and everlasting shame, if we do not do what is expected of us. This horrendous doctrine would make all God's saints mercenaries, inspiring obedience and faithfulness by either the threat of punishment or by the promise of reward. I challenge anyone to find a single example of such base, carnal threats against redeemed sinners in the New Testament. Such doctrine is as offensive as it is unscriptural, because both dishonours our God and assumes that God's people do not really love Christ, that they are not motivated, inspired, and governed by that love and by their hearts' concern for the will and glory of God.

2. This base, carnal doctrine of earned reward in heaven robs Christ of the glory of his grace and makes room for human flesh to boast before God

If you and I do something that puts God almighty in obligation to reward us, then we have a right to boast in his presence. If we do something by which we merit a higher standing than others in glory, why should not we boast about it?

3. The doctrine of degrees in glory has the obnoxious odour of works about it; and there is no room for works in the kingdom of grace

The God of Glory will not be worshipped upon an altar of hewn stone (Exodus 20:25). He will not be worshipped upon an altar built by our hands. There is no room for the baggage of works in the strait and narrow way.

One text

There is one text of scripture, which both destroys the doctrine of degrees of reward and assures every believer of an everlasting fulness of joy in glory. The text is Revelation 21:4: – 'And God shall wipe away all tears from their eyes; and there shall be no more death, neither sorrow, nor crying, neither shall there be any more pain: for the former things are passed away'.

Heaven is a place of joy without sorrow, laughter without weeping, pleasantness without pain. In heaven there are no regrets, no remorseful tears, no second thoughts, no lost causes, no sorrows of any kind.

Will you be among the blessed company of the redeemed? Will you be with Christ in glory? You will only enter into glory if you are worthy of heaven. You can only be made worthy by the merits of Christ. If you are worthy of everlasting glory, you shall have all the glory of heaven itself, without degrees, perfectly. The very glory that God the Father gave to the God-man Mediator, that great Mediator has given to his people (John 17:5; 22). Trust Christ and all the glory of Christ in heaven is yours. All who believe on the Son of God are heirs of God, and more, we are joint heirs with Christ!

'God shall wipe away all tears from their eyes; and there shall be no more death, neither sorrow, nor crying, neither shall there be any more pain: for the former things are passed away'.
(Revelation 21:4)

Chapter 72

No Tears – No Exceptions

Every saved sinner has learned by the effectual teaching of God the Holy Spirit what Jonah learned in the whale's belly. Every sinner who has experienced God's omnipotent, saving operations of grace gladly confesses with Jonah, 'Salvation is of the Lord!' For believing men and women, that blessed fact of grace, that universal declaration of holy scripture cannot be stated too fully, too frequently, or too emphatically.

Salvation is, in its entirety, the work of God's free and sovereign grace in Christ. That is the foundation upon which we build all our doctrine. That is the hermeneutic principle upon which we interpret scripture, because it is the hermeneutic principle laid down in scripture.

Salvation is by grace alone, through faith alone, in Christ alone. No part of salvation can be, in any measure, attributed to the will, worth, or works of man. The language of Inspiration could not be more emphatically clear in this regard (2 Timothy 1:9-10; Ephesians 2:8-9; Romans 11:6).

Salvation involves

Be sure you understand this: – Salvation involves all that is required to bring a sinner from the ruins of the fall into the glory of heaven. There is no aspect of salvation, no part of the package, neither on this side of eternity nor on the other, which depends upon or is in any way, or to any degree, determined by man.

God's election of some to salvation is the election of grace. Divine predestination is 'to the praise of the glory of his grace'. Our redemption by the precious blood of Christ, that redemption which purchased and secured for us the forgiveness of all sin forever, was effectually accomplished for us 'according to the riches of his grace'. We are 'justified freely by his grace'. We were born again by the power of God's grace. Our faith in Christ is the gift and operation of the grace of God. We are sanctified by that same free grace. If we persevere unto the end, it will be by that grace of God, which keeps us in grace and faith, being sealed by his Holy Spirit, 'unto the redemption of the purchased possession', that is to say, 'until the day of our resurrection'. When, at last, we stand before our God and Saviour in heaven, we shall possess all the glory of our heavenly inheritance forever, as 'heirs of God and joint-heirs with Jesus Christ', by free grace alone.

When our great God and Saviour says, 'Time shall be no more', when he makes all things new; when he presents us before the presence of the glory of God, holy, unblameable, and unreproveable, without any trace of sin upon us; when he who made all things for himself brings forth the chief cornerstone and puts it in the place of everlasting pre-eminence and glory before heaven, earth and hell, we will shout with Zerubbabel, 'Not by might, nor by power, but by my Spirit, saith the Lord of hosts … crying, Grace, grace unto it!' (Zechariah 4:6,7).

No tears

Because this great and glorious thing we call salvation is all of grace, from start to finish, we are assured that it shall be equally, fully, and perfectly possessed by all who are the heirs of it. So thorough, so complete, so full is God's salvation that when it is finished, there will be absolutely no regrets, no sorrows, and no tears in eternity for God's elect. Difficult as that may be for us to grasp, it is plainly revealed in holy scripture.

'And God shall wipe away all tears from their eyes; and there shall be no more death, neither sorrow, nor crying, neither shall there be any more pain: for the former things are passed away' (Revelation 21:4). Isaiah tells us the same thing. 'He will swallow up death in victory; and the Lord God will wipe away tears from off all faces; and the rebuke of his people shall he take away from off all the earth: for the Lord hath spoken it' (Isaiah 25:8).

Notice the very slight, but very significant difference in the way the two texts (speaking of the same promise) are worded. Isaiah tells us that God will wipe away 'tears from off all faces'. He promises us that God will wipe tears from the faces of all who possess eternal life with Christ in everlasting glory. But in Revelation 21:4, the apostle John tells us that, 'God shall wipe away all tears from their eyes'. By divine inspiration, he gives an added touch of grace. He tells us that our God is not only going to wipe tears from the eyes of all his people, but also that 'God shall wipe away *all tears* from their eyes!'

Put the two texts together and you have the glorious promise of God in the gospel to every believing sinner. It is just this: – when our great and glorious God is finished with all things, he will have so thoroughly and completely saved all his people from all sin and from all the evil consequences of sin forever that there will never be a tear in our eyes again!

Who can grasp the fulness of this promise? It is too great, too broad, too incomprehensible for our mortal brains. Yet, it is gloriously true! Our great God shall, in heaven's glory, remove us from all sin, remove all sin from us, and remove us from all the evil consequences of sin. He will remove us from every cause of grief. He will bring us at last into the perfection of complete salvation and every desire of our hearts will be completely gratified. God's salvation is so perfect and complete that when he is finished, we will not even have the slightest tinge of sorrow for anything.

An implication

Revelation 21:4 clearly implies that there is much weeping in the way to heaven, and there is. Faith in Christ brings deliverance from all curse and condemnation, but not from pain and sorrow. There are many things which believers suffer in this world along with other men. Because the world is a world of sin, it is a world of sorrow. Believers suffer physical pain and sickness, domestic trouble and heartache, financial losses, bereavements and many, many other things, just like all other men and women in this world.

There are many things that bring tears to our eyes about which the world knows nothing. The world knows nothing of the warfare that rages in our souls between the flesh and the spirit. The world knows nothing of our struggles with and weeping over inward sin, unbelief, hardness of heart toward God, and overmuch love of the world and of self. The world knows nothing of our nights of weeping and days filled with sorrow because of our lack of consecration to our God, our lack of devotion to our Saviour, and our lack of submission to the direction of the blessed Holy Spirit.

There are even some precious tears, tears we shed here that will be dried on the other side of Jordan. Here we shed many tears of repentance, many tears of sympathy, many tears of concern for the souls of men and the glory of God, and many tears of longing for the manifest presence of Christ. But all these tears, too, shall be dried forever, once we have been delivered from this world of sin and sorrow.

Present comfort

Do not misunderstand my meaning. Even now, our heavenly Father does much to dry our tears. The believer's life is not a morbid, sorrow-filled existence. Not at all! We do have our sorrows. Yet, even in the midst of sorrow our Lord gives us great comfort (Isaiah 43:1-6).

> But now thus saith the LORD that created thee, O Jacob, and he that formed thee, O Israel, Fear not: for I have redeemed thee, I have called thee by thy name; thou art mine. When thou passest through the waters, I will be with thee; and through the rivers, they shall not overflow thee: when thou walkest through the fire, thou shalt not be burned; neither shall the flame kindle upon thee. For I am the LORD thy God, the Holy One of Israel, thy Saviour: I gave Egypt for thy ransom, Ethiopia and Seba for thee. Since thou wast precious in my sight, thou hast been honourable, and I have loved thee: therefore will I give men for thee, and people for thy life. Fear not: for I am with thee: I will bring thy seed from the east, and gather thee from the west; I will say to the north, Give up; and to the south, Keep not back: bring my sons from far, and my daughters from the ends of the earth.

Even here, our heavenly Father gives us a measure of resignation to his will. He teaches us to trust his providence. He reminds us of his gracious purpose (Romans 8:28-32). He causes us to remember his promises. He blesses us with the sense of his presence. He floods our hearts with the knowledge of his love (Ephesians 3:19). He reminds us that the cause of our pain is his own loving hand (Hebrews 12:5-12). He comforts us by fixing our hearts on better things above (Colossians 3:1-3; 2 Corinthians 4:15-18).

Our prospect

Yet, in heaven's glory our God will wipe all tears from our eyes. Impossible as it is for us to imagine, there is a time coming when we shall weep no more, when we shall have no cause to weep! Heaven is a place of sure, eternal, ever-increasing bliss; and the cause of that bliss is our God! Remember what we have already learned. Heaven is a place of joy without sorrow, laughter without weeping, pleasantness without pain! In heaven there are no regrets, no remorseful tears, no second thoughts, no lost causes, no sorrows of any kind!

If God did not wipe away all tears from our eyes, there would be much weeping in heaven. We would surely weep much over our past sins, unconverted loved ones forever lost in hell, wasted opportunities while we were upon the earth, our many acts of unkindness toward our brethren here, and the terrible price of our redemption! But God will wipe away all tears from our eyes – all of them! In heaven's glory there will be no more death to part loving hearts. There will be no more sorrow of any kind. There will be no more crying for any reason. There will be no more pain of any sort. Why? How can these things be? – 'The former things are passed away!'

Our great God shall, in heaven's glory, remove us from all sin, remove all sin from us, and remove us from all the evil consequences of sin. He will remove us from every cause of grief. He will bring us at last into the perfection of complete salvation and every desire of our hearts will be completely gratified. Then we will be like Christ. We will be with Christ. We will see Christ. We will love Christ perfectly. We will serve Christ unceasingly. We will worship Christ without sin. We will rest in Christ completely. We will enjoy Christ fully. We will have Christ entirely. These things shall be our everlasting experience, without interruption!

'And round about the throne were four and twenty seats: and upon the seats I saw four and twenty elders sitting, clothed in white raiment; and they had on their heads crowns of gold ... The four and twenty elders fall down before him that sat on the throne, and worship him that liveth for ever and ever, and cast their crowns before the throne, saying, Thou art worthy, O Lord, to receive glory and honour and power: for thou hast created all things, and for thy pleasure they are and were created'.
(Revelation 4:4, 10, 11)

Chapter 73

Believers and their Crowns

Let us take a glimpse, just a glimpse, within the veil. Without the evil of vain curiosity or speculation, but with faith, hope, and expectation, I want us to look into some of those things which concern our eternal estate in the glory of heaven.

I realize that we know very little about heaven and the eternal bliss of God's elect there. We know that there is a place of eternal bliss in the presence of God and the holy angels where the people of God shall dwell when time is no more. We know that heaven is a place of happiness, bliss, glory, peace, and love, a place of perfect righteousness and truth, where neither sin nor sinners can enter. Beyond these things, we know little. The Holy Spirit has saved up the details of the next world, refusing to reveal them until we get there. 'As it is written, eye hath not seen, nor ear heard, neither have entered into the heart of man, the things which God hath prepared for them that love him' (1 Corinthians 2:9). We do not know where heaven is. We do not know what our heavenly bodies will be like. We do not know what the events of eternity will be.

We know much about what will not be in heaven. There will be no sickness, no sorrow, no sin. There will be no darkness, no disappointment, no death. There will be no corruption, no care, no crying. There will be no trials, no temptations, no tears. But we really know very little about what there will be in heaven. For now ignorance is best for us. If we knew more about our heavenly inheritance, we would most likely neglect our earthly responsibilities. If all the glory of heaven was revealed our feeble hearts and minds could not now contain it. If we knew more of the future we would probably neglect the present; and that must not be.

However, there are some things plainly revealed about the believer's eternal inheritance in heaven. Those things that are revealed are revealed for our present encouragement, enjoyment, and consolation. The text that heads this chapter speaks of the people of God before the throne, in the presence of our great and glorious Redeemer, the Lord Jesus Christ.

The 'four and twenty elders' represent the whole company of the redeemed in heaven. They are representatives of the whole church of Christ, the whole company of God's elect. They represent all of those who were chosen of God, redeemed by Christ, regenerated by the Holy Spirit, and glorified in the resurrection. These twenty-four elders bear the characteristics of all the saints in their glorified state. They reveal seven things about our eternal bliss in heaven. They tell us seven things which are true of all the people of God in the eternal glory.

1. They are all clothed with white raiment: – The righteousness of Christ.
2. They all worship the Lamb (5:8).
3. They are all redeemed by the blood of the Lamb.
4. They are all around the throne.
5. They are all kings and priests unto God.
6. They shall all reign with Christ on the earth, and
7. They shall all have 'on their heads crowns of gold'.

According to the revelation given in holy scripture, all the people of God shall have crowns of gold on their heads in the beginning of heaven's glory.

What are these crowns?

There are five separate and distinct crowns promised to believers, which the Lord God shall give to his saints. Paul speaks of an incorruptible crown that shall be the reward of perseverance (1 Corinthians 9:24-27). Like runners in a race, the believer must press on, persevering unto the end. He that finishes the race wins the prize. There is no reward to those who give up and fall by the wayside (Philippians 3:13-14; Hebrews 12:1-3).

A crown of life is promised as the reward of faithfulness to the Lord (Revelation 2:10; James 1:12). Those whose trials destroy their faith never really had any true faith. They shall perish. But those who are faithful in their trials prove that their faith is genuine. They shall have the crown of life.

When he was about to leave this world, Paul encouraged himself and found great solace in anticipating that crown of righteousness, which is the reward of those who love Christ at his appearing (2 Timothy 4:6-8). He had every reason to expect it upon his arrival in glory. He tells us, by divine inspiration, that this crown of righteousness is a crown 'which the Lord, the righteous judge, shall give me at that day: and not to me only, but unto all them also that love his appearing'. All who are born of God love Christ and love his appearing (1 John 4:19; 1 Corinthians 16:22; Titus 2:11-14). The Holy Spirit assures us in 2 Timothy 4:8 that all who love Christ and love his appearing shall receive the crown of righteousness.

There is a crown of rejoicing awaiting the Lord's servants (his people), which is the reward of those who seek the salvation of God's elect (1 Thessalonians 2:19-20). 'Children's children are the crown of old men' (Proverbs 17:6). When our Lord Jesus Christ comes in his glory to gather his elect from the four corners of the earth, and he presents them all to his Father, saying, 'Behold, I and the children which God hath given me' (Hebrews 2:13), as he rejoices in the salvation of his elect and the fulness of his body (Ephesians 1:23), the church, so will we. Paul did not glory and rejoice in the fact that he was the instrument of God used to accomplish the conversion of his elect in Thessalonica (cf. 1 Corinthians 3:7). Rather, he gloried and rejoiced in the salvation of God's elect, because the salvation of God's elect is the glory and joy of Christ'.

The scriptures also speak of a crown of glory that is the reward of the believer's union with Christ (1 Peter 5:4). When Christ comes, we shall be like him, for we shall see him as he is. He said, 'The glory which thou gavest me I have given them; that they may be one, even as we are one' (John 17:22).

These five crowns are spoken of distinctly in the New Testament: the incorruptible crown, the crown of life, the crown of righteousness, the crown of rejoicing, and the crown of glory. What are these crowns? Isaiah 28:5 indicates what is clearly the teaching of the entire volume of inspiration in this matter. These five crowns are one crown, and that one crown is the Lord Jesus Christ himself! It is written, 'In that day shall the Lord of hosts be for a crown of glory, and for a diadem of beauty, unto the residue of his people'.

Christ is the prize we seek. Christ is the crown we shall wear. Christ is the reward of his people. What more could we need or desire? Christ is heaven. If we have Christ, we have all. We can want no more! He is our glory. He is our joy. He is our righteousness. He is our life. He is our incorruptible crown. In heaven's eternal glory, 'Christ is all!'

Who shall wear the crowns?

The vision given in Revelation 4 shows all the saints in heaven as kings and priests unto God. They all are crowned as such; and all their crowns are the same: – 'crowns of gold'. That doctrine that teaches that there are degrees of reward in heaven, degrees of glory, and degrees of happiness among the redeemed is totally without foundation in holy scripture. It is nowhere written or implied in the Word of God!

Upon the very surface of things, such doctrine is apparently false. It promises a reward of debt. It promotes pride and self-righteousness. It says that some things are earned by human works as wages that God is obliged to pay. It makes our acceptance and joy in heaven dependent upon our own works, not upon the grace of God. It gives man honour, praise, and glory. Let this heresy be rooted out and dashed to pieces once and for all!

The notion that there will be degrees of reward in heaven runs contrary to everything that is most plainly revealed in the gospel (1 Corinthians 4:7). Our salvation and acceptance before God is a matter of pure, free grace (Ephesians 2:8-9). All the blessings of God were given to all of God's elect in Christ before the world began (Ephesians 1:3; 2 Timothy 1:9). God never accepts, much less rewards, anything but perfection and our perfection is in Christ. Perfection requires a perfect reward; and in Christ all the redeemed are perfect (Colossians 2:10). Our Lord plainly states that our reward shall not be based upon the merits of our service, but upon the purpose of his grace (Matthew 20:1-16).

The Lord God alone shall have the praise of heaven. When we have done the very best that we could do, it is infinitely less than we should have done. We are all unprofitable servants. Would any sane human being really want God to reward him according to his personal merits? Who can stand before Him? – 'He that hath clean hands and a pure heart'.

We do not serve our God being motivated by a desire for gain. We serve the Lord our God being motivated by love and gratitude (2 Corinthians 5:14). God will never reward greed!

The bliss, the glory, the happiness, and the reward of God's elect in heaven shall be equal to all and full in all God's elect. All are equally loved of God. All are equally redeemed by the blood of Christ. All are equally righteous in Christ. All are equally heirs to the covenant of grace and all God's promises (Ephesians 2:11-13).

Who shall wear these crowns of gold? – All the true people of God. Not one of God's elect shall be robbed of any heavenly blessing or privilege.

How do we obtain these crowns?

We see the twenty-four elders around the throne with crowns on their heads. God's elect in heaven, those who have been redeemed by the blood of Christ out of every tribe and tongue and nation in the world, are wearing crowns of pure gold. But how did they get those beautiful crowns of glory?

They got their crowns by the grace of God (Ephesians 1:3). They got their crowns by hereditary descent (Romans 8:16-17). There are none in heaven but the sons of God; and the sons of God shall have their rightful inheritance. They got their crowns by sovereign predestination (Ephesians 1:11-12). They got their crowns by rightful claim. These crowns were purchased for them by the blood of Christ. They were earned for them by the obedience of Christ in the establishing of perfect righteousness. The saints in heaven have been made worthy of these crowns by the imputed righteousness of Christ (Colossians 1:12; Ephesians 5:25-27). Christ himself has already claimed them in the name of all his people (Hebrews 6:20).

Children of God, rejoice, laugh in the face of your trials and troubles here. Soon you shall wear a crown! God will see to it.

What shall we do with these crowns?

'The four and twenty elders fall down before him that sat on the throne, and worship him that liveth for ever and ever, and cast their crowns before the throne, saying, Thou art worthy, O Lord, to receive glory and honour and power: for thou hast created all things, and for thy pleasure they are and were created' (Revelation 4:10-11).

No sooner shall the Lord God place the crowns on our heads than we will willingly, gladly take them off our heads, bow before the feet of our God and Saviour, and cast them down at the foot of the throne of his sovereign majesty and grace, saying, 'Not unto us, O Lord, not unto us, but unto thy name give glory, for thy mercy, and for thy truth's sake' (Psalm 115:1). Why? Because Christ alone is worthy of honour, praise, and glory. He chose us. He redeemed us. He called us. He has preserved us. He shall bring us to glory.

We will cast our crowns before his throne, because we will have a solemn reverence for him. We shall see him as he is, and we will say, 'That no flesh should glory in his presence'. 'He that glorieth, let him glory in the Lord'. We will cast our crowns before his throne, because we will be filled with a deep sense of sincere humility. Each will know then, far better than now, and each will gladly confess, 'I am nothing. I have done nothing (Matthew 25:34-40). I deserve nothing'.

We will cast our crowns before his throne, because we will have a deep sense of gratitude to him. We will acknowledge then perfectly what we know now: – 'By the grace of God I am what I am'. In short, we will cast our crowns before his throne, because we will love him intensely.

> In mansions of glory and endless delight,
> I'll ever adore thee in heaven so bright;
> I'll sing, as I cast down
> the glittering crown from my brow,
> If ever I loved thee, my Jesus, 'tis now.

Do you have such a hope and expectation as this? Do you expect to enter heaven by the grace of God through the blood of Christ and be crowned with everlasting glory? Are you anxious to cast your crown at the feet of Christ? Begin now to do so. Give the Lord the praise and honour due unto his name. Worship him with reverence. Humble yourself before him. Show your gratitude to Christ by your zeal for his glory. Show your love to Christ by your self-sacrificing, self-denying service and devotion to him. Soon, perhaps very soon, we will meet around the throne of our Redeemer, where we shall cast our crowns at his feet and say: – 'Worthy is the Lamb that was slain to receive power, and riches, and wisdom, and strength, and honour, and blessing'.

'And I saw a great white throne, and him that sat on it, from whose face the earth and the heaven fled away; and there was found no place for them. And I saw the dead, small and great, stand before God; and the books were opened: and another book was opened, which is the book of life: and the dead were judged out of those things which were written in the books, according to their works. And the sea gave up the dead which were in it; and death and hell delivered up the dead which were in them: and they were judged every man according to their works. And death and hell were cast into the lake of fire. This is the second death. And whosoever was not found written in the book of life was cast into the lake of fire'. (Revelation 20:11-15)

Chapter 74

The Great White Throne Judgment

When will the day of judgment be? Who will be judged? Who will be the judge? Will there be one judgment or two? Will there be one judgment for believers and another for unbelievers? Will we be judged first by Christ for our sins and second for our works as believers? These are questions about which there is much needless confusion. A careful study of the teachings of the Word of God about the day of judgment will help to clarify our thinking about that great day. No text in the Bible more clearly teaches us what will happen on that day than the passage which heads this page – Revelation 20:11-15. Read it carefully.

This is the throne of judgment, before which we all must appear in the last day. It is called 'a great white throne', to set forth the power, holiness, and sovereignty of the One who sits upon it. It is called 'great' because it is the throne of the omnipotent God. It is called 'white' because it is pure, spotless, righteous, and just. Nothing proceeds from this throne but justice and truth. It is called a 'throne' because the Judge who sits upon it, before whom we all must stand, is the holy, sovereign Lord God. In the last day, when time shall be no more, we all must appear before the august, great, white throne to be judged of God, to be judged according to the strict and exact righteousness and justice of the thrice holy God!

While the Word of God constantly warns the wicked of the terror of divine judgment and the everlasting wrath of God, the day of judgment is never described as a terror to believers, or even a thing to be dreaded by us. Rather, for the believer the day of judgment is always set forth as a matter of anticipated joy and glory. On this earth God's saints are constantly misjudged. His servants are maligned and slandered by reprobate men. In that last great day, God almighty will vindicate his people and he will vindicate his servants (1 Corinthians 4:3-5). In the Word of God, we do not find God's saints dreading that day, but looking forward to it, even anticipating it, with peace. If, as believers, as sinners saved by God's free and sovereign grace, through the sin-atoning blood and imputed righteousness of the Lord Jesus Christ, we understand what the Bible says about that great day, we will look forward to it, too. With those things in mind, let us see what the Bible teaches about the great white throne judgment. I do not claim to be an expert on prophetic matters. But I do know that there are five things clearly revealed in the Word of God about things to come.

Christ's coming

First, the Lord Jesus Christ is coming again. Do not concern yourself about the signs of the times and those things that men imagine are indications of the last days. There is very little, if anything, of spiritual value to be gained by studying all the books ever written on prophetic issues. They all have to be rewritten as soon as the predicted events have failed to come to pass! We are never commanded to look for signs of our Lord's coming. We are commanded to be looking for him to come!

Get this one blessed fact fixed in your mind: – Jesus Christ, our Lord, our Saviour, the Son of God, is coming again! The Son of God is personally coming again to this earth (Acts 1:9-11). That very same God-man who was born at Bethlehem, who lived as our Representative and died as our sin-atoning Substitute on the cross is coming to this earth again. He said, 'I will come again' (John 14:3). The Apostle Paul wrote, 'The Lord himself shall descend from heaven' (1 Thessalonians 4:16). He said, 'The Lord Jesus shall be revealed from heaven' (2 Thessalonians 1:7; Job 19:25-27).

He came once in weakness. He is coming again in power. He came once in humiliation. He is coming again in glory. He came once to be despised. He is coming again to be admired. He came once to suffer. He is coming again to conquer.

The second coming of Christ will be sudden, unannounced, unexpected, and climactic. Christ will come as a thief in the night, without warning (1 Thessalonians 5:2). He said, 'I will come on thee as a thief, and thou shalt not know what hour I will come upon thee' (Revelation 3:3). The Lord does not tell us to look for the tribulation, or the regathering of Israel, or the rebuilding of a Jewish temple. He tells us to look for him! If you look for signs, and times, and seasons, you will be shocked when Christ comes.

The only thing mentioned in the Word of God that will announce the Lord's coming will be 'a shout, the voice of the archangel and the trump of God' (1 Thessalonians 4:16). No man knows the day or hour of our Lord's coming; and that is best (Matthew 24:36; Mark 13:32; Acts 1:7). If we knew the day or hour, we would become irresponsible and negligent with regard to our daily duties. Do not seek to know when Christ is coming. Be content with his promise, and wait for his appearing.

Yet, we must always look for our Lord Jesus to appear at any moment. 'Behold, he cometh' (Revelation 1:7). Look for him upon the tiptoe of faith and expectation. All will be taken by surprise except those who are expecting him to appear. Like those Thessalonians who believed God, we must constantly 'wait for his Son from heaven' (1 Thessalonians 1:10). Faith is ever 'looking for that blessed hope and the glorious appearing of the great God and our Saviour Jesus Christ' (Titus 2:13). Christ is coming now. Soon he shall appear and when he does he will bring with him a crown of righteousness, immortality, and life for all who love him and look for his appearing (2 Timothy 4:8; James 1:12).

General resurrection

Second, when Christ comes, there will be a great, general resurrection of all who ever lived upon the earth (Revelation 20:13; John 5:28-29). All who have died in faith shall be raised from the grave. All will be raised. But the saints of God will have distinct priority in the resurrection. 'The dead in Christ shall rise first'. The bodies of God's saints shall be raised from their graves and reunited with their souls (1 Thessalonians 4:13-18). All the Old Testament saints and all the saints and martyrs of this age, all who sleep in Jesus, shall be raised from their graves!

Then, immediately after the sleeping saints rise, all believers living on earth will be changed and caught up to meet the Lord in the air (1 Corinthians 15:51-58). As our Lord descends in the brilliant glory of his second advent, we shall go out to meet him and return with him, as he comes with all his saints to burn up the earth, destroy the wicked, and make all things new. What a day that will be!

After that, after the Son of God has gathered all the ransomed bodies of his elect from the earth, after he has destroyed all the wicked with the brightness of his coming, all the wicked shall be raised. There is a resurrection for the wicked, too. But, for those who believe not, there is no music in the resurrection. The Lord himself shall issue a summons they cannot resist. They will stand in terror before him whose grace they despised and against whom they sinned! The body and soul now united in sin shall be united in horror to be judged of God and suffer his wrath forever in hell!

The judgment

Third, immediately after the resurrection we must all be judged according to the record of our works (Revelation 20:12-13). 'It is appointed unto men once to die, but after this the judgment' (Hebrews 9:27). The Judge before whom we must stand is the God-man, whom we have crucified (John 5:22; Acts 17:31; 2 Corinthians 5:10). We will be judged out of the books, according to the record of God's strict justice.

When the books are opened, what shocks of terror will seize the hearts and souls of those who have no righteousness and no atonement before the holy Lord God! With the opening of the books, every crime, every offence, every sin they have ever committed, in mind, in heart, and in deed shall be exposed! 'Judgment was set; and the books were opened' (Daniel 7:10).

I realize that this is figurative language. God does not need books to remember man's sins. However, as John Gill wrote, 'This judgment out of the books, and according to works, is designed to show with what accuracy and exactness, with what justice and equity, it will be executed, in allusion to statute-books in courts of judicature'. In the scriptures God is often represented as writing and keeping books. According to these books we all shall be judged.

What are the books? – The book of divine omniscience (Malachi 3:5) – The book of divine remembrance (Malachi 3:16) – The book of creation (Romans 1:18-20) – The book of God's providence (Romans 2:4-5) – The book of conscience (Romans 2:15) – The book of God's holy law (Romans 2:12) [This book of the law has two tables. The first table contains all the sins of men against God (Exodus 20:3-11). The second table contains all the sins of men against one another (Exodus 20:12-17)] – The book of the gospel (Romans 2:16).

But there are some against whom no crimes, no sins, no offences can be found, not even by the omniscient eye of God himself! 'In those days, and in that time, saith the LORD, the iniquity of Israel shall be sought for, and there shall be none; and the sins of Judah, and they shall not be found: for I will pardon them whom I reserve' (Jeremiah 50:20). Their names are found in another book, a book which God himself wrote and sealed before the worlds were made. It is called, 'The book of life'. In this book there is a record of

divine election, the name of Christ our divine Surety, a record of perfect righteousness (Jeremiah 23:6, cf. 33:16), a record of complete satisfaction, and the promise of eternal life.

The question is often raised, 'Will God judge his elect for their sins and failures, committed after they were saved, and expose them in the day of judgment?' The only reason that question is ever raised is because many retain a remnant of the Roman doctrine of purgatory, by which they hope to hold over God's saints the whip and terror of the law. There is absolutely no sense in which those who trust Christ shall ever be made to pay for their sins! Our sins were imputed to Christ and shall never be imputed to us again (Romans 4:8). Christ paid our debt to God's law and justice; and God will never require us to pay. God who has blotted out our transgressions will never write them again. He who covered our sins will never uncover them!

The perfect righteousness of Christ has been imputed to us. On the day of judgment, God's elect are never represented as having done any evil, but only good (Matthew 25:31-40). The day of judgment will be a day of glory and bliss for Christ and his people, not a day of mourning and sorrow. It will be a marriage supper. Christ will glory in his Church. God will display the glory of his grace in us. We will glory in our God.

The righteous

Fourth, those who are found perfectly righteous, righteous according to the records of God himself, shall enter into eternal life and inherit everlasting glory with Christ. They that have done good, nothing but good, perfect good, without any spot of sin, wrinkle of iniquity, or trace of transgression, shall enter into everlasting life. (Revelation 22:11).

Who are these perfectly righteous ones? They are all who are saved by God's free and sovereign grace in Christ (1 Corinthians 6:9-11; Romans 8:1, 32-34). Though there shall be degrees of punishment for the wicked in hell, because there are degrees of wickedness, there shall be no degrees of reward and glory among the saints in heaven, because there are no degrees of redemption and righteousness.

Heaven was earned and purchased for all God's elect by Christ. We were predestined to obtain our inheritance from eternity (Ephesians 1:11). Christ has taken possession of heaven's glory as our forerunner (Hebrews 6:20). We are heirs of God and joint-heirs with Jesus Christ (Romans 8:17). Our Saviour gave all the glory he earned as our Mediator to all his elect (John 17:5, 20). In Christ every believer is worthy of heaven's glory (Colossians 1:12).

Glorification is but the consummation of salvation; and salvation is by grace alone! That means no part of heaven's bliss and glory is the reward of our works, but all the reward of God's free grace in Christ! All spiritual blessings are ours from eternity in Christ (Ephesians 1:3).

The wicked

Fifth, all who are found guilty of sin in that great and terrible day of judgment shall be cast into the lake of fire and there be made to suffer the unmitigated wrath of almighty God forever! One by one, God will call the wicked before his throne and judge them. As he says, 'Depart ye cursed', he will say to his holy angels, 'Take him! Bind him! Cast him into outer darkness!'

In that day there will be no mercy, no pity, no sorrow, no hope, and no end for the wicked! To hell they deserve to go! To hell they must go! To hell they will go! Let all who read these lines beware. Unless you flee to Christ and take refuge in him, in that great day the wrath of God will seize you and destroy you forever! I beseech you now, by the mercies of God, be reconciled to God by trusting his darling Son! In that great and terrible day let us be found in Christ, not having our own righteousness, but the righteousness of God in Christ.

'For I am jealous over you with godly jealousy: for I have espoused you to one husband, that I may present you as a chaste virgin to Christ. But I fear, lest by any means, as the serpent beguiled Eve through his subtlety, so your minds should be corrupted from the simplicity that is in Christ'.
(2 Corinthians 11:2-3)

Chapter 75

Four Great Dangers

Natural men and women, unsaved, unregenerate professors of religion, sometimes become excited and zealous about Christ and the gospel of God's free and sovereign grace in him. In a sense, they often get just as excited about the doctrines of grace as true believers do, maybe even more so, at least for a while. But after a while the lustre and beauty of grace grows dim in their eyes, the glory of substitution is lost to them. After a while, the lost religionist gets tired of the gospel of Christ. He wants something new, something more profound, something mysterious. Like the children of Israel in the wilderness, the natural man has no real taste and relish in his soul for the manna of heaven. He soon longs for the leeks and onions of Egypt.

Such people may or may not openly deny the gospel. But, in time, they get tired of hearing the sweet message of Christ crucified. They grow weary of hearing about grace; free, sovereign grace, and nothing but grace. The manna of heaven tastes stale to them. I have seen this happen so many times that it frightens me. I am fearful for you who read these lines, just as Paul was for the Corinthians (2 Corinthians 11:2-3).

Satan is a crafty, subtle deceiver. He does not care what the issue is by which men and women are beguiled, so long as they are beguiled. He does not care what he gets you to embrace, so long as he gets you to turn away from Christ. When the fiend of hell turns anyone away from Christ, he has won the day. That frightens me.

There are four dangers to which we are all naturally susceptible, four snares of Satan by which multitudes have been deceived. Many men who were once so promising, so encouraging, so impressive have been turned away from Christ by one of these four satanic snares. Mark them and be warned.

Worldliness

Worldliness is a very great danger. We are warned to beware of it in the strongest terms possible (Matthew 13:22; 1 John 2:15-17). The care of this world and the deceitfulness of riches, the love of the world (its riches, its power, its acceptance, its pleasures), have slain many in time. Usually, these weeds do their work slowly, but they do it effectively. Beware of worldliness!

Arminianism

Arminianism is also a great danger to us, because we are all proud Arminians by nature. No matter how thoroughly convinced we are of free grace, our proud, sinful nature still cries up free will. We all want to build the altar at which we worship by our own hands (Exodus 20:24-25). We all want to think that salvation, at least some part of salvation, at least in some measure, is of our own doing.

Arminianism is a monster with many heads. Every time it raises one of its ugly heads, cut it off quickly. Do not endure for a moment any thought that promotes man's dignity, or any thought that robs God of his glory: – 'Salvation is of the Lord!' – 'It is not of him that willeth, nor of him that runneth, but of God that sheweth mercy!'

Intellectualism

Being proud, arrogant worms, we all have to face the danger of intellectualism, too. Satan knows how proud we all are of our puny brains. Because we are so very proud of our mental abilities, we vainly imagine that by much study and diligent research we can find out all things. We foolishly imagine that we can by searching find out God! I have even heard some men boast that they came to know the gospel, not by divine revelation, but by their own great brilliance and disciplined study!

Proud flesh always loves to study and learn 'some new thing'. So we give ourselves to answering one question, then another, and then another. How often individuals, pastors, churches, and denominations become consumed with the study of prophecy, creeds, morality, church order, political issues, family issues, etc. Those who give in to this lust of the flesh soon make the gospel of Christ a sideline, because there is no end to foolish questions. When the gospel of Christ becomes a sideline in any church or ministry, Satan has won the day (1 Timothy 1:4; 2 Timothy 2:23; Titus 3:9).

Legalism

We also face the constant danger of legalism. It is more difficult for a person to be weaned from legalism than from any other tendency of human nature. The spirit of bondage and legality is more frequently and more forcefully dealt with in the New Testament than any other error. To one degree or another, worldliness, Arminianism, and intellectualism all have their roots in the spirit of legality.

Let me be crystal clear. When I use the term 'legalism', I am referring to any doctrine or religious system that teaches that man can be justified before God by something he does, or makes sanctification and holiness something a man does for himself, or teaches that man can put God under obligation to him, that man can, by something he does, merit God's favour. Legalism is any attempt to bring the people of God back under the bondage of the law.

This demon of legality must be exposed and eradicated. The Holy Spirit says, 'Cast out the bondwoman and her child'. Nothing is more harmful, or more deadly than this foolish attachment of sinful men to the law. It promotes pride and self-righteousness. It turns a man's eyes away from Christ to himself. It causes strife and division among God's people, causing sinful man to think he is something when he is nothing! It destroys every foundation of true peace and assurance before God. It is in direct opposition to the plainest statements of holy scripture.

Legalism, in any form, to any degree, is totally contrary to the gospel of Christ. Law and grace simply will not mix. We who believe on Christ, we who are saved by the free grace of God in Christ are not under the law in any sense, to any degree, for any reason. We will not, we must not allow anyone to bring us under the yoke of bondage to the law. (Romans 6:15; 7:4; 10:4; Galatians 3:1-3, 13, 24-25; 5:1-4; 6:12-13; Colossians 2:16-17; 1 Timothy 1:5-10).

> Free from the law, O happy condition!
> Jesus hath bled; and there is remission!
> Cursed by the law and bruised by the fall,
> Christ hath redeemed us, once for all!

In Christ we fulfil the law by faith, by believing on him who fulfilled the law for us (Romans 3:31). In Christ we have no curse from the law (Galatians 3:13). In Christ we have no covenant with the law (Romans 7:4). In Christ we have no constraint by the law (2 Corinthians 5:14). In Christ we have no commitment to the law!

We are saved by grace. We are justified by grace. We are sanctified by grace. We are kept and preserved by grace. We are motivated by grace. We are governed by grace. We shall be glorified by grace. There is no room in the household of grace for the whip of the law.

I use great plainness of speech because I want to be understood. Let men call me a foul, base antinomian and promoter of licentiousness as often and as loudly as they please. I will not be moved. There is no room for Hagar in Sarah's house! We cannot rest on Zion's hill of grace until we quit trying to climb Sinai's dark, high mountain. Ishmael shall never be heir with Isaac.

You can have either grace or works, but not both. You can have either Moses or Christ, but not both. You can either work or rest, but you cannot do both! Any mixture of law with grace is a total denial of grace. If you cling to the one, you cannot hold the other! It is written, 'If by grace, then is it no more of works: otherwise grace is no more grace. But if it be of works, then is it no more grace: otherwise work is no more work' (Romans 11:6). I urge you, do not allow anyone, or anything, to take you away from Christ (Galatians 5:1-4).

'Assemble yourselves and come; draw near together, ye that are escaped of the nations: they have no knowledge that set up the wood of their graven image, and pray unto a god that cannot save. Tell ye, and bring them near; yea, let them take counsel together: who hath declared this from ancient time? who hath told it from that time? have not I the LORD? and there is no God else beside me; a just God and a Saviour; there is none beside me. Look unto me, and be ye saved, all the ends of the earth: for I am God, and there is none else. I have sworn by myself, the word is gone out of my mouth in righteousness, and shall not return, That unto me every knee shall bow, every tongue shall swear. Surely, shall one say, in the LORD have I righteousness and strength: even to him shall men come; and all that are incensed against him shall be ashamed. In the LORD shall all the seed of Israel be justified, and shall glory'.
(Isaiah 45:20-25)

Chapter 76

When God Gets Done

Here the Lord God himself speaks to sinners about who he is, what he is determined to do, and how we may be saved by him. He tells us here how things shall be when he gets done with all things.

God's description of lost men

In Isaiah 45:20, the Lord God describes lost, unbelieving men and women who worship at the altar of a 'god' who cannot save as those who have no knowledge: – 'Assemble yourselves and come; draw near together, ye that are escaped of the nations: they have no knowledge that set up the wood of their graven image, and pray unto a god that cannot save'.

All men and women are religious. Everyone has some kind of religion. Everyone has some concept of God, and some form of religious faith and hope. The fact is most people are very religious. I do not suggest for a moment that they are spiritual, or that they are saved; but most people are very religious. The vast majority of the people we meet and do business with, most of our friends, and most of our relatives are described by our Lord as people who have entered the wide gate and walk in the broad way that leads to destruction. They have entered into and walk in 'a way that seemeth right unto a man, but the end thereof are the ways of death' (Proverbs 16:25).

In this twentieth verse of Isaiah 45, the Lord God tells us three things about all lost, unregenerate, religious people.

1. 'They have no knowledge'

We are not told that they have a little knowledge or misguided knowledge; but that 'they have no knowledge'. Lost, unregenerate, religious people have absolutely no spiritual knowledge. Their ignorance is blatantly manifest almost every time they open their mouths. In order for a person to know anything spiritual, he must be born again (John 3:3-7). He must be taught of God. He must have the mind of Christ imparted to him in regeneration (1 Corinthians 2:14-16).

It does not matter how religious people are. It does not matter how long they have studied the Bible and studied what men say about the Bible. It does not matter how much experience they have, or how phenomenal their experience is. Natural, unregenerate people have no knowledge of themselves, or of God, or of sin, or of righteousness, or of salvation in and by Christ.

2. They 'set up the wood of their graven image'

They all worship a god that they have whittled out of the dark forests of their own depraved minds (Romans 1:21-23). I realize that refined, civilized, educated people do not worship images carved from tree stumps, chiselled from granite, or moulded even from gold and silver. Yet, the vast majority of people in the world (judging by the words of their own mouths and by the statements of the world's religious leaders) worship a little, peanut god which they have whittled from their own little, peanut minds, a god that no more resembles the God of the Bible than does a gnat.

3. They worship, serve, and 'pray unto a god that cannot save'

The god of this age (call it by whatever name you will) is 'a god that cannot save'. The Holy Spirit told us plainly that in these last days 'perilous times shall come'. He told us that in these perilous times men and women everywhere would have 'a form of godliness' (religious exercise), while denying the true power of true godliness. Then, he commands, 'from such turn away' (2 Timothy 3:1-5).

Our Lord Jesus said to the Jews and religious leaders of his day, 'Ye do err, not knowing the scriptures, nor the power of God' (Matthew 22:29). That is exactly what is wrong with the religious world in which we live. The Apostle Paul describes all legalistic, Arminian, free will, works religion as 'another gospel', the preaching of another god, another Jesus, another spirit, and another salvation. He calls it a religion that is a mere 'form of godliness'; and he declares that it is a mere form of godliness, because it denies the power of God.

The power of God, the power of godliness, in this context, is the gospel, which is the power of God unto salvation. Lost religionists do not deny the omnipotence of God, but the gospel of God! Pastor Henry Mahan had an article in his church bulletin[1] several years ago dealing with this very issue. He listed five areas in which the religion of our day is but a mere form of godliness.

1. A form of godliness says, 'God wills to save all men'. Then denying his power adds, 'but he cannot save unless men open their hearts to him'.
2. A form of godliness says, 'God has a wonderful plan for men and women'. Then denying his power adds, 'but you must allow him to have his will and way'.

---

[1] The Thirteenth Street Baptist Church Bulletin, Ashland, Kentucky.

3. A form of godliness says, 'Christ died on the cross for all the sins of all the sons of Adam that all might be saved'. Then denying the power of his blood adds, 'but his blood has no power or efficacy to save anyone until man releases it to work'.

4. A form of godliness says, 'The Holy Spirit knocks at everyone's heart with a desire to enter and work repentance and faith'. Then denying the power adds, 'but you must open the door'.

5. A form of godliness says, 'Salvation is of the Lord'. Then denying the power adds, 'but those whom he saves may fall away and perish'.

A god that cannot save is no god at all. Any who worship such a god, are not saved. Any who preach such a god are to be identified and marked as false prophets. How are we to treat such religion? How are we to deal with those who preach it and promote it to the everlasting ruin of men's souls? Paul tells us plainly, 'from such turn away!'

God's description of God

In Isaiah 45:21 the Lord God contrasts himself with the gods of men who cannot save. He tells us that he is a God who can save; and in this verse he asserts his own glorious, saving character. This is God's description of God. He who is God indeed is sovereign, just, and saving! – 'Tell ye, and bring them near; yea, let them take counsel together: who hath declared this from ancient time? who hath told it from that time? have not I the LORD? and there is no God else beside me; a just God and a Saviour; there is none beside me.

Look at this verse closely. Too often we read a familiar text too quickly and miss the full scope of its teaching. In this verse of scripture the Lord God declares five things about himself, five things which identify him as God. Observe what the text says. If the god you worship, if the god to which you pray, if your idea and concept of God lacks any of these five characteristics, then your god is but a graven image, a useless, imaginary god. This, I repeat, is God's description of God.

1. He who is God has an absolute, unalterable, sure purpose, by which all things are governed

In the opening part of verse twenty-one, the Lord God challenges men to bring all their peanut gods and let them all take counsel together. I challenge you to do the same. Gather up all the gods of men, the Baptist gods, the Mormon gods, the Catholic gods, the Protestant gods, the Russellite gods, Hindu gods, Islam gods, Jewish gods, and all the other gods of men.

Let them all take counsel together. Find me one in the whole bunch who has declared absolutely, from ancient times, from eternity, all things that are, have been, and shall hereafter be. He who is our God has (Isaiah 14:24, 27; 46:9-11). He who alone is God has an absolute, unalterable purpose; and he 'worketh all things after the counsel of his own will'.

2. He who is truly God truly is God, he declares himself to be, 'I the LORD'

Do you see that? He is not a lord. Our God is 'the LORD'. He is the only LORD. He is LORD everywhere, at all times, over everything. He controls the universe absolutely. He has his way in the whirlwind. The clouds are the dust of his feet. The thoughts of men's hearts, the roll of the dice, and the paths of the fish in the sea are all under his total rule (Isaiah 45:5-7, 12; Psalm 76:10; 115:3; 135:6). This God truly is God!

This great and glorious God, whom we worship, is the absolute, sovereign monarch of the universe. He is sovereign over all men. He is sovereign over all the events of the universe. He is sovereign in the salvation of his people.

3. He who is God is God alone

He declares there is none with him, none like him, and none but him. Most people are really pantheists and polytheists. They believe God is in everything and everybody. They believe that just about every man's notion of God really is God: Buddhists, Mohammedans, Jews, Papists, Mormons, Barbarians, and Baptists; but most people are wrong. There is but one God.

4. He who is God is a just God

Much could and should be said about God's justice; but I will say just two things regarding it here. These two things simply must be understood. (1) A just God must and shall punish all sin. (2) A just God cannot save sinners apart from the satisfaction of his justice. 'By mercy and truth iniquity is purged' (Proverbs 16:6), but not by any other means.

Blessed be his name, the justice of God has been satisfied for sinners by the obedience and death of the Lord Jesus Christ his dear Son! In him mercy and truth have met together. Righteousness and peace have kissed each other. Therefore, upon the grounds of Christ's obedience and death as the sinner's Substitute, the Lord God declares this fifth thing about himself.

5. He who is God indeed is both 'a just God and a Saviour'

That is exactly what the Lord told Moses about himself back in Exodus when he showed him his glory; and that is exactly what Paul tells us in the third chapter of Romans (Exodus 33:19, 34:5-7; Romans 3:24-26).

God's description of faith

In Isaiah 45:22 this great and glorious Lord God, who is both a just God and a Saviour, shows us the salvation he performs. The only way any sinner can ever be saved is by looking to this great and glorious God, who reveals himself in Christ. The Lord God, our great Saviour, says, 'Look unto me, and be ye saved, all the ends of the earth: for I am God, and there is none else'.

Salvation is Christ. He alone is the Saviour of men. The only way sinners can get God's salvation is by looking to him! We are saved by 'looking unto Jesus, the Author and Finisher of our faith'. Look to Christ. Look to Christ alone. Look to Christ for everything (1 Corinthians 1:30-31). Look to Christ always. As the children of Israel looked to that brazen serpent in the wilderness and lived, so every sinner who looks away to Christ shall be saved by the grace and power of this great God, who is our Saviour. This thing we call 'salvation', insofar as our experience of it is concerned, begins looking to Christ (Isaiah 45:22). It is sustained looking to Christ (Hebrews 12:2). It shall be consummated looking to Christ (1 John 3:2).

God's description of providence

Read Isaiah 45:23-25, and learn this: – When God gets done with this world, everybody is going to know who he is: – 'I have sworn by myself, the word is gone out of my mouth in righteousness, and shall not return, That unto me every knee shall bow, every tongue shall swear. Surely, shall one say, in the LORD have I righteousness and strength: even to him shall men come; and all that are incensed against him shall be ashamed. In the LORD shall all the seed of Israel be justified, and shall glory'.

God almighty raised up Pharaoh and destroyed him for the saving of his people, to make all men know who he is. When God was done, at the end of the day, everybody in Egypt as well as Israel knew who God is. They did not all know him; but they all knew who he is. God raised up Cyrus to deliver Israel out of Babylon. He was a splendid type of Christ. But God raised him up to deliver Israel and to deliver them in a specific way, for the reason stated in verse 6: – 'That they may know from the rising of the sun, and from the west, that there is none beside me. I am the LORD, and there is none else'. Indeed, God created, rules, and disposes of all things in the universe, for this one great reason, that everyone may know him and glorify him in the salvation of his people (Isaiah 45:7-18). That which he has purposed, he will do. Nothing in earth or in hell can prevent it, or even hinder it.

Our God is the God of purpose. He is accomplishing his purpose. Here the Lord God declares to the assembled angels and men before his august, sovereign and holy throne exactly what he is going to do. You can mark it down. When God gets done with this world, these five things will be accomplished. God has bound himself with an oath to do them!

1. Every knee shall bow to the Lord Jesus Christ, acknowledging him as Lord (Isaiah 45:23; Philippians 2:8-11).

2. The Lord Jesus Christ shall have a people to worship and serve him forever: – There shall be a people called out of this world who shall confess that Christ is all their righteousness and strength. 'Surely shall one say, in the Lord have I righteousness and strength' (v. 24).

3. All God's elect shall come to Christ: – 'Surely shall one say, in the Lord have I righteousness and strength: even to him shall men come' (v. 24; John 6:37-40).

4. Every rebel in the universe, both men and devils, will lick the dust before the throne of Christ in utter shame and confusion of face: – 'Even to him shall men come; and all that are incensed against him shall be ashamed'. All will bow to Christ. Some will bow in repentance by the power of his grace, and some in terror before the throne of his holy justice; but all will bow!

5. Every chosen sinner will be saved, and being saved by grace alone, they will all glory in the Lord forever (Romans 11:36; Jeremiah 9:23-24; 1 Corinthians 1:30-31): – 'In the LORD shall all the seed of Israel be justified, and shall glory'.

Then, and not until then, shall our Lord Jesus Christ stand up in the midst of glory, and say to all his creation: – 'Behold, I make all things new. And he said unto me, Write: for these words are true and faithful. And he said unto me, It is done. I am Alpha and Omega, the beginning and the end. I will give unto him that is athirst of the fountain of the water of life freely' (Revelation 21:5-6).

'Then cometh the end, when he shall have delivered up the kingdom to God, even the Father; when he shall have put down all rule and all authority and power. For he must reign, till he hath put all enemies under his feet. The last enemy that shall be destroyed is death. For he hath put all things under his feet. But when he saith all things are put under him, it is manifest that he is excepted, which did put all things under him. And when all things shall be subdued unto him, then shall the Son also himself be subject unto him that put all things under him, that God may be all in all'.
(1 Corinthians 15:24-28)

Chapter 77

'The End'

I like to get to the end of things. I try, as much as possible, to consider what the end of a thing will be before I do it. I try to consider what the end of my words will be before I speak them. From her earliest childhood, I taught my daughter never to think about her actions and words for the immediate time, but to consider what the end will be. I think she learned the importance of that instruction even as a child.

Immediate gratification often ends in pain and destruction. Immediate pain may in the end preserve life and give gratification. The drug addict finds immediate gratification in his needle; but pain and destruction are sure to follow in the end. The cancer patient finds immediate pain in his surgery and treatments; but life and gratification in the end make the pain insignificant.

In the natural world, nothing is more important than a thoughtful consideration of and regard for the end of things. All our words and deeds, even all our thoughts and attitudes have certain, inevitable consequences. If you take fire to your bosom, you are going to get burned. If you sow to the wind, you are going to reap the whirlwind. The end of anything is far more important than its beginning.

In spiritual matters, too, the end of all things is far more important than their beginning. When everything has run its predestined course, when time shall be no more, when this earth is dissolved in a ball of fire, the resurrection is past, and the judgment is over, we read, 'Then cometh the end!' The text might better be translated: – 'Then, the end!'

Though creation has revolted against God and sin has marred his handiwork, though it appears that everything here is in utter chaos, though antichrist seems to reign among men without rival, though Babylon (the great whore of free will, works religion) has made all the earth drunk with the wine of her fornications, there is a day coming called 'the times of the restitution of all things, which God hath spoken by the mouth of all his holy prophets since the world began' (Acts 3:21).

Though today all the world, all men, and all events appear to be set in direct opposition to Christ, there is a day coming called 'the dispensation of the fulness of times', in which the Lord God will 'gather together in one all things in Christ, both which are in heaven and which are on earth, even in him' (Ephesians 1:10).

Though all men by nature despise his rule, there is a day appointed by God, in the which 'at the name of Jesus every knee shall bow, of things in heaven, and things in earth, and things under the earth; and every tongue shall confess that Jesus Christ is Lord, to the glory of God the Father' (Philippians 2:10-11).

Though all men by nature are the enemies of God, though Satan and all the demons of hell oppose his purpose, though men and devils unite as one, in thought, word, and deed, to rob the triune God of his glory, in the end, through the blood of his cross, by our

Lord Jesus Christ, almighty God shall 'reconcile all things unto himself, whether they be things in earth or things in heaven' (Colossians 1:20).

In Isaiah 45:20-25 the Lord God himself tells us how things will be in the end. We would be wise to hearken unto the gracious counsel he gives in that place.

> Assemble yourselves and come; draw near together, ye that are escaped of the nations: they have no knowledge that set up the wood of their graven image, and pray unto a god that cannot save. Tell ye, and bring them near; yea, let them take counsel together: who hath declared this from ancient time? who hath told it from that time? have not I the LORD? and there is no God else beside me; a just God and a Saviour; there is none beside me. Look unto me, and be ye saved, all the ends of the earth: for I am God, and there is none else. I have sworn by myself, the word is gone out of my mouth in righteousness, and shall not return, That unto me every knee shall bow, every tongue shall swear. Surely, shall one say, in the LORD have I righteousness and strength: even to him shall men come; and all that are incensed against him shall be ashamed. In the LORD shall all the seed of Israel be justified, and shall glory.

In the end, every creature in heaven, earth, and hell, every deed performed in God's creation, by men, angels, devils, and Satan himself, (every deed!) great and small, good and evil, and every event of providence shall magnify, honour, exalt, and praise our great and glorious God.

As we come now to the end of this study of Bible doctrine, I think it will be helpful to conclude the study by seeking to know and understand the teaching of holy scripture regarding the end of all things. May God the Holy Spirit graciously turn our hearts and minds away from the cares and burdens, heartaches and sorrows, trials and temptations, difficulties and disappointments of this world of time and sense. May he even take our hearts away from the pleasures, joys, and comforts of this world and this brief existence. Come, O Spirit of God, come! Set our hearts and minds this hour, and set them permanently, upon 'THE END'.

When everything that shall be has been, when everything that must be has come to pass, when all the will, purpose, desire, and pleasure of the triune God has been perfectly accomplished and fulfilled in all things and by all things, the scripture declares, 'Then cometh the end!' Let me show you five things from the Word of God about 'the end'.

All things temporal

If we would apply our hearts to wisdom, we must learn and constantly remind ourselves of this first fact: – Everything in this world is temporal and must soon come to an end. 'The fashion of this world passeth away' (1 Corinthians 7:29-31).

I wonder if we will ever learn that everything here is just temporary. Time is not endless. This world is not eternal. Everything in this world had its beginning and shall have its end. The beginning and the end of all things have been ordained and fixed by God's unalterable decree from eternity. God made you and me for a specific purpose. When God's purpose for us, and concerning us has been perfectly and completely accomplished, 'then cometh the end'. Then our end shall be either eternal bliss or eternal woe. Will you think about that fact?

We live in a world in which all things are temporal and passing away. Everything around us is decaying, dying, and coming to an end. That man must be truly blind who does not see that everything here is only momentary. We are creatures created by God with immortal souls in a world where everything is mortal, temporal, and perishing. All property, all talents, all relationships, all evil, all good, all opportunities, all things in this world are temporary! Nothing temporal can ever satisfy our immortal souls.

We are all moving rapidly to a world in which everything is eternal. As was just stated, you and I are men and women with immortal souls. We live in a world where everything constantly changes. But we are going, and going rapidly, to a world where nothing changes and nothing ends. That great, unseen world which lies beyond the grave, whatever else it is or is not, it is eternal (2 Corinthians 4:18). Hell is eternal. Heaven is eternal (Mark 8:36-37). Everything here is vanity. Only that which is eternal is of any real meaning, significance, consequence, and value. I urge you, for your soul's sake, count nothing on this earth more valuable and precious now than you will in that day when you must leave it.

> All things here will soon be past.
> Heaven and hell alone will last.
> Will you, for trinkets of a day,
> Eternally be cast away?
>
> Immortal souls, can't you see,
> All things here are vanity?
> Should you gain the world's store,
> Is it really worth your soul?
>
> Set your heart on Christ alone,
> Trust the work which He has done;
> And when this world has passed away,
> You'll never miss the melting clay.

The Lord Jesus Christ alone can prepare us for eternity. Our happiness or misery in eternity depends entirely upon and will be determined entirely by our relationship with the Son of God now (John 3:36; 6:47; 1 John 5:10). Only the blood of Christ can wash away our sins. Only the righteousness of Christ can give us acceptance with God. Only faith in Christ can fetch the merits of his blood and righteousness to our souls. Only the Spirit of God can give us faith.

I cannot press with sufficient urgency the need ever to beware of 'the cares of this world, and the deceitfulness of riches, and the lusts of other things (which) entering in, choke the word, and it becometh unfruitful' (Mark 4:19).

All things of God

Second, if we would live peaceably in this world, we must learn that the beginning, the accomplishment, and the end of all things are of God: – 'All things are of God' (2 Corinthians 5:18). All things in heaven, all things in earth, and all things in hell, all things good and all things bad, all things pleasant and all things painful, all things temporal and all things eternal. 'All things are of God' (Isaiah 14:26-27; 45:2-13; 46:9-11; Romans 8:28; 11:36).

God predestinated all things according to the good pleasure of his will. God created all things according to the good pleasure of his will. God rules all things according to the good pleasure of his will. God disposes of all things according to the good pleasure of his will. God shall have the praise of all things according to the good pleasure of his will (Psalm 76:10; Proverbs 16:4; Ephesians 1:11).

Christ reigns

Third, I want you to see that the Lord Jesus Christ, God's Son, our dear Saviour must reign until the end comes: – 'He must reign' (1 Corinthians 15:24-26). That Man who lived and died for us, as our Mediator, Surety, Representative, and Substitute, that he might save us and bring us to heaven is himself God almighty, who rules all things. He earned the right to reign over all things as a Man, as our Mediator and Surety, to be the sovereign Governor of the universe, by his obedience to his Father. He forever possesses the power of absolute, unrivalled, sovereign dominion because he is God the Son. Observe what the text says.

Our Lord Jesus Christ must reign because he is God. A god who does not reign is no God at all (Psalm 115:3; 135:6). He must reign because his dominion is the reward of his obedience (Psalm 2:8; 14:9; Romans 14:9; Philippians 2:9-11). He must reign because the salvation of God's elect and the glory of God depend upon it (John 17:2-4). He must reign because no one is able to stop him!

Our great and glorious Saviour will soon appear to put down forever all rule, authority, and power. All civil rule, authority, and power. All domestic rule, authority, and power. All ecclesiastical rule, authority, and power. All satanic, demonic, hellish rule, authority, and power.

The Lord Jesus shall soon put all enemies (his and ours) under his feet. He will graciously, effectually conquer the hearts of all his elect, bring them to his feet, make them willing in the day of his power to be there, and cause them to bow in subjection to him, to his sceptre as their King, and to obey his gospel and his ordinances.

Those he does not conquer by his grace, the Son of God will conquer by his wrath. All will bow to him, either as willing servants saved by his grace, or as conquered vassals compelled to acknowledge the dominion, the rightful dominion of that King whom they despise.

He shall put our enemies under his feet, too; and if they are put under his feet, they are put under our feet. Sin, with all his misery, shall soon be put under our feet. Soon, the world, with all its influence, shall be put under our feet. Death, with all its fear and in all its forms (judicial death, spiritual death, physical death, the second death), shall be put under our feet. Even Satan, shall soon be bruised beneath our feet by the God of all grace (Romans 16:20).

Kingdom delivered up
Fourth, when the end comes, the Lord Jesus Christ shall deliver up the kingdom unto God the Father: – 'Then cometh the end, when he shall have delivered up the kingdom to God, even the Father; when he shall have put down all rule and all authority and power ...

And when all things shall be subdued unto him, then shall the Son also himself be subject unto him that put all things under him, that God may be all in all' (1 Corinthians 15:24, 28).

What do those two verses mean? First, let me show you what they most certainly do not mean. When the scriptures here declare that the Son shall deliver up the kingdom unto the Father, they do not teach, suggest, or in any way imply that Christ is not God (1 Timothy 3:15), or that the Son of God is in any way inferior to the Father (1 John 5:7), or that Christ will cease to be Prophet, Priest, and King over his church and kingdom (Hebrews 1:8).

What does Paul mean, then, when he tells us that Christ shall deliver up the kingdom unto God, even the Father, and shall be subject to him? When the resurrection is over, when the great white throne judgment is done, and all things are created new, when all God's elect are saved, there will be one final work to be done by our Lord Jesus Christ as Jehovah's Servant, as the Surety and Mediator of the covenant.

The Lord Jesus Christ will present all the elect unto the Father, holy, unblameable, unreproveable, and perfect (John 10:16; Ephesians 5:25-27; Hebrews 2:13; Jude 24-25). The Shepherd will present his sheep. The Saviour will present his church. The Son will present his brethren. The King will present his kingdom to God, even the Father. Augustus Toplady wrote,

> I take the kingdom to consist of that innumerable company whose names were written in heaven; and which, when their numerical fulness is completed, the Son of God, who graciously consented to become the Son of Man for their sakes, will present in one, entire, and glorified body to the Father.

In that great day, in the end, Christ will stand before his Father and our Father, with all his elect by his side in the perfection of his holiness, and say, Lo, I and the children which thou hast given me.

All are here. Not one is lost! All, my Father, you chose and gave to me, all you trusted me to redeem, here they are, just as I promised. They are holy, unblameable, unreproveable, washed in my blood, robed in my righteousness. All that I redeemed, every blood bought soul is here. All those who have been regenerated, called, and sealed by the blessed Holy Spirit are here.

He will, no doubt, go on to say. Now, my Father, all the purpose of grace is fulfilled. All the counsel of peace is accomplished. All that we agreed upon in the everlasting covenant of grace is done. In all things, our great purpose in predestination is now fully accomplished. Now grace reigns through righteousness unto eternal life!

God all in all

Fifth, this is the end of all things: 'that God may be all in all!' God almighty has from eternity ordained everything that comes to pass in time to make himself an everlasting and a glorious name (Isaiah 63:12, 14), that in all things Christ might have the pre-eminence (Colossians 1:18). In the end, God, the triune God, Father, Son, and Holy Spirit, as he is revealed, known, loved, and worshipped in the Person and work of Christ, our God-man Mediator, shall be 'all in all'.

There are three things in this last phrase of 1 Corinthians 15:28 I want you to see.
1. The works and purpose of the triune God shall be perfectly accomplished (Ephesians 1:3-14; 2:4-7).
2. God in Christ shall be all. The Lord Jesus Christ, our great God and Saviour, shall be all meat, clothing, and shelter for our bodies, all life, joy, peace, glory, and satisfaction for our souls, all sun and moon and light forever!
3. God in Christ shall be all in all. God, the triune God, shall be all in all things. God, the triune God, shall be all in all his people. God, the triune God, shall be all in all the praises of all saints and angels forever!

The delivering up of the kingdom to the Father will not put an end to it, but eternally establish it in a new and more glorious form. Christ shall not cease to reign, though the mode of his administration will be different. As a divine Person, he will always be one with the Father. Even as the incarnate God-man, he will continue forever. It is only in Christ the Word that we can see and know God. The effects of his mediatorial kingdom will abide forever. There will never be a time when the God-man will be cast aside, or hidden in the shadows. Our Lord Jesus Christ will never be less than he is now: The Image of the Invisible God!

Is this the goal for which we labour? Is this the burden, care, concern, and prayer of our hearts? That our 'God may be all in all'. Do we not, from the depths of our souls, pray, as our Saviour taught us, 'Our Father, which art in heaven, 'Hallowed be thy name. 'Thy kingdom come … Thy will be done'? If this is indeed the thing for which we most ardently labour, the thing we desire, for which we earnestly pray, then we have every reason to take heart and be of good courage: – 'Therefore, my beloved brethren, be ye stedfast, unmoveable, always abounding in the work of the Lord, forasmuch as ye know that your labour is not in vain in the Lord'.

AMEN

Index of Scriptures

Old Testament

New Testament

Matthew

		11:26	101
		11:28	518
1:20	97	11:28-30	212, 342, 472,
1:20-23	40		495, 507
1:21	83, 84, 239, 274,	11:29-30	508, 518
	391	12:31-32	44, 348, 349, 350
3:10	95	12:37	337
3:13-17	532	13:22	604
3:15-17	40	13:44	263, 296
5:14	167	15:1-6	359
5:16	167, 439	15:6-9	16
5:20	471	15:17-19	377
5:21, 27, 38, 43, 48	377	15:19-20	202
5:45	64	16:12	16
5:48	63, 329	16:18	530, 558
6:4, 6, 8, 18	62	16:21	253, 304
6:9	368	17:3	552
6:9-10	140	17:5	143
6:28-30	448	18:20	530, 534, 558
6:33	155	19:17	64
6:34	448	19:26	63
7:3-5	491	20:1-6	591
7:22-23	196	20:1-16	577
8:20	299	20:15	110
9:2	339	20:28	227, 256, 269, 270
10:20	427	22:14	381
10:22	103, 575	22:29	611
10:27	385	23:37	384
10:30	115, 456	23:37-38	106
10:40	384	24:23-24	85
10:42	574	24:24	215
11:20-23	303	24:31	215
11:20-24	348	24:36	557, 597
11:25	408	25:1, 6	571
11:25-27	541	25:31-40	600

Index of Topics

www.ingramcontent.com/pod-product-compliance
Lightning Source LLC
Chambersburg PA
CBHW030942150426
42812CB00062B/2693